Attitude Change: A Critical Analysis of Theoretical Approaches

SERIES IN PSYCHOLOGY

ATTITUDE CHANGE

A Critical Analysis of Theoretical Approaches

CHARLES A. KIESLER
Yale University

BARRY E. COLLINS
University of California, Los Angeles

NORMAN MILLER
University of Minnesota

JOHN WILEY & SONS, INC.

NEW YORK · LONDON · SYDNEY · TORONTO

Library of Congress Catalog Card Number: 68-56162

SBN 471 47465

Printed in the United States of America

In recognition of the debt we owe to the persons
most influential in our graduate training, the
three of us would like to dedicate this book to
DONALD T. CAMPBELL *and* LEON FESTINGER.

Preface

THE origin of this book can be traced to 1964 when we were all teaching at Yale University. In thinking about the various theoretical approaches to attitude formation and change we had each noted that there has been relatively little conceptual or empirical confrontation among them. To a considerable extent, each of the theories has led its own private existence—a vein to be mined only by those who were already stockholders in the enterprise. Therefore, with notable exceptions, surprisingly little detailed criticism of individual theories or comparison among the several disparate approaches was available.

We are indebted to a bookman, who traveling down our shared third floor corridor in the Institute of Human Relations (IHR) informed us that Collins and Miller on the one hand, and Kiesler, on the other, were talking about writing very similar books. We were delighted to discover a mutual concern with theoretical issues in attitude change. After discussing our respective plans, we decided that because each of us held distinct theoretical biases—and we cared who was right—it would be an intellectual challenge to us, and possibly result in a better book, if we were to collaborate.

We have tried to inspect the formal and informal properties of each theory thoroughly. We have consistently asked ourselves: What are the assumptions of the theory? What predictions can it make (and have they been empirically supported)? Which data does the theory not account for easily? We hope that our efforts will clarify old theoretical issues, pose new ones, and most importantly, lead to attempts at empirical resolutions.

There are those who may say that we have been too critical of each theory. It is true that we tried to be *very* critical—but constructively and dispassionately so. There is a fine line between constructive criticism and unfair attack, and we have at least tried to stay on the right side. If this book at all stimulates our colleagues or provokes theoretically oriented research, we will regard ourselves as successful.

The chapters on theories are written at a relatively high level. However, the first two chapters contain considerable material that should introduce the area, even to someone with little background. Consequently, we think the book could easily serve in an advanced undergraduate course.

We are indebted to *Psychological Reports,* John Wiley and Sons, *Public Opinion Quarterly, Journal of Conflict Resolution,* W. B. Saunders, University of Chicago Press, Yale University Press, Addison-Wesley, *Journal of Experimental Social Psychology, Psychological Review, Journal of Abnormal and Social Psychology,* Stanford University Press, *Journal of Personality and Social Psychology,* Holt, Rinehart and Winston, *Sociometry, American Sociological Review, Journal of General Psychology, Journal of Social Issues,* and McGraw-Hill for permission to use copyrighted material. A number of colleagues were kind enough to make their work available to us prior to publication. Work on several chapters was facilitated by National Science Foundation Grant GS-1194, Barry E. Collins, principal investigator, and NSF Grants GS-478 and GS-1000, Norman Miller, principal investigator. In addition, Madeleine Hays deserves special thanks for assistance in writing portions of Chapter 3.

Daniel Katz and Jonathan Freedman each read the entire manuscript and provided us with many thoughtful criticisms. The book was clearly improved as a consequence of their efforts. In addition, Linda Fleischer, Melvin Manis, Muzafer Sherif, Harry Upshaw, Charles Ward, and James Whittaker read a draft of Chapter 6 and provided many useful comments and criticisms. Besides those credits that have been specifically mentioned, the final form of this book has benefited by the exchange and discussion of ideas with many of our other colleagues. Their names are too numerous to mention, but their wisdom and advice also importantly contributed to the final form of the book. Obviously, however, the responsibility for the finished product must rest with the authors.

Our effort in writing this book was clearly mutual and a collaborative one. Although each of us had responsibility for individual chapters, extensive criticism, discussion, and revision by the others makes this truly a joint enterprise. Even approaching our joint task from this cooperative stance, however, some residual differences in emphasis, preference, or interpretation sometimes remained. In such cases, we typically deferred to the author who took initial responsibility for a particular chapter. Consequently, each of us could undoubtedly find sections or instances where our own individual interpretation or emphasis might differ somewhat from the final version. Nevertheless, we feel that the final product reflects the thorough interdependence of three authors. Furthermore, we judge our individual efforts as essentially equivalent. In this spirit, the order of authorship represents the ordering of three hands of poker dealt for just that purpose.

1968

CHARLES A. KIESLER
BARRY E. COLLINS
NORMAN MILLER

Contents

Attitude Change: A Critical Analysis of Theoretical Approaches

Chapter 1

The Concept and Measurement
of Attitudes

THE concept of attitude has played a central role in the development
of American social psychology. Before World War II social psychologists
devoted a large part of their efforts to attitude measurement and scaling.
Postwar psychologists have been equally dedicated to theoretical and
empirical issues in attitude change. In this book we compare and contrast
several definitions and theories of attitude change. There has been, however, no single definition of attitudes acceptable to all who do research
on attitude change. Thus we have deliberately refrained from taking
a single theoretical and definitional point of view in writing this book.
Our definition of attitude inevitably shifts slightly from chapter to chapter as we assume the role of different theorists. Although we are convinced that further quibbling over the definition of attitudes would produce little progress, we feel some preliminary definitional discussion of
attitudes is necessary before discussing theories of attitude change. As
indicated, however, it is our explicit intention to avoid taking a stand
on a single definition of attitudes; the following discussion should indicate
some of the issues involved.

Some Problems in the Definition of Attitude

Krech and Crutchfield (1948) define an attitude as ". . . an endur-
ing organization of motivational, emotional, perceptual, and cognitive

1

processes with respect to some aspect of the individual's world" (p. 152). In his pioneering article, "Attitudes Can be Measured" (1928), Thurstone advocates a broad definition; however, he later reports that he wished he had retained a more limited definition contained in an earlier draft of the 1928 paper. "I defined attitude as the intensity of positive or negative affect for or against a psychological object. A psychological object is any symbol, person, phrase, slogan, or idea toward which people can differ as regards positive or negative affect" (Thurstone, 1946, p. 39). This definition is adopted by Edwards (1957) in his *Techniques of Attitude Scale Construction*. As will become apparent in the subsequent chapters of this book, these more or less cognitive definitions are most typical in theories of attitude change.

Donald Campbell (1950) uses a more behavioristic language in his attempt to find a common ground in the various definitions of attitude.

"Research on social attitudes has been justly criticized for a lack of common definition of the concept, and for a failure to integrate definition and measurement procedures. This diversity of definition has been in odd contrast with the obvious similarity of research procedures. This paradox arises from definitional attempts which confound *explanations* of the phenomena with the process of *pointing* to the phenomena. It is the contention of the present writer that agreement on the implicit operational (or pointing) definition of attitudes is already present. As a tentative formulation the following is offered: *A social attitude is (or is evidenced by) consistency in response to social objects.* If we look at those definitions utilizing concepts of set, or readiness to respond—for example, Allport's (1935) 'An attitude is a mental and neural state of readiness, organized through experience and exerting a directive or dynamic influence upon the individual's response to all objects and situations to which it is related'—and ask for the evidence of a 'mental and neural state of readiness,' the symptoms of a 'directive or dynamic influence,' criteria as to the 'objects and situations to which it is related,' these evidences will be, in final analysis, consistency of predictability among responses. *An individual's social attitude is a syndrome of response consistency with regard to social objects.* And even those whose behavioristic orientation leads to a rejection of such mentalistic definitions as Allport's—and who would say with Bain (1928) and Horowitz (1944, p. 142), 'essentially . . . the attitude must be considered a response rather than a set to respond'—in research practice do not equate *isolated* responses with attitudes; but on the contrary, look for the appearance of *response consistencies.* This is dramatically evidenced by Horowitz's (1936) use of the appearance of consistent differentiated response to photographs of Negro and white children to mark the occurrence of race prejudice in children" (Campbell, 1950, pp. 31–32.)

This analysis has been in large part accepted by Bert Green in his chapter in the 1954 *Handbook of Social Psychology*. He adds a useful analysis in terms of Guttman's (1950b) concept of an attitude universe:

"It is apparent from these examples that the concept of attitude implies a consistency or predictability of responses . . .

"This definition does not divest attitudes of their affective and cognitive properties, which may be properties of, or correlates of, the responses which comprise the attitude . . .

"The content of an attitude is determined by the responses which constitute it. The set of behaviors comprising an attitude will be called an *attitude universe.* . . .

"Conceptually, then, attitude measurement involves sampling a behavior universe, and measuring the universe by means of a sample. This means that the sample of elements should be representative. . . . From a sample of verbal responses to questions about opinions, one should not make inferences about behavior other than verbal responses to similar verbal questions. It may be that responses to these verbal questions are correlated with responses in nonverbal situations, but this must be determined experimentally" (Green, 1954, p. 336).

We are in complete agreement that the *definition* of attitudes should correspond closely with the operational definitions used to measure the attitude.

In his chapter in the 1968 *Handbook of Social Psychology,* McGuire uses Allport's (1935) definition to indicate five of the dimensions of disagreement among definitions of attitude. First, there is disagreement about the psychological locus of attitudes. Allport stated that attitudes were "mental and neural states." Krech and Crutchfield (1948) defined it as "motivational, emotional, perceptual, and cognitive." Campbell and Green, in preceding the quotes, argue that an attitude exists as a collection of responses. A second dimension of disagreement concerns whether attitude should be defined as a response or as a readiness to respond. McGuire (1968) discusses four distinct theoretical positions on this continuum. A third issue concerns the degrees to which attitudes are organized. To what extent is a single attitude made up of separate components? And to what extent are these components organized in the same way for attitudes toward different objects? Many of these issues are discussed in Chapter 7 on "Functional Theories of Attitude Change."

A fourth dimension of disagreement among definitions concerns the extent to which attitudes are learned through previous experience. That attitudes are forged out of previous experience is perhaps the least controversial issue in American social psychology; it was one of the few points of agreement in the cognitive versus behavioristic argument between Doob (1947) and Chein (1948). A fifth issue concerns the extent to which attitudes play a directive-knowledge or a dynamic-motivational function.

McGuire (1968) goes on to discuss some of the distinctions that have been made to differentiate attitude from other psychological concepts —again demonstrating that there is relatively little agreement on the substance of the distinctions. The distinction between attitudes and opinions, for instance, seems to be "a situation involving names in search of a distinction, rather than a distinction in search of a terminology." One might argue that "attitudes" should be defined as a general orientation and "opinions" are the more specific manifestation (Hovland, Janis, and Kelley, 1953). Or one might argue that opinions should be defined as an overt expression of the covert attitude (as mentioned in the Measurements section of this chapter).

Others have attempted to distinguish between attitudes and knowledge. Should attitudes be limited to a purely directive function (such as the "habit" concept in stimulus-response psychology) or should attitudes also be imbued with dynamic, drive properties? McGuire suggests that the attitude-knowledge continuum is similar to a propaganda-persuasion versus education-instruction dimension. Similarly, we may be "educating" when the audience has no initial stands on an issue but persuading when the audience does have an initial stand.

It would appear that most of these issues are theoretical and empirical issues. They should be resolved by data rather than philosophical argument. All too often, social psychologists have tried to make their definition of attitude both a definition *and* a theory of the concept. Whether or not the various operational procedures typically used to measure "attitudes," "overt behavior," "perceptions," "motivational states," etc., constitute a single syndrome is a theoretical and empirical matter not resolved by creating a definition. Definitions should be intimately bound up in the measurement techniques; material about the function of attitudes within the personality and society is theory *about*—not measurement *of*—attitudes.

Our primary criterion for evaluating theories of attitude change in the following chapters is the extent to which theoretical notions can stimulate research and predict the empirical data of attitude change. Many of the issues briefly reviewed above will be discussed in later chapters when these "definitional" issues are relevant to the predictive ability of a theory. Our purpose thus far has been to provide a quick overview of the kinds of issues that are discussed in the social attitude section of good introductory social texts and handbook chapters. In the following sections of this chapter we briefly review the historical roots of the concept of attitude, provide an overview on techniques of measuring attitude, and conclude with a somewhat longer section on the literature relating behaviors and attitudes.

Historical Beginning of the Concept of Attitude

In 1935, Allport termed attitude "the most distinctive and indispensable concept in contemporary social psychology." In spite of the fact that the philosophy and epistemology of the authors writing about attitudes differ widely, theorists continue to find the concept of attitude useful. Although the use of the experimental laboratory as a tool for the investigation of attitude was probably unanticipated by early writers in the field, our current theorizing about attitudes has been sufficiently influenced by these earlier conceptions that a brief review will provide insight into "attitude's" current usage.

Gordon Allport (1935) traces the study of "attitudes" to 1888, when L. Lange discovered that a subject who was instructed to concentrate on being ready to press a key at the onset of a stimulus responded more rapidly than a subject who was instructed to concentrate on the incoming stimulus itself. The response was at least a part of a "set" within the individual. This phenomenom was called the subject's *aufgab*—or task-attitude.

A second historical root is found in American psychology's fascination with individual differences. Individual differences is probably the major theme throughout the intellectual history of the concept of attitude. Scientists have felt the need for a concept to name and explain a consistency in individual behavior across a variety of situations; and many have chosen the concept of "attitude" for this purpose. Whether it was a nineteenth-century psychologist interested in individual differences in reaction time or an astronomer recording a stellar event, a sociologist interested in individual differences of a Polish immigrant as he is immersed in a new culture, or the contemporary psychologist's concern with attitudes toward minority groups and a potential cure for the common cold—all have found the concept of attitude useful.

According to Allport, Freud's followers filled in many of the dynamic attributes which are currently ascribed to attitudes, "identifying them with longing, hatred and love, passion and prejudice, in short, with the onrushing stream of unconscious life" (Allport, 1935, p. 801). Although the concept of attitude per se is seldom used by classical Freudians, the highly influential *Authoritarian Personality* (Adorno, Frenkel-Brunswik, Levinson, and Sanford, 1950) and the work by Katz and Sarnoff reviewed in Chapter 7 present an extensive application of psychodynamic concepts in the analysis of attitudes toward minority groups.

But it is probably the sociologists who added the important dimensions to the concept of attitude and gave it the richness that makes it so popular in contemporary American social psychology. In one of the most influential social science books of this century, *The Polish Peasant in Europe and America,* Thomas and Znaniecki (1918, 1927; see also Blumer, 1939) took the position that social psychology *is* the scientific study of attitudes. Whereas many traditional sociological analyists had limited themselves to the objective and sociological conditions impinging on a society, Thomas and Znaniecki argued that it was necessary to consider psychological variables, i.e., differences between individuals, in order to understand social change.

The Thomas and Znaniecki definition of attitude reflects the emphasis on conscious experience that pervaded American psychology early in the twentieth century: An attitude is "a process of individual consciousness which determines real or possible activities of the individual in the social world" (p. 22). As Blumer (1939) states, " 'attitudes' become seemingly blanket terms for all phases of mental life or psychological processes" (p. 21). Since they were developing an integrated sociological theory, Thomas and Znaniecki were careful to state that an attitude is not simply a psychical state in the abstract. "The psychological process remains always fundamentally *a state of somebody;* the attitude remains always fundamentally *an attitude toward something*" (Vol. I, p. 23). Thus, although attitudes are defined with words referring to conscious experience, their primary theoretical function is to explain individual differences in reaction to socially significant objects such as outgroup persons, legislation, countries, and institutions.

We can discover a little of the flavor of early quantitative research and attitudes by reviewing the treatment of "Social Attitudes and Their Measurement" in Murphy, Murphy, and Newcomb's *Experimental Social Psychology* (1937). Perhaps more aptly named *empirical* social psychology, the 1937 edition represented a revision of an earlier (1931) edition. The major part of the book is concerned with the process of socialization and the genetic study of social behavior. Typical chapter headings are "Nature and Nurture in Relation to Social Differences," "The Development of Social Behavior in Early Childhood," and "Some Adult Behavior Patterns in Our Own Society."

Although the last of 13 chapters, the chapter on "Social Attitudes and Their Measurement" begins with the statement, "Perhaps no single concept within the whole realm of social psychology occupies a more nearly central position than that of attitudes" (p. 889). Attitudes are defined "as verbalized or verbalizable tendencies, dispositions, or adjustments towards certain acts" (p. 889). A distinction is then drawn between sociological and psychological analyses: attitudes may be related to sociological variables such as size of community or psychological variables such as personality traits.

Following a discussion on attitude measurement, Murphy, Murphy, and Newcomb began a major section on "Attitudes and Individual Characteristics." As is typical of most new endeavors in science, investigators began with questions which turned out to be too simple; as of 1937 it was already apparent that it would be impossible to make sweeping generalizations about attitudinal differences between individuals of different age, intelligence, radicalism and conservatism, and other values.

The next major section of the attitudes chapter deals with "The Experimental Modification of Attitudes." Murphy, Murphy, and Newcomb summarize the results of 34 studies in chart form. Typical is a study by Caldwell and Lumdeen (1933) in which a high school class in biology was exposed to instruction in unfounded beliefs in science; it was apparently successful in decreasing unfounded beliefs and in increasing factual knowledge. Kornhauser (1930) found that a year's course in economics produced less uniformity, undecidedness, and extremeness, and more liberalism. These changes were, however, less than the corresponding changes in information. Other investigators studied the attitudinal impact of other college courses, modified curriculum in civics classes, four consecutive weekly radio addresses, radical motion picture propaganda, and an extensive antiprejudice program which included two weeks in Harlem with parties, teas, home visits, personal contacts, and speeches.

Murphy, Murphy, and Newcomb conclude the chapter on attitudes with a discussion of "Attitudes as Determined by Life Experiences." They summarize research on such variables as education, Reserve Officers Training Corps, classes, college fraternity life, familiarity and contact with respect to race and nationality attitudes, home and family, religious institutions, racial or national backgrounds, socioeconomic status, and communities or certain geographical areas.

With a few exceptions, such as the study by Saadi and Farnsworth (1934), which experimentally paired some statements with a liked, or disliked, or a neutral author, this research posed unsophisticated questions. Very few of the studies are truly experimental in the sense that subjects are randomly assigned to treatment and control conditions. Furthermore, variables such as "a year's course in economics" are of such a gross and "shotgun" nature that it is difficult to ascertain which aspect or facet of the complex manipulation is actually responsible for the results. The basic analytic procedure of science is the attempt to manipulate a single variable—either in isolation or orthogonally to all other variables. A major role of theory, in fact, is to specify those specific aspects in a complex situation that contribute to attitude change.

In summary, investigators interested in *aufgabe* or task-sets in reaction time, the acculturation of Polish peasants, the effectiveness of a year's course in economics, and anti-Semitism, have been drawn to the concept of attitude. The common theme drawing these investigators together is a concern with the importance of individual differences or the tendency of different individuals to behave differently in the same situation and for the same individual to behave similarly in different situations. Thus social philosophers and action-oriented pragmatists have used the concept of attitude because it offered a theoretical explanation for socially significant *behaviors*. The emphasis on behavior in most definitions of attitude can be traced to these historical roots. These theoretical discussions and definitions have been a strong influence in the evolution of the concept of attitude—an influence which has stressed the behavioral relevance of attitudes and their importance in the analysis of socially significant problems.

Brief Review of Attitude Measurement Techniques

There is a second, somewhat independent influence on our current conceptions of attitude—an influence stemming from the literature on attitude measurement. In contrast to the definitions and theoretical discussions, the literature on measurement techniques has contributed to the evolution of the concept of attitudes by stressing self-report aspects of attitude. Whatever the *definition* or theory, the most common *measure* of attitude is a pencil and paper instrument—a measurement technique which does not make direct use of overt behavior. As is not unusual in science, technological innovations often determine the direction of scientific investigation; areas which lack sophisticated research tools often remain unexplored. (Attitude test responses are, of course, a kind of behavior too; and we will discuss that point later.)

We have included a brief review of attitude measurement procedures for historical and methodological purposes. But we should offer fair warning; it is rare for one of the laboratory studies reviewed in the following chapters to use any of the methodologically sophisticated attitude scaling techniques described below. The typical laboratory investigation of attitude change employs one or two simple, unpretested pencil and paper questions which reflect little of the theoretical emphasis on behavioral implications of attitudes or the methodological emphasis on elaborate measurement techniques. Attitude measurement represents an important part of the scientific history of attitudes; no other facet of attitudes had been subjected to so much sophisticated work at the beginning of World War II. But the postwar *theory-testing* experiments have made little, if any, use of the elegant measurement techniques. The following review of attitude measurement techniques is only potentially relevant to experiments testing theories of attitude change. Thus, in contrast to our heavy emphasis on methodology elsewhere, the following sections are only brief overviews.

Following the taxonomy of Cook and Selltiz (1964), we distinguish five general categories of attitude measures in this section.

1. Measures in which inferences are drawn from self-reports of beliefs, behaviors, etc.

2. Measures in which inferences are drawn from the observation of ongoing behavior in a natural setting.

3. Measures in which inferences are drawn from the individual's reaction to or interpretation of partially structured stimuli.

4. Measures in which inferences are drawn from performance of "objective" tasks.

5. Measures in which inferences are drawn from physiological reactions to the attitudinal object or representations of it.

The following sections discuss each category separately; but almost all of the studies reviewed in later chapters use self-report techniques and our discussion here will reflect this emphasis.

SELF-REPORT MEASURES

In 1925 Floyd H. Allport and D. A. Hartman published an article which proved to be the first step in a series that led to techniques for the quantification of attitude measurement. Allport and Hartman began by asking 60 upper-class students to write their personal views on several topics including prohibition. "The resulting opinions on each issue were then carefully sifted and the distinct and relevant views were assembled. Keeping the issues separate, these views were printed on slips of paper and arranged independently by six judges, teachers of political science and psychologists, in order of their logical position in a scale ranging from one extreme on the issue in question to the opposite extreme" (Allport and Hartman, 1925, p. 736). A somewhat larger sample of underclassmen were then asked to "check the one statement which most nearly coincided with his or her own views."

Compared to the traditional attitude measures in which the respondent indicates a "yes" or "no" vote for a proposition, this technique divides the subjects into a number of subgroups, which are rank ordered with respect to the attitudinal dimension. But we do not know anything about the relative distances between the Allport and Hartman scale positions (subgroups). Few persons would classify themselves in any one of a finely graded series of distinctions, but a large number of people would be forced to place themselves in a broad category. Thus any distribution shape could be evoked by making the distinctions broad or fine at a particular point on the curve. Hence one could construct a "test" which would appear to indicate that almost everyone was opposed to capital punishment by providing many fine distinctions on the "pro" side of the scale and only a single broad, vague response alternative on the "anti" side. The "pro" people would spread themselves thinly among the several "pro" alternatives, but all "anti" persons would be forced to choose the single "anti" alternative.

Note that Allport and Hartman replaced the traditional question "Are you for or against prohibition?" with a somewhat different question. Rather than probe directly into the underlying attitude, they asked the subject which of the following opinions best characterized his attitude. Thurstone (1928) was quite careful to point out that the opinion statements are only used as "indicants" or "methods of diagnosing" the underlying attitude and are not the attitude itself. Edwards (1957) has made this assumption—fundamental to most self-report techniques of attitude measurement—quite explicit: "One of the major assumptions involved in the construction of attitude scales is that there will be differences in the belief and disbelief systems of those with favorable attitudes towards some psychological object, and those with unfavorable attitudes" (pp. 10–12). Not all opinions and beliefs, of course, are expected to differ among persons with different attitudes toward social objects. But, if there are some statements of belief that are symptomatic of an underlying favorable or unfavorable attitude toward an object, these beliefs can be used in a technique of measurement for the underlying attitude.

The psychophysical model (thurstone). The first step in Thurstone's technique of scale construction is to scale the attitude *statements* along the attitude continuum. (It will be remembered that, eventually, we are interested in scaling people and not statements.) This task is approached, as in psychophysics, by asking a number of "judges" to evaluate the stimuli (opinion statements in this case) along some continuum. Again as in psychophysics, there is a variety of specific experimental procedures by which the judges can be asked to evaluate stimuli.

Although there are theoretical advantages to the mathematically sophisticated method of paired comparisons, practical considerations led Thurstone and Chave (1929) to use the less cumbersome technique of "Equal Appearing Intervals." The statements are printed on cards and the judges are asked to sort the statements into 11 piles. The leftmost pile represents the most unfavorable statements and the rightmost pile represents the most favorable statements. The judges are instructed to make the intervals between the piles equal—i.e., the difference between the second and third pile should represent as large a difference on the underlying continuum as the difference between the eighth and ninth. This method—the method of Equal Appearing Intervals—was that actually used by Thurstone and Chave in 1929 in a monograph which has become the standard handbook for preparing Thurstone attitude scales.

Thurstone proposed criteria for eliminating items that were *ambiguous* or *irrelevant*. Ambiguous items are eliminated because the judges are not able to agree reliably on their placement along the continuum. After the ambiguous items have been eliminated one is left with a series of opinion statements which have been "measured" or "scaled" along an attitudinal continuum. Although the opinion statements have been ordered along an attitudinal continuum, we do not yet know that the statements differ only with respect to the attitude in question. The judges have been instructed to focus on only one aspect of the items (e.g., their bigotry, pro-unionism). The items could differ in many additional aspects to which the judge's attention was not directed in the instructions for the original judging.

Therefore Thurstone proposed a second criterion which must be met by an item—irrelevancy. It will be remembered that the judges used for the original scaling of the opinion items were instructed to attend those aspects of the item relevant to the particular attitude continuum. But the instructions given to subjects who take the attitude scale simply ask the subject to check all statements with which he agrees; his attention is not focused on the underlying attitudinal continuum of interest to the investigator. Since the attention of the subject is not explicitly focused on the attitudinal dimension by the experimenter's instructions, he may agree or disagree with an item *for some reason other than its position on the underlying attitude scale*. Thurstone proposed and used a statistic for measuring this relevance and suggested rejecting irrelevant items (Thurstone and Chave, 1929).

METHOD OF SUMMATED RATINGS (LIKERT). Although Thurstone (1929) described a procedure whereby the scale scores for items could be inferred from the attitudinal responses without first asking judges to sort the items among the attitudinal dimension, it was Likert's (1932) monograph that received the greatest attention among psychologists who wished to score attitudes directly from the attitudinal responses without recourse to a panel of judges. By far the great majority of studies reviewed in this book rely on Likert-type scales to measure attitudes.

The first difference between Likert's technique and Thurstone's original procedure is the item format and instructions to respondents. Whereas the respondent to a Thurstone attitude scale is asked to check all of the opinion statements with which he agrees, the respondent in the Likert is asked to indicate the degree of agreement or approval to all items on a five-point scale. For each attitude item, five response categories are provided: strongly approve, approve, undecided, disapprove, strongly disapprove. On an a priori basis, the investigator determines whether a disapproval or an approval response indicates a large amount of the attitude in question. One end of the scale is assigned an arbitrary value (e.g., the numeral one), the next category is two, the next is three, the next is four, and the next is five. Each individual, then, has a score for every item in the test ranging from one to five. His scale score is then simply the sum of the scores he received on each item.

Items are eliminated if they do not empirically tap the same attitude as the other items in the scale. The advent of computer technology has increased the popularity of indices such as correlations among items or the correlation between a single item and the score for the total scale to help make these judgments. Likert originally proposed a criterion based on a simple critical ratio. On the basis of the total score the top 25% and lowest 25% of subjects were selected. The mean on each item was then determined for the top 25% and the lowest 25% of the subjects. An item was accepted or rejected depending on its ability to discriminate the top 25% from the lowest 25%—i.e., the mean difference divided by its standard error.

It should be stressed, however, that a seven-point agree-disagree scale is not a Likert scale. The Likert technique requires an item analysis to demonstrate that all the items measure the same attitude. Most of the empirical studies reviewed in this volume use the format of a Likert scale. The investigator thinks up one or two generalizations apparently relevant to the attitude and tacks on a seven-point agree-disagree scale. These items use the Likert item format; but, without item analysis, they are not Likert scales. More complete theoretical and "how-to-do-it" discussions are available in Torgerson (1958), Edwards (1957), Green (1954), and Scott (1968).

SCALOGRAM ANALYSIS (GUTTMAN). The scalogram analysis (1950a, 1950b) is based upon a notion of testing which might be called the "successive hurdles" analogy of testing—a notion which also underlies the Stanford-Binet intelligence test. Binet's theory of intelligence was that the process of development was characterized by the continuing acquisition of new capabilities. Once a child had mastered a particular task such as discriminating visual forms (squares, circles, triangles), it was assumed that he maintained this skill and went on to approach new problems. Thus the typical four-year-old can complete a drawing of a man, discriminate visual forms, recall immediately nine and ten word sentences, and answer such questions as "Why do we have houses?" By five and a half he has acquired additional skills that allow him to define such simple words as "ball," copy a square successfully, and count four objects. The increasingly difficult tasks constitute higher and higher hurdles or problems which the child must overcome.

Guttman scale analysis is usually applied to dichotomous data. Dichotomous data are data with only two values, 0 and 1, yes and no, agree and disagree, etc. Dichotomous data do not easily lend themselves to many of the common statistical techniques (the Pearson product moment correlation, which typically forms the basis for factor analysis, for instance). But the scalogram analysis capitalizes on the dichotomous form of the data to provide an elegantly simple and straightforward criterion of unidimensionality. Although the Guttman scalogram is not limited to dichotomous data (e.g., Torgerson, 1958), that is its most convenient and frequent application. Both the development of the scalogram technique and Guttman's persuasive arguments have contributed to increasing importance placed on unidimensional attitude scales; but it cannot be argued that one of the unique advantages of the Guttman technique is that it tests for unidimensionality. There are techniques available to test for unidimensionality in both Thurstone and Likert scaling techniques also.

The basic definition of unidimensionality in a Guttman scale—simple definition—is that once a person has overcome a difficult hurdle, he should be able to overcome all simpler ones. Thus we expect the responses to the test item to have a very straightforward pattern. The respondent will be able to "pass" or answer in the affirmative *all* questions until a certain point of difficulty (or extremity of attitude). After that point he will be unable to "pass" or answer affirmatively *any* of the more difficult items. This will be true only to the extent that the items tap a single unidimensional skill. If, as is more likely, the items require both motor and cognitive skills, then a child might pass a "difficult" item because of advanced motor skills but fail an "easy" item which placed more emphasis on skill. If the items tapped only cognitive skill (or if motor and cognitive skills were perfectly correlated), then the child should pass all items up to a certain point of difficulty, and then fail all the more difficult items.

A classic example of a Guttman-type scale is the Bogardus social distance scale, which was actually developed before Guttman's formalization of the scalogram technique (Bogardus, 1925). Instructions of the scale state: "According to my first feeling reactions, I would willingly admit members of each race (as a class, and not the best members, nor the worst members) to one or more of the following classifications under which I have placed a cross." The respondent was then asked to indicate if he would admit the members of the racial or ethnic group in question to: (1) close kinship by marriage; (2) his club as personal chums; (3) his street as neighbors; (4) employment in his occupation; (5) citizenship in his country; (6) his country as visitors; or (7) would he exclude them from his country.

These items were constructed so that the Guttman-Binet logic is appropriate. The more favorable the attitude of the respondent, the more situations will he check. And, more important, if he is willing to admit a Negro to, say, employment in his occupation, we expect that he would be willing to admit the Negro to hold citizenship in the country, to be a visitor in his country, and would not exclude him from the country. We expect this pattern of responses, however, only if the testee is responding to those aspects of the item which are relevant for his attitude toward Negroes. To the extent that he has heavy financial investments in his home (and believes the influx of ethnic groups would lower property values) his response to item number 3 may be determined by factors other than the attitude in question (i.e., favorability toward Negroes in general)—and thus not fall into the pattern prescribed by Guttman. Responses to the Bogardus social distance scale, then, will exhibit the cumulative pattern prescribed by Guttman only if they tap a unidimensional attitudinal continuum—just as the Binet scale would exhibit the cumulative properties only if the testee's test performance is the function only of some unidimensional aspect of his intelligence and not of irrelevant factors such as practice on particular tasks.

The logic of the Guttman scale is important because many behavioral measures are dichotomous. As we shall see, they may appear to be inconsistent with pencil and paper measures when in fact they form perfect Guttman scales.

THE UNFOLDING TECHNIQUE (COOMBS). Coombs (1964) describes a technique of attitude scaling that derives information on the unidimensionality and relative spacing between the attitude items. The respondent is required to indicate which item he feels best represents his own position, the item next closest, and so on to the item he finds most discrepant with his own position. We will not discuss the mathematical procedures, but Coombs' technique can provide information with respect to both unidimensionality and the relative spacing among items without recourse to the panel of judges required in Thurstone's psychophysical method.

SELF-REPORT TECHNIQUES NOT DEPENDENT UPON OPINION STATE-MENT. The semantic differential, as described by Osgood, Suci, and Tannenbaum (1957), calls for a direct evaluation of the attitudinal object. The semantic differential consists of a series of bipolar adjectives such as hot-cold, fair-unfair, valuable-worthless. Each pair of adjectives is typically separated by seven intervals. The subject is asked to indicate where along the continuum between the two pairs of adjectives the attitude object lies. By means of factor analytic procedures, Osgood and his colleagues found that one dimension of meaning accounted for a large proportion of the variance—the evaluative factor. The particular adjectives making up the evaluative factor may be expected to vary somewhat depending on the particular object being rated, but the most common adjective pairs are fair-unfair, valuable-worthless, pleasant-unpleasant, clean-dirty, and good-bad. Scores on the evaluative factor of the semantic differential are frequently reported to be highly correlated with other measures of attitude toward a particular social object (Osgood et al., 1957).

Taylor and Parker (1964, pp. 37–42) questioned the necessity of inferring attitude from opinion statements. They discuss a type of question which they call the "attitude report question." The attitude report question is little more than the old self-rating scale, which was widely used in the early days of personality and social measurement prior to the more sophisticated attitude scaling techniques already reviewed. "Such a question may be defined as one which subsumes all other attitude items in the same attitude universe. The difference between an attitude report question and the usual scale item is exemplified in the difference between asking, 'Do you feel that Jews corrupt everything with which they come into contact?' (Eysenck and Crown, 1949, p. 75) and asking, 'In general, how do you feel about Jews?' with the degree of favorability being rated on a graphic scale" (p. 37). The authors conclude that such items as the preceding general question and other general questions as "How do you feel about treating emotionally disturbed patients?" and "In your opinion, how adequate has been your overall training in dealing with emotionally disturbed patients?" are at least as reliable as four-, five-, and six-item Guttman scales. Reliability was estimated from a factor analysis including all Guttman scales and attitude report questions.

Even though this is the only research known to the present authors dealing with the comparative reliability and validity of such attitude report, graphic attitude items, the typical laboratory or experimental study of attitude change is much more likely to use such an item than to use a preconstructed Guttman, Likert, or Thurstone attitude scale. As Taylor and Parker point out, the major disadvantage is that there is no method to assess whether or not a single item is tapping a unidimensional attitude, whereas several internal consistency checks of unidimensionality are possible with all four of the attitude scaling techniques discussed and also the semantic differential. With respect to reliability, the Taylor and Parker results would also seem to contradict the widely accepted mathematical postulate that the reliability of the scale is increased with the number of items in the scale. It is possible that the single-question technique gains as much reliability with its directness of questioning, which bypasses the belief structure, as it loses by being only one item.

OBSERVATION OF OVERT BEHAVIOR

If the phrase "observation of overt behavior" brings to mind such techniques as recording actual participation in protest marches or observing how an executive actually deals with his subordinates, we can report little, if anything, in the way of research along these lines. Attitude research on voting, for instance, must inevitably be based on *self-report* of voting since the psychologist cannot gain access to the polling booth to record the actual overt behavior. In sharp contrast to the highly sophisticated methodological work on attitude scaling from self-report, behavioral measures of attitude remain relatively crude. In fact, the present authors are unaware of a single instance in which investigators were able to report reliability for their behavioral measures. Even the clinical psychologist—who certainly deals with "behavioral problems"— typically relies on self-report or the report of observers for his information about what his patient actually does. It is possible that a careful scholar would find interesting examples of behavioral measures of attitude in the small-group literature. Any of the indices which can be formed from the Bales' interaction process analysis (Bales, 1950), for instance, are probably very useful for inferring attitudes of particular group members toward other group members or the task under consideration. But the concept of attitude is not very prevalent in the small-group literature, and the present authors are not aware of any particular examples where the interaction scores have been used to infer the existence of an attitude.

Cook and Selltiz (1964) have suggested that attempts to develop behavioral measures fall into three general categories. In the first, subjects are presented ". . . with standardized situations that they are led to believe are unstaged, in which they believe that their behavior will have consequences, and in which the attitudinal object is represented in some way other than by the actual presence of a member of the object-class" (p. 44). Any self-report attitude instrument, administered under instructions that the responses are to have real-life consequences, would, by this definition, constitute "behavior." There is only a shade of difference, for example, in asking subjects whether they would be willing to have a picture taken with a Negro of the opposite sex to be used for various purposes, and asking the subject to sign a statement that he will, in fact, do so (as in the subsequently described experiments by De Fleur and Westie, 1958). Although Milgram himself (1963; 1964; 1965) has not used the concept of attitude explicitly, his general experimental paradigm would presumably fall in this category. Subjects are led to believe that they are administering electric shocks to a fellow subject in another room. Since the subjects presumably believe that the consequences of their action are real, differences in the number of shocks delivered to, say, white Anglo-Saxons, Protestants, Negroes, Jews, etc., could be used as an index of attitudes toward these groups. Marlowe, Frager, and Nuttall (1965) asked their subjects to volunteer as guides to show Negro students around the Harvard campus and used this response as a measure of attitude toward Negroes. The experimenters did not actually observe the students conducting tours around the Harvard campus, but we may consider the agreement to volunteer a "behavioral" response because the subjects were led to believe that the volunteering response would have real-life consequences.

According to Cook and Selltiz (1964), "Another approach is to present the subject with an admittedly staged situation and ask him to play a role—perhaps to behave as he would in such a situation in real life, perhaps to take the part of someone else or to act in some specified way" (pp. 44–45). They cite a study by Stanton and Litwak (1955) in which foster parents were asked to play roles in various stressful situations. Evaluations of these role-play experiences proved useful in predicting success as a foster parent; and with a little charity, we can see the relevance of this to the diagnosis of attitude.

Finally, Cook and Selltiz discuss a third behavioral approach which is used in the study of attitudes toward social groups: ". . . (the tester asks) . . . for sociometric choices among individuals some of whom are members of the object group, preferably under circumstances that lead the participants to believe that such choices will have consequences in the form of subsequent assignment in some situation" (Cook and Selltiz, 1964, p. 45).

REACTION TO OR INTERPRETATION OF PARTIALLY STRUCTURED STIMULI

"The common characteristic of techniques in this category is that, while there may be no attempt to disguise the reference to the attitudinal object, the subject is not asked to state his own actions directly; he is ostensibly describing a scene, a character, or the behavior of a third person" (Cook and Selltiz, 1964, p. 47). In other words, he is using projective techniques. The literature on projective techniques is extensive, and the reader is referred to other sources (e.g., Campbell, 1950; Cook and Selltiz, 1964; Zubin, Eron, and Schumer, 1965) for a review. With few exceptions (e.g., Katz and his colleagues, see Chapter 7), experiments testing theories of attitude change seldom have used projective techniques to measure attitudes.

PERFORMANCE ON "OBJECTIVE" TASKS

"Approaches in this category present the respondent with specific tasks to be performed; they are presented as tests of information or ability, or simply as jobs that need to be done. The assumption common to all of them is that performance may be influenced by attitude, and that a systematic bias in performance reflects the influence of attitude" (Cook and Selltiz, 1964, p. 50). Just as Thurstone had suggested that some statements of "fact" might characterize persons of either positive or negative attitude, testers in this tradition assume that the direction of "error" the subject makes in answering a factual question is indicative of his attitude. There is some support for the assumption in studies of attitude toward Russia by Hammond (1948) and Weschler (1950) and in a study by Rankin and Campbell (1955) on attitudes toward Negroes.

Also in this category are studies that assume that a subject is able to remember information consistent with his attitude longer (Levine and Murphy, 1943; Jones and Kohler, 1958) or makes systematic mistakes in his reasoning (Watson, 1925; Morgan, 1945; Thistlethwaite, 1950). It is possible to infer the subject's own attitude—particularly if it is an extreme attitude—when he is ostensibly engaged in an objective judgment task such as the first stage of Thurstone scaling. This phenomenon will be discussed in the chapter on judgmental theories on attitude change. We might also include the Horowitz and Horowitz (1938) pictures test in this category. Subjects are asked to select, from a group of pictures, which persons belong together. Decisions about characterization—i.e., characterization by race rather than sex or age—have been used to make inferences about attitudes.

PHYSIOLOGICAL REACTIONS

Rankin and Campbell (1955) had subjects attached to a galvanic skin response apparatus they wore while engaged in an experimental task. An experimenter—either Negro or white—entered the room ostensibly to adjust the apparatus. GSR scores were related to verbal measures of attitude. Westie and De Fleur (1959) report a significant relationship between GSR, vascular constriction in the finger, and a pencil and paper test of attitude. There has been some suggestion that physiological arousal occurs to both positively *and* negatively evaluated attitude statements. Katz, Cadoret, Hughes, and Abbey (1965) and Dickson and McGinnies (1966), to consider two examples, find increased physiological arousal associated with both agreeable and disagreeable attitude statements.

Some provocative studies by Eckhard Hess (1965; Hess and Polt, 1960) suggests that pupil dilation may be correlated with the interest value of the stimuli. Woodmansee (1965) reports some evidence of greater dilation in response to Negro content pictures among anti-Negro subjects. But Collins, Diebold, and Helmreich (1967) fail to find evidence of within-subject correlations between the evaluative scale of this semantic differential and pupillary dilation to attitude-relevant stimuli. Thus this study finds no relationship between pupillary dilation and a traditional measure of attitude.

Physiological measures are seldom used in the experiments reviewed in the later chapters of this book. Readers interested in these measures are referred to the collection of papers in Leiderman and Shapiro's *Psychobiological Approaches to Social Behavior* (1964).

SUMMARY

A review of the attitude measurement literature reveals a considerable amount of effort and accomplishment in self-report attitude scale construction. But the sophistication of this literature should not create a false sense of complacency about the attitude measures in the experiments reviewed later. First, remember that very few laboratory investigations of attitude are based on these sophisticated, pretested attitude scales. Second, the preoccupation with pencil and paper measures of an attitude (at the expense of alternate methods of measurement) has resulted in an "operational drift." Our operational measurement procedures have drifted away from our theoretical notions of attitude. Almost every paper using a technique other than self-report is a methodological paper, published just to prove it is possible to measure an attitude without self-report. Every theory of attitude change in this book rests on an empirical foundation of pencil and paper. Webb, Campbell, Schwartz, and Sechrest (1966) have presented a number of nonquestionnaire techniques of measurement. But their book is not a presentation of alternative techniques of attitude measurement which can be immediately substituted for verbal self-report measures in the standard laboratory experiment on attitude change. Instead, it is admittedly an attempt to stimulate the creativity of psychologists and lessen their dependence on the questionnaire, a most worthwhile aim.

But social scientists have stopped asking the question: "Can attitudes be measured?" The standard measurement techniques have been accepted—assumptions and all. This uncritical acceptance of attitude measurement techniques has had a strong impact on the contemporary conceptions of attitude. While the historical influences such as the emphasis on behavior and the emphasis on socially important topics remain, much of the research reported in later sections of this book appears to assume that an attitude is: "Whatever is measured by my pencil and paper test." We shall discuss this problem in detail in the next section. However, in defense of this common practice by active researchers, we shall discuss now some of the justifications that they muster on their own behalf. There are two major portions of an experiment between which effort can be divided—the independent manipulation and the dependent measurement. If an experimental test fails because it is insensitive, the insensitivity may stem from weak manipulations of the independent variable or, instead, from unreliable dependent measures. Since the day-to-day realities of the working researcher inevitably impose a compromise with ideal practice, every experiment necessarily represents an accord between effort and a thoroughly adequate test of a theoretical proposition. Thus the practical experimenter often must decide whether to spend time strengthening his independent manipulation or refining his dependent variable.

Whether as a result of considered judgment or reliance on tradition, many researchers prefer to put more of their energies into creating a powerful independent manipulation rather than refining their attitude measures. In the extreme case, they may use only a single attitude item—although researchers more commonly use multiple items. In their defense, these researchers would argue that their experimental designs most frequently deal with current or locally relevant attitude dimensions (in an effort to add "meaning" or "interest" for the subject) and for these dimensions there are no extant attitude scales which have been carefully constructed. Furthermore, and perhaps more importantly, they would stress that they are not interested in a careful measurement of individual differences but rather in detecting treatment differences. Since their treatments are designed to be maximally or highly potent, perhaps they are correct in minimizing the need for a tuned measuring device. Additionally they would point out that even when previously constructed measures are topical for a particular experimental design, their substantial length may preclude their use; the induction of the independent treatment may by itself tax the subject's tolerance for fatigue.

Nonetheless, the present authors do not recommend that attitude change studies use only a single attitude item as a dependent variable. A small scale has greater reliability than a single item; thus the experimenter could achieve standard levels of statistical significance with fewer subjects or a weaker manipulation. Furthermore, the use of a small scale increases our confidence that the results will generalize to a universe of attitude items.

Behaviors and Attitudes

Both theories and definitions of attitude have been strongly influenced by the need for a concept that would account for individual differences in behavior. In spite of this historical and theoretical pressure in the direction of a behaviorally defined attitude, attitudes are almost universally measured by pencil and paper or verbal report techniques. The highly sophisticated and specific techniques for the measurement of attitudes typically lack the global scope implied by many of our definitions and most of our theory about attitudes.

Considered in this context, the title for this section, "Attitudes and Behavior" is paradoxical. To begin, an attitude response (whether verbal or pencil and paper) is a kind of behavior. On the one hand, then, we could argue that attitude test responses *are* behavior. By this line of reasoning, attitudes would be a subclass of behavior, and our title should be "Some Kinds of Behavior and Other Kinds of Behavior."

We can arrive at the same conclusion by starting at the other end. Most definitions of attitudes tell us that attitudes contribute to overt behavior. If we hold the stimulus condition constant, individual differences in behavior should correspond to individual differences in attitude. By this reasoning, all behaviors are measures of attitude; thus the title of this section might be "One Measure of Attitudes and Another Measure of Attitudes."

But ask any social psychologist about the relationship between behavior and attitudes and you are likely to start a lively discussion. Clearly, then, the phrase "behavior and attitudes" must mean something. What has happened is that social scientists have, almost without exception, settled on pencil and paper or interview techniques for the *measurement* of attitudes while retaining a *theory* that specifies behavioral implications for attitudes. The properly pedantic title for this section should be something like "The Relationship Between Certain Kinds of Behavior, Arbitrarily Designated by Most Social Scientists as Measures of Attitude, and Other Kinds of Behavior Which, According to Theory, Should Be Influenced by the Attitude in Question." In the next two sections we will first discuss the evidence for an inconsistent relationship and then the evidence supporting a consistent relationship.

EVIDENCE FOR ATTITUDE-BEHAVIOR INCONSISTENCY

It is commonly assumed that attitudes and behaviors are closely related in natural settings. Nonetheless, there are several studies often cited to demonstrate an inconsistent relation between attitudes and behavior. We will postpone the question of whether attitude *change* is related to behavior *change* for the last section. Undoubtedly the most frequently discussed study under the heading "Behavior and Attitudes" is one by La Piere (1934). It deals with the apparent inconsistency created when motel or restaurant proprietors actually served a Chinese couple even though they said they would not do so when asked by letter.

We will offer several criticisms of this experiment later, but the response to the letter is, somehow, more like an "attitude" and less like a "behavior" than what the desk clerks and waitresses did when the Chinese couple arrived on the premises; but, in another sense, both are very much "behavior." The response to the letter—accepting or rejecting a request for reservations—is very much overt behavior, very much a part of the "real life" activities of an entrepreneur, and in no sense a laboratory situation.

La Piere (1934) reports on his travels with a Chinese couple:

"In something like ten thousand miles of motor travel, twice across the United States, up and down the Pacific Coast, we met definite rejection from those asked to serve us just once (p. 232). . . . To provide a comparison of symbolic reaction to symbolic social situations with actual reaction to real social situations, I 'questionnaired' the establishments which we patronized during the two year period. . . . To the hotel or restaurant a questionnaire was mailed with an accompanying letter purporting to be a special and personal plea for response. The questionnaires all asked the same question, 'Will you accept members of the Chinese race as guests in your establishment?' (p. 233) . . . 92% of the (restaurants and cafes) and 91% of the (hotels, auto-camps and tourist homes) replied 'No.' The remainder replied 'Uncertain; depend on circumstances'" (pp. 233–234).

Another study frequently cited in support of the contention that attitudes are not correlated with behavior is a study by Ralph D. Minard (1952) on "Race Relationships in the Pocahontas Coal Field." Minard notes some striking differences in the patterns of racial behavior during working hours in the coal mine and nonworking hours in the community.

"The boundary line between the two communities is usually the mine's mouth. Management assists the miners in recognizing their entrance into the outside community with its distinctions in status by providing separate (racially segregated) baths and locker rooms. . . .

"There is a difference in men, and not all of them adjust to the shift in community patterns outside the mine in the same way. Probably about 20 per cent of the men have favorable attitudes toward Negroes reasonably free from prejudice both within and without the mine. There are another 20 per cent whose attitude both inside and outside the mine is strongly prejudiced and changes little with shift in community relationship. It is the remaining 60 per cent who tend to shift their role and status upon passing from the mine's mouth into the outside world . . ." (Minard, 1952, p. 31).

What we actually have here is not an inconsistency between attitudes and behavior. If anything, it is an "inconsistency" between behavior in two different situations.

EVIDENCE FOR ATTITUDE-BEHAVIOR CONSISTENCY

Perhaps the most fertile ground for evidence suggesting a consistent relation between attitude and behavior is found in studies using the "known group method" for validating attitude scales. Groups which are "known" to have extreme attitudes on a particular issue are administered an attitude scale. Thus prejudice scales are frequently validated by administering them to Northern and Southern whites, or to whites and Negroes. Nettler and Golding (1946), for instance, report that items of their Thurstone scale on attitudes toward the Japanese successfully discriminated between members of avidly pro-Japanese and members of avidly anti-Japanese organizations. Similarly, Sherif and Hovland (1961) have found that members of prohibitionistic organizations (the joining of which can be regarded as "behavior") indicated attitudes significantly different from members of other organizations. That is, people who attend Catholic churches hold Catholic beliefs, etc.

It should be pointed out that, statistically, any relationship will be exaggerated when the selection groups for either attitudes or behavior are chosen from the extreme ends of the continuum, as in the "known group method." An effect that is small in the general population will be shown more dramatically than it would be shown with a similar sized group of subjects sampled randomly from the entire continuum.

One of the most directly relevant studies on the relationship between attitude and behavior is a study by De Fleur and Westie (1958). "Each subject . . . was conducted to an interview room where a variety of questions, devices and situations were presented to him regarding his feelings about Negroes" (p. 669). From these procedures a verbal measure of "attitude" was constructed.

The measure of "behavior" illustrates how a clever experimenter can capture a "real-life" variable in the laboratory.

"In the laboratory session, and in earlier phases of the interview, each subject had viewed a number of colored photographic slides showing interracial pairings of males and females. Some of these slides portrayed a well-dressed, good looking, young Negro man paired with a good looking, well-dressed, young white woman. Others showed a white man similarly paired with a Negro woman. The background for all of the slides consisted of a table, a lamp, and a window with a drapery, giving an effect not unlike that of a living room or possibly a dormitory lounge. The persons in the photographs were seated beside each other in separate chairs and were looking at one another with pleasant expressions . . . .

"To present the overt action opportunity, the interviewer told each subject that another set of such slides was needed for further research. The subject was first asked if he (or she) would be willing to be photographed with a Negro person of the opposite sex. . . . Then . . . the subject was presented with a mimeographed form and informed that this was 'a standard photograph release agreement, which is necessary in any situation where a photograph of an individual is to be used in any manner.' The photograph release agreement contained a graded series of 'uses' to which the photograph would be put . . . , ranging from laboratory experiments, such as they had just experienced, to a nationwide publicity campaign advocating racial integration. They were to sign their name to each 'use' they would permit.

"In American society, the affixing of one's signature to a document is a particularly significant act. The signing of checks, contracts, agreements and the like is clearly understood to indicate a binding obligation on the part of the signer to abide by the provisions of the document" (De Fleur and Westie, 1958, pp. 669–670).

The attained relationship between pencil and paper measure of attitudes and the behavioral measure (number of "permissions") is indicated in Table 1.1.

While the relationship between the "attitude" and "behavior" is significant statistically, it should be noted that 14 subjects, or nearly a third of the sample, behaved "inconsistently." Five subjects indicated

TABLE 1.1.   RELATIONSHIP BETWEEN RACE ATTITUDES AND LEVEL OF
SIGNED AGREEMENT TO BE PHOTOGRAPHED WITH NEGRO

		Subject Attitude	
		Prejudiced	Unprejudiced
Behavioral	Prejudiced	18	9
Measure	Unprejudiced	5	14

Adapted from De Fleur and Westie (1958).

a high degree of verbal prejudice but gave a large number of permissions. Another nine subjects indicated relatively little verbal prejudice but signed only a few permissions.

In summary, there are data on both sides of the question. Some studies seem to indicate no relationship between behavior and attitude, whereas others indicate a positive relationship. Typically, most of the evidence falls between—suggesting that it is possible to predict behavior from attitudes but without a great deal of precision.

FACTORS AFFECTING THE RELATIONSHIP BETWEEN ATTITUDES AND BEHAVIOR SITUATIONAL DIFFERENCES

The important question, then, is not "Are attitudes and behavior correlated?" Rather, we should ask, "When are attitudes and behavior correlated?" and "What factors affect the size of the correlation when and if it is found?" This section examines factors that might be expected to facilitate or inhibit the correlation between attitude and behavior.

A correlation between attitudes and behavior rests on the stability of individual differences—a tendency for an individual to respond somewhat consistently from one situation to another. The problem of correlating attitudes and behavior is no different from the problem of correlating behavior in one situation with behavior in another situation. Beginning with the astronomer's personal equation and continuing through the development of various intelligence tests, psychologists of individual differences have found that they could detect a certain amount of consistency in the behavior of individuals from situation to situation.

Seldom, however, has this consistency been large enough so that it can be seen by a casual observer. More frequently, statistical indices are needed to reveal the consistency. The following example may help to illustrate how differences in behavior from situation to situation can obscure stable individual differences. If we construct a table listing a wide variety of imaginable situations or environments across the top (such as a first date, a visit to a library, a twenty-fifth wedding anniversary, and a visit to a nuclear submarine) and if we arrange widely different attitudes along the rows, it seems probable that the behavioral differences from situation to situation would be much larger than the behavioral differences from attitude type to attitude type. In fact, it would take a practiced eye indeed to detect the attitudinal contributions to behavior in these diverse situations.

Three studies from the literature on attitudes and behavior illustrate the problem of predicting from one situation to another. La Piere reports his intuitive hunches that nonattitudinal factors such as luggage and demeanor contribute to the proprietor's behavior when the oriental couple requests service:

"In the end I was forced to conclude that those factors which most influenced the behavior of others towards the Chinese had nothing to do with race. Quality and condition of clothing, appearance of baggage (by which, it seems, hotel clerks are prone to base their quick evaluations), cleanliness and neatness were far more significant for person-to-person reactions in the situations I was studying than skin pigmentation, straight black hair, slanting eyes, and flat noses. . . . A supercilious desk clerk in a hotel of noble aspirations could not refuse his master's hospitality to people who appeared to take their request as a perfectly normal and conventional thing . . . " (La Piere, 1934, p. 232).

Minard's description of the differences in the working and town situations in the Pocahontas coal field is another example of how situational differences contribute to behavior. In the mine the workers are dramatically separated from the "outside world" by the mine shaft, engaged in a common activity, and under pressure from management to eliminate status differences based on race which might interfere with productivity. "On top," however, there is no shared task and no pressure from management; the interaction is more likely to be in the more sensitive socioemotional areas than in the task areas. With the segregated locker rooms at the mouth of the mine to help make the transition, it is not hard to understand why, for 60% of the miners at least, it is easy to establish different behavior patterns in the two situations.

Lohman and Reitzes (1954) describe another set of workers who fail to exhibit consistency in the work situation and the residency situation. The "Civic Club" in the neighborhood fostered anti-Negro behaviors. The union in the work situation fostered pro-Negro behaviors.

"The 151 individuals within the neighborhood selected for study were all members of a labor union with a clear, implemented policy of granting Negroes complete equality on the job (the job situation). The neighborhood in which they were residents and of which they were an organic part, however, was strongly anti-Negro with respect to the movements of Negroes into the neighborhood. . . . The study of the neighborhood indicated that in the center of the organizational pattern of the community was the deliberately organized property owners association, called the Civic Club (the neighborhood situation). This Civic Club can be considered a key factor in explaining the action of individuals toward Negroes as neighbors. . . . By being in the center of the organizational structure of the community, the club was able to define and structure any situation which involved Negroes as neighbors. . . .

"The Civic Club's definition of the situation—rejection of the Negroes as neighbors—provided the individual with well formulated statements, reasons, and justification for specific actions in specific situations involving the individual's interests in the neighborhood situation.

"The same individual *in a different context* (emphasis added) for example, at work, with a corresponding organizational structuring of the specific situation, acts in terms of this definition of the situation by another deliberately organized collectivity. In neither case does the individual act out any abstract, generalized attitudes toward Negroes, which could become important only when the deliberate definition is absent" (Lohman and Reitzes, 1954, pp. 342–343).

Situational differences, norms, and expectations can vary while the attitude remains constant. These differences in norms for behavior create differences in behavior unrelated to the attitude—which runs counter to the usual notion that behavior is a more "valid" measure of attitude. Lohman and Reitzes present data to support the notion that the situations or relevant norms contributed significantly to attitudes and behaviors toward Negroes. On the basis of interview material, they identified people who were strongly involved in the neighborhood and others who were not so strongly involved. "It was those persons most involved in the (anti-Negro) neighborhood who voiced the greatest objections to Negroes as neighbors."

This suggests that those individuals closely in tune with the environmental pressures for rejection of Negroes as neighbors hold the most negative attitudes. Similarly, individuals classified as highly involved in (pro-Negro) union activities were likely to accept Negroes at work. Also consistent with the interpretation that attitudes and behavior toward Negroes are determined largely by the situations is the fact that acceptance of the Negro at work was uncorrelated with acceptance of the Negro as a neighbor.

These discrepancies between work and neighborhood behaviors are not indicative of a low correlation between attitudes and behavior. They illustrate that the normative differences from one environment to another are often so large that behaviors are not always correlated with behaviors, and attitudes are not always correlated with attitudes. We will not find a high correlation between attitude and behavior if situational pressures substantially contribute to the observed behavior—and they almost always do.

RELIABILITY. Consider the problem of trying to predict the baseball batting averages recorded by a fatigued (or intoxicated) scorekeeper who occasionally assigns a hit to the wrong player, thus giving one player fewer hits than he deserves and another player more hits than he deserves. Even if you did a perfect job of predicting the *actual* batting performance, you would fail to accurately predict the *recorded* batting average. We never predict the "actual" behavior or "actual" attitude. We predict a measurement of behavior or a measurement of attitude, and any imprecision (low reliability) in our measuring technique—situational variances, ambiguous test items, careless respondents, drunken scorekeepers, or what have you will lower our predictive precision.

ITEM DIFFICULTY. Even though measuring techniques produce highly reliable measurements for both attitudes and behavior, two measurements may fail to correlate because they make discriminations at different extremes of the attitude or behavioral continuum. Consider two items from an arithmetic test: (1) 2 plus 2 equals ?; and (2) differentiate the expression sin $X^{-\frac{1}{3}}$. Suppose that 98% of our respondents successfully answered the first question and 2% successfully answered the second. Suppose further that our test is a perfectly reliable and valid measure of mathematical ability—i.e., it was indeed the least apt respondents who failed to answer the first question and the most skilled respondents who answered the second. The two items would be measuring the underlying ability continuum with perfect accuracy and validity. In spite of this fact, the correlation between the scores on the two items would be very low. The best that we can do is say that 2% of the people failing the first item will not be the same 2% who pass the second item. For the other 96 people, no prediction can be made from one item to the other.

This problem is limited to measures that are scored dichotomously and that make discriminations near the end of the continuum. The use of a Guttman score composed of several dichotomous items making discriminations at different points on the continuum would eliminate the problem. But, unfortunately, the use of a single dichotomous item making a discrimination near the extreme is common in the literature on behavior and attitudes.

If the behavior "test" discriminates between the extremely prejudiced and the moderately prejudiced, then everyone from moderate prejudice on down is classified as "nonprejudiced." If the attitude item discriminates between the "no prejudice whatsoever" and the "just a tiny bit prejudiced," then everyone from just the tiny bit prejudiced on up is classified as prejudiced. Many people classified not prejudiced by the behavior item must be classified prejudiced by the attitude item. This does not mean attitude and behavior are not correlated—it just means that the attitude item makes a dichotomous distinction at one end of the continuum and the behavior item makes its distinction at the other end of the scale.

The two measures of "attitude" and "behavior" used by Kutner, Wilkins, and Yarrow (1952) in their replication of the La Piere study illustrates this problem. For the behavioral criterion the procedure was as follows:

"Three young women, 2 white and 1 Negro, all well-dressed and well-mannered, entered 11 individual restaurants in a fashionable Northeastern suburban community, Subtown. In each case, the white women entered first, asked for a table for three and were seated. The Negro woman entered a short while later, informed the hostess or head waiter that she was with a party already seated, found the table and sat down" (Kutner et al., 1952, p. 649).

The behavioral "test" was structured so as to minimize the possibility of refusal—in other words, it would take an extremely high amount of prejudice to reject the Negro woman. The women were well dressed and the white women of the party were actually seated by the time the Negro woman arrived on the scene. It is perhaps not surprising, then, that the women were served in all 11 establishments.

Consider, on the other hand, the difficulty level of the attitude "test" in Kutner et al.

"Two weeks following each visit, a letter signed with an assumed name was sent to each establishment. . . . The letter read as follows:

"Dear Sir:
"A group of friends and I are planning a social affair to be held in Subtown in the near future. I should like to make reservations to have them for dinner at your restaurant. Since some of them are colored, I wonder whether you would object to their coming.
"Could you let me know if the reservations may be made so that I may complete the arrangements as soon as possible?
Yours truly," (p. 649).

In marked contrast to the behavioral test, the letter does much to maxi-mize the possibility of refusal. Reservations are not requested in a straightforward manner, and the manager is almost invited to refuse: "Since some of them are colored, I wonder whether you would object to their coming."

Seventeen days after the letters were sent out, no replies of any kind had been received. A follow-up telephone call indicated considerably less receptiveness on the part of the restaurant managers than a control call which merely requested the reservations for a party of friends to be held in the near future.

The study dramatically demonstrates that restaurant managers will behave in a prejudiced way in some situations and not in others. Because of the extreme difference in the item difficulty—no prejudice on the behavioral measure and almost complete prejudice on the attitudinal measure—the study does not have any bearing whatsoever on the ques-tion of the relationship between attitude and behavior. Even if there were a *perfect* correlation between attitude and behavior, it could not be demonstrated with items so structured that they classify 100% of the subjects in a single category.

A similar argument holds when the difficulties are less extreme. Campbell (1963) has argued that the behavior patterns in the La Piere study with the Chinese couple and the Minard study on the Pocahontas coal field do not indicate a true inconsistency:

"In La Piere's . . . study, he and the Chinese couple were refused ac-commodation in .4 percent of places stopped. The mailed questionnaire reported 92.5 percent refusal of Chinese. The first thing we note is that the two diagnostic situations have very different thresholds. Apparently it is very hard to refuse a well-dressed Chinese couple traveling with a European in a face-to-face setting, and very easy to refuse the Chinese as a race in a mailed questionnaire. . . . But this is no evidence of in-consistency. Inconsistency would be represented if those who refused face to face accepted by questionnaire, or if those who accepted by questionnaire refused face to face. There is no report that such cases occurred" (Camp-bell, 1963, p. 160).

A similar argument can be made for Minard's description of prejudice in the town and prejudice in the mine. The town situation represents an "easy item"—a situation with such a low threshold that citizens with even moderate amounts of prejudice exhibit the prejudice in their be-havioral pattern. The mining situation can be regarded as a more difficult item or a situation with a higher threshold. It requires a higher degree of prejudice to overcome the situational pressures for equality. Using Minard's statistics, 20% of the workers are so prejudiced that they exhibit prejudicial behavior both inside the mine and out. Sixty percent are of a moderate degree of prejudice, such that they exhibit prejudice in the low threshold town situation but not in the high threshold mine situation, and the remaining twenty percent are so unprejudiced that no prejudicial behavior occurs in either town or mine. An inconsistency would be noted if someone were prejudiced in the mine but not prejudiced in the town—and Minard reports no such behavior patterns.

CATEGORY WIDTH. Most of our behavioral measures of attitude make relatively few discriminations along the attitudinal continuum; typically, persons are divided into 2, 3, 4, or 5 categories. Pencil and paper measures, on the other hand, are typically more nearly continuous—making many fine discriminations along the attitude continuum. Two persons who fall in separate, narrow categories on the pencil and paper measure might fall into the same, broad category on the behavioral measure. Similarly a manipulation might create a small amount of attitude change which would be detected by the precise pencil and paper measure but merely produce an undetected change within one of the broad categories of the behavioral measure.

A CHANGE IN THE ATTITUDE OBJECT. We can expect a high correlation between pencil and paper measures of attitude and behavioral responses only when both behaviors are elicited by the same stimulus (or attitude) object. A frequent reason for nonexistent or low correlations between attitude measures and behavioral measures may well stem from the fact that most attitude questionnaires measure responses to the generalized "typical Negro" or "Jews in general." It is difficult for even the most ingenious experimenter, however, to find some way to observe overt behavior in response to the "typical Negro" or to "Jews in general." As a consequence, most attitude responses are to some culturally defined stereotype, whereas most behavior observed by social psychologists is in response to a particular and specific social object. The La Piere study and its replication by Kutner et al. are, of course, subject to this criticism.

Even if the experimenter attempts to hold the social object constant from attitude testing to behavior testing situations, the "meaning" of the attitude object may be altered by the different context of the behavior and attitude testing situations. For instance, Soloman Asch (1940) asked his respondents to rank order several professions in terms of their prestige. Unlike most attitude testers, however, Asch asked the subjects to give specific examples of what they had in mind while they were rating the professions. In this way Asch was able to ascertain the specific social objects which the subjects were evaluating in the questionnaire. Politicians are ranked rather low on the list and were described as "ward heelers," "party hacks," etc.

At a later time Asch presented subjects with a rank order of the same ten occupations which had presumably been obtained from a large sample of fellow college students. Asch deliberately had incorrectly listed the profession of politicians very high in the rank order. As is typical in conformity studies, Asch's subjects increased their evaluation of "politicians." But when Asch again asked the subjects to give specific examples of the professions, he found that the subjects listed respected national statesmen. It seems plausible that the context provided by the false norms about politicians for the conformity group changed the specific attitude object being rated.

CHANGE IN THE SALIENCE OF VARIOUS ATTITUDES TOWARD THE ATTITUDE OBJECT. Most of the attitudes that are measured actually represent a summary or composite evaluation which could be broken down into several components. This is because most of the objects evaluated in attitude questionnaires could be broken up into many specific components, and in many cases the respondent can be found to have a separate attitude toward each aspect of complex attitude objects. Attitudes toward "Negroes" can probably be broken down into many separate and smaller attitudes. To consider just two, the suburbanite may have a favorable attitude toward Negroes because he considers himself a liberal and feels that it is both his and society's obligation to right wrongs done toward a disadvantaged racial group. As a suburbanite with most of his savings tied up in his home, he may also believe—"unpleasant as the social realities may be"—that his property value would be significantly lowered if Negroes were to move into his neighborhood. Continuing with this simple example, his composite or overall attitude toward Negroes would then be made up of two parts, a favorable attitude on the basis of his philosophical liberalism, and an unfavorable attitude based on his economic interest in his home. Presumably, if an attitudinal question is couched in general and philosophical terms, his favorable attitude will be heavily weighted in his response. If the test situation deals specifically with Negroes moving into his neighborhood, on the other hand, then his unfavorable attitude would be weighted heavily in the response.

Some attitudes may be salient in the paper and pencil test, while other attitudes are salient in the behavioral situation. This situation arises quite frequently in correlations between attitude and behavior because attitudinal measures frequently make broad and philosophical attitudes salient, whereas behavioral measures make specific and immediately personal attitudes salient. We can expect a low correlation between attitude and behavior in those cases where one set of subattitudes is salient in the testing situation, whereas another set of subattitudes is salient in the behavioral situation.

FACTOR STRUCTURE OF ATTITUDE AND BEHAVIORAL SYNDROMES. Intuitions gained from observation of our own behavior and the behavior of others allow us to make fairly competent intuitive guesses about when two stimulus situations are similar and when two responses are similar, i.e., under what circumstances we should expect correlation between two attitudes or two behaviors. But factor analyses of attitude items frequently fail to confirm our intuitive notions of which items would "hang together" in a single syndrome. Most of the research in this area has been directed toward the discovery of unitary syndromes of mental abilities, personality traits, and attitudes, but we should expect much the same state of affairs to appear when we are trying to discover uniform and internally consistent *behavioral* syndromes.

Triandis (1964) asked a small number of University of Illinois undergraduates how they would behave toward certain stimulus persons, such as a 50-year old Negro, Roman Catholic, male physician, or a 20-year old white, Jewish, female soda fountain clerk. They were asked to rate the extent to which they would or would not engage in certain behaviors with 34 different kinds of stimulus persons described by the various possible combinations of the adjectives in the above examples. They were asked whether they would admire the character of, be commanded by, physically love, kiss the hand of, go fishing with, prohibit from voting, discuss moral issues with, lose a game to, treat as subordinate, etc.

For the white, Protestant, male sample of respondents, five separate factors were discovered (Triandis, 1964). What is the meaning of the fact that there are five *separate* factors? The behaviors within a factor probably make up a highly intercorrelated syndrome. If one of Triandis' subjects stated that he would admire the character of a particular stimulus person, he is also very likely to cooperate in the political campaign of a certain person, obey him, and ask his opinion. Since admiring the character of and falling in love with a person are two *different* factors, we do not expect to find a strong correlation between admiring the character of and falling in love with the same person. Thus, although you may know that one friend admires the character of another, that knowledge does not allow you to predict that your friends are likely to fall in love. Nor does the knowledge that a friend admires the character of someone give you any information about whether he would be likely to be partners with him in an athletic game (factor three), be permitted to do your friend a favor (factor four), treat him as a subordinate (factor five). Therefore we might feel that admiring the character of, falling in love with, being partners with, allowing favors to be done for us by, and treating as a subordinate, should form a single consistent pattern of behaviors; but Triandis (1964) found that these five behaviors were parts of relatively separate and distinct clusters.

With this background we can return to our major point: When should we expect attitudes and behavior to be uncorrelated? Our intuitive ideas about what attitudes should be correlated with each other are frequently in error; our intuitive ideas about what behaviors should be correlated with each other are frequently in error. It should be even less surprising that our intuitions about which attitudes should be correlated with which behaviors also should be in error. No matter how strong our hunch is that a Southern restaurant owner's general evaluation of Negroes should be correlated with his behavior when a Negro enters his restaurant, empirical investigation could well demonstrate that serving behavior is not included in the same syndrome as general evaluative attitudes for Negroes in southern United States. For the sake of argument, for example, it could well be that the serving behavior is part of a cluster or syndrome which includes attitudes toward the federal government and law violations rather than the syndrome which includes evaluative attitudes toward Negroes.

In summary, our notions that a *particular* attitude correlates with a *particular* behavior may be incorrect, not because of a general failure of attitudes to have any relationship to behavior, but because our intuitive notions about which attitudinal factors are correlated with which behavioral factors are incorrect. While our theoretical analysis of attitudes definitely commits us to a position that attitude factors should, in general, be correlated with *some* behavioral factors, it does not commit us to a position that each attitude factor should be correlated to *all* behavioral factors. It does not commit us to the position that a particular attitude factor should be correlated with a particular behavioral factor—even if the logical and intuitive arguments that a particular attitude and behavior belong in the same factor are very compelling.

NONATTITUDINAL CONTRIBUTIONS TO THE RESPONSE. As we will discuss in the methodology chapter, a response to a "test item" is influenced by factors other than the attitude. Although the experimenter attempts to eliminate competing motivations of habits and attitudes in the testing situation, he frequently seeks out "real life" situations for his behavioral test. The behavioral response is fully immersed in the cross-current of extra-attitudinal pressures on the response. In a later chapter we shall discuss in detail the fact that the ebb and tide of day-to-day life frequently lead an individual to emit a response which he would not have emitted in the absence of counterattitudinal pressures. With only a brief reference to scientific justification, an experimenter can elicit behaviors quite foreign to the subject's underlying attitudes such as telling a lie to an attractive coed (Festinger and Carlsmith, 1959) or administering presumably dangerous shocks to a fellow subject (Milgram, 1964, 1965).

To the extent that the extra-attitudinal factors involved in the "attitude response" are different from the extra-attitudinal factors involved in the "behavior response," we can expect an attenuation (or elimination) of the correlation between attitude and behavior. Conversely, to the extent that the extra-attitudinal factors are similar in the two testing situations, the correlation between attitude and behavior will be artificially inflated.

ATTITUDE CHANGE AND BEHAVIOR CHANGE

Festinger (1964) has focused attention on the problem of relating attitude change to behavior change. "The fact that existing attitudes relate to overt behavior does not tell us whether or not an attitude *change* brought about by exposure to a persuasive communication will be reflected in a *change* in subsequent behavior" (Festinger, 1964, pp. 406–407). His literature search turned up only three studies relevant to this problem—and even then he had to stretch the interpretation of Janis and Feshbach to make the data relevant (Maccoby, Romney, Adams, and Maccoby, 1962; Fleishmann, Harris, and Burtt, 1955; Janis and Feshbach, 1953). The three studies reviewed do not find a relationship between attitude change and behavior change; in fact, the relationship is sometimes slightly negative. Subsequently Greenwald (1965, 1966) reports several experiments designed to investigate the problem directly. He reports that students who worked on vocabulary problems (as opposed to those working on current affairs) also rate the vocabulary problems as more important on the posttest under most conditions. Since working on the vocabulary problems is a behavior, we have evidence that attitude and behavior change are correlated in some circumstances. Greenwald also reports that subjects committed in advance to a position contrary to the communication show significant belief change but non-significant behavior change.

Chapter Summary

Theoretical works and definitions of attitude have stressed the import-ance of attitudes in the explanation of individual differences. Two indi-viduals may make different responses in the same social setting—indi-cating that a psychological (individual difference) variable like attitude is necessary because sociological or environmental variables are not them-selves sufficient to explain behavior.

A number of highly sophisticated techniques for measuring attitudes have been developed; but most of the sophisticated methodological work (and practically all of the substantive work reported in this book) is based on pencil and paper self-report measurement techniques. Our con-ceptions of attitude have been influenced by both the historical emphasis on behavioral implications of attitudes and the methodological emphasis on pencil and paper, self-report techniques.

Finally, we review the evidence of a relation between pencil and paper self-report measurement techniques and measurements more closely allied to overt, socially important behavior. It is concluded that the studies claiming to demonstrate that attitudes and behavior are inconsistent do not accomplish what they claim. A number of factors that might attenuate or obscure the relationship between attitude and behavior are reviewed.

Chapter 2

Evaluating Theories of Attitude Change

How do we evaluate theories of attitude change? To start, we will briefly describe the general structure of a scientific theory[1] and comment on the characteristics of social psychological theorizing. The ideal provides a sobering standard for evaluating social psychology's more meager achievements toward a formal theory of attitude change. But even if a theory had all the characteristics of a *formal* theory, it might not be a *good* theory. No matter how crude or elegant the deductive system in a theory, the value of that theory ultimately rests in its ability to predict the data. Thus this chapter contains a heavy methodological emphasis, bordering on the "how-to-do-it."

A theory cannot be predicted without evaluating the experiments that generated the supporting data. Just as optical illusions dramatically show that our eyes can misinform us, flaws in scientific procedures also introduce scientific misinformation. A particular empirical outcome may *seem* to confirm the predictions of a theory; but we must be confident that the data are scientifically sound before we take them as added support for a theory. We begin this chapter with a brief discussion of the formal properties of a good theory. The second, much longer section is devoted to methodological problems in experiments on the social psychology.

[1] More comprehensive and detailed treatments of theory construction are readily available elsewhere (e.g., Braithwaite, 1953; Campbell, 1920; Kaplan, 1964; Margenau, 1950; Nagel, 1961; and Deutsch and Krauss, 1965).

Formal Theory and the Theories of Attitude Change

Looking back on the spectacular success of physics and chemistry in the nineteenth century, philosophers of science have tried to reconstruct the rules by which science ought to proceed. With respect to the study of attitudes—and probably with respect to the whole of psychology—these conceptions of science represent goals for a formalized discipline, but they are probably not obtainable in the near future. We begin with a discussion of the nature of theory as it has been sketched by these philosophers of science. Then—since these goals turn out to be so far from the relatively humble theoretical attempts to be reviewed here—we will describe a few intermediate goals for which current theories of attitude change are immediately striving.

A theory, as such, takes (1) a set of theoretical constructs and (2) a set of linking statements. The linking statements define the formal relations among the constructs. The statements of relationship should be made in a language or abstract calculus which allows one to deduce new relationships among the constructs which were not explicitly specified in the first statement of the theory. The rules of algebra represent one of the best known examples of an abstract calculus. The rules define the relationship among the theoretical constructs and specify the manner in which new information may be deduced, or old information translated into a more useful form. The physical sciences have made great strides by translating their theories into the language of algebra, and then making use of the powerful rules for deduction and manipulation provided by the algebraic system to discover new relations among the constructs. A chemical engineer can actually construct a working model (i.e., theory) of the larger chemical industrial facility and then use the behavior of the model to predict the behavior of the larger facility. The social psychologist must build his theory with the far less precise language of everyday life. These verbal models have less deductive power than mathematical models or the chemist's pilot plant. Since theories of attitude change are composed of a group of words, they can never be more precise than the inevitably imprecise language of which they are composed.

DEFINING THE CONSTRUCTS

Before a theory can have any predictive or explanatory usefulness, we must be able to translate from the abstract symbols, linking statements, and logical rules of manipulation into the arena of events we wish to explain or predict. To borrow an example from Deutsch and Krauss (1965), the theoretical concept of distance (as in the expression $D = \frac{1}{2}GT^2$) is of little empirical use until we specify that distance may be quantified by such methods as a tape rule, a yardstick, and trigonometric triangulation. As it, turns out, the problem of specifying how concepts are to be measured is a problem for theories of attitude change. In fact, for the workaday scientist in attitude change the major part of his theoretical and empirical endeavors are devoted to a specification of exactly which procedures do and do not measure a particular theoretical construct. The most common fault of the theories reviewed in this book is a failure to specify *in advance* why a particular operational procedure is not a test of the theory, i.e., to specify in advance why the theory cannot be generalized to a new setting or procedure.

One technique for dealing with this problem has been the use of two types of definitions: a literary or conceptual definition and an operational definition (Underwood, 1957b). An operational definition defines a concept by specifying the procedures used to measure the concept. One operational definition for the concept "dissonance" (see Chapter 5), for instance, is to induce an individual publicly to say that a dull task is interesting (Festinger and Carlsmith, 1959). Unfortunately, it may not be readily apparent to the uninitiated that this particular measuring operation is designed to produce the same "dissonance" which has been more formally defined by the statement: *"Two elements are in a dissonant relation if, considering these two alone, the obverse of one element would follow from the other"* (Festinger, 1957, p. 13) And, as the reader will discover in the chapters to follow, dissonance is one of the better defined of the concepts used to theorize about attitude change.

One useful way to conceptualize the problem of operational definitions is to assume that there is a universe of operational definitions for each concept. The function of a literary or conceptual definition, then, is to define the boundaries of this universe in such a way that *another* scientist can generate new operational definitions which are acceptable to the author of the theory. The previously cited definition of dissonance illustrates the use of a literary definition to specify the universe of possible operational definitions. The italicized sentence quoted above is followed by three pages of further attempts to clarify and explain the concept which Festinger had in mind. He goes on to say: "To state it a bit more formally, X and Y are dissonant if not-X follows from Y. Thus, for example, if a person knew there were only friends in his vicinity and also felt afraid, there would be a dissonant relation between these two cognitive elements. Or, for another example, if a person were already in debt and also purchased a new car, the corresponding cognitive elements would be dissonant with one another" (p. 13).

For even the simplest concept there is almost an unlimited number of potential operational definitions. Technically, the description of an operational definition would involve a complete delineation of *all* conditions of measurement. These include the particular subjects mentioned, the lighting conditions in the experimental room, clothes worn by the experimenter, time of day, mood of subjects, current international situation. Unfortunately, this requirement is not academic; a number of such background factors can be shown to crucially affect the outcome of experiments.

These problems illustrate the difficulty in making the transition from the literary definition to an operational definition. The limitations of the everyday language make it doubtful that any author can ever present his concept so clearly (or anticipate every limiting condition so accurately) that other scientists can generate new operational definitions without error. Nonetheless, the prime requirement of a scientific theory is that it be public; we must evaluate an author's literary definition by the degree to which it stimulates his colleagues to generate acceptable operational definitions.

Any particular operational definition should represent, *in principle at least,* a random sample from the universe of available operational definitions. It is important to stress that, when empirical evidence suggests that a particular operational definition does not belong in the universe, it is not sufficient to generate another definition and try again. The original literary definition must have been at fault if it led the theoretician or one of his colleagues to generate an incorrect operational definition. The fact that an incorrect operational definition was generated reflects back on a weakness in the literary or conceptual definition which should be remedied. The literary definition should be reformulated in such a way that scientists are less prone to develop inappropriate operational definitions.

Lacking a special language, theories of attitude change can never exceed the precision of everyday language. At present, therefore, we must be content with lengthy literary definitions in which an author may frequently revert to examples in order to convey the meaning of his concept. The minimum requirements of a literary definition are that it be publicly recorded and that it be sufficiently clear to enable others in the scientific community to generate satisfactory operational definitions. Ideally, a satisfactory operational definition is one which both the original author and the rest of the scientific community accept as indeed implied by the literary definition.

LINKING STATEMENTS. The social psychology of attitude change is presently limited to linking statements, which are seldom more precise than "A whole lot of this leads to more of that." For example, under certain conditions, "high dissonance leads to large amounts of attitude change." Thus social psychologists temporarily bypass specifying just how much a "lot of this" is and quantifying the amount of a "whole lot more of that."

Even the best developed of our current theories of attitude change do not adequately specify the conditions under which their predictions should hold true, and the conditions under which the theoretical processes are either not relevant or are cancelled out by some other process. A *slightly* more complete statement of the preceding prediction from dissonance theory including a few limiting conditions is: "High amounts of dissonance will produce a large amount of attitude change, when other means of dissonance reduction are relatively unavailable."

THEORY BUILDING IS AN ANALYTIC PROCESS. Science is essentially a series of analytic steps in which a complex phenomenon is broken down into simpler processes. To the extent that theories contribute to this scientific process, they must also be analytical. In 1930 it might have been of interest to know that a course in race prejudice could alter the responses in subjects on a particular scale. Once such a finding becomes a part of the scientific literature, however, progress of science demands that theoreticians and experimenters alike ask, "Why?" Was the whole course necessary? Or did some aspect of the course decrease prejudice, others leave it totally unaffected, while some actually increased prejudice? Do the changes really represent a fundamental attitudinal reorganization? Both the empirical and theoretical progress of science demand that the gross phenomena (such as a semester course that produces changes in questionnaire responses) be broken down into unitary conceptual pieces; those smaller pieces must be further broken into smaller pieces, etc.

One of the major by-products of such an analytical approach is that the scientist is able to specify the limiting conditions as well as the generality of his theoretical predictions. If a social psychologist knows just what features of the course in prejudice are crucial for attitude change, he can then predict that attitude change will occur in those courses if those features are present, and will not occur if those features are not present.

Furthermore, by identifying the critical causal aspects of the communication which are necessary for attitude change, science has also gone a long way toward achieving a subjective feeling of explanation. Why did attitude change occur? It occurred because a particular set of necessary and sufficient conditions was created by this particular communication—the same set of necessary and sufficient conditions which had been theoretically specified and empirically verified to produce attitude change in other situations.

Experimental Methodology and Theories of Attitude Change

RANDOM ASSIGNMENT OF SUBJECT AND THE EXPERIMENTAL METHOD

There are a number of techniques for exploring the nature of reality, and many of them have been used to obtain data relevant to theories of attitude change. But to the extent that a data gathering technique does not provide an unambiguous causal interpretation of the results, the data are less relevant to theory. The *sine qua non* of unambiguous causal attribution is random assignment of subjects to experimental conditions. If subjects are not *randomly* assigned to conditions, an unambiguous causal interpretation is impossible. We do not know, for instance, whether the pro-administration attitude of those listening to a presidential speech on television stems from the speech itself, or from the fact that persons with a pro-administration attitude are more likely to expose themselves to the speech. Most of the empirical investigators in this volume have been drawn into the experimental laboratory for their theory testing in order to gain the control necessary to assign subjects randomly to conditions and the control necessary to create the conditions required for theory testing.

Random assignment assures that, within the statistical limits, the various experimental groups were comparable before the experimental manipulation was administered. Any differences among the groups can be attributed to "something" that happened after the random assignment. Data gathered from other sources are substantially less relevant to causal hypotheses. It is almost inevitable, then, that a book concerned with theory should concentrate on data from experimental studies. The experiment is unsurpassed as a source of causal and theory-testing data, yet we cannot ignore the problems created by such a heavy emphasis on a single, fallible channel of knowledge about the "real world."

OVERVIEW OF METHODOLOGICAL SECTIONS

At this point we make an abrupt transition from the philosophy of science to the actual methodological details recurring constantly in theory-testing experiments. The rest of this chapter deals with methodological problems in the procedures used to gather empirical support for theories of attitude change. The measured response in a test situation reflects several factors other than the underlying attitude; so we begin with a discussion of responses confounded with the attitudinal response. Such factors as (1) norms of self-presentation, (2) characteristics of the experimental design, (3) characteristics of the experimenter, and (4) the format of the measuring instruments making the meaning of our dependent variable ambiguous.

Many of the same problems appear again when we turn our attention to the independent or manipulated variable. The next two sections deal with two broad problems involved in the interpretation of independent manipulations: internal and external validity.

Internal validity is concerned with the interpretation of the results of a particular experiment. Can the observed effects be unambiguously attributed to the *intended* aspects of the independent variable? Random assignment gives us confidence that posttest differences can be attributed to *something* which takes place between assignment of subjects and the posttest, but several common design faults can make it impossible to be sure that that something is the same thing the investigator had in mind when he designed the experiment. Perhaps the results were caused by something happening after random assignment other than the intended manipulation. The section on internal validity will cover such topics as history, testing, mortality, regression, instrument decay, selection, and maturation—any one of which can present a rival alternative explanation for obtained differences if the proper safeguards are omitted. Readers familiar with the writings of Donald Campbell (1957; Campbell and Stanley, 1963) will recognize his contributions to these discussions.

External validity refers to the extent to which the observed phenomena, law, results, or psychological process will generalize to other settings. Low incentives produce more attitude change as a result of counterattitudinal behavior in one experiment (see Chapter 5); but over what range of incentives, experimenters, subject populations, counterattitudinal behaviors, etc., will the effect be observed? These epistemological limitations of the laboratory experiment will be discussed under the heading of external validity—the extent to which laws observed in the laboratory reflect those of the "real world." Note that it is the laws which we hope are general, not the particular experimental procedures. A highly general law may be discovered in a contrived and artificial experimental setting.

After a discussion of factors affecting internal and external validity, we discuss some varying strategies for research. For instance, should the experimenter strive for a constant stimulus situation for each subject or should he allow the stimulus situation to vary from subject to subject to gain a similar psychological impact? Finally, we conclude with a few comments on the use of the word "change," the interpretation of interactions, some overlooked statistical designs, and an emphasis on alternative explanations. The chapter is then concluded with Campbell's effort to integrate various approaches to the study of attitude change.

RESPONSES CONFOUNDED WITH THE ATTITUDINAL, DEPENDENT VARIABLE RESPONSE

Consider the junior executive, at lunch in the company cafeteria, who is asked by his boss to express his attitude toward a painting prominently displayed in his superior's office. The young man undoubtedly feels that his response has consequences far beyond that of indicating his "true" or "private" attitude toward the painting. He feels that his response is one of the many that are instrumental toward a rewarding state of affairs—eventual promotion, a salary raise, or, more immediately, the esteem of someone higher in the status hierarchy. Similarly, he has information not only about his "true" or "private" evaluation of the painting but also about the likely consequences of any number of statements he might make. He may assume that the prominent placement of the picture indicates a positive attitude toward it by his boss, or he may know that his boss violently disagrees with the taste of the interior decorator hired to refurbish the senior executive office suite. He may decide that honesty is the best policy, and that he should express himself frankly. Or he may realize that the question was a rhetorical one and called for no answer whatsoever. Finally, aside from any considerations about this particular picture, he may know that "rising young executives" in this particular company either "do" or "do not" like modern art.

It should be clear that his response to the lunchroom question will be a function of many determinants. The response to *any* attitude measure is determined partly by the attitude in question and partly by other, irrelevant factors. It is never possible to present an attitude object in complete isolation; any response to the attitude object contains contributions from other elements in the measuring situation. Although attitude testers have developed a number of techniques to minimize the contribution of these other factors, we would have to have both head and shoulders in the sand to blind ourselves to their presence.

The notion that there are nonattitudinal contributions to the attitude or test response is not new. In his "Attitudes Can Be Measured," L. L. Thurstone (1928) reasoned:

"There comes to mind the uncertainty of using an opinion as an index of attitude. The man may be a liar. If he is not intentionally misrepresenting his real attitude on a disputed question, he may nevertheless modify the expression of it for reasons of courtesy . . . . But his actions may also be distortions of his attitude. A politician extends friendship and hospitality in overt action while hiding an attitude that he expresses more truthfully to an intimate friend. Neither his opinions nor his overt acts constitute in any sense an infallible guide to the subjective inclinations and preferences that constitute his attitude" (p. 532).

For a more complete discussion of discrepancies between overt behavior and private opinion see Kiesler's (1968) review of the conformity literature.

There are four types of nonattitudinal contributions to the attitude measures. These are irrelevant contributions stemming from (1) norms of self-presentation which specify the "appropriate," "expected," or "socially desirable" response; (2) characteristics of the experimental design; (3) the experimenter; and (4) the format of the measuring instruments.

NORMS OF SELF-PRESENTATION. According to Erving Goffman (1955), each individual communicates his view of himself in addition to substantive information in most interpersonal communications. Since the attitude response is an interaction or "communication" between the respondent and the attitude tester, the respondent will be concerned about the face he presents as well as the "true" information about his attitude. The problem of self-presentation is particularly acute for most of the attitudes of interest to social psychologists. There are descriptions or norms which specify how an individual ought to respond for most of the important social objects in our environment. For a variety of reasons, an individual may learn that certain responses to the attitude stimulus are socially desirable (Edwards, 1957; Crowne and Marlowe, 1964). And his notions of what is socially desirable have no necessary relation to his "true" or private attitude.

While the typical scientific data-gathering procedure avoids the irrelevant pressures acting on the junior executive in the preceding example, efforts to "purify" the testing situation may actually accentuate some of the nonattitudinal contributions to the attitude response. Most attitude testing situations probably emphasize rather than de-emphasize the self-presentational aspects of the attitude response. First, the fact that the test is being given by a "psychologist," or "scientist," means that the average respondent is communicating upwardly to someone of higher status. The subject is communicating to a scientist who is qualified, and, indeed, explicitly motivated to diagnose or evaluate the respondent. (See Riecken, 1962, on this point.) Second, attitude tests are explicitly designed for the purpose of describing or diagnosing some socially significant aspects of the respondent. (See, for example, Zimbardo, 1960, on response involvement; and Rosenberg, 1965, on evaluation apprehension.)

Several of the standard techniques used by attitude testers can be viewed as an attempt to minimize the contribution of self-presentation needs to the attitude measurement. Experimenters often preface the test with a set of instructions designed to minimize the evaluative or diagnostic aspects of the test responses. The experimenter may stress the scientific nature of the experiment. He may straightforwardly ask that the subjects disregard the consequences of their responses and "be truthful" for the sake of science; or the experimenter may assure respondents that the answers will remain anonymous. The experimenter may also try to argue that the responses to these particular test items are not relevant to any norms or prescriptions which might specify the "correct" answer. Thus the experimenter may state that there is no right or wrong answer;

he may stress that people differ in their views and that any response is acceptable; and he may stress that he, the experimenter, doesn't care how the subject responds.

A second technique that does not explicitly request the subject's cooperation disguises the normative implications of the attitude response. An attitudinal response may have implications for the tester which it does not have for the subject. For instance, Kelman (1953) did not ask his subjects to give their own reactions to jungle and fantastic hero comic books, rather he asked them to evaluate the suitability of material for younger readers. It may not require much sophistication to realize that the psychologist can infer one's own attitude toward comic books from a knowledge of one's "suitability ratings" for younger children; but Kelman's grade school population may not have realized that Kelman planned to make inferences about their attitudes from their ratings of the books. In any event, it seems plausible that Kelman reduced the self-presentational implications of his measurement when he did *not* ask the subjects to give their own direct reactions to the material. Other techniques used to gain information from the respondent without his knowledge were discussed in the measurement section of Chapter 1 and in Webb, Campbell, Schwartz, and Sechrest (1966).

A third approach is to deal with attitudinal responses not under the conscious control of the subject. Although certain physiological responses are probably the best example of responses not under the conscious control of the subjects, these responses are not necessarily correlated with the attitude we want to measure. (See, for example, Schachter, 1959.)

A fourth approach, which has received more attention in personality measurement than it has in attitude measurement, is an attempt to counterbalance the normative or self-presentational pressures on the attitude response (Edwards, 1957). In this way, if he is clever enough, the experimenter may be able to design two items so that—although both are socially desirable in the sense that they conform to the relevant norms and prescriptions—one item indicates a high amount of the attitude in question and the other a low amount. Thus Christie did not try to eliminate social desirability and acquiescence response sets from his "Mach" scale (Christie & Geis, in press), rather he designed his test so that these self-presentational motives are counterbalanced and do not bias his total attitude score in either direction.

If we grant that the subject molds his test response items to some extent in order to make his desired presentation of self, what are the implications for experiments on attitude change? The implications depend on the assumptions we make about the relation between the self-presentational contribution and the attitudinal contribution to the measured response. Let us first consider the simplest assumption: self-presentation motives add a more or less "constant error" to every subject's response. A constant error limits the interpretations we can make of the subject's position relative to the neutral point. A procedure which actually makes very prejudiced people slightly less prejudiced might, because of a constant error in the attitude measure, *appear* to be making unprejudiced people even more unprejudiced. This would occur when a constant error made everyone (open-minded and bigoted alike) appear more open-minded than they really were.

The crucial fact is that a constant error in both pretest and posttest would not hide true change. The state of attitude measurement—like most measurement in psychology—has not really reached the point where we can place interpretation on the absolute value of the score. It is much more typical to convert an attitude score to percentiles or standard scores. Then the neutral zone dividing the prejudiced from the nonprejudiced has no more meaning beyond the fact that it is the median or average attitude of the particular sample tested.

A more serious problem arises when self-presentational norms vary from condition to condition. A communication advocating that a cure for the common cold is indeed in sight might change the subject's strategy of self-presentation. He might decide that the appropriate response is to agree with the attitude statement, whereas he previously thought the appropriate response was to disagree. In this case, a change in attitude on the posttest would reflect a changed notion of the most appropriate self-presentation rather than a changed attitude about the probability of a cold cure. Self-presentational norms would be a rival hypothesis to explain the impact of the independent manipulation. Another way to state the problem is to say that there is an interaction between the experimental manipulations and the norms salient for self-presentation—i.e., the impact of the manipulation is to make one set of norms relevant in one condition and another set relevant in the other. For example, subjects in an "ego threat," "insult," or "low self-esteem" condition might be more concerned with self-presentation than subjects in the "no threat" condition. Or evaluation from a female accomplice might lead a male subject to decide that his "snow job" self-presentation (usually held in reserve for first dates) should be substituted for the "detached and uninvolved" self-presentation which had previously seemed appropriate for the experimental setting. Differences between the "evaluation" and "no evaluation" conditions could stem from differences in the relevant self-presentation norms rather than a "true" difference in attitude. In summary, every experimental manipulation should be examined to see if it might produce a change in the norms of self-presentation, which might form an alternate explanation for the hypothesis.

CHARACTERISTICS OF THE EXPERIMENTAL DESIGN. The major emphasis in the previous section was on general social norms of self-presentation, where the subject might use cues from the particular experiment to decide which norms were salient. Martin Orne (1962) has presented similar argument which deserves separate treatment. He argues that subjects treat an experiment as a problem or test and search the procedure for cues about the response the experimenter is "looking for"—just as students search an exam question for cues about what the instructor is "looking for." Here the subject might give a confederate a high rating, not because he thinks every Red Blooded American Boy should express attraction to someone who does a good deed, but because the procedure has tipped him off that the experimenter anticipates his subjects will be attracted to the confederate in those circumstances. The problem is that the experimenter wants to know what the subject really thinks of the confederate, not what he thinks he *ought* to think.

According to Orne, "The experimental situation is one which takes place within the context of an explicit agreement of the subject to participate in a special form of social interaction known as 'taking part in an experiment.' Within the context of our culture the roles of subject and experimenter are well understood and carry with them well-defined mutual role expectations" (Orne, 1962, p. 777). The subject has agreed to perform a very wide range of actions on request without inquiring into their purpose. Orne states that when he began a request for friends or acquaintances to do five push-ups with the statement "Would you do me a favor?" none complied. If, however, he first asked the subjects to participate in a short experiment and then asked them to do five push-ups, their typical response was "Where?" This suggests that the special experimenter-subject role relationship does create certain prescriptions for compliance. Subjects are more likely to "be persuaded" or "conform" in an experiment than elsewhere.

Orne's second argument is somewhat more complicated. He first assumes that the subjects share with the experimenter a certain amount of faith in science and that they think the present experiment will advance science and mankind. In fact, when experimenters attempt to recruit volunteers for experiments, they frequently appeal directly to such values. It follows that the subjects have a stake in the outcome of the experiment, and they are motivated to contribute their own responses to this endeavor. "Admittedly, subjects are concerned about their performance in terms of reinforcing their self-image [i.e., are concerned about their self-presentation]; nonetheless, they seem even more concerned with the utility of their performances" (Orne, 1962, p. 778). As the next link in his chain of logic, Orne argues that most subjects will try to enact the role of a "good subject" by validating the experimental hypothesis.

If we grant that subjects are trying to confirm the experimental hypothesis, Orne's next point is compelling. Subjects do not passively respond to the experimental manipulation; the whole experiment takes on aspects of a problem-solving experience in which the subject must first discover the experimental hypothesis and then produce the anticipated behavior. "Viewed in this light, the totality of cues which convey an experimental hypothesis to the subject become significant determinants of subjects' behavior. We have labelled the sum total of such cues as 'demand characteristics of the experimental situation' (Orne, 1959a)" (Orne, 1962). We shall return to Orne's argument later when we are discussing the external validity or generalizability of the experimental result. The threat to internal validity stems from the fact that the different manipulations may lead the subjects to choose different "solutions" to the "test question" defined by the experimental procedure; one manipulation makes one answer appear "correct," and another manipulation makes another answer appear "correct."

We do not need to assume, as does Orne, that this problem-solving set stems from constructive, helpful motivations on the part of the subject. General contrariness, a desire to be the exception to the rule, or a motivation to reduce the status between experimenter and subject by refuting the experimenter's hypothesis would also lead the subject to ferret out the solution and to produce its opposite.

One solution is for the experimenter to try to conceal the aspects of the design which would give the subject cues about the intent of the experimental manipulation or the experimenter's hypothesis. Perhaps more effective is the creation of a cover story transparent enough so that all subjects are able to ascertain some "true purpose" of the experiment that is irrelevant to the one the experimenter has in mind.

Another solution is to design experiments with "experimental realism." These experiments would "hit the subject squarely between the eyes," involve him, force him to take it seriously, and have impact on him. This experimental realism might so absorb and involve the subject in the experiment that he would have no time to play games with the experimenter or engage in a problem-solving exercise. Cover stories used to create this experimental realism also have the effect of disguising the experimenter's true interest. It is an empirical question as to whether compelling cover stories in deception experiments increase or decrease the subject's problem-solving activities, but the argument seems reasonable. There is, however, one possible unfortunate long-range impact caused by these deception designs. As more and more are conducted, written up in popular magazines, and passed around the community by word of mouth, the general problem-solving set of all subjects in all psychological experiments seems to increase. Subjects may learn that all social psychologists lie. They may become so sensitized to deception that even the best of cover stories could not allay their suspicion and problem-solving efforts. Thus the short-range cure could eventually kill the patient.

Another technique which probably attenuates the impact of demand characteristics in a design is the disguised posttest. The posttest can be disguised by using the indirect measurement techniques discussed in Chapter 1 or by separating the posttest from the experimental procedures. The posttest may be irrelevant to the experimental procedures (an afterthought, part of another study, etc.) or the posttest data may not be seen by the experimenter (a second, presumably independent experimenter collects the data as in Festinger and Carlsmith, 1959; Rosenberg, 1965; Carlsmith, Collins, and Helmreich, 1966). If the posttest is not a part of the experiment, the subject will not use the posttest to communicate his "solution" to the experimenter. Three more solutions are suggested by Aronson and Carlsmith (1968). If the manipulation is introduced as an accident—an event presumably unique to this particular subject—the subject may exclude the manipulation from his definition of the problem to be solved. Similarly, if the manipulation is introduced by a confederate, it may be regarded as a unique happening and not a part of the game between subject and experimenter. Finally, if the subject is recruited as an "experimenter" he may exclude his activities in that role from his activities as a subject.

The best procedure is probably to prevent the subject from labeling the subject-experimenter relationship as an "experiment" in the first place. This may be one of the strongest arguments for naturalistic experiments such as those by Blake and Mouton (1957), where a well-dressed confederate is sent out into the Texas traffic against the light. There are, however, serious ethical problems created when an experimenter intrudes into the privacy of his subjects, if they are unaware they are taking part in an experiment.

However, even if we were able to prevent the subject from finding cues which define the "correct response," the fact that he was *looking* might limit external validity. It seems likely that results obtained from a group of problem-solving subjects intent on discovering the "right thing to do" would not generalize to persons in a setting that does not elicit the problem-solving set.

CHARACTERISTICS OF THE EXPERIMENTER. Orne's discussion of demand characteristics emphasizes the active problem-solving behavior of the subject and his use of cues provided by the design itself. In contrast, Rosenthal (1964, 1966) emphasizes another aspect of the experimenter-subject interaction: experimenters often obtain data confirming their expectations. Whereas Orne speaks of analyzing the demand characteristics which are more or less inherent in a design and procedure (and are relatively unaffected by the experimenter), Rosenthal presents data indicating that two experimenters (working with the same design and procedure) will obtain different outcomes if their expectations differ. The experimenter's expectations, then, can contribute a component to the attitude test response independent of the demand characteristics of a particular design.

The term experimenter *bias* must be distinguished from experimenter *effects*. Experimenter bias refers to differences in the experimenter's behavior from condition to condition which are produced by his different expectations. Thus the groups differ not only with respect to the intended manipulation, but also with respect to subtle differences in the behavior of the experimenter. Experimenter bias constitutes a threat to the internal validity of the experiment; we do not know whether observed differences are created by the manipulations in the script or differences in the behavior of the experimenter corresponding to his expectations.

Even if the experimenter behaves identically (apart from the differences specified by the design) when running subjects in various conditions, the results he obtains may not generalize to a specified universe of experimenters. The particular experimenter may have some idiosyncratic characteristics which interact with the experimental conditions to produce the obtained outcome. Other experimenters may obtain no difference or the opposite results with the same experimental procedure. An experimenter *effect*, then, constitutes a threat to the external validity of the experiment and will be discussed along with other limitations on generalization such as the subject population, testing procedures, and other context variables.

It is possible, however, that Rosenthal's experimental procedures may exaggerate the impact of experimenter bias:

". . . virtually all of Rosenthal's findings have occurred in contexts which are essentially different from the usual laboratory experiment—and that difference is one that *invites* bias. In Rosenthal's paradigm, each experimenter runs only one of the experimental conditions. For example, in the learning experiment, an experimenter ran either a "bright" or "dull" rat. This does not occur in an actual experiment; here the same experimenter usually runs subjects in all conditions. It is our contention that it is easier for an experimenter to bias a subject's behavior, without being aware of it, if he is running only one condition. Consider the learning experiment. If an experimenter felt that he were running a bright rat, he might be inclined to handle the rat with respectful gentleness. Moreover, his criteria for success might be lenient; i.e., if the rat moved his nose toward the correct stimulus and then withdrew, the experimenter might be inclined to consider this a successful trial. Our point is that it would be more difficult for him to do this if he were running *both* maze dull and maze bright rats. I.e., he might catch himself handling different rats differently or using different criteria for different rats. It is easier to be biased if all of the bias for all subjects consists of the same judgment or behavior on the part of the experimenter" (Aronson and Carlsmith, 1968).

Our own guess is that Aronson and Carlsmith (1968) are probably correct in assuming that it is far easier for an experimenter to make a constant error than to make differential errors which exaggerate treatment effects. On the other hand, we doubt that the problem can be eliminated by having the same experimenter run all conditions. Assuming that the integrity of serious researchers need not be questioned, there may still be a variety of unconsicous behaviors on the part of the experimenter (e.g., differential smiling), which may interact with treatments. In some cases, the experimenter may unconsciously assume that these unscripted behaviors constitute legitimate reinforcing improvisations that add impact to the scripted version of the manipulation—although they may never get reported in the procedure section of the research report. Not all of such experimenter biases need operate to exaggerate treatment effects in the predicted direction. Some experimenters, perhaps in overzealous conscientiousness, may develop unconscious behaviors that actually diminish predicted treatment differences. Furthermore, we judge these problems to be more severe in social psychological or personality research than in animal research.

There are no instant cures for experimenter bias. Hiring experimenters (presumably) unaware of the hypotheses built into the design does not look promising. First, the typical person hired for this task (a graduate or undergraduate in psychology) probably develops hypotheses of his own after becoming familiar with the whole design. Furthermore, Rosenthal (1958, 1963, 1964, 1966) demonstrated that experimenters tend to perpetuate the hypothesis formed on the basis of trends in the data of the first few subjects. Finally, conducting experiments in ignorance of the hypothesis would be poor training for the graduate and undergraduate students, many of whom are apprentice psychologists.

A separate posttest administered by someone "blind" to the subject's condition limits the opportunities for bias. Rosenthal's procedures consist largely of testing sessions with relatively little time devoted to building a cover story, inducing a manipulation, etc. This makes it plausible that much of the bias he reports is communicated during the posttest. A posttester ignorant of the subject's condition could not systematically bias the subject's response.

If several experimenters each administer one of the manipulations in a factorial design and all are blind to all manipulations except their own, bias cannot produce an interaction between two manipulations administered by different experimenters. In order to produce an interaction between two variables, an experimenter would have to know exactly what condition of the factorial the subject was in. If he knows only about one variable (i.e., only which row *or* which column of a two-dimensional experiment), the most he can bias is a main effect. Similarly, if all manipulations are administered simultaneously by using printed instructions or automated equipment, bias is unlikely. Finally, if the decision as to what condition a subject is in is postponed as long as possible, bias opportunities are minimized.

It is possible to make an eloquent argument for a "live experimenter" as a means for achieving impact and experimental realism (e.g., Aronson and Carlsmith, 1968). But the problems of both experimenter bias and experimenter effects argue strongly against live experimenters. Automated procedures such as audio and videotape of experimenter activities minimize the opportunity for experimenter bias. It is not clear that automated procedures must, of necessity, limit the impact of an experiment. Finally, automated data-recording procedures would reduce biased "errors" in data recording and analysis. Even with a completely automated experiment, however, an experimenter may be more likely to check for errors when the data fail to confirm the hypothesis. Hypothesis-confirming errors may be less likely to be discovered.

FORMAT OF THE MEASURING INSTRUMENT (RESPONSE BIAS). The format of an attitude test item systematically contributes to the attitude response—more or less independently of the specific attitude object. Two "response sets" or "response styles" will serve to illustrate this nonattitudinal contribution to the attitude test response.

In his early work on the development of objective classroom tests, Cronbach (1941, 1942, 1946, 1950) discovered that a tendency to guess "true" as opposed to "false" when in doubt about a true-false test item would artifactually lower test scores under certain circumstances. He noticed that students were consistent in their guessing habits from test to test; students likely to guess "true" he labeled "acquiescent," and those who tend to guess "false," "critical." As Rorer (1965) has indicated, the extension of this concept to attitude questionnaires and personality inventories where the correct response for a particular individual is not known creates certain logical difficulties. Nonetheless, there is a considerable amount of evidence that the agreement-disagreement format of many attitude test items contributes to the attitude response, possibly independent of content. Empirically keyed tests such as the MMPI and the F scale, for instance, which are developed by selecting those items that empirically predict certain criteria—psychiatrists' ratings or scores on the E (ethnocentrism) scale—frequently have either very few or very many items scored so that agreement with the item has a common meaning; in other words, agreement indicates either a high or low score on the test scale. Since such a state would seldom occur by chance, the predictive value of the item is partly dependent on the format (i.e., an agreement or disagreement response is called for) as well as their specific content.

There is some disagreement in the literature concerning the interpretation of the acquiescence set (Couch and Keniston, 1960, 1961; Taylor,

1961; Edwards and Walker, 1961; Rokeach, 1963; Rorer, 1965). There is argument about whether the acquiescence effect is produced by a generalized tendency to agree or disagree with a statement no matter what its content, or by a desire to endorse those items that are socially desirable. Nor is it clear whether the tendency toward acquiescence represents a generalized personality trait, or even represents a general tendency which can be observed consistently over a wide range of item content and item format. However, it is very clear that the language and format of the items contribute to the response.

Another type of response set or style has to do with the extremity of the subject's response. It seems likely that some individuals consistently choose the very high or very low scores, whereas others prefer to indicate their responses with numbers at or near the middle of the continuum. In the posttest of a study on forced compliance (Carlsmith, Collins, and Helmreich, 1966) an "independent" posttester asked the subjects to indicate their evaluation of the experimental task on an 11-point scale (-5 to $+5$). As a part of the cover story involved in the posttest, the subjects also rated several selections of recorded music on an 11-point scale. Subjects rated each of five selections on four scales such as "How much would you like to dance to it?" and "How much would you like to study to it?" Some subjects preferred the middle of the scale, small numbers ranging around zero, whereas others consistently preferred the extreme ends of the scale, numbers around $+5$ or -5. The rating of each record was scored as an absolute number. A person scoring at either extreme, $+5$ or -5, was given a score of 5. Neutral subjects were given a score of 0. A summed "extremity score" for all of the record ratings correlated with the extremity of the subject's response on the dependent variable. Peabody (1962) argues that the extremity response bias is so extreme that items should be scored dichotomously so that the total scores reflect direction of the response from the neutral point but not extremity from the neutral point. Miller (1965) reports that experimentally induced "involvement" in an issue *produces* a more extreme response on that issue. If a measurement procedure made an issue more salient or increased involvement, attitude responses would be more extreme.

INTERNAL VALIDITY

At this point we turn our attention from the focus on dependent variables in the previous section to a discussion of independent variables.

There will be two major sections on independent variables—internal validity and external validity.

"*Internal validity* is the basic minimum without which any experiment is uninterpretable: Did in fact the experimental treatments make a difference in this specific experimental instance? *External validity* [discussed in the next section] asks the question of *generalizability:* To what populations, settings, treatment variables, [i.e., experimental manipulations] and measurement variables can this effect be generalized? Both types of criteria are obviously important, even though they are frequently at odds in that features increasing one may jeopardize the other" (Campbell and Stanley, 1963, p. 175).

A number of factors may produce differences between two experimental groups even when the intended manipulation has no effect (or the opposite effect). If two groups differ in some respect other than the one deliberately introduced by the design, internal validity is threatened. The confounding difference may be responsible for the observed difference in the dependent variable. The results may not be produced by the variable the experimenter had in mind when he designed the experiment.

The confounding variables constitute challenges to the internal validity of the experiment—the extent to which observed differences were actually produced by the intended manipulation. Much discussion about internal validity takes place in later chapters because the discussion of the theoretical implications of an experiment naturally leads to a careful evaluation of the experimental manipulations responsible for the observed difference. Nonetheless, a brief overview of some of the major challenges to internal validity provides a useful methodological checklist.

History. Anything that happens to an experimental group after subjects have been randomly assigned can create a difference at post-test time. Experimental procedures frequently involve elaborate experiences for the subject—any one of which could be responsible for observed differences. Thus the most desirable control group is one in which there are as few differences between experimental and control group as possible. When an experiment contains several experimental groups as in a factorial analysis of variance design, or several different levels of one manipulation, the control group is frequently omitted. This procedure is perfectly acceptable as long as the experimenter limits his inferences to the *differences* between the experimental conditions; he cannot, however, make statements about how experimental subjects differ from untreated subjects without an "unmanipulated" control.

TESTING. The pretest experience is a part of the history of subjects. Thus a comparison between a group which has had both pretest and manipulation and a group which has had neither pretest nor manipulation provides an ambiguous test. Any differences may be attributed to either the testing or the manipulation. A control group with pretest and no manipulation measures the effect of testing. When the experimental group is contrasted with a pretested control, any difference must be a function of the manipulation since both groups were pretested. As previously mentioned, a pretest control group should be composed of subjects randomly sorted into control and experimental groups; and control subjects should be treated identically with experimental subjects, omitting only the crucial aspects of the manipulation.

As long as the procedures of testing do not differ among experimental and control groups, we can be confident that observed differences are not produced by the testing procedures. As Campbell has indicated (1957; Campbell and Stanley, 1963), the major threat of testing is limited to external validity—i.e., the extent to which observed phenomena can be generalized to populations of persons who have not experienced the testing procedures. The research on the way in which testing procedures can limit the generality of an experimental result is discussed in the section of this chapter on external validity.

MORTALITY. The essential feature of an experimental design is the random assignment of subjects to groups. It is an unfortunate, but apparently inevitable, feature of psychological research that data cannot always be obtained from all randomly assigned subjects. Rats die in the experimental laboratory, subjects fail to show up for the posttest, experimenters make mistakes, subjects become "suspicious," etc. Since it is difficult to argue that this subject loss is random, any experiment with a subject loss is not a true experiment.

But such a strict criterion cannot be used for experimental research in psychology; so we make do as best we can. Following a line of argument suggested by Campbell (1957, 1963; Webb et al., 1966), we pay serious attention to subject loss only when it constitutes a *plausible* rival hypothesis. In other words, the critic must develop an argument based on data and careful reasoning in which he explains just how the particular pattern of subject loss could result in the obtained data.

The studies in forced compliance (see Chapter 5) illustrate the plausibility of mortality as a rival hypothesis. In these experiments subjects are offered large and small inducements to perform some behavior inconsistent with their measured or presumed attitudes. If more subjects in the low-incentive condition refused to comply with the experimenter's request than did subjects in the high-incentive condition, we would have a rival hypothesis to explain the apparently greater attitude change of the low-incentive group. Since subjects with extremely negative attitudes are least likely to agree to perform a counterattitudinal act (Collins and Helmreich, 1969; Kelman, 1953), these extremely negative subjects would drop out of the low-incentive condition but remain in the high-incentive condition. When the group is measured at posttest time, the positive attitudes of the low-incentive group could be attributed to the fact that the experimental procedures eliminated all the subjects who were negative on the pretest. Mortality presents a particularly serious problem in connection with regression because mortality often eliminates subjects who are extreme on the dependent variable. Regression is a problem whenever subjects are "selected" or "retained" for being extreme on some dimension because they will *appear* to be less extreme the next time they are measured (Campbell and Stanley, 1963).

Fortunately it is not always the case that more subjects refuse in low- than in high-incentive conditions of the forced compliance studies to be reviewed later. Experimenters on forced compliance, aware of the very problem we have just illustrated, usually take great efforts to see that few subjects refuse to emit the counterattitudinal behavior.

It is important to stress again that mortality refers only to subject biases arising *after* random assignment of subjects to conditions. Given random assignment of subjects to conditions, the use of subjects who are extreme on any subject variable (e.g., subjects who are unintelligent, high in achievement needs, volunteers) can never constitute a threat to internal validity.

INSTRUMENT DECAY, SELECTION, MATURATION. Instrument decay is a change in the measuring instrument over time. It is most likely to occur in social psychology when human observers change their standards over time. Middle-class observers, who are initially shocked at the antisocial behavior of juvenile delinquents, for instance, may come to rate certain behaviors as less extreme after they have been exposed to the lower-class culture for a while. Selection represents a rival alternative hypothesis whenever subjects were not assigned randomly. Maturation covers those effects that are systematic with the passage of time.

It is not a serious problem in the relatively brief periods typically observed in laboratory experiments on attitude change, but adequate controls would be needed to separate effects attributable to the natural unfolding or growth of the subject between pretest and posttest for long-term studies.

EXTERNAL VALIDITY

Now we turn our attention to factors that limit the generalizability of the *phenomena* or *laws* discovered in experiments. The results of an experiment might have poor external validity because the results are specific to the particular experimenter, the particular operational definition of the independent variable, the particular measurement techniques used, the particular subject sample, etc. One strategy of research to maximize external validity is to utilize settings with maximum similarity to the real world. This has been labeled "mundane realism" by Aronson and Carlsmith—a phrase accurately connoting the low regard in which they hold it. They point out that mundane realism is not necessary to achieve experimental realism or psychological impact, and we agree. We simply add that mundane realism probably facilitates external validity and it does not preclude successful experimentation.

But external validating is an inductive, empirical problem. There is no certain basis for stating that the results of one experiment are more general than the results of another. Just because an experimental setting appears similar to the "real world" we cannot be sure that the phenomena discovered in that setting will generalize to the real world. Nor does it follow that, just because experimental procedures appear to be atypical, the phenomena discovered in the experimental setting will not generalize. There is, of course, a certain amount of face validity in experimental settings which are typical of settings in the universe to which we want to generalize. It should be stressed, however, that many of the phenomena that interest us are atypical in the real world. The fact that we are seldom confronted with a unanimous disagreement from our peers on a simple physical judgment does not diminish the value of Asch's (1952, 1956) work on conformity. The universe to which we want to generalize may be only a small—but nonetheless important—niche in the real world. The point here is that our aim as scientists is not to create, with full complexity and richness, a laboratory reproduction of "real world" events. The theoretical propositions we test are abstractions of the real world. Thus, for instance, the external validity of the law of gravity does not rest on whether conditions of free fall in a true vacuum can indeed be found in the "real world."

Mundane realism *is* particularly valuable if the similarity to the real world conceals the fact that the subject is participating in an experiment. This does much to eliminate the threat to external validity created by the demand characteristics which become salient if an "experiment" is labeled as such by the subject. Noteworthy is an experiment by Brock (1965) in which the manipulation was introduced into the ongoing merchandising process of a retail paint department. Another example is Miller and Levy's (1967) "inadvertent" delivery of an insult to women in shopping plazas.

In the following sections we consider several factors affecting external validity: (1) the experimenter, (2) the testing procedures, (3) subject populations, and (4) the specific experimental procedures and operational definitions. As a final point on external validity, we summarize Hovland's (1959) explanation of the discrepancy between field and laboratory studies.

THE EXPERIMENTER AS A CONTEXT VARIABLE. Rosenthal's discussion of the experimenter's expectations as a threat to internal validity is an alternative explanation of the results. The attention and concern which have been aroused by Rosenthal's (1966) data and arguments about the relevance of the experimenter's *expectations,* however, may have tended to obscure the fact that many aspects of the experimenter, other than his expectations about outcome, influence the experimental results. (See Kintz, Delprato, Mettee, Persons, and Schappe, 1965, for a review.) Experimenters do differ—they are, after all, only people; the marked variation among people was one of psychology's first discoveries. McGuigan (1963) has stated the problem well in the title of his article: "The Experimenter: A Neglected Stimulus Object."

Although often not as complete as those in the *Journal of Experimental Psychology,* method sections in social psychology journals frequently describe in detail the physical setting of the experiment, the nature of the apparatus used, and often include a verbatim script. Seldom, however, is any mention made of the person who delivered the script. But the same experimental setting, the same script, and the same equipment do not have the same psychological *impact* in the hands of two different experimenters.

The most serious threat to external validity is an interaction between experimenter and manipulation such that the cell means have a different rank order for different experimenters. The ideal state is a complete lack of interaction between manipulations and experimenters; but interactions where all experimenters produce different magnitudes of the same effect are not particularly bothersome at the present level of development. If all experimenters produce the same effect, the theoretical prediction has been confirmed for each experimenter. The presence of an interaction with the experimenter does mean that the theory has failed to specify how the predicted effects will interact with specified experimenter characteristics. But the theory is right so far as it goes; each experimenter produces differences in the predicted direction. Experimenter main effects offer no threat to the theory. The lack of an interaction means that the effects of the manipulations are similar for all experimenters.

Ideally, experiments would be run in several replications, each with a different experimenter. If the experimenter is treated as a random factor in a factorial design, statistical statements can be made about whether the results are likely to generalize to a universe of experimenters (as well as a universe of subjects, as in the more conventional statistical tests). It is true that this procedure may be very expensive if highly trained experimenters are required. And it is true that experimenter differences are difficult to interpret if obtained. But it is a fundamental requirement that a phenomenon generalize across experimenters—or that the theory explicitly specify the universe of experimenters to which its predictions are relevant. Of what use are results, possibly unique to a particular set of experimenters—no matter how cheaply they were generated in a single-experimenter experiment? Whatever is gained by designing complex experiments that require highly trained experimenters may be lost through decreased external validity. Of course the solution of using multiple experimenters is not the simple panacea that it may appear to be. Even when an experimenter uses several trained graduate student experimenters, we must still ask to what universe of experimenters we can generalize. We have to face the external validity problem because we rarely (if ever) use a random sample of experimenters; few if any experiments are designed to use an untrained random selection of experimenters. But, if experiments were designed to allow a random sample of experimenters, the results would certainly have greater external validity.

Aronson and Carlsmith (1968) stress that it is easy to "louse up" an experiment and that we should not be overly depressed by a failure to replicate by an unskilled experimenter. The point is well taken. It is probably easier to fail to replicate than to succeed; we should be more impressed with success than failure, particularly if the replicator is theoretically motivated not to replicate. On the other hand, it should be stressed that the fewer the similarities between an original experiment and a replication, the greater our confidence in the external validity of the finding. Obviously the theoretical motivations of the experimenter are only one of the many factors that produce replication failures. Since there is often more to a theory than is publicly recorded, an experimenter "trained" in a theoretical tradition is probably more likely to replicate than an investigator who must rely on publicly recorded versions of the theory. But ideally we should be able to specify *in advance* what credentials are required to conduct a test of theory. Lacking that, it is too easy to dismiss failures to replicate as the folly of inept experimenters.

The seriousness of this problem is magnified by the fact that many of the people who make theoretical contributions are more interested in exploring new theoretical frontiers than in replicating their own research. Since science is public enterprise, more effort should be made to publicly record *all* of the prerequisites for empirical confirmation. These include the typically unpublished trivia of the procedure—if any of those trivia are required for replication. It is also necessary to include the many characteristics of the experimenter necessary for replication.

So far, the data on the experimenter effect in actual experiments do little more than say that experimenters can produce different results. Older literature on interviewer effects, however, has left us with a few generalizations about the relationship between specific characteristics of the interviewers and their contribution to the test response. Cantril (1944) and more recently Athey, Coleman, Reitman, and Tang (1960) have demonstrated that the race of the interviewer contributes to the attitudinal response. Riesman and Ehrlich (1961) report results consistent with our earlier discussions of the experimenter as an authority figure. Questions asked by young interviewers elicited more responses "unacceptable" to the interviewer than did the same questions asked by older interviewers. Interviewers have also obtained different results as a function of their religion (Robinson and Rohde, 1946; Hyman et al., 1954) and social class (Riesman, 1956; Lenski and Liggett, 1960). As a final example, Benney, Riesman, and Star (1956) report an interaction between the age and sex of the interviewer. Additional interviewer biases are discussed by Hyman et al. (1954) and by Kahn and Cannell (1957). Unfortunately, none of these references bear directly on the problem of whether or not these experimenter characteristics would interact with standard attitude change manipulations. It is important to stress, then, that we do not have empirical evidence that different experimenters produce a different rank order of the experimental conditions. For instance, even though young experimenters might indeed elicit more "disagree" or "unacceptable" answers, it does not necessarily follow that bias would be more pronounced in some experimental conditions than others. Only when this tendency to elicit more "disagree" answers is *not* uniform or consistent over experimental treatments do we worry about internal validity.

THE INTERACTION OF TESTING PROCEDURES AND MANIPULATIONS. Testing procedures are a second factor threatening external validity. The possibility that the pretest constitutes a manipulation which has an independent effect on the dependent variable (posttest) was discussed under internal validity. In this section we are concerned with the possibility that the pretest and manipulation, *in combination,* produce an effect different from either the pretest or the manipulation taken independently.

In the most common pretest design, subjects are randomly assigned to two groups and both groups are given a pretest. Only one of the groups is given the manipulations, but both are given a posttest. Since the two groups have the same experimental history except that one has been given the manipulation and the other has not, any differences between the experimental and control groups can be attributed to the presence of the experimental manipulation.

Although this design produces no threats to internal validity, a number of investigators (Solomon, 1949; Campbell, 1957; Campbell and Stanley, 1963) have been concerned that the observed difference might be produced by the *combination* of experimental manipulation and pretest which would not have been produced by the manipulation alone. In other words, the observed results may not generalize to a universe of subjects who did not receive a pretest. This problem is eliminated in a posttest-only design since neither experimental nor control subjects are pretested—any differences can be unequivocally attributed to the manipulation alone. The posttest-only design *eliminates* the possibility for a testing by manipulation interaction, but additional groups allow us to *test* for its presence. If a pretest-posttest control (with no manipulation) is compared with a posttest-only control (also with no manipulation), then the differences can be attributed to a simple, main effect of the pretest. If the posttest scores of a pretest-manipulation-posttest control are different from the scores of a pretest-posttest control and different from a manipulation-posttest control, then there is evidence that pretest and manipulation produce an effect in concert which neither produces independently.

Robert Lana (1959a, 1959b) fails to find evidence of a testing-manipulation interaction in a persuasion study. One-half of the subjects receive a pretest twelve days before the manipulation while the other half of the subjects receive no pretesting. Subjects are then exposed to a persuasive communication and posttested immediately. Lana's failure to find evidence for a testing × manipulation interaction should provide some comfort for investigators favoring the pretest. But his design, on an a priori examination, seems less likely to produce a pretest × manipulation interaction than many experiments in social psychology because first, there is a 12-day separation between pretest and manipulation, and second, the study involves a minimum amount of deception (Lana was not concerned that the pretest might allow subjects to see through his cover story).

In his studies on the primacy and recency effect, Lana (1964) reports a clear primacy effect for subjects exposed to a pretest and no order effects in conditions not exposed to a pretest. In another paper, Lana (1966) re-analyzes two of his primacy-recency studies (Lana and Rosnow, 1963; Lana, 1964). Since two-sided presentations are used in primacy-recency studies, Lana used absolute change scores as his measure of opinion change—a subject changing in either direction from his pretest was scored as showing opinion change. Lana reports that the presence of a pretest inhibits the amount of attitude change produced by a manipulation, and that an undisguised pretest inhibits attitude change when compared to a disguised pretest. Other investigators (Solomon, 1949; Entwisle, 1961) report an interaction of pretest and other variables in educational training studies, but these studies do not use attitude change as a dependent variable.

Interaction between pretest and manipulation is probably more serious than these few references indicate. There have been very few studies which include the appropriate control groups required to test for the interaction (pretest-manipulation-posttest, manipulation-posttest, and pretest-posttest); most studies are either posttest-only or pretest-posttest designs. The seriousness of the problem has been recognized; many investigators use a posttest-only design in situations where the pretest might interact with the manipulation. In many deception studies, for example, pretest × manipulations interactions would probably be discovered if pretest conditions were added to the typical posttest-only conditions. These investigations have eliminated (but not tested for) the interaction by using posttest-only designs.

In summary, there is relatively little published evidence demonstrating the presence of an interaction between a pretest and a manipulation, but that is little reason for complacency. The possibility that the obtained results might not generalize to unpretested subjects remains a serious threat to the external validity of pretest studies which omit the control groups needed to test for pretest-manipulation interactions. Finally, we should again state that a main effect of testing is not a threat to internal validity.

SUBJECT POPULATION. Critics of contemporary psychology frequently remark that we have a "psychology of the college sophomore with occasional excursions to the high school student." The problems associated with subjects from the introductory psychology pool are particularly serious for the social psychologist. Deception and elaborate cover stories often make experiments on attitude change particularly vulnerable to the sophisticated student who is currently learning about the shenanigans of experimental psychologists from his instructor. Obviously, social psychologists should seek out heterogeneous subject populations. Some designs are by necessity tailored to a specified age group or subject population; but alternate designs not so limited have a greater potential for external validity.

SPECIFIC EXPERIMENTAL PROCEDURES AND OPERATIONAL DEFINITIONS. Among those who experimentally study attitudes, two investigators might agree completely on the variable they want to study but arrive at quite different procedures for manipulating the variable. Consider the slightly facetious case where a dozen social psychologists are given a concept to manipulate experimentally. Spectators are then shown film clips of the actual experimental procedures and are asked to "name the variable" being manipulated. At this state in social psychology we doubt that even the close colleagues of the original investigators would achieve a perfect score in reconstructing the literary definition which had been used to generate various operational procedures.

The gap between a theoretical proposition and the operational procedures used to test it can create a problem of generalization. Since a particular operational definition is only one of many implied by a literary or theoretical definition, the same results might not be obtained with another operational definition. A good theory must contain theoretical and literary definitions such that one's colleagues could generate satisfactory operational definitions. This is not to say that all operational definitions should appear similar. Two experiments on the same variable giving the same results with markedly different operations give greater confidence in the underlying theoretical variable, thus leading to a more powerful inference than if the experiments were carried out with methodologically similar operations. The greater the difference in methodology between two separate confirmations of a theory, the stronger the support for the theory.

It is often difficult to distinguish where the cover story stops and the manipulation begins because most cover stories are closely wed to the manipulation. This interweaving of cover story and manipulation probably does contribute to impact and control, but it is another example of how "precision," "control," and "impact" may be bought at the price of external validity. The fact that a cover story and manipulation are closely interwoven makes it difficult to test a theory with two different methodologies; the cover story limits the range of methodological innovations possible. To the extent that the cover story contributes to the observed phenomena, the results may not generalize to other cover stories.

RESULTS FROM FIELD AND LABORATORY STUDIES IN ATTITUDE CHANGE. The results of investigators who use the survey research procedures to "go out into the real world and study the really important problems of our ongoing society" do not always coincide with the results of those who "bring the problem into the laboratory in order to analyze it and gain a scientific understanding of the processes." Survey researchers usually find less evidence of attitude change than do laboratory workers. The following paragraphs briefly review an analysis of differences between field and laboratory research made by Carl Hovland (1959). He points out that there are a number of substantive differences between the typical "field" and "laboratory" studies. It is important to keep in mind that Hovland is comparing studies conducted in the field and laboratory. The difference between correlational and experimental research is a separate issue.

An important difference between studies done in the field and in the laboratory is the condition of exposure to the persuasive communication. In the laboratory, subjects are exposed to a communication in a context which is either similar to the academic lecture situation or emphasizes the "scientific nature" of the experiment. These procedures provide many motivations extrinsic to the persuasive communication itself. In contrast, naturalistic studies of attitude change usually limit themselves to audiences which have chosen to expose themselves to the communication. If this self-selection resulted in an audience already in favor of a communication, then there would be little room for attitude change. This point of Hovland's is reinforced by the recent literature on demand characteristics. In the laboratory the effect of demand characteristics is probably to provide an apparent increase in attitude change. The problem-solving subject asks himself, "Why would he read me that communication, if he didn't want me to agree with it?" But in the field, the respondent is frequently cast in the role of an expert: "We are interested in what you think."

A noninherent difference between field and laboratory research is the length of time separating the communication exposure and the attitude measurement. While there are exceptions, experimental studies usually test attitudes immediately after the communication exposure, and field studies typically involve a somewhat longer interval. There is some evidence that attitude change may actually increase if the time interval between persuasion and measurement is increased (Katz, 1960; and the low communicator credibility condition in Hovland and Weiss, 1951). But the more typical result is a sharp decrease in attitude change as time between exposure and testing increases (the high credibility condition in Hovland and Weiss, 1951; Kelman and Hovland, 1953). There are similar differences in the type of subjects used. Practical convenience has led the experimental psychologist to concentrate heavily on college sophomores and high school students, whereas survey researchers typically utilize a much more heterogeneous sample—thus increasing the size of the error term.

The types of issues used in the two approaches is a distinguishing factor. Although there is little systematic evidence on the point, it seems reasonable that the "central" or important attitudes which draw the interest of survey researchers are less amenable to change than are the topics experimental scientists use, which are specifically chosen because they are susceptible to modification through communication.

In other words, Hovland has argued that the field and laboratory are not inherently different sources of data. He identified a number of substantive variables which happen to confound most field versus laboratory comparisons. For a more complete discussion of field versus laboratory and correlations versus experimental research see Campbell (1957), Campbell and Stanley (1963), and Aronson and Carlsmith (1968).

THE NEED FOR HETEROGENEITY OF IRRELEVANCIES

Considerations of the sort that we have just discussed led a number of psychologists (Campbell, 1957, 1963; Cook and Selltiz, 1964; Webb et al., 1966, for instance) to enter a plea for multiple measurements of attitude. We cannot completely eliminate all of the irrelevant features of the testing situation such as general standards of socially desirable behavior, demands implicit in procedure and design, expectations of the experimenter, and the context of the item wording and format; so the next best approach is to employ several different attitude indicators. All the measures should have in common the attitude object (or, more typically, a symbolic representation of the attitude object), but they should differ maximally in the irrelevant features contributing to the response—i.e., there should be a heterogeneity of irrelevancies.

It is impossible to avoid the undetachable accountrements added to the attitude object by the testing procedure; but there is no need to limit our perspective by measuring attitudes through only one, inevitably biased method. Paradoxically, this may mean that we often choose to employ a set of measurements with maximally different methods. This would be so even though the dissimilar measurement techniques have lower reliability (as measured by the standard reliability estimates) than another set of methods more homogeneous in their bias. One reason two items may appear on the same factor (they may be highly correlated and have high "reliability") is that they share a common method bias—and not that they both validly measure the same attitude. Since shared method bias inflates reliability (but not validity), standard measures of reliability may lead some investigators to choose measurement techniques similar rather than dissimilar in their irrelevant characteristics.

There are, however, a number of methodological problems with multiple response measures. In the first place, repeated measures may arouse suspicion in deception experiments. This is also a criticism of deception designs which cannot stand up under multiple response measures. Multiple response measures are another example of how external validity must often be bought at the price of control, impact, and experimental realism. Nevertheless, a creative experimenter may gain both if he begins his initial design plans on the assumption that multiple response measures would be desirable if possible. Multiple response measures also create statistical problems. The measures cannot be analyzed independently since they are correlated. With five items in the same format, the scores could be summed to form a single index; but it is difficult to form a single index from items with different formats. Techniques for multiple, correlated response measures on the same subject are just now being developed (see, for example, Bock, 1963).

A heterogeneity of irrelevancies is required for independent manipulations as well as the dependent variable. A heterogeneity of irrelevancies increases our confidence in the translation of a theoretical concept into an experimental manipulation. If two manipulations are both derived from the same theoretical proposition and both produce the same results, we make stronger inferences the greater the methodological *dissimilarity* of the manipulations. We can best generalize when we have developed a program of research establishing a number of variables, a number of measurement techniques, and a number of different operational definitions of the same independent variable. These replications within heterogeneity of irrelevancies give us knowledge of the conditions under which relationships hold.

SOME STRATEGIES FOR RESEARCH

Stimulus control versus psychological control. The experimenter in social psychology must decide whether he wants to produce identical psychological states among subjects by tailoring his procedure to fit each subject, or whether he should attempt to make the objective conditions or stimulus presentation identical for all subjects. The first condition results in uncontrolled variation in stimulus variables to achieve a uniform perception life space, or psychological state in the subject. The second allows variations in individual reactions to the manipulations in order to achieve a constant stimulus situation.

The solution to this dilemma is obviously affected by one's broader theoretical position. Lewinians, Gestaltists, phenomenologists are theoretically drawn to procedures that produce a uniform psychological state, whereas learning theorists and other "S-R" or "objective" psychologists are drawn toward a uniform stimulus presentation. Consistent with their broader theoretical orientation, Aronson and Carlsmith argue that "people are different, and . . . the same instructions do not mean the same to all subjects." Carlsmith even argues that it would be appropriate to use "procedures which might entail the presentation of dramatically different stimuli to different subjects." Likewise, consistent with his broader theoretical orientation, Donald Campbell (1957, 1963; Campbell and Stanley, 1963) takes a stand closer to the uniform stimulus presentation end of the continuum. The dilemma is, in part, a substantive theoretical difference rather than a methodological one.

But the problem is also relevant to several methodological problems. First, the greater freedom given the experimenter to interpret the script, the less accurately the *publicly* recorded procedure reflects what actually happened. Thus replications that essentially follow the published script may fail because they did not duplicate some nuance of tone of voice, gesture, etc., unrecorded in the publicly available version of the procedures. If experimenters are told that they cannot deviate from the public version of the script, they are motivated to make sure that everything they want to accomplish is represented in the written script. If the experimenter is required to abide closely by the script, he will probably devote more skill and craftsmanship to the script and less to unrecorded improvisations. In short, the more complete and accurate is the publicly recorded procedure section, the greater the likelihood of an accurate replication. An explicit license to the experimenter to deviate from the script probably leads to important omissions in the written description of the procedure.

The major thrust of the argument for a flexibility in delivering prepared scripts deals with the problem of clarity and understanding. ". . . Although instructions should be clear and repetitious, it is unwise to make them too repetitious, lest the brighter subjects become bored or annoyed. Moreover, regardless of how clear or repetitious a set of instructions are, there are bound to be some subjects who miss the point. Thus, the same instructions may simultaneously escape some subject and annoy others by being too simple" (Aronson and Carlsmith, 1968). Most would agree that some flexibility is needed in order to increase clarity and understanding; the difference is probably one of emphasis. The psychologist interested in uniformity of the objective procedures is more likely to formally program repetition and clarification into his script. A common procedure is to introduce points into the script where, at the experimenter's discretion, he either repeats or delivers a prepared rephrasing. In this way, the clarifications and repetitions are built into the publicly recorded script for future replicators to see, and the objective stimulus presentation is kept as constant as is possible consistent with needs for clarity and understanding. The essential point is that a complete and explicit script should be prepared before the experiment is run. It should be a guide to experimenters and not just an "after-the-fact" summary.

The dilemma is not an either-or confrontation between the objectivist and the subjectivist. There is a continuum ranging from Carlsmith's "dramatically different stimuli" to a totally automated procedure using tapes or films, during which the subject never interacts with a live experimenter; and the authors of this volume are in disagreement about the optimum place on this continuum. We do agree, however, that experimenters should be aware of the possibility of costly loss to analysis replication, and external validity. The impact gained by flexible instructions may not compensate. We also agree that the ideal state is a combination of the two positions—unvaried stimuli with strong impact.

IMPACT, CONTROL, AND ANALYSIS-REPLICATION

Aronson and Carlsmith's "Experimentation in Social Psychology" (1968) offers the rare opportunity to look over the shoulders of two skilled experimenters whose work is frequently presented in this book. As students and colleagues of Leon Festinger, they make explicit the values and strategies that have been associated with that prolific theoretical group.

Early in their chapter they identify two problems: "control" and "impact." "One of the major limitations on control which concerns us is the extent to which unmeasured individual differences may obscure the results of an experiment." The problem of control is particularly severe for the social psychologist, who is unable to minimize biological differences by controlling the heredity of his subjects. The second problem is impact. The experimenter in social psychology is severely restricted by "the relatively narrow limitations imposed on the kinds of experimental treatment" he can use. Thus the laboratory social psychologist must use relatively weak manipulations and must overcome appreciable noise in order to produce statistically reliable findings. These two problems jointly interfere with the likelihood of obtaining a measurable and statistically significant effect from the independent manipulation.

The experimenter must first achieve a high degree of *control* over the stimulus situation so that all subjects are in as nearly identical environments as is possible. Similar stimulus situations minimize the error variance contributed by environmental differences. Secondly, the experimenter must exercise the utmost in craftsmanship to achieve the maximum psychological *impact* from the relatively weak stimulus manipulations which ethics and practical considerations allow him.

The solutions to the problems of impact and control, however, are sometimes incompatible.

"We see this as the basic dilemma of the experimental social psychologist. On the one hand we want maximal control over the independent variable. We want as few extraneous differences as possible between our treatments. We want to specify as precisely as possible the exact nature of the treatment we have administered and its exact effect upon the subject. This leads us to try to develop manipulations which are highly specifiable, in which the differences between treatments are extraordinarily simple and clear, in which all manipulations are standardized, in short—to an approximation of something like a verbal learning experiment. On the other hand, if the experiment is controlled to the point of being sterile, it may fail to involve the subject, have little impact on him, and therefore may not affect his behavior to any great extent" (Aronson and Carlsmith, 1968).

Aronson and Carlsmith argue that, if control and impact can be achieved, many other problems of experimentation in social psychology disappear. For instance, if an experiment has sufficient impact, they argue that the subject will become so involved with the experiment that he does not have time to engage in guessing games with the experimenter. Thus impact eliminates suspicion among subjects in a deception design and minimizes the impact of the demand characteristics of the design.

There is at least one difficulty in this approach, however. Many of their specific recommendations to increase impact and control may lower the external validity; impact and control procedures may make it difficult to replicate the experiment. An experiment cannot be replicated unless the experimenter has specified exactly which aspects of a complex stimulus manipulation are responsible for the difference in the dependent variable. This is accomplished by analyzing the stimulus situation into smaller and smaller parts in order to specify each aspect, element, or facet of the manipulation that is a necessary prerequisite for the observed changes in the dependent variable. This can be accomplished, on the theoretical side, by a scientific analysis which decomposes complex phenomena into simpler ones and, on the empirical side, by a series of modified replications which focus on the relevant and eliminate the irrelevant components of the experimental manipulations.

The importance of this aspect of experimentation for theory-making and testing leads us to suggest a third goal for experimentation in social psychology: *analysis-replication*—the need for analysis or decomposition of complex phenomena into simpler phenomena. Analysis and replication is closely related to the problem of control. Thus, like control, the needs of analysis and replication often enter into a strain with impact. Let us consider some specific examples.

THE COVER STORY. Aronson and Carlsmith argue eloquently that the experimental manipulations and testing procedures should be embedded in a compelling cover story which involves the subject (thus creating impact) and makes plausible the manipulations and testing procedures (thus eliminating suspicion).

"It is perhaps already clear that what we have called 'setting the stage' not only leads into the independent variable, but is often a part of it. . . . Indeed, in a well built experiment it is often difficult to determine where the one leaves off and the other begins" (Aronson and Carlsmith, 1968).

There seems little doubt that such a procedure increases the impact of a manipulation; but the impact has been achieved at the cost of analysis-replication. First, to the extent that the manipulation and cover story are inexorably intertwined, it is difficult, conceptually or empirically, to analyze or decompose the experiment into the relevant and irrelevant parts. Furthermore, the marriage of cover story and manipulation makes systematic replication difficult.

"Thus, a replication of the Aronson-Mills (1959) study, for example, might necessitate a major change in the context of the experiment. If the subjects were asked to perform 30 push-ups (instead of reading obscene words), one could hardly maintain the format of a group discussion on the psychology of sex without straining the credulity of the subjects. Even the most naive of subjects would have second thoughts about doing push-ups as a screening device for discussion on sex. Thus, one must often re-do the entire experiment—changing not only the particular operations used in setting up the independent variable, but also the general setting, the experimental instructions, the stimulus to be rated, the measurement of the dependent variable, etc." (Aronson and Carlsmith, 1968).

Thus deception experiments with elaborate cover stories aggravate the difficulty of theoretical analysis and systematic replication and lower the external validity of the experiment. It may also make it difficult to theoretically analyze the manipulation into its component parts. Furthermore, as we have already pointed out in the section on demand characteristics, it may be important to consider the long-run impact of deception experiments on the "problem-solving" stances of our subjects. To what extent do our current research procedures generate "feelings of being manipulated" or general resistance in future subjects? If they do, this too may create replication difficulties.

Pilot experiments and pretesting. Psychologists usually do extensive pretesting and frequent pilot studies. Certainly no one would argue with the necessity for pilot studies and pretesting. Subjects just do not understand, they see through the cover story, manipulations are either too strong or too weak or just do not work at all.

There are at least two very serious problems with a strategy of running a number of successive pilot studies and fiddling with the manipulations until they work. If we throw dice to generate our data, we expect one out of every twenty t tests to reach "significance" at the .05 level. Unless the experimenter is pretesting procedures which are somehow worse than chance, he should expect one out of every twenty of his pilot studies to achieve significance. The .05 level just is not the .05 level if a successful experiment has been preceded by even a single unsuccessful pilot study. The more elaborate and complicated is the experiment, the greater the need for pretesting, and the more likely is a statistical artifact.

This statistical problem is particularly aggravated if the experimenter runs a few subjects and then analyzes the data to see if they conform with his hypothesis. If they do not, he makes a revision in the procedure and starts over again. If they do, he continues to run subjects and includes the data from the "pretest" subjects who confirmed his hypothesis. This procedure capitalizes on chance even more blatantly than the successful pilot study procedure. It is as though the experimenter ran successive groups of twenty subjects in the same procedure, stopping and starting over again every time the first twenty subjects fail to confirm the hypothesis and continuing with the experiment only in the event that the first half of his subjects confirmed the hypothesis. He has waited until chance favors the hypothesis for the first half of his subjects.

There are no cut-and-dried solutions to this statistical problem. At the very least, the experimenter is honor-bound to report the number of previous unsuccessful tries when he publishes his success. Secondly, a replication is probably required if the success follows several unsuccessful pilot studies. And it would help if pretest subjects were separated from experimental subjects. Data which are used as a basis for deciding whether or not to continue with a particular design should not be included in the final statistical analysis.

There is a more subtle difficulty created by pretesting which is not so frequently discussed. If the literary or conceptual statement of a theory leads an experimenter to formulate a procedure that does not work, the problem may well rest with the original theory. If the theory leads investigators to generate a number of operational definitions, (pilot studies) and only 20% (or even only 90%) of these procedures work, then the fault may lie with the original theoretical statement rather than the practical problems in the procedures that failed. In other words, if an experimenter tries out four operational procedures and succeeds on the fifth, there is reason to doubt that he would succeed again if he tried a sixth and seventh. This is an important point. When a theory generates an operational procedure that fails to work, the theory should be modified. And, importantly, the modified theory should no longer generate inappropriate procedures.

In this connection, there is some presumption for established theories. If the theory has successfully generated operational procedures in the past, we are more likely to attribute a current failure to technical difficulties unrelated to the theory than if we are starting with a new theory or a theory with a past record of failures.

A FEW REMAINING COMMENTS ON THE METHODOLOGY OF ATTITUDE CHANGE EXPERIMENTS

USE OF THE WORD "CHANGE." Use of the word attitude *change* is often mistakenly reserved for the pretest-posttest design. A posttest-only experimental design can be supplemented with a control group which receives a test at the same point in time when experimental and control groups have been treated identically. It is then correct to infer that the unmeasured pretest attitudes of experimental subjects are, within statistical limits, identical to the measured attitudes of the control group. If the posttest scores of the experimental subjects are significantly different from the test scores of control subjects, it is correct to infer that his experimental subjects indicated a significant *change,* even though a change score was not computed for each individual.

If the experimenter chooses to perform internal analyses on his data, however, correlations, or breakdown between high and low changes, are impossible in a posttest-only design. Since we do not have a score for each individual, we do not know whether a high posttest score is high because the individual began the experiment with a high score or because the experimental manipulation produced a change to that high level. Internal analysis often provides useful insights, but any internal analysis which selects subjects *because* they are extreme invites regression artifacts.

INTERPRETATION OF INTERACTIONS. We will dwell briefly on a mistaken statistical inference we occasionally discovered in our review of the literature. First, consider the case of an interaction in a simple 2 × 2 analysis of variance. As can be seen in Fig. 2.1, the lines are not parallel; so, if the error variance is small enough, we would expect a significant interaction. The significance of that interaction allows us to say that the *difference* between points *a* and *c* is significantly different than the *difference* between points *b* and *d* (or that the difference between *a* and *b* is significantly different than the difference between *c* and *d*). In Fig. 2.1, for instance, it is apparent that the large positive difference of *b* minus *d* may reasonably be significantly different from the small negative difference between *a* and *c*. The significant interaction *does not*, however, allow us to infer that points *b* and *d* are significantly separated. It is thus an *incorrect* summary of the significant interaction to say that "point *b* is higher than *d*, while point *a* is lower than point *c*." Until the appropriate *t* test has been done demonstrating that *b* is significantly higher than *d* and that *a* is significantly lower than *c*, the preceding statement cannot be made. As a matter of fact, a likely outcome from a set of data such as those illustrated in Fig. 2.1

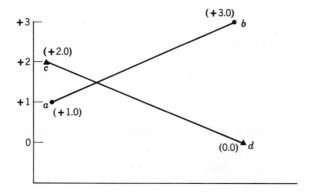

FIGURE 2.1. Example of an interaction.

would be a statement that b is significantly higher than d, whereas a and c are not significantly different. A significant interaction refers to significant *difference of differences*. No statement about significance of the difference between cell means can be made on the basis of any interaction; an appropriate t test is required to make significance statements about cell means. In summary, an interaction in and of itself allows only *one* conclusion, not two or four or whatever.

Some overlooked designs for attitude change research. Investigators in the area of attitude change appear to be overly enamored with the "change score." Posttest values are subtracted from pretest values to create a single change index for each subject, and the numbers are plugged into standard statistical designs. The analysis of co-variance with the pretest as a co-variant and the posttest as a dependent variable represents a statistically powerful analysis; it should be used more frequently.

If the experimenter has access to the pretest scores before assigning subjects to experimental conditions, the "treatments by levels" or "randomized blocks design" is appreciably superior to the co-variance analysis for pretest-posttest designs. Subjects with similar pretest scores are sorted into several groups, which are then relatively homogeneous on the pretest. Subjects within each of these groups are then randomly assigned to experimental conditions. The procedure is repeated for each of the homogeneous pretest groups. Pretest level is then treated as one factor in the analysis of variance design. This procedure has a number of impressive advantages:

1. It assures that all experimental conditions will be equal on the pretest.

2. As long as the pretest categories are fairly small so that all subjects in a group have almost identical pretest scores, this design has a greater statistical power than a change score analysis. It even has greater statistical power than the co-variance analysis if the relationship between pretest and posttest is not linear.

3. This method of analysis provides an explicit test for an interaction between pretest position and the experimental manipulation.

4. Since extreme subjects were randomly assigned to experimental and control conditions, there are no regression artifacts in comparisons among experimental conditions for subjects on either extreme of the pretest distribution.

As a practical note, it is not necessary to collect all the pretest data prior to running the subjects. If the experimenter has a reasonable notion of the pretest distribution before he collects the data, he can divide the distribution into a priori categories and determine a random sequence of experimental conditions *for each pretest category*. Since this amounts to a random assignment of subjects to experimental conditions within each pretest category, the data can be analyzed using pretest as a factor in the analysis of variance.

ALTERNATIVE EXPLANATIONS. A review of the literature on attitude change makes it all too apparent that few investigators consider alternative explanations *before* they gather their data. If the experimenter solicits alternative explanations from himself, colleagues, and students, he may be able to make alterations in the design, eliminating these alternative explanations. Perhaps a sort of "brainstorming" session where only alternative explanations can be discussed would help regain the perspective that is frequently lost as investigators gain the momentum to carry them through pretesting, subject-running, and data analysis. Indeed, one can argue that training in considering alternative explanations should be an integral part of the graduate school experience. A dispassionate view of one's own data is part of the scientific attitude.

Social Attitudes and Other Acquired Behavioral Dispositions (Campbell)

The rest of this book subdivides the various theoretical approaches by category into separate chapters. These theories, our discussion of them, and the data gathered to test various theories tend to emphasize the differences between any two given theories. This stress on the differences among theories is partly forced on the present authors by the organization of this volume. As a partial counterweight to this emphasis, we present Donald T. Campbell's framework for theoretical integration.

In a paper published in Volume 6 of Sigmund Koch's *Psychology: A Study of a Science,* Campbell (1963) presents a theoretical statement on the nature of attitudes. In contrast to most of the theoretical approaches discussed in this book, which stress the differences among theories, Campbell attempts to reconcile and integrate the behavioristic and cognitive or phenomenological approaches to attitudes.

We should make it clear at the beginning that it was not Campbell's purpose to set forward a theory of attitude *change*. We will abstract a few of his points most relevant to the process of attitude change, but they should be placed in perspective by outlining Campbell's broader purposes. He argues that a large number of concepts (including attitudes, valence, set, habits, learning) can be subsumed under the category of "acquired behavioral dispositions;" the proliferation of concepts within social psychology is at least in part a function of the proliferation of social psychologists rather than a proliferation of phenomena to be named. A first, and major, purpose of his paper is to establish the essential similarity among a large number of concepts which, according to their dictionary definitions, might seem incompatible.

"It is a commonplace observation that for human and other organisms, *behavior is modified as a result of experience,* that somehow a person *retains residues of experience of such a nature as to guide, bias, or otherwise influence later behavior.* This pervasive fact has been noted and conceptualized by most social scientists. Individually and collectively, they have given the process many and diverse labels. Today there is a surfeit of such concepts, and each new theoretical effort seems to increase the number" (Campbell, 1963, p. 97).

According to Campbell the major difference between cognitive and behavioristic theories is the connotation of the theoretical terms. The fact that a theory is couched in a language with "objective" connotations (i.e., implicit response) is usually taken as a sure sign that the theorist has taken sides in the conflict between the cognitive and behavioristic psychologists. Similarly, language with subjective connotations (i.e., cognition, perception) places the theorist clearly on the other side of the fence.

Campbell argues that, whether the connotation is subjective or objective, the languages of most theories are *functionally* equivalent. He would argue, for instance, that the statement "I perceive that the current administration is dishonest and incompetent" is functionally equivalent to the statement "I voted against the current administration." And both would be functionally equivalent to the statement of an outside observer, "He sent money to a political party" or "I received a letter of approval of disapproval."

All three of the preceding statements (statements describing perception, statements describing own actions, and statements by an objective observer describing overt behavior) diagnose or measure the same underlying acquired behavioral disposition—a tendency to respond negatively and avoid the class of stimuli that fall into the category "the current administration."

Campbell argues further that different techniques of *data collection* have contributed to the spurious differences in connotation between cognitive and behavioristic theories. The behavioristic psychologist—both by inclination and by necessity when working with infrahuman organisms—is most likely to use data gathered by an objective observer. Since the objective observer has no access to subjective information from his subjects, he must couch his descriptions and theorizing in terms of overtly observable stimuli and overtly observable behaviors.

The cognitive psychologist—both by inclination and as a result of the practical difficulties of following his subjects around to observe how they respond to various stimuli—is most likely to rely on subjective, self-report sources of information. These self-report or "conscious experience" sources of data, Campbell argues, lead the cognitive psychologists to couch his theory in perceptual terms or notions of the nature of the object. Campbell would argue, for instance, that a subject is much more likely to say "Squash is bad" than he is to say "I don't eat squash." He is more likely to say "My mother is an old scold" than he is to say "In the presence of my mother, I show avoidance reactions."

In summary, the behavioristic and cognitive *connotations* of theories in psychology do not prevent them from being functionally equivalent. Statements of perception, of behavioral intent, and of observed behavior all imply that the organism will respond in a consistent manner to a certain category of stimuli. Cognitive psychologists depend heavily on (human) verbal self-report and the behavioristic psychologists depend heavily on observation of overt behavior as a source of data. This bias in data collection procedures is reflected in a biased objective or subjective connotation of their theories.

MODES OF ACQUIRING BEHAVIORAL DISPOSITIONS

Behavioristic theories of attitude change build upon a foundation of data gathered from infrahuman subjects, which are incapable of verbal communication. But independent manipulations in attitude change experiments are usually verbal communications, and the typical dependent variable (pencil-and-paper tests) also depends on verbal communication. Thus the first, and crucial, step in building a behavioristic theory of attitude change is to liberalize the parent behavioristic theory so that it includes verbal communication as both a stimulus variable and a response category. Perhaps more than any of the other theorists in the next chapter, Campbell has paid explicit attention to this problem. He begins by listing six modes of acquiring behavioral dispositions.

1. Blind trial and error-locomotor exploration. Habits are acquired through blind trial and error when a blindfolded college sophomore shuffles through Warner Brown's (1932) human maze (a trough maze with three-inch high pathway edges through which one shuffled). They are also acquired in this manner when a blindfolded child explores Miller and Dollard's (1941) room with boxes containing candy and when animals explore tunnel mazes or puzzle boxes where vision is useless. Campbell (1956, 1963) argues that "this is the only mode of learning that is systematically investigated in learning theory—perhaps on the grounds that the simplest processes should be studied first. While this approach is clearly not modal for the socialized human being, it does seem in some sense basic, the ultimate resort" (1963, p. 107).

2. Perception. "Were one not blinded in Warner Brown's maze, one [would acquire] the appropriate behavioral disposition so rapidly that the process [would] elude study" (p. 107). Campbell wants to state explicity that an acquired behavioral disposition acquired through blind trial and error is, for most purposes, functionally equivalent to one acquired through perception. Consider a subject who is "allowed to see the maze, explore it visually, and then run the maze blindfolded, as does the person running the maze by blind trial and error. Could observing diagnosticians distinguish the final behavioral dispositions had they not seen the acquisition trials?"

3. Perceptual observation of another person's responses. It is also possible to learn by observing another organism's responses to stimuli; this is the traditional process known as imitation. "By memorizing the responses and then imitating them, the observer might acquire behavioral disposition externally identical to that which others had acquired by a perception of the maze or by blind trial and error" (p. 108).

4. Perceptual observation of the outcomes of another's explorations. The previous mode refers to a blind copying of the habits of another; it represented a learning of *responses* only. It is also possible to learn by observing the stimulus conditions under which another

behaves and the consequences of that behavior for that stimulus situation. "This is vicarious trial and error in its most literal sense, i.e., letting a Vicar do one's exploring" (p. 108).

5. Verbal instruction about responses to stimuli. In this mode of acquiring behavioral dispositions, previous modes of learning can be skipped by giving the subject explicit instructions about how he should behave in the presence of certain stimuli.

6. Verbal instruction about the characteristics of objects. ". . . It should be emphasized that behavioral dispositions can be verbally induced by means of descriptions of the object with no mention of the responses. Instead of saying 'turn right,' one can say 'the left path is blocked, the right one is open' " (p. 109).

With these six different techniques for acquiring a behavioral disposition (attitude, valence, set, etc.), Campbell greatly extends the array of stimulus or input manipulations typically used in behavioristic learning experiments. He argues that the diagnostician is frequently unable to distinguish among acquired behavioral dispositions that were acquired through each of the different modes. From the point of view of the diagnostician (attitude tester), all six techniques are equivalent forms of imparting knowledge, changing attitudes, teaching acquired behavioral dispositions, etc.

MODES OF EXPRESSING ACQUIRED BEHAVIORAL DISPOSITION: DIAGNOSTIC SYMPTOMS

"For the socialized human being, many behavioral dispositions can be expressed by locomotor behavior, by verbal statements of stimulus-response sequences, by verbal descriptions of the environment and the objects in it. Once a child has, as by blind trial and error, learned about the boxes, he can express the acquired dispositions by locomoting around and manipulating the boxes or by reporting what he does when he comes to a given box or by reporting what the boxes are like. He can instruct another person about the maze he has learned through statements about responses to make or about the nature of the maze parts" (Campbell, 1963, p. 111).

It is here that Campbell makes his major theoretical contribution with a point somewhat different from most of the other behavioristic viewpoints discussed in Chapter 3. Consistent with his methodological arguments (Campbell and Fiske, 1959) Campbell argues that a wide variety of verbal statements and overt responses can serve as symptoms or techniques of *measurement* of an acquired behavioral disposition. None of the measuring techniques completely defines attitude; overt behavior, verbal statements with connotation of perception, verbal statements with connotation of behavior, value descriptive verbal statements, and statements of behavioral intention—all are means of expressing (and consequently of measuring or diagnosing) the same acquired behavioral disposition. The reader is referred to the section on "Behavior and Attitudes" in Chapter 1 for several of Campbell's arguments in support of the equivalence of various modes of expressing an acquired behavioral disposition, attitude, habit, etc.

SUMMARY AND EVALUATION

The authors of this volume are in agreement that at least some of the conflict between "cognitive" and "behavioristic" theories of attitude change is a conflict over what kinds of language should be used rather than a conflict over what predictions should be made. Our position on the relationship between behavior and attitudes in Chapter 1— that attitudes and behavior are consistently related in the absence of situational pressures to the contrary, or difficulties in measurement techniques—is consistent with the Campbellian formulation.

Campbell (1961) has demonstrated that most of the results in the conformity literature can be ordered about his theoretical premises. There has been, however, no data gathered specifically to test the Campbellian formulation. In this sense, the theory is not actively in competition with the theories to be discussed in subsequent chapters. This is not to say that the formulation does not make impressive strides toward the broader goals outlined at the beginning of this section.

Campbell does not attempt to subsume the other theories into his formulation. Rather he tries to illustrate how learning theory must be expanded if it is to deal with the phenomena of attitude change and other "cognitive" problems. It is, in his words, an "exercise in translation." Although more behavioristic than cognitive in its final form, Campbell's effort illustrates that all theoretical effort need not be devoted to searching for differences among theories. Although we have stressed the differences, the theories in this book are probably more similar than different. To the extent that the language of these theories creates the appearance of difference when difference does not exist, Campbell's point is well taken.

Chapter Summary

We began this chapter with a few comments on the nature of formal theory. A theory, as such, is (1) a set of theoretical constructs and (2) a set of linking statements. The linking statements define the formal relations among the contsructs. Ideally, the linking statements should be stated in a language which allows one to deduce new predictions not explicitly present in the original formulation. But, since our theories of attitude change are couched in the rather imprecise language of everyday usage, few of the theories in this volume allow for a rigorous deduction of new predictions. Concepts are defined by two techniques: a literary or conceptual definition and an operational definition. A literary definition defines the boundaries of the concepts in such a way that another scientist can generate new operational definitions which are acceptable to the author of the theory. An operational definition defines the concept by specifying procedures which are used to measure the concept.

Following a brief introduction to the nature of formal theory, the main body of this chapter has been concerned with experimental methodology in theories of attitude change. The major criterion for the success of a theory is the extent to which it predicts empirical data, so the reader must be able to judge the methodological soundness of the data supporting the various theories in this book. The measured response in a test situation reflect several factors in addition to the underlying attitude. Such factors as (1) norms of self-presentation, (2) characteristics of the experimental design, (3) characteristics of the experimenter, and (4) response bias often make the meaning of our dependent variable ambiguous. Several ways in which these factors can make an empirical test of a theory of attitude change ambiguous are discussed.

The next sections of the chapter discuss internal validity and external validity. Internal validity is concerned with the interpretation of results of a particular experiment. If an experimental manipulation is so complex that the experimental results can be attributed to any one of several possible factors, internal validity is threatened. The section on internal validity covers such topics as history, testing, mortality, regression, instrument decay, selection, and maturation. External validity refers to the extent which the observed phenomena, law, results, or psychological processes will generalize to other settings. External validity is *not* the same as mundane realism. We do not guarantee that our results will generalize if the experimental procedures are similar to those found in the real world; similarly, laws discovered in contrived settings may have great generality. Several factors may limit the external validity, or generalizability of an experiment: (1) the particular experimenter, (2) the particular testing procedures, (3) the particular subject populations, and (4) the specific experimental procedures and operational definitions used. As a final topic under external validity, we review a paper by Hovland on the differences between field and laboratory research. Hovland points out that there are several substantive differences between field and laboratory research. Thus the different findings in the field and in the laboratory do not necessarily imply that laboratory research does not generalize the field.

We then turn to some issues involved in experimental research on attitude change. We discuss the issues of stimulus control versus psychological control. We also discuss the incompatible requirements of impact, control, and analysis-replication. Many of the methodological problems are resolved if the subject can be genuinely involved in the experimental procedures. But several techniques commonly used to gain impact may threaten external validity, or generalizability. Elaborate cover stories and extensive pilot experiments in pretesting, for instance, make it hard to identify the exact facet of the experimental manipulation that is crucial for the obtained results.

The next section presents a few comments on the use of the word change, the interpretation of statistical interactions in analysis of variance designs, the "treatments by levels" or "randomized blocks design," co-variance analysis, and the need for alternative explanations.

The chapter concludes with a summary of Campbell's "Social Attitudes and Other Acquired Behavioral Dispositions." Campbell's presentation is included to help offset the stress on *differences* among theories presented in this book. Using a somewhat behavioristic vocabulary, Campbell tries to demonstrate the *similarities* among the various theoretical approaches to the study of attitudes.

Chapter 3

Stimulus-Response and Behavioristic Theories of Attitude Change

THEORIES of learning have had a marked influence on psychologists—particularly American psychologists. Not only have American psychologists expended enormous amounts of effort in the development and refinement of the theories per se—more experimental data have probably been collected for the purpose of sorting among these theoretical explanations of learned behavior than for any other psychological purpose. One only has to recall the arguments among Hull, Tolman, Guthrie, Skinner, and their peers to imagine what might be called the golden era of intellectual and theoretical excitement in American psychology. The emphasis on formal theories of learning and the interaction between data gathering and theorizing in learning conditions continues, most notably by Spence (e.g., 1956), Miller (e.g., 1959), and their students.

Many psychologists look back upon the theoretical efforts of this era as a model for theory development in other areas. The theoretical analysis of learning represents a genuine interaction between the theoretician and the data gatherer. Experiments were done specifically to "test" one theory or another and to pit the predictions of one theory against the predictions of another, and theories were extensively modified as the data began to come in.

We can distinguish the various learning theories along so many dimensions that it can almost be said that there are as many learning theories as there are learning theorists. But there are a number of common characteristics—in addition to a focus on the learning process—which allow us to group them together for purposes of this chapter.

For one thing, nearly all behavioristic theorists share a Darwinian interest in the adaptive aspects of human behavior. This emphasis has led learning theorists to a very pronounced interest in the "objective" environment (i.e., stimulus) and the "objective" feedback (i.e., reward and punishment) which are provided to the organism. This set of interests leads those behaviorists who think about attitude change to place far more emphasis on the stimulus characteristics of the communication situation than is provided by other theoretical approaches. Thus the early research done by Hovland and his associates emphasized the dimensions they felt to be objectively quantifiable of the communication (e.g., the order and arrangement of persuasive arguments), of the communicator (e.g., credibility), and of the audience (e.g., age and education) (Hovland, Lumsdaine, and Sheffield, 1949; Hovland, Janis, and Kelley, 1953). It would be a mistake to underemphasize the importance of this preference for certain kinds of variables in the development of a theory. In fact, perhaps the most salient characteristic of the research discussed in this chapter, which distinguishes it from the research in other chapters, is the substantive interest in quantifiable stimulus characteristics of the communication situation.

This interest in the covariation among the objective stimuli and the overt responses was strengthened by certain developments in the philosophy of science. Philosophers of science argued that a psychological concept was "defined" completely by the procedures which are used to measure it. This "operationalism" lent a certain methodological elegance to research which dealt with the easily qualifiable stimulus and response variables.

This substantive and methodological interest in a high degree of control over the environment has had an unfortunate side effect—unfortunate at least to those of us who would look toward theories of learning for insight into the process of attitude change. Practical and ethical considerations have led most learning theorists into the animal laboratory. The early development of learning theories depended on research on organisms lower in the phylogenetic order than the typical attitude change subject. The theories were designed with the notion that they would receive their testing in the animal laboratory, and the modifications in the theory produced by animal data further fostered a certain provincialism in the theory.

GENERALIZING FROM THE ANIMAL LAB

The problems of generalization from animal laboratory to attitude change may not be quantitatively different or greater for learning theory than for any other theory. But the quantitative problems are large. The jump from psychophysics to attitude change made by the judgment theorists (Chapter 6), for instance, is markedly less than the transition learning theory must make from a foundation built of Y-mazes, Skinner boxes, and Lashley jumping stands. The predictive power of any theory suffers as we move away from those situations involved in the original theory construction. For behavioristic theories of attitude change the distance is so far that the theory of attitude change is typically called a "translation" or "analogy" rather than the extension or generalization of the original theory.

These problems of translation raise four particularly bothersome problems. First, it is often unclear whether a particular experimental test is a test of the original theory or of the translation. The basic postulates of a learning theory are firmly established on their own home ground in the animal laboratory. Negative results in an attitude change experiment often lead to the conclusion that the *translation* rather than the theory itself was wrong. But a theory is not a theory unless it is capable of being disproved. Each of the behavioristic approaches to attitude change must be evaluated as a unitary theory. To the extent that theories fail to make correct predictions in the arena of attitude change, we must conclude that there is something wrong with the theory—no matter how adequate a record the prediction may have had in the other empirical testing grounds.

Suppose an experimenter were to test the statement that receiving a smile from another person is a reinforcing event. Suppose further that we run an experiment in which every time the subject expresses a favorable opinion toward capital punishment the experimenter smiles. In the event that we find no increase in favorable attitude toward capital punishment, what do we conclude? One probable conclusion would be "a smile is not really a reinforcer in this situation"—i.e., I have made an inappropriate translation of the general theoretical position that reinforcements change attitudes. But there is another conclusion from the data that is equally tenable, i.e., that reinforcing events do not necessarily change attitudes. There are considerable data that suggest, in fact, that the delivery of verbal or monetary incentives for the overt statement of an attitude does not necessarily produce any consequent attitude change.

A second problem posed by the translation from learning theories to the attitude situation stems from the heterogeneity of the learning theories themselves. All too often a "learning theory of attitude change" is based upon a drastically oversimplified common theme garnered from several different learning theories. While gaining a certain consensus among learning theories, such an oversimplification loses the precise predictive power inherent in the idiosyncrasies of each theory.

A third problem has already been mentioned. To jump from animal laboratory investigations on the learning of overt responses to the investigation of the change of already learned nonovert attitudes in human beings is a large one.

Finally, there is very little horizontal interaction among the various behavioristic theories of attitude change. Each theorist begins anew on the foundation of learning theory. There has been little attempt to specifically compare and contrast—either verbally or impirically—the several independently derived behavioral theories of attitude change discussed below.

In this chapter we first review "implicit response" theories of attitude change. These include the work of Leonard Doob, the Lotts, the Staats, and William Scott. Although it is not a full-blown formal theory, we next review the "working assumptions" used by Hovland, Janis, and Kelley in their *Communication and Persuasion* (1953). We then discuss the theoretical presentations of Robert Frank Weiss and Daryl Bem. A brief review of McGuire's theoretical work is the last substantive section. The final section raises the methodological and theoretical issues associated with awareness. We should forewarn the reader of the eclectic nature of this chapter. Many of the theoreticians we have grouped together would not approve of our categorization; it is an exception if the various theorists even cite each other. There is, therefore, a minimum of continuity from section to section. Throughout this chapter, we assume the elementary knowledge of instrumental and classical conditioning available in any introductory psychology text.

Attitude as an Implicit Response: Leonard Doob

In Doob's (1947) analysis, an attitude is viewed as an implicit, mediating response—a hypothetical construct or intervening variable between an objective stimulus and an overt response. The attitude response, although unobservable by an outside observer, is both a response to the observable stimulus and a stimulus to the observable response in a sort of "chaining" mechanism. Both of these stimulus → response bonds (observable stimulus → attitude and attitude → objective response) are assumed to obey "all the laws of behavior theory."

To be more precise, Doob defines an attitude as *"an implicit drive-producing response considered socially significant in the individual's society"* (1947, p. 136, Doob's italics). Let us look more closely at the elements of Doob's definitions. By "implicit" Doob means that the response is not directly observable: it may effect overt behavior, but it is not overt behavior. The response "may be conscious or unconscious, distinctly verbal or vaguely proprioceptive" (p. 136).

Doob assumes that the implicit response (attitude) is both cue- and drive-producing. With respect to the cue properties, an individual can discriminate the presence-absence and the varying levels of intensity of an implicit response, just as he can discriminate the presence-absence and intensity of an overt stimulus. Explicit is the assumption that any response that can be learned to (connected to) an overt stimulus can also be learned to an implicit response. Some learning theorists have stressed the independence of (1) the overt stimulus → implicit response bond learning from (2) the implicit response → overt behavior bond learning (especially in avoidance or fear conditioning; see Miller, 1951). But Doob relies on an older analysis in which the learning of the implicit response is chained backward from the learning of the overt response. Consistent with some of Hull's (1932) observations, Doob assumes that responses occurring nearest in time and space to a reinforcement are learned first and that the learning then moves backward in both time and space away from the reinforcement. An implicit response is learned then, because it is part of a sequence of behavior which eventually leads to the reinforced overt response. Weiss (1962) also holds this chaining view of attitude learning.

Doob also asserts (consistent with several other treatments of learning theory, e.g., Miller, 1951; Miller and Dollard, 1941) that the implicit response has energizing characteristics which can motivate the external response. Consistent with earlier attempts to delineate a place for the concept of attitude among the other concepts of psychology and sociology (e.g., Faris, 1925), Doob limits the term to those implicit responses which mediate "socially significant behavior." "Socially significant behavior" is used qualitatively to set attitudes apart from other habits and associative bonds. Thus the distinction is not critical to the theory because attitudes and other habits obey the same empirical laws.

There are six characteristics of an attitude according to Doob's theoretical analysis:

1. The goal response. This consists of those overt behaviors that are the end result of the overt stimulus → implicit response → overt behavior sequence.

2. Perception (or attention). Doob assumes that there is some drive which motivates the individual to attend to the overt stimulus which sets off the entire sequence.

3. Afferent-habit strength. This is the strength of the bond between the overt stimulus and the implicit response.

4. Efferent-habit strength. The strength of the bond between the implicit response and the overt behavior which it mediates is efferent-habit strength.

5. Drive strength. This is the intensity of motivation or the energizing capability of the implicit response.

6. Interaction. Although not previously mentioned, Doob also stresses that the overt response is a function of many determinants in addition to the particular implicit response (attitude) under consideration. The particular behavior that occurs will be a function of the attitude in question as well as all the other stimuli, drives, habits, and attitudes present in this particular situation. The principle of interaction has two major consequences. (a) It will not always be possible to predict overt behavior from a single attitude without knowing the other determinants of behavior. (b) It is never possible to attain a perfect measure of an attitude since the overt behavior involved in the measuring technique is a function of other determinants than the attitude in question. Other attitude change theorists make an assumption similar to Doob's interaction assumption, but none make it quite as explicit.

A crucial step in Doob's theoretical analysis (as with all of the learning theory approaches to attitude change) is the concept of generalization. Doob emphasizes the flexibility given to learning theory by the concept of generalization. Since a response can generalize to stimuli not involved in the original learning, the implicit response can become attached to a variety of related stimuli or stimulus patterns. Also, considering the role of the implicit response as a cue- and drive-producing stimulus, we may expect an overt response to generalize to a variety of similar implicit responses. The complicating issue of response generalization (Osgood, 1953) is left untouched by all the learning theory approaches to attitude change reviewed here.

We have now briefly discussed Doob's theoretical analysis of attitude and attitude change. Later we shall return for a more critical view of his theory, but for the moment let us look at some of the data related to the theory. Actually, Doob's theory has provoked little experimentation specifically designated to test the theory or to pit it against other theories, but we shall look at several experiments that specifically treat an attitude as an implicit, cue-producing response.

LOTT

Lott (1955) taught young children to respond to geometric figures (e.g., a triangle) with particular names (e.g., egg). In a second training session, she taught the children to apply the same names to particular color stimuli; in the same session she trained her subjects to find a marble (assumed to be a reward) under one of the figures used in the first session. In Lott's terms, the choice-response to a particular geometric figure stimulus was reinforced. For some groups, these three stimulus-response sequences (shape → name; color → name; and shape → choice-response) were subjected to further practice.

Note that at no time had the sequence color → choice-response been allowed (or reinforced). Lott theorized that the dual use of naming response—e.g., the word "egg," for both the color and shape stimuli—would result in a mediated generalization. In a derivation from Doob's theory, she expected that the "favorable attitude" (presumably reflected by the choice response) created when subjects were reinforced for choosing the triangle would be conditioned not only to the triangle stimulus but also to the "internal mediating naming response" (egg). Thus any stimulus, however unlike a triangle in its physical characteristics, which evokes the (implicit) egg response should also evoke the favorable attitude (shape → name → choice-response). Lott used several different generalization test situations and the results were as expected. For example, when the children were asked to choose a colored object in anticipation of a marble (reinforcement), they reliably chose that colored object which had the same *name* as the previously reinforced *shape*.

This is an interesting experiment, but there are aspects of it that suggest some degree of caution in generalizing from this experiment to other attitude change data. First, does the choice response in Lott's experiment reflect an "attitude," as that term has been here presented, or does it merely reflect the degree to which subjects learned what the experimenter's expectations of him were? As we stressed in our discussion of demand characteristics in Chapter 2, all experiments take on features of a problem-solving situation or game in which the subject tries to produce the "appropriate" response—whether that be defined by the experimenter's expectations, general norms about self-presentation, or special responses which are "demanded" by the particular experimental design and procedure. Lott's experiment seems particularly vulnerable to this criticism. The whole experiment sounds like a children's game presented by the experimenter, in which the subject is supposed to guess how to win (get a marble). The subject then attends to whatever clues the experimenter gives him (ah, both called egg!) about how to obtain the marble. This issue of subject awareness is critical for most behavioristic theories of attitude change; we have devoted a special section at the end of this chapter to the issue.

These two explanations of the results, fortunately, can be distinguished empirically. The Lott-Doob explanation assumes that the choice response has been attached to the implicit response (egg), which is, in turn, attached to the overt stimuli (color or shape in this case). The demand characteristic explanation assumes that the choice response occurs because the subject decides that the response is somehow appropriate in this experimental context. It should not be difficult to design an experiment which maintains the learning situations necessary for the Lott-Doob prediction but which manages to create the impression that some other response is "appropriate" (e.g., desired by the experimenter). Greenwald (1965) reports a series of experiments that pit some aspects of the demand characteristics against his hypothesis. This procedure is especially desirable in designs such as Eisman's, which provide the subject with so many cues that might lead him to conclude that some responses are more appropriate than others.

STAATS AND STAATS

We are fortunate to have two recent reviews (Staats, 1967, 1968) to help in organizing the several experiments by Staats and Staats. While the general theoretical framework is more or less similar to that of Doob's, Staats argues that the learning of the (1) overt stimulus → implicit response (attitudes) bond takes place separately from the learning of the (2) implicit response → overt behavior bond.

In particular, Staats argues that the *acquisition* of attitudes or affective and emotional "meaning" for a social object or word takes place through classical conditioning. Many stimulus events in our environment elicit emotional and affective responses in a particular individual. New stimuli (conditional stimuli, or CS) attain the power to elicit these same emotional and affective responses if the new stimulus is consistently paired with the old stimulus (i.e., the unconditional stimulus, or UCS). Since words and social objects are frequently paired with important environmental events, it is not surprising that many words and social objects attain the ability to evoke emotional and affective responses. "It may be suggested that a word becomes meaningful when it comes to elicit a conditional response through classical conditioning."

In order to demonstrate this phenomenon in the laboratory, Staats, Staats, and Crawford (1962) report a classical conditioning paradigm in which certain words (CS) were paired with shocks or loud, harsh sounds (UCS). Three findings support Staats' argument that attitudes are formed by classical conditioning: (1) during test periods, the word which had been paired with the shocks or loud harsh sounds was found to evoke galvanic skin responses (GSR); (2) the word which had been paired with shock or loud noises was also rated lower on the evaluation scales of the semantic differential; and (3) there was a correlation between the magnitude of the galvanic skin response to the word and the extremity of the verbal rating. The last finding suggests that both verbal rating and galvanic skin responses are measures of the degree to which the classical conditioning procedures have been successful. Similar data are presented in a useful review by Maltzman (1968). Maltzman conditions both galvanic skin response (GSR) and word meaning to a neutral word. When the intensity of the UCS was varied, the more intense UCS produced a greater GSR to the conditioned stimulus (a previously neutral word) in the test period and also a stronger negative, verbal, evaluative rating of the word. Demand characteristic or awareness explanations for these experiments are discussed in a special section at the end of this chapter.

HIGHER-ORDER CONDITIONING. Staats argues that the principle of "higher-order conditioning" further extends the generality of his theory. If a word has attained the ability to produce a certain emotional and affective response because it has been paired with some significant event in the environment, then still a third word or event can come to produce the emotional and affective responses if it is paired with the conditioned stimulus.

In order to test this hypothesis, Staats and Staats (1957) projected a nonsense syllable onto a screen. The subject was led to believe that the study concerned two kinds of learning—looking at nonsense syllables and hearing words. This apparently plausible explanation is at least a step in the right direction toward making this study less vulnerable to the demand characteristics or "awareness" alternative explanation.

On a basis of pretest material, Staats was able to compile a list of words (beauty, whim, sweet, gift, etc.) that elicited generally favorable responses in most subjects. Similarly, it was possible to develop a list (bitter, ugly, sad, sour, etc.) that elicited negative responses in most subjects. A third list was made up of words which, on the basis of the pretest material, elicited neither negative nor positive reactions.

It should be stressed that this procedure does not present a true case of "higher-order conditioning." In other words, Staats did not, *in his laboratory,* imbue the word "beauty" with the ability to evoke a positive response or the word "bitter" with the ability to evoke a negative response. It is only if we agree with Staats' previous theory—i.e., that all words have attained their power to elicit emotional and affective responses through previous classical conditioning—that we can regard the present study as an example of "higher-order conditioning." Without that assumption, the study is merely another study of classical conditioning where a UCS (i.e., words such as beauty or bitter) is known to produce an unconditioned response at the begining of the experiment.

The results support Staats' hypothesis, whether we regard the study as one of first-order or higher-order conditioning: the subjects were conditioned to feel the same way about the nonsense syllables which had been projected on the screen as they did about the affective meaning words with which the syllables had been paired (Staats and Staats, 1957).

A follow-up paper (Staats and Staats, 1958), reports two experiments which condition affect to national and individual names. Subjects were presented with a series of national names (e.g., "Dutch," "Swedish") on a projection screen. During the presentation of each slide, the experimenter said a word aloud (e.g., gift), after which each subject repeated the word. The subject was told to concentrate on learning the list of national names but to concentrate simultaneously on pronouncing the words aloud to himself. In the first experiment, the name "Swedish" was presented in conjunction with positive words (e.g., gift, happy) and the name "Dutch" was presented with negative words (e.g., bitter, ugly, failure). The subjects then filled out the semantic differential on the national names (and the words). The second experiment was quite similar to the first, excepting that male first names (e.g., Tom, Bill) were used instead of the national names. In both cases the predictions based on the classical conditioning paradigm were confirmed. That is, subjects gave a more positive evaluation on the semantic differential for the (national and male) names that were presented contiguously with positive words than they did for those names presented with negative words (Staats and Staats, 1958).

The parallel between classical conditioning and attitude formation is extended by three further studies. The known semantic differential ratings of words can be modified by pairing these words with other words which have different semantic differential ratings (Staats, Staats, and Biggs, 1958). Also, the number of conditioning trials affects the strength of the conditioned meaning (Staats and Staats, 1959).

In another paper (Staats, Staats, and Heard, 1960), a dimension of reinforcement ratio was added to the paradigm. There were three conditions of either 100, 50, or 0% reinforcement. Higher ratios of reinforcement produced better "conditioning."[1] However, since they used the *difference* between positive and negative words as a dependent variable, it is impossible to say whether the results are due to punishment, reinforcement, or both.

This classical conditioning analysis of attitudes, quite typically for a stimulus-response orientation, has focused almost entirely on the process of attitude *formation*. Staats (1968) extends his formulation somewhat further by speculating about the functions which an attitude might serve for an individual. Since a word or social object can gain the functional properties of a reinforcer or a punisher by being associated with the original reinforcer or punisher, these words and social objects should be able to serve as rewards and punishments in their own right (secondary reinforcement). This interpretation is tested in a study by Finley and Staats (1967). On the basis of ratings on the semantic differential, the authors selected three groups of words which had different meanings for sixth graders: one group with positive evaluative meaning, a second group with negative evaluative meaning, and a third group without

---

[1] Staats and Staats (1958) discarded the results from subjects who indicated they were aware of the systematic word-name relationships (17 out of a total of 89). However, in later papers this type of datum is retained in the analysis; the data from the aware subjects are not presented separately. See the awareness section at the end of the chapter for further discussion of these issues.

evaluative meaning as measured by the semantic differential. In a button-pushing apparatus, some subjects heard a "negatively valued word" when they pressed a certain button, other subjects heard a "positively valued word," and others a "neutrally valued word." As predicted, the results indicated that the words rated positively on the semantic differential increased the frequency of the button-pressing response, negatively rated words decreased the button-pressing response, and neutrally evaluated words acted as neither reinforcers nor punishers.

The logic used by Staats and Staats has been extended by Das and Nanda (1963) to include sensory preconditioning. For any given subject each of two tribes (Ho or Munda) was paired with a nonsense syllable. The two words, tribal name and nonsense syllable, were read out 60 times by the experimenter and the subjects were asked to repeat the pair each time. After a pause, the subjects then underwent a 200-trial probability learning sequence—one of the two nonsense syllables was presented and they were asked to guess which of two words was "correct." They were told the correct answer following each trial. One of the nonsense syllables was paired with "good" for .85 of the trials and the other was paired with "bad" for .85 of the trials. (In both cases the opposite word was used on the remaining .15 of the presentations.) Note that the tribal names were never directly paired with "good" or "bad." Subjects then rated the tribal names on a 5-point scale ranging from "extremely bad" to "very good," which is similar to the evaluative scale of the semantic differential. Subjects were also asked to pick the 10 adjectives from a list of 20 which were most appropriate to the tribal names.

The authors assume that their probability learning procedure established the response "good" or "bad" to the nonsense syllables. The data from ratings of the nonsense syllables on the posttest support this assumption. In Doob's language, the training established an overt stimulus → implicit (attitudinal) response bond. The authors then refer to a phenomenon in classical conditioning—sensory preconditioning. They reason that if two stimuli (say, nonsense syllables and tribal names) are first associated, then a response learned to one (say, a nonsense syllable) will also occur to the other (tribal names). And this is what they found. Both the adjective checklist and the five-point good-bad scale show that the tribal name was rated similarly to the nonsense syllable with which it had been associated in the first phase of the experiment.

We must be careful about attributing these findings to sensory precon- ditioning. It may be, of course, that the responses "good" become attached to the nonsense syllable. Or it could be that the subjects rea- soned something like the following: "He held up those same cards 60 times, and they said the same thing nearly every time. Maybe he is trying to tell me something—that good and that funny words go to- gether." It is not much of an intellectual leap to figure out that the experimenter was trying to say that all three words—the nonsense syl- lable, the tribal name, and "good"—are all supposed to "go together."

This specter of demand characteristics is the same one we brought up in discussing the similar studies by Staats and Staats. But "Demand Characteristics" is not a phrase which, like a wand, can be waved over somebody's data to make them disappear. The present authors do feel, however, that the effort of the subject to respond "appropriately" is a very plausible alternative hypothesis to many of these conditioning experiments—especially where the design and procedure provide many cues or hints about what the "appropriate" response should be. But, although not without alternative interpretation, these data were spec- ifically collected to test predictions made from a position much like Doob's, and the results are in line with the predictions. The problems of awareness and demand characteristics in these "conditioning" para- digms are general to several of the theories in this chapter; as indicated, further discussion of the general problem has been postponed until the end of the chapter.

SCOTT

The previous studies supporting Doob's position work within a classical conditioning paradigm. Investigators first create a stimulus → implicit response bond (or else they work with bonds already established to such stimulus words as good, gift). Then, in the standard classical condition- ing paradigm, the first stimulus is paired with a second, and the second stimulus comes to evoke the same responses previously attached only to the first stimulus. Although quite consistent with Doob's formulation, these studies do not deal with the backward chaining process of instru- mental learning to which Doob gives the greatest emphasis.

Scott, on the other hand, focuses on just this process. "It is conceivable that an opinion be expressed initially, in the absence of a supporting attitude, but if the verbal behavior is rewarded, the corresponding atti- tude may develop and mediate subsequent opinion expressions in the presence of similar cues" (1957, p. 72). Thus the "expression" of the attitude is equated with Doob's overt response, and a reinforcement of the overt response is assumed to work back to strengthen the stimulus → attitude connection as well as the attitude → expression connection. Conversely, punishment of the overt expression leads the subject to "revert to his formerly preferred response disposition" (p. 72).

Scott (1957, 1959) utilized a debate setting in which subjects were required to uphold a particular viewpoint in a debate. They then either won or lost the debate. "The vote of 'win' is presumed to have reinforced the verbal behavior and with it the accompanying implicit responses—attitudes and cognitive support for them. The vote of 'lose' presumably weakened whatever response tendencies had been established by the overt behavior . . ." (1957, p. 74). The results were as predicted: "winners" changed their attitude in the direction they advocated in their speech; "losers" did not change.

Scott tested the effects of the entire sequence of events involving preparation for and delivery of the debate speech as well as winning and losing. Dahlke (1963) tried to separate out the effects of winning per se by including a control group which debated but neither won nor lost. Males showed no attitude change in any condition. Female debaters who won were not different from the no-feedback controls; female debaters who lost showed significantly less attitude change than the no-feedback controls. Thus Scott's results are not replicated for males; there is no evidence for a reinforcing effect of the win; but females do evidence a punishment effect as a result of losing. Kiesler (1965) obtained results precisely opposite Scott's, i.e., losers changed more than winners; but a comprehensive explanation for the Kiesler data remains to be found. There is, then, some empirical confusion surrounding Scott's (1957, 1959) experiments.

SUMMARY

The preceding is a fair representation of the research relevant to Doob's theory. Though there are other experiments (e.g., Rhine, 1958, 1960; Rhine and Silun, 1958; Singer, 1961), the total amount of research is small. In some ways this is to be expected. Doob's theory is stated rather generally and all-inclusively. Although he does discuss a large number of terms originally derived to account for experimental data in learning, he does not give a great many suggestions on precise translations of these terms operationally for research in attitude change.

In fairness to Doob, however, several things should be kept in mind. First, his article was written in 1947, long before a large percentage of the existing literature on attitude change had been accumulated. He lacked the vision of hindsight enjoyed by later theorists. More importantly, prior to that time, with the exception of F. H. Allport (1924), much of the theorizing in attitude formation had not utilized a learning theory analysis; Doob made a contribution just by suggesting that behaviorism could be made relevant to the study of attitudes.

But do these theories really make an important contribution to the social psychology of attitude change? Several factors limit the generality and importance of the behavioristic approach. First, they employ a somewhat more restricted definition of attitude than other theories of attitude change. Second, their experiments are usually more contrived and further removed from the propaganda situations of real life than the other theories reviewed. Finally, the theory has been relatively unsuccessful in stimulating theory-testing experiments. Whatever their values as formal theories, the behavioristic theories in this chapter are, in their present state, relatively limited in scope. These criticisms also apply to most of the rest of the theories discussed in this chapter.

The Yale Communication and Attitude Change Program

WORKING ASSUMPTIONS

Hovland, Janis, and Kelley's book, *Communication and Persuasion* (1953), was the first of a highly visible series of research monographs. We will use it as a basis for discussing the "Yale Program"—one of the major forces shaping contemporary research and theory on attitude change. The book does not represent theory construction in the sense in which we commonly understand the word. Indeed, the authors themselves explicitly state that they "shall not attempt to present a systematic theory of persuasive communication." Instead, they present a program of empirical research organized around the theme sentence, "Who says what to whom with what effect?" (Smith, Laswell, and Casey, 1946). We shall, nevertheless, use their introductory comments to illustrate the framework, approach, or theoretical orientation which governed the type of research subsequently pursued by the Yale researchers. We should stress again, however, that the "working assumptions" and research reviewed in this section do not constitute a formal theory.

Communication and Persuasion opens with a discussion of the nature of opinion change and the types of variables involved in persuasive communications. The S-R tenor of their approach is seen in the definition of opinion:

". . . verbal answers that an individual gives in response to stimulus situations in which some general question is raised" (p. 6).

Both "opinion" and "attitude" refer to implicit responses, and, in theoretical terms, are intervening variables. The relationship between the two is an intimate one.

". . . while the term opinion will be used to designate a broad class of anticipations and expectations, the term attitude will be used exclusively for those implicit responses which are oriented toward approaching or avoiding a given object, person, group or symbol" (p. 7).

With reference to Doob's (1947) early article, the authors indicate that their conception of an attitude implies that an attitude has drive value. They suggest that opinions may be verbalizable, but the term attitude is not restricted to verbalizable attitudes. The concept of attitude includes unconscious or nonverbalizable avoidance tendencies. In addition, the authors maintain the distinction between the answer which an individual may give to another individual and the "implicit" response which he gives to himself when faced with the stimulating question.

"We assume that opinions, like other habits, will tend to persist unless the individual undergoes some new learning experiences. Exposure to a persuasive communication which successfully induces the individual to accept a new opinion constitutes a learning experience in which a new verbal habit is acquired" (p. 10). With these sentences the authors clearly identify the process of attitude change with "the process of learning." One can safely assume that the authors anticipate that the laws governing the "learning" of an overt response are quite similar to those which are involved in the "change" of an attitude. Hovland, Janis and Kelley then go on to outline a few of the general factors which affect the learning of an attitude.

First they suggest that the "recommended opinion" which the communicator presents in his communication is one of the key elements in the attitude learning situation. In some way, either by direct questioning or a more subtle approach, the communicator must present a stimulus which evokes an "answer response" in the listener.

"When exposed to the recommended opinion, a member of the audience is assumed to react with at least two distinct responses. He thinks of his own answer to the question, and also the answer suggested by the communicator. The first response results from the previously established verbal habit constituting the individual's original opinion; the second response is assumed to result from a general aspect of verbal behavior, namely, the acquired tendency to repeat to oneself communications to which one is attending. Hence, a major effect of the persuasive communication lies in stimulating the individual to think both of his initial opinion and the new opinion recommended in the communication" (p. 11).

The notion that attitude learning (i.e., attitude change) involves some kind of "mental rehearsal" or "practice" of the attitude response is a key element in any stimulus-response theory of attitude change—an element largely absent in most other approaches to attitude change. Stimulus-response or behavior theorists have probably paid more attention to the practice or rehearsal variables than any other single class of variables in their analysis of animal and human behavior. It is not at all surprising, then, that the notion of mental rehearsal of the attitude response should be a primary component of a behavioral or stimulus-response theory of attitude change.

Second, the authors of *Communication and Persuasion* introduce "incentive" as another important variable in the attitude learning process. "Practice, which is so important for memorizing verbal material in educational or training situations, is not sufficient for bringing about the *acceptance* of a new opinion. We assume that acceptance is contingent upon *incentives,* and that in order to change an opinion it is necessary to create greater incentives for making the new implicit response than for making the old one" (p. 11). Analogous to Hull's distinction between skill (H) and incentive motivation (K), Hovland, Janis, and Kelley stress that it is not sufficient that a response be learned—that an individual understands or is capable of making the attitude response to certain stimuli. It is also necessary that he have some motivation for choosing that particular response to the attitude question in preference to other available responses. "A major basis for acceptance of a given opinion is provided by arguments or reasons which, according to the individual's own thinking habits, constitute 'rational' or 'logical' support for the conclusions" (p. 11).

Three main classes of variables influence the extent to which an individual is motivated to make one attitude response in preference to another. (1) "The observable characteristics of the perceived source of the communication." (2) "The setting in which the person is exposed to the communication, including, for example, the way in which other members of the audience respond during the presentation." (3) The communication stimuli, including content elements such as "arguments" or "appeals."[2]

ILLUSTRATIVE RESEARCH

The relatively straightforward and empirical approach which Hovland, Janis, and Kelley chose to follow renders the present authors' attempt to elevate the introductory comments to a "theory" a little presumptuous. But the general approach developed by Hovland with the support of his colleagues and students so thoroughly dominated the field during the '50s that some acknowledgment of their "working assumptions" is mandatory. And though the general approach was presaged in *Experiments on Mass Communication* (Hovland, Lumsdaine, and Sheffield, 1949), *Communication and Persuasion* is clearly the most influential book.

Given the strong empirical orientation of Hovland, Janis, and Kelley's approach, its flavor can perhaps best be captured by summarizing the empirical issues and results they discuss. Its impact and thrust is best conveyed by presenting some of the hypothesis suggested in the empirical chapters of *Communication and Persuasion*. The scope of *Communication and Persuasion* is as broad as its title; there are few issues in the current work on attitude change which Hovland, Janis, and Kelley did not touch in 1953. Although occasionally we cannot resist discussing subsequent work, our main purpose is to illustrate the "Yale Approach" to attitude change with a few concrete examples. Therefore the readers should remember that most of the theory and data presented has been extensively modified and criticized in the last 15 years.

---

[2] Although clearly present in the introductory chapters, the emphasis on acceptance—as opposed to learning—is often not found in the subsequent research. For instance, Hovland, Janis, and Kelley seemed surprised to find that communicator credibility produced greater attitude change but did not produce a more accurate learning of the arguments in the communication.

Communicator credibility. As indicated, the theme sentence "Who says what to whom with what effect?" provides the organization for the book. The first chapters explore the effect of the communicator or source. Two aspects of credibility are explored—expertness and trustworthiness. By expertness they refer to the extent to which a communicator is perceived as the source of valid or correct assertions. Trustworthiness refers to "the degree of confidence in the communicator's intent to communicate the assertions he considers most valid." This second factor implicitly emphasizes some of the motives that underlie the communicator's persuasive attempt. Thus, in discussing a study of the effect of the film, "The Battle of Britain," Hovland, Janis, and Kelley note that soldiers' interpretations of the film's *purpose* were crucial. The persuasive impact of the film was less for those men who judged its intent to be manipulative rather than informative. Such kernels of research ideas continue to have impact (e.g., Walster et al., 1966; Brock, 1967).

In general, Hovland et al. found greater acceptance of the communication when the communicator had high credibility (although there are some exceptions; see Smith, 1961; Zimbardo et al., 1965; Powell, 1965). But they found difficulty in disentangling the effects of the two main components of credibility which they studied, namely, trustworthiness and expertness. In some instances they found that while trustworthiness did affect judgments about the fairness of the presentation, there was little effect on the amount of opinion change. In other instances, however, trustworthiness seemed to be responsible for somewhat sizeable differences in opinion change. Further research is needed to extricate the crucial variables interacting with trustworthiness to produce these different outcomes. Perhaps they can be traced to interactions with content of the communication, organization of the arguments within the communication, or audience factors such as familiarity with the arguments for and against the issue.

In attempting to account for the increased attitude or opinion change found when the communicator is highly credible, it is not surprising that Hovland et al. emphasized learning or attentional factors. They initially suspected that a low credibility communicator undermines an audience's attention to the content of the message, and that low credibility communicators produce misinterpretation and miscomprehension of the meaning of what is being said. However, in their measurements of learning or recall of content, they rarely found differences sizeable enough to readily explain the credibility effects that they obtained. Thus they came to emphasize the motives of the audience to accept or believe what the communicator recommends rather than learning factors per se. But, as noted, there is a strong hint that Hovland et al. considered the motives of the source to ultimately be behind the effect. Persuasion is increased "when a recommendation is presented by a person who is believed to be informed, insightful and *willing to express his true beliefs and knowledge*" rather than trying further his own ulterior ends by manipulating the audience.

Most interesting, perhaps, is the research showing that credibility effects are short-lived. When opinions were measured three or four weeks after the presentation of the communication they found that the credibility effects had dissipated. The increased persuasion produced by a high credibility source disappears. Similarly, the decreased persuasion produced by low credibility source vanishes; this latter phenomenon is the "sleeper effect." The net persuasion returns to an equivalent and intermediate level for both high and low credibility groups. They attributed these effects to disassociation of the communication content from the source. This is not to say that the audience does not remember who initially presented the communication. On the contrary, they find that the audience can indeed remember the particular communicator. Instead, they point to a tendency to no longer spontaneously associate the source with the message. In other words, even though the audience knows from whom they previously heard the communication if they are asked, nevertheless, they tend not to make this association *unless* asked. When the association between source and content is specifically reinstated, the prestige or credibility effects reappear.

Though the Hovland, et al. approach is presented as one that stems from learning theory, their treatment of prestige effects may superficially appear to be more closely allied to cognitive theory than learning theory. After all, as they point out, the prestige effects are not to be attributed simply to the forgetting of the source. Subjects apparently learned who the source was and this learning was intact at the time of the second testing some several weeks later. The cognitively oriented psychologist would infer that some cognitive reorganization accounts for the shift in persuasion between the immediate and delayed post measures.

But it is equally easy to explain these data within learning theory. Consider the advocated position of the communication as the response to be learned and the communicator as a stimulus. What Hovland et al. note is that while the stimulus is adequately learned, its hookup with the response is inadequately learned. Underwood and Schultz (1960; also see McGuire, 1961) have spoken of such a two-stage process in treating the learning of paired-associates in the verbal learning situation. The first stage of the process is "learning the stimuli." Subsequently, the responses can be tied to the stimuli—the "response hookup phase." If this analogy is correct, it suggests that prestige effects need not always be short-lived. That is, the Hovland data are merely a consequence of specific situations in which the learning of "*who* said what" was incomplete. By altering the experimental circumstances, the short-lived impact of prestige factors could presumably be increased.

An alternative and perhaps simpler interpretation of these effects focuses upon the demand characteristics of the experimental situation (see Chapter 2). Subjects may treat the prestige manipulation as a cue to what the experimenter expects him to do. A laudatory description of the communicator may merely tell the subject that the experimenter wants him to change his position. The "reinstigation" procedure just prior to the delayed measurement reasserts the experimenter's intent. Festinger (1955) has also suggested that the same results would be produced if subjects in the two conditions discussed the experiment before the delayed posttest.

FEAR-AROUSING APPEALS. In a second chapter, Hovland et al. consider fear-arousing appeals. In retrospect this has turned out to be one of the more controversial chapters in the book. We include only a brief review to continue our illustration of the "Yale approach." Hovland, Janis, and Kelley note that the characteristics of the appeal could differentially affect the three stages of the communication process—attention to the content of the communication, comprehension of the content, and acceptance of its conclusions. They initially speculate that "emotional" appeals would increase an audience's motivation to accept the conclusion since acceptance of an effective recommendation would be associated with drive reduction. It is hard to understand, however, why the effects of fear on other stages were dismissed. It seems likely that at least for some audiences, high emotionality would also increase attention.

In one experiment (Janis and Feshbach, 1953) high school freshmen were exposed to one of three communications on dental hygiene which differed in the level of fear they induced. As anticipated, greater arousing content in the communication produced more worry in subjects immediately after the communication. Speculating further about the effect of fear, they imply that the mention of highly specific dangers may result in *less* worry than a "less frightening" appeal in which the threatening material is ambiguous and vague. The specificity of the danger implies the correct concrete curative act. They also presage the experimental work by McGuire (to be reviewed later in this chapter) on inoculation against persuasion by suggesting the possibility of "emotional inoculation." By this, they refer to the possibility that the effects of a communication presenting a threatening or pessimistic event may be dissipated by prior exposure to material which discusses or predicts the event in advance. However, if true, this may be a simple consequence of adaptation level theory (Helson, 1948, 1959).

Given the fact that a high threat appeal does generate more worry or fright, it still may not elicit greater acceptance of the content of the communication or greater compliance with the behavior it advocates. Analysis of the effect of the dental hygiene communications showed that this was indeed the case. They found an inverse relation between amount of fear or worry elicited by a communication and subsequent acceptance of the position advocated. Futhermore, the minimal fear appeal, which produced greatest adherence to the dental hygiene recommendations, produced greatest resistance to subsequent counterpropaganda.

Several possibilities could produce such an outcome. When high drive (anxiety) is aroused, (1) it is sometimes difficult to attend to what is being said; (2) well-practiced defenses which are prepotent over the response advocated by the communication may be aroused; (3) the negative aspects of the communication may generate hostility toward the communicator, thereby impeaching his credibility and leading the listener to reject the recommended stand or behavior.

If a high-fear communication distracts subjects, they should show poorer learning (or retention) of the content. Though no such differences were found in the dental hygiene study, those results should not be taken as a fatal disconfirmation of the "inattention explanation" in that the recall measures used by social psychologists are often insufficiently sensitive to detect differences between treatment groups even if such differences do exist. Indeed, a later study (Janis and Milholland, 1954) did give a wisp of support. While no overall differences in retention were detected between high fear and low fear groups, there were differences in the *type* of content retained. The minimal fear group retained more information concerning the causes of the threat, whereas the high fear group tended to more accurately remember the consequences of the threat. However, though these differences appear to provide some support for the notion that the presence of fear arousing content can affect what is attended to in a communication, they may alternatively simply reflect the true differences between the two communications.

To examine the defensiveness explanation, Janis and Feshbach performed an internal analysis of their data. They found some evidence to suggest that the high fear appeal was particularly ineffective for those subjects who were high in chronic anxiety. This hypothesis was later confirmed more directly by Goldstein (1959). Subjects were classified into two types by scores on an Incomplete Sentence Test—those who typically dealt with threatening material by confronting it directly and those who avoided, misperceived, or denied the presence of threat. Although the "take measure" failed to indicate difference in fear arousal, a high fear appeal was, as expected, particularly ineffective for "avoiders." For the "copers" the effectiveness of high and low fear appeals was essentially equivalent. Other studies also provide support for the defensive avoidance hypothesis (Janis and Terwilliger, 1962; Nunally and Bobren, 1959).

Hovland, Janis, and Kelley suggest a variety of hypotheses about the effects of threat on persuasion, only some of which were experimentally tested. However, those that subsequently were tested by other researchers have not consistently received unequivocal support. For instance, Hovland et al. hypothesized (as did Janis and Feshbach, 1953) that the adequacy or effectiveness of the precautions mentioned in a high fear appeal would control the effectiveness of a high fear appeal. Yet three recent experiments (Leventhal, Singer, and Jones, 1965; Leventhal, Jones, and Trembly, 1966; Dabbs and Leventhal, 1966) yield no support. Similarly, the hypothesis that a high fear appeal would be more effective in implementing immediate as opposed to delayed action was not supported (Leventhal and Watts, 1966; Leventhal and Niles, 1965). Furthermore, even the initial Janis and Feshbach finding of decreased persuasive effectiveness with greater fear arousing content has not received consistent support. Haefner (1965), Leventhal and Niles (1965), Niles (1964), Leventhal and Singer (1966) all found the opposite effect and Leventhal, Singer, and Jones (1965), Leventhal, Jones, and Trembly (1966), and Leventhal, Watts, and Pagano (1967) found no difference. Clearly, however, even though the hypotheses proposed have not generated the simple consistency in outcome that one might wish, they have generated a substantial amount of systematic research. Consistent with our goal to use this research to illustrate the "Yale approach," we have not attempted an integrating review of the subsequent research on fear-arousing communications, but such reviews are available elsewhere (Leventhal, 1965; McGuire, 1968; Janis, 1967).

ORGANIZATION OF PERSUASIVE ARGUMENTS. In their next chapter, Hovland, Janis, and Kelley consider the organization of persuasive arguments. Once again their treatment rests heavily upon the concepts of contemporary experimental psychology—attention, perception, motivation, and learning. More specifically, they consider such problems as: whether a major argument should be used at the outset or saved for the climax; the relative superiority of a one-sided communication versus a two-sided communication which mentions some of the points one's opponent might present; the merits of explicitly spelling out the conclusion one wants the audience to accept or letting the audience infer their own conclusion from the material presented; and lastly the old question of primacy versus recency—does the first of two speakers or the second have some advantage over and above the relative effects of their persuasive material. For each of these questions, some research evidence is presented; but by no means are the empirical questions around each of these issues thoroughly resolved. Thus, even though Hovland and Mandell in the one experiment presented on "explicit conclusion drawing" find that over twice as many subjects change their opinions in the direction advocated by the communication when the conclusion was explicitly drawn, Hovland, Janis, and Kelley note that explicitly drawing a conclusion will not invariably produce superiority. They go on to discuss how this effect might be altered with different kinds of communicators, a different type of audience, and with a different type of issue. Each of these sections contain interesting untested hypotheses.

One question not dealt with by Hovland, Janis and Kelley is the extent to which the operation of demand characteristics controls the outcome in the Hovland and Mandell experiment that they report. When the direction of effect is such that more persuasion occurs when a communicator explicitly enunciates the conclusion, it is easy to interpret any treatment advantage as simply reflecting more precise or obvious instructions by the communicator regarding what it is he wants the subjects to do on the dependent measure. Those subjects who heard the conclusion rather than having to infer it would have had more accurate knowledge of "the correct way to respond" on the final dependent measure.

The experiments on one-sided versus two-sided arguments show advantage to a two-sided presentation in the long run, provided that at some time in the future the audience is likely to be subjected to counterpropaganda. The comparative effectiveness of one-sided versus two-sided presentations is also shown to interact with audience factors.

GROUP FACTORS. Hovland et al. next explore resistance to opinion change when a person is in a group. This chapter can be thought of as being more concerned with social influence than with attitude change in that it focuses on the pressures toward conformity that group members exert on the individuals comprising the group. However, the relation to opinion change is obvious. When individuals are subject to the stabilizing effects of the group's opinion, the influence of external persuasive attempts will be diminished.

They spell out two types of conformity: normative conformity, which is based on what is socially accepted or desired by group members, and informational conformity, which is based upon information about reality conveyed by other people's opinions. They note three factors that cause a person to seek or maintain membership in a group: first, positive attractions within the group such as friendship or achieving status or desired group activities; second, threats or deprivations which can be avoided by seeking or maintaining group membership; and third, group restraints or sanctions which function to maintain membership. All three of these factors can lead to susceptibility to influence by the group. To the extent that the person is strongly motivated to maintain or obtain membership, he will conform to group norms.

Five factors are cited as inducing or maintaining conformity: the individual's knowledge of group norms, the extent to which he values group membership, his social status or rank within the group, particular situational cues, and the salience of the group, i.e., the degree to which a specific group is present or dominant in the person's awareness at the time the counterpersuasion is delivered. The consequence of conformity is that when the group is exposed to a counternorm communication, members will resist change. In fact, when group membership is extremely valued, boomerang effects may occur.

Other things being equal, the highly ranked (highly valued) individual should value group membership more strongly in that for him, membership is particularly reinforcing. Furthermore, as pointed out by Hittes and Campbell (1950), highly ranked members have more information about what the group norms actually are. Both the valuation of membership and knowledge of group norms should make him more resistant to counternorm persuasion. However, Hovland, Janis, and Kelley hypothesize that though the person who most highly values group membership will be more resistant to persuasion or opinion change, he will be *more* easily changed independently of changes among other members. Thus the highly ranked person would be a key person in initiating opinion change among group members because of his greater freedom for change. (In later years Hollander—1958, 1961, 1964—has termed this freedom of the highly ranked member "idiosyncrasy credit.")

PERSONALITY AND PERSUASIBILITY. The next chapter examines the relation of persuasibility to personality factors. The material in his chapter stimulated research reported in a later volume of the Yale Communication series. The authors cite three types of personality traits characteristic of those who resist social influence: (1) persistent aggressive motives toward others; (2) social withdrawal and isolation; and (3) acute psychoneurotic symptoms. These three different characteristics may operate to reduce persuasion in different ways. The persistently aggressive person may resist persuasion by derogating or impugning the speaker's credibility. Thus, if the communicator has impeccable credibility, personality differences in this trait presumably should not yield large differences in persuasion, whereas, when the communicator's credibility is more fallible, differences in this trait should yield differences in persuasion. For those who differ in their tendency toward social withdrawal, we hypothesize that differences in persuasion are mediated by differences in attention and input of information. Thus complexity of the message and the extent to which acceptance of the conclusion depends on comprehension of a set of arguments should interact with this personality dimension. The third factor—the presence of acute psychoneurotic symptoms—should interact with the topic of the communication. Topics that invoke long-standing defense mechanisms should produce large persuasibility differences among psychoneurotics, whereas for communications on relatively neutral topics, messages should be equally persuasive for those with and without psychoneurotic symptoms. These hypotheses, though implicitly suggested by Hovland, Janis, and Kelley, remain untested.

As McGuire (1967) recently pointed out, the relation between personality and persuasibility may be much more complex than was initially imagined. He suggests that personality probably interacts in different directions with different stages in the flow of input to consequent responses. Thus, for instance, a person of low intelligence would tend to be uncritical of the communicator. In assigning greater credibility to the source, he would thereby inflate the persuasive impact of the communication. On the other hand, countering this tendency is the greater likelihood of the unintelligent person to miscomprehend the persuasive material contained in the communication.

ACTIVE PARTICIPATION. Hovland, Janis, and Kelley then consider the effects of active participation. They present evidence (Janis and King, 1954; King and Janis, 1956) that a person who is induced to actively assert the essential points of a communication as if they represented his own opinion is more persuaded than controls who listened to the communication. This process of overt verbalization was labeled role-playing.

One suggested explanation of the greater effectiveness of persuasion when the subject role-plays a position is that of extraneous rewards. Thus anticipated social approval for the role-play performance may reinforce the *implicit* attitude response as well as the overt role-play performance. King and Janis (1956) interpret their results as inconsistent with the satisfaction hypothesis since subjects in the improvisation condition showed more attitude change but were less satisfied with their performance. But, as Zimbardo (1965) has pointed out, the dissatisfaction in the improvisation condition might have been created by the negative feedback given to one-third of the subjects in the improvisation condition. Hovland, Janis, and Kelley also rule out increased attention and better learning of the communication as explanations of the advantage of improvisation.

The authors conclude that the most likely explanation rests in the fact that subjects in the improvisation condition must make up *new* arguments and reorganize the old material. Since the subject is most likely to use new arguments and organizations he finds persuasive, the resulting communication would be tailored to a particular audience of one—the subject himself. The issues raised by this role-playing research have generated considerable additional research and are relevant to other considerations discussed in greater detail in Chapter 5. (Also see reviews by Aronson, 1966; Elms, 1967; Carlsmith, 1968; Collins, 1968.)

RETENTION. In their last chapter Hovland, Janis, and Kelley consider factors affecting the retention of opinion change. Their discussion benefits heavily from prior research in the area of verbal learning. Quite clearly, however, retention differences are typically due to differences in the initial learning of the communication content. As Underwood (1957a; also see Underwood and Schulz, 1960) has emphasized, it is important that one keep separate learning and retention as variables. If differences on a retention test simply reflect past differences in initial learning, we cannot talk about a variable which has affected retention. Since almost no variables have been shown to influence retention aside from proactive and retroactive interference (Underwood, 1957a), it is not likely that social-psychological variables will be shown to violate this general finding.

CRITICISM

A number of critical points can be made. The most obvious one has already been reiterated persistently throughout this section—*Communication and Persuasion* does not qualify as a formal theory. As Deutsch and Krauss state: "Hovland and his associates have not developed any systematic theory of the persuasion process . . . ." Furthermore, it can be argued that their approach is not even closely wedded to S-R psychology. Few of the experiments reported in *Communication and Persuasion* even manipulate the classical variables that appeared in the major contemporaneous presentations of S-R theories of learning. Not a single experiment manipulates frequency, the most potent variable in the S-R account of behavior; no experiments test the interaction of drive with frequency; the interaction of drive with complexity of task (comprehension difficulty or complexity of the communication) also remained untested; the effects of irrelevant incentives were only tested later (Janis, Kaye, and Kushner, 1965; Janis and Dabbs, 1965), etc. To push things still further, it can be argued that even the theoretical terms invoked to explain their findings as well as the language on which they are based are not consistently drawn from the S-R vocabulary.

None of these criticisms of the formal *theory* detract in any way from the importance of the empirical *research;* the individual studies rank among the best. We merely state that the "working assumptions" are just that—a general approach and set of assumptions used by some people who did good research on attitude change. But as Hovland, Janis, and Kelley themselves state, they did not even attempt to build a formal theory.

With a paucity of any real theoretical structure and an absence of theoretical tests, there is indeed little to criticize from a theoretical standpoint. The comparative fruitfulness of a strategy of emphasizing S-R terms in preference to those of some other "System" cannot easily be evaluated. Had Hovland preferred some other linguistic system, it is doubtful that it would have mattered much. The entire program of experiments could easily have been performed if the introductory "theoretical" chapter had never been written.

Whether regarded as a theory or not, the "Yale Communication Research Program" is homogeneous enough to be classified as an "approach" to the study of attitude change. In their book *Theories in Social Psychology,* Deutsch and Krauss (1965) include the "Yale Communication Program" as one of the six chapter subheadings in the chapter on reinforcement theory, noting that "they have been guided by the central notion of learning theory . . . ."

As Roger Brown observes, "The work has been well done, especially the studies constituting the Yale Series . . . but it lacks something of intellectual interest because the results do not fall into any compelling pattern. They summarize a set of elaborate contingent, and not very general, generalizations" (1965, p. 549). The research reported by Hovland and his colleagues was clearly problem-oriented rather than theory-oriented. Nearly all of the topics that were treated in *Communication and Persuasion* (Hovland, Janis, and Kelley, 1953) (e.g., characteristics of the communicator, types of persuasive appeal, effects of group conformity pressures) were discussed almost two decades earlier in Murphy, Murphy, and Newcomb's (1937) review of the research on attitudes.

In addition to its problem orientation, probably the most salient characteristic of the research is its emphasis on an analytic experimental study of attitudes. In a historical context where investigators had been content to show that a year's course in economics had some impact, Hovland, Lumsdaine, and Sheffield (1949) were able to make a strong argument for the "experimental investigation of a single variable by controlled variation"—even in the context of a wartime program to evaluate the effectiveness of instructional material. The subsequent volumes which comprise the Yale studies in attitude and communication (*The Order of Presentation and Persuasion,* Hovland et al., 1957; *Personality and persuasibility,* Janis et al., 1959; *Attitude Organization and Change,* Rosenberg et al., 1960; and *Social Judgment,* Sherif and Hovland, 1961) initially continued in this enthusiastic, but relatively atheoretical, empirical attack on the classical problems of attitude change. (Only the last two volumes deviate from this approach, and they cannot be classified as stimulus-response theories of attitude change. *Social Judgment,* the most theoretical of all the works, is discussed in Chapter 6 on judgmental theories of attitude change. *Attitude Organization and Change* is treated in Chapter 4 on balance theories.) Throughout the 1950s this theoretically uncoordinated attack on the currently important problems of attitude change probably stimulated more good research on attitude change than any other orientation, and reestablished the study of attitudes as a central endeavor for scientific social psychologists. But the lack of a more dominant theoretical orientation has, for some psychologists, left the work bereft of elegance. There can be no doubt, however, that the quality of the empirical research was outstanding. It identified important variables, stimulated research, and focused scientific attention on the study of attitudes.

Persuasion and the Acquisition of Attitude: Models from Conditioning and Selective Learning

Weiss builds his theory on a close analogy with the Hull-Spence version of behavior theory (Spence, 1956). He argues that the metamorphosis of the Hull-Spence learning theory into a theory of persuasion and the acquisition of attitudes is so great that a completely new theory emerges. ". . . It seems prudent to distinguish between a theory of conditioning and selective learning and a theory of persuasion based on analogies with conditioning and selective learning" (Weiss, 1962, p. 710). Thus, whatever its intellectual debts, Weiss' theory must stand or fall on its own ability to predict data on human attitudes.

Weiss first identifies those elements of the persuasion situation that parallel the more frequently studied forms of learning. With regard to instrumental and selective learning Weiss says:

"Consider a persuasion communication consisting of three elements: (1) An *opinion statement:* (2) An *argument,* information which supports the opinion, but does not repeat the opinion statement; and (3) some *neutral material* which neither repeats, supposts, nor contradicts the opinion. If these elements are arranged in the communication so that the opinion statement is followed by some neutral material and then by the argument, then, an *S* required to read the communication aloud would first see the communication, then state the opinion, read some neutral material, and finally, state an argument supporting the opinion. This sequence of events may be regarded as analogous to the sequence: Stimulus, response, delay, reinforcement. . . . The sight of the communication (including the sight of the written opinion statements) is the stimulus, the opinion is the response to be learned, the argument is the reinforcement, and the interval between the opinion statement and the argument is the delay of reinforcement" (1962, pp. 710–711).

This analysis allows Weiss to argue that the communication situation is basically a "learning situation" containing all of the ingredients necessary for learning. Two comments are in order before we proceed toward a more detailed description of Weiss' presentation. First, Weiss does not deal with the question of what leads the individual to make an opinion response initially. He simply assumes that some characteristic of the communication (or test) situation leads the subject to make an opinion response (as do Hovland, Janis, and Kelley, 1953). Second, Weiss' contention that an argument constitutes a reinforcer is not based on any theoretical argument. Weiss utilizes the "weak" form of the empirical law of effect, arguing "in terms of the empirical law of effect, any event which follows a response and increases the strength of that response on the next trial is called a reinforcer . . . . It seems reasonable to expect that a communication in which the opinion to be learned is followed by a convincing argument will be more effective than one which does not include any support for the opinion" (Weiss, Rawson, and Pasamanick, 1963, p. 157).

HULL-SPENCE BEHAVIOR THEORY

Four additional concepts from Hull-Spence and learning theory (Spence, 1956) are needed in order to understand the predictions which Weiss makes for attitude change.

THE BEHAVIOR EQUATION. In the Hull-Spence scheme, the response strength is represented by "effective excitatory potential" $\bar{E}$. As in all of the Hull-Spence variables, $\bar{E}$ is a theoretical construct. That is, it has a theoretical existance of its own, and is not definitionally equivalent to any particular measure of overt response. The theoretically defined measures of $\bar{E}$, moreover, vary somewhat from learning situation to learning situation. Thus the correct measure for $\bar{E}$ differs for each of the three classes of learning to be discussed later: selective learning, instrumental learning, and classical conditioning.

Setting aside for the moment the problems of the measurement of $\bar{E}$, the theory states that $\bar{E}$ is a function of four other theoretical variables.[3]

1. Habit strength H. The theoretical, or intervening, variable of habit strength is an increasing negatively accelerated function of reinforced trials. H represents the skill or practice aspect of learning; and the theory says that "skill" increases with each reinforced trial and that reinforced trials early in the learning experience produce a greater increase in H than reinforced trials later in the experience. To be accurate, however, it should be noted that in Spence's (1956) recent statement H is defined simply as the number of times a response has been emitted (without any stipulation about reinforcement).

2. Drive D. D represents a generalized level of energy or arousal. All sources of motivation combine into a single theoretical term; experiments on rats, for instance, have shown that increasing the thirst of animals running for food reinforcement and increasing the hunger of animals running for water reinforcement increases the running speed—even though the drive being manipulated is not relevant to the reinforcement received.

3. Incentive motivation K. K is a variable which entered into Hull's scheme rather late and is a theoretical repository for most of the manipulations involving reinforcement (e.g., magnitude, delay, and number of reinforcements).

4. Inhibitory potential I. Generally, inhibitory potential is theoretically related to fatigue in the learning process and is used to account for the extinction and spontaneous recovery of the learned response.

MULTIPLICATIVE D. As can be seen by the equation at the top of Fig. 3.1, the excitatory potential (i.e., the response strength) is assumed to be attained by *multiplying* (rather than by adding) drive × habit variables. An increase in habit strength will have a much greater influence on effective excitatory potential for high levels of drive than it does for low levels of drive.

It should be stressed that the absolute *difference* between the response strengths ($\bar{E}$) associated with each of two habits depends upon the drive level. Consider a numerical example. Habit A has an H strength of 2, and habit B has an H strength of 3. Ignoring K for a moment, a drive level of 2 would mean that habit A would produce an effect

---

[3] A complete version of this theory would include oscillatory and threshold intervening variables, but Weiss omits them for simplicity.

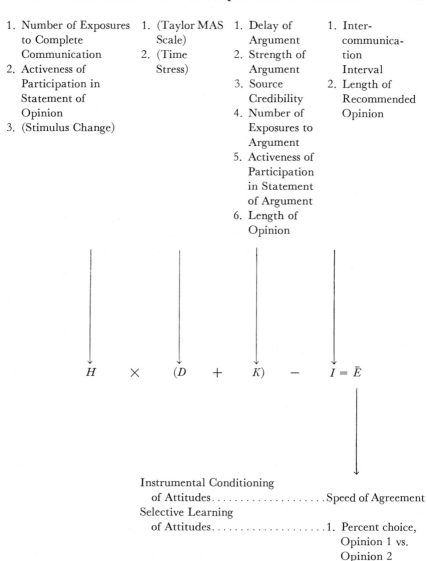

1. Number of Exposures to Complete Communication
2. Activeness of Participation in Statement of Opinion
3. (Stimulus Change)

1. (Taylor MAS Scale)
2. (Time Stress)

1. Delay of Argument
2. Strength of Argument
3. Source Credibility
4. Number of Exposures to Argument
5. Activeness of Participation in Statement of Argument
6. Length of Opinion

1. Inter-communication Interval
2. Length of Recommended Opinion

$$H \quad \times \quad (D \quad + \quad K) \quad - \quad I = \bar{E}$$

Instrumental Conditioning
of Attitudes. . . . . Speed of Agreement
Selective Learning
of Attitudes. . . . . 1. Percent choice, Opinion 1 vs. Opinion 2
2. Speed of Agreement with Each Opinion

Figure 3.1. Instrumental persuasion: relations assumed among independent, intervening, and dependent variables (From Weiss, R. F., 1962).

of excitatory potential of 4, and habit *B* would produce an effect of excitatory potential of 6. There would be a *difference* of 2 units.

Let us assume that we increase the drive strength to 5. Now the excitatory potential associated with habit *A* is 10 and that associated with habit *B* is 15. Both habits are associated with increased response strength, but the gain of the initially strongest habit is *relatively* greater. The difference between the two excitatory potentials is 2 units at a drive level of 2, and 5 units at a drive level of 5.

CLASSIFICATION OF LEARNING. Spence (1956, p. 27) distinguishes among three kinds of learning: selective learning, instrumental learning (conditioning), and classical learning (conditioning). The basic characteristic of selective learning is that the stimulus situation evokes a large number of alternative responses and learning is primarily "the process whereby the alternative members in the response hierarchy change in their relative strength."

"In both instrumental and classical conditioning the aim of the experimenter is to arrange for the occurrence of but a single response or response chain which is followed by reinforcement. . . . Instead of choosing a response relatively low in the initial response hierarchy as is typically done in selective learning, the experimenter attempts to choose the strongest response, i.e., the one most likely to occur is the one to be reinforced. In this manner he hopes to limit the investigation to the study of the strengthening of this single response" (Spence, 1956, p. 37–38).

One of the primary consequences of the distinction between selective learning and instrumental conditioning is that an increase in drive will have a different impact for the two types of learning. Since an increase of drive typically increases the relative dominance of the strongest response, an increase in drive should facilitate learning in the instrumental situation where the dominant or only response is being strengthened. But in a selective learning situation, where a response low in the response hierarchy is the focus of attention, an increase in drive will contribute less to this low order response than to the high order responses. Thus an increase in drive for selective learning should inhibit learning.

OPERATIONAL DEFINITIONS OF INDEPENDENT VARIABLES AND THE GENERAL EXPERIMENTAL PARADIGM

As can be seen in Fig. 3.1, delay of argument, strength of argument, source credibility, number of exposures to argument, activeness of participation and statement of argument, and length of opinion should produce an attitude change because they change the level of incentive motivation (K) for the opinion response—and thus should behave according to the functional laws ascribed to K in the Hull-Spence learning theory. As can also be seen from Fig. 3.1, seven additional variables are assumed to affect attitude change through H, D, or I.

The typical experiment (e.g., Weiss and Pasamanick, 1964) is represented to the subjects as a study of "speaking ability and personality." Subjects are requested to read several short passages into a microphone "with as much expression and conviction as possible." The individual manipulations are introduced by varying the nature of the passages which the subjects read.

OPERATIONAL MEASUREMENT OF ATTITUDES

As is indicated in Fig. 3.1, the effectiveness of the communication would be measured by (1) the speed of agreement with the opinion (for instrumental conditioning) and (2) either the percent choice of opinion one versus opinion two, when the two opinions are presented simultaneously or the speed of agreement with each of the opinions when they are presented separately (for selective learning). Although it seems plausible that speed of agreement is related to the standard pencil and paper tests of attitude, we do not have any *data* to indicate that speed of agreement is highly correlated with the more standard measures of attitude. Should further investigation prove that speed of agreement represents a new measure of "attitude" unrelated to those previously used by attitude theorists, then Weiss would merely have developed an "island of theory." His theory would be valid so far as it goes, and it would qualify as an extension of the responses considered by previous attitude theories. But it would not compete with the other theories in this book because Weiss and the other theorists would not be using the same empirical base.

Weiss has designed a simple apparatus to obtain the speed of agreement measure.

"[The subject] was seated in front of a gray panel in which two glass screens were set at eye height. Below this was a lever (normally in a center position) which could be moved 14 in. in either direction. Opinion statements could be projected on one or both of the screens by means of two synchronized slide projectors located behind the panel. In instrumental attitude conditioning only one screen was used. When an opinion statement was projected on the screen, Standard Electric timers began to measure latency of agreement. If S agreed with the statement, he moved the lever toward the screen, all the way to the end of the slot . . . . Just as in instrumental conditioning, zero super threshold excitatory potential (no opinion) or the presence of strong competing responses (incompatible opinions) are reflected in failure to respond within the time allowed (45 sec)" (Weiss, 1962, p. 720).

When the apparatus was used to study selective learning, the two opinions were projected on different screens, one on the screen to the right and one on the screen to the left. The subject indicated the opinion he agreed with by moving the lever toward his preferred opinion.

EMPIRICAL SUPPORT

1. INSTRUMENTAL CONDITIONING: DELAY OF ARGUMENT. Weiss, Buchanan, and Pasamanick (1965) found that speed of agreement was significantly faster for a group persuaded with a 4-second delay of argument than for a group persuaded with a 20-second delay when neutral material was used to create the delay. Weiss (1967) reports similar results using five delay intervals ranging from 0 to 55.5 seconds. Speed of agreement decreases with longer delays. But when the delay was created by interrupting the subjects, speed *increased* with longer delay (Weiss, Buchanan, and Pasamanick, 1965). The authors try to explain the data by arguing that "Most subjects have a learning history in which interruption (by parents, teachers, etc.) indicates behavior regarded as incorrect, inadequate, or otherwise disapproved." They argue that the long interruption represents a delay of punishment, and therefore the long delay (of punishment) should lead to increased speed of agreement. But this assumes that the punishing aspect of punishment occurs at the end of the interruption only. If the interruption itself is the punishment, then a long interruption would be a large punishment rather than a long delay. If so, speed should decrease with larger punishment (longer interruptions)—just the opposite of the results. In summary, whatever the explanation for the interruption method, several studies demonstrate the effectiveness of short delays with the neutral material method.

2. INSTRUMENTAL CONDITIONING: ARGUMENT STRENGTH AND DRIVE. Weiss, Rawson, and Pasamanick (1963) chose subjects who indicated that they had "no opinion" on (i.e., no response associated with) the statement "The British House of Lords should be reorganized." Weiss is careful to point out that the definition of instrumental conditioning

(Spence, 1956) limits it to "the strengthening of an opinion which [the subject] already holds, or to the establishment of a learned opinion in [subjects] who have no previously learned opinion on a given topic" (Weiss, 1962, p. 718). An experiment on selective learning, for which there are different predictions, is reviewed in paragraph 4 following.

Subjects were told that the experiment concerned speaking ability and personality, and they were asked to read a communication aloud. All subjects read a communication that began with the opinion statement "The British House of Lords should be reorganized." In the weak argument condition the opinion (attitude response) was followed by a brief, or weak, 23-word argument. In the strong argument condition the opinion (attitude response) was followed by a somewhat stronger, 72-word argument (see Weiss et al., 1963, p. 159). Each of these two experimental groups were then divided into subjects who indicated a high generalized drive level (i.e., received high scores on the Taylor Manifest Anxiety Scale) and subjects who indicated a low level of generalized drive. As is quite straightforwardly predicted from Fig. 3.1, subjects with the strong argument (higher K) indicated faster agreement than those subjects with the weaker argument. Subjects with high manifest anxiety (high D) also indicated a higher level of agreement. As is also predicted by the equation in Fig. 3.1, the two variables combined additively, i.e., the difference between strong and weak arguments is identical at low and high drive levels.

3. Instrumental conditioning: argument strength and number of exposures to the persuasive communication. In a similar general paradigm, Weiss and Pasamanick (1964) manipulated two levels of argument strength (as in the previous study) and presented the communication either once or twice. Although subjects responded with greater speed when the argument was repeated, the increased effectiveness of strong arguments which was reported in the previous study was not replicated. The results also failed to confirm the predicted interaction between argument strength and number of repetitions. It might be noted that Weiss analyzes data only for those subjects who "learn the response." In other words, the speed measures reflect differential speeds of agreement among subjects who agree; this analysis would be insensitive to any mechanism of attitude change which increased the percentage of subjects who agree with the communication.

4. Selective learning: delay of argument and drive. We now turn our attention to selective learning situations where the impact of

drive differs from the instrumental learning situation. Weiss, Rawson, and Pasamanick (1963) used subjects who indicated "no opinion" on both of the two topics under consideration. In contrast to the instrumental learning paradigm (paragraph 1 above), in which only one communication was used, subjects read *two* persuasive communications on two different topics. One communication argued that the British House of Lords should be reorganized, and the second argued that water rights in the southwest should be regulated by the Commerce Department. By inserting some neutral material between the opinion and the supported material (argument-reinforcement), the experimenters manipulated the delay of reinforcement. When one communication used a short delay, the other used a long delay. Subjects in both delay sequences were selected for high or low scores on the Taylor Manifest Anxiety Scale. The equation in Fig. 3.1 clearly predicted that the response reinforced after a short delay would be preferred to the response reinforced after a long delay. This prediction was confirmed by Weiss et al. (1963).

As has been previously indicated, high drive may inhibit learning in the selective learning situation where two or more responses are evoked by the test stimulus. According to Spence, ". . . there will be an *inverse* [emphasis ours] relation between performance (percent choice R_s) and drive level under conditions which keep the reaction potentials in the low range . . . . Thus, it would be expected that a differential in favor of lower drive groups would tend to be present in the early stages of training and at low absolute levels of drive" (Spence, 1956, p. 217). These conditions are met in the study by Weiss et al., since subjects were chosen who had no initial position (i.e., low initial habit strength). As Spence predicted, the effects for drive in this selective learning situation are different from the simpler instrumental conditioning situation reported previously. In the high drive condition (i.e., for subjects with high manifest anxiety) there was no preference for the opinion response reinforced with the short delay; subjects chose the short delay opinion 50% of the time. In the low drive condition the opinion reinforced with a short delay was chosen with the 70.8% frequency. There was a significant tendency to prefer the short delay opinion under *low* drive conditions. Furthermore, subjects in the lowest quartile on the manifest anxiety scale prefer the short delay opinion at a rate of 66.7%, those in the lower fourth at 83.3% and those among the lowest sixth (N-8) at 100%. In summary, drive, as predicted, inhibited learning in a selective learning paradigm. Unfortunately for Weiss' argument, however, none of the experiments on instrumental conditioning in paragraphs 1 to 3 are exact counterparts to this final experiment on selective learning. The experiment in paragraph 1 manipulates delay but does not manipulate drive; the experiment in paragraph 2 manipulates drive but does not manipulate delay. We do have data to indicate that drive does not interact with argument *strength* (paragraph 2); but there is no data to indicate that drive does not interact with argument *delay* in instrumental conditioning as well as in selective learning. Also, the theoretical importance of these findings would be strengthened if found with a manipulated drive as well as the predispositional generalized drive (manifest anxiety). But the obtained results are reasonably clear and predicted quite straightforwardly from the Spence theory. The validity of an analogy between argument strength and magnitude of reward and between delay of argument and delay of reward has received support.

CRITICISM

It should be noted that only three of the thirteen analogies between the Hull-Spence intervening variables and the attitude change manipulations suggested by Weiss in Fig. 3.1 have been in any way tested to date. Since the other ten were not involved in the theoretical deductions made for the research done so far, that aspect of Weiss' theory cannot be considered to have received any support yet. Also, just where Weiss' theory fits into the general scheme of attitude theories—whether it represents exploration of a novel empirical area as yet uncovered by attitude theories or whether it represents a competing theory to explain the same empirical data—depends largely on the currently untested relationship between Weiss' "speed of agreement" measure and the more traditional indices of attitude strength.

Furthermore, Weiss' efforts to date have concentrated on subjects who have no attitude on the topic, i.e., they are neutral. Weiss' theory would presumably make predictions about changing already formed attitudes, but under the provocative requirement that this be viewed as habit reversal or selective learning. This requirement provides the basis for a host of experiments. For example, in Weiss' first experiment described above, high drive should produce less attitude change for subjects who have the opposite position on the issue.

Weiss does not discuss the concept of extremeness. It would be possible to equate the notion of extremeness (or some correlated notions, e.g., intensity) with habit strength. If the persuasive attempt were treated as habit reversal, however, recourse could be made to the fact that habit reversal is more rapid for well learned habits. [See Rhine's (1958) discussion of a concept formation approach to attitude change.]

The most impressive support for the theory is probably the differential impact of drive variables in instrumental conditioning versus selective learning paradigms. In this connection, the failure to find an interaction between argument strength and number of exposures (paragraph 3 above) is particularly disappointing. Missing also is a test of the complexity $\times$ drive interaction commonly made from Hull-Spence learning theories for subjects who do not begin with "no opinion."

But we must again ask of this behavioristic theory, "Does the theory really make a contribution to the social psychology of attitude change?" The interaction with drive may be interesting, but the other variables of the theory are less interesting. It is not an impressive theoretical contribution to say that strong arguments produce more attitude change. Furthermore, the theory is limited in scope. It seems likely that the dependence on the basic Hull-Spence behavior formula must inevitably exclude many of the interesting phenomena covered by other theories in this book. The limited definition of attitude also limits the range of applications. Finally, the theory has not stimulated much research.

But, by and large Weiss' theory comes out rather well as a formal theory. It has stimulated only a small amount of research in its rather short life, but the theory, as a theory, does an excellent job specifying boundary conditions, making specific and precise predictions, and clearly specifying appropriate conditions for empirical tests. Weiss' theory may well receive considerable attention in the future. It is a good beginning.

Skinnerian "Radical Behaviorism" (Bem)

A SKINNERIAN ANALYSIS OF "SELF-DESCRIPTIVE" VERBAL BEHAVIOR (I.E., ATTITUDES)

Working within the framework proposed by Skinner (1953, 1957), Bem (1965, 1966, 1967) uses a behavioristic vocabulary to discuss attitude change. He does not depend on phenomenological concepts such as "insight," "self-concept," "self-awareness," or attitude. In the opening sentence of his 1965 article, for instance, he defines self-awareness as "one's ability to respond differentially to his own behavior and its controlling variables . . . ." (p. 199).[4] Later he says: "Among the responses that comprise self-awareness [note that self-awareness is defined in terms of objective response] verbal statements that are self-descriptive are perhaps the most common . . ." (Bem, 1965, p. 199).

Following Skinner's (1957) analysis, Bem argues that the processes by which an individual learns to label internal stimuli *private,* are the same processes by which an individual learns to label *public* external stimuli, which are available to the socializing community. Note the implicit assumption, common to nearly all behavioristic analyses, that current self-descriptive statements—attitudes—have been learned as a result of previous experience with one's human and nonhuman environment.

According to the Skinner-Bem analysis, the socializing community can easily provide the kinds of discrimination learning needed to teach a child to appropriately label a cat, a mother, etc. The stimuli being labeled are available both to the infant and to the socializing community. Since the socializing community can distinguish between mother and Aunt Ethel, the socializing community can also determine whether the stimulus immediately at hand has been correctly labeled, and it can provide appropriate rewards and punishments.

"The community, however, faces a [unique problem] in training the individual to make statements describing internal stimuli to which only he has direct access . . ." (Bem 1965, p. 199). The socializing community must, for instance, reward and punish the self-descriptive statement "I am hungry" without access to any of the internal stimulation available to the infant. Thus the socializing community is forced to use criteria other than privately available internal stimuli when it teaches the child the appropriate circumstances under which to describe himself as "hungry."

---

[4] As we indicated in the introductory material for this chapter, the preference of a behavioristically oriented attitude change theorist for words with an "objective" connotation is one of the most distinguishing characteristics of behavioristic and neobehavioristic attitude theorists. But the reader should be careful that he does not confuse differences in literary or philosophical predilections for an "objective" or "phenomenological" vocabulary as any more than just that—a difference in the connotation rather than the denotation.

Bem does not deny that the socializing community may be so clever in guessing whether the internal cues of hunger are present or absent that the child will eventually learn to correctly label certain of these private, internal states of stimulation. He does argue, however, "that many of the self-descriptive statements that *appear* [emphasis added] to be exclusively under the discriminative control of private stimuli may, in fact, still be partially controlled by the same accompanying public events used by the training community to infer the individual's inner states" (1967, p. 185). In other words, the socializing community will have used certain cues—external to the individual and publicly available to the socializing community—in order to reward and punish the individual as he learns to make self-descriptive statements. Thus, whenever a child is rewarded for stating, "I am hungry," it will be because some external cue available to the socializing community led the community to *guess* that the appropriate internal stimulation was present. Private stimuli therefore may play a smaller role in descriptive statements than the individual himself expects. Bem cites the example of the study by Schachter and Singer (1962) which argues that subjects make extensive use of external cues when they label the private, internal stimulation provided by their emotional state.

It follows from this analysis that self-descriptive statements (i.e., attitudes) are based on an individual's observations of overt behavior and the external stimulus conditions in which it occurs. In other words, you must depend on the same kind of information in order to make descriptive statements about yourself that I would use in order to make descriptive statements about you. It is this assertion, that *self-perception is limited to the same set of public cues used in interpersonal perception,* which constitutes Bem's distinctive theoretical contribution.

Bem traces his anslysis to Skinner's distinction between a mand and a tact:

"A descriptive statement, a verbal response that is under the discriminative control of some portion of the environment, is classified as a 'tact' (Skinner, 1957). A speaker is trained to describe or 'tact' his environment for the benefit of his listeners who provide generalized social reinforcement in return. . . . Verbal responses that are under the control of specific reinforcing contingencies are called 'mands.' A speaker who emits a mand is asking for, requesting, or 'manding' a particular reinforcer. . . . Mands are often disguised as tacts, as in 'I believe you have the sports page' or as in the case of the television announcer who praises the product he is selling; his verbal behavior is a mand for the salary he receives and may not at all be under the actual discriminative control that features the product he appears to be tacting. . . .

"It is clear, then, that in attempting to infer a speaker's 'true' beliefs and attitudes, the listener must often discriminate the mand-tact characteristics of the communication" (Bem, 1965, pp. 200–201).

The control over an individual's beliefs and attitudes exerted by his overt behavior is mitigated to the extent that cues are present implying that the behavior is deceitful or, more generally, is being emitted for immediate specific reinforcement.

EMPIRICAL SUPPORT FOR THE BASIC THEORETICAL PREMISES

The basic premise of Bem's theory of attitude change is that certain combinations of external cues and one's own overt behavior will lead to changes in one's attitudes or self-descriptive statements, whereas other combinations will not. ". . . An individual bases his subsequent beliefs and attitudes [self-descriptive statements] on . . . self-observed behaviors to the extent that these behaviors are emitted under circumstances that have in the past characteristically set the occasion for telling the truth" (Bem, 1966, p. 707).

In order to provide direct support for his formulation, Bem (1965) reports a study in which he "raised stimuli from birth" in the laboratory. If Bem creates one stimulus characteristically associated with "lying" and another stimulus characteristically associated with "truth-telling," then those stimuli will facilitate or hinder the extent to which future behaviors have an impact on one's self-descriptive statements or attitudes.

Bem (1965, pp. 210–217) presented the subjects with a looseleaf notebook containing cartoons which the subject had previously rated as neutral on a scale ranging from very unfunny to very funny. After subjects had been seated in an acoustically tiled recording room, they received the following instructions over an intercom:

". . . [We] are going to be examining an individual's ability to judge whether the speaker on the tape is telling the truth or not. To do this, some of the things you will say on the tape will be true statements; others will be untrue. . . . After I ask you a question, I will start the tape recorder and you should answer the question into the microphone in front of you. Whenever I turn on the tape recorder, one of the two colored light bulbs in the ceiling fixtures will also go on automatically. If the amber light goes on . . . , you should make up an untrue answer and speak it into the microphone as convincingly and naturally as possible . . . . The lighting circuitry is set to select the two colored lights automatically and in random sequence" (Bem 1965, pp. 212–213).

This first part of the procedure was to "raise in the laboratory" *external* stimuli which had, in the past, been associated with truth-telling or lie-telling. The next part of the procedure was designed to have the subject make factual statements in the presence of these external stimuli. Subjects again looked at some of the same cartoons and announced their personal decision that it was funny. The truth (or lie) light was turned on "Just so you will know when I turn the tape recorder on and off . . . " Once the tape recorder (and the truth or lie light) was turned on, the subject then stated his previous decision aloud into the tape recorder.

Subjects were then asked to re-rate the cartoons on a six-point scale. Seven of the eight subjects were persuaded to a greater extent by comments made in the presence of the truth light than by comments made in the presence of the lie light. In other words, when forced to make an extreme judgment of funniness on a cartoon previously rated neutral, subjects were much more likely to "internalize" their extreme judgment if it was made in the presence of a stimulus which had been previously associated with truth-telling.

The basic postulate of Bem's theory thus receives strong support. The extent to which a person utilizes the information from his own behavior depends on the presence of external cues that have, in the past, been associated with truth-telling.

In a second experiment subjects went through a training procedure similar to that described in the preceding experiment; they answered a factual question untruthfully when the green light was on and truthfully when the amber light was on. False statements made in the truth light led to significantly more recall errors than either (1) a false statement in the presence of the lie light or (2) no false statement at all.

CRITICISM

As is always the case when a relatively straightforward instrumental or classical conditioning paradigm is applied to human subjects, the problem of demand characteristics arises. The critical reader must consider the possibility that the results are due to some sort of high-level cognitive problem solving; the subjects may have guessed the "correct answer" "desired" by the experimenter. But Bem's two studies seem less susceptible to these criticisms than most human studies of instrumental or classical learning. First, he does provide an explanation for the lights. The amber and green lights did serve *two* functions in the first part of the experiment: (1) to indicate whether the subject was to lie or tell the truth and (2) to indicate when the tape recorder was turned on. Bem's explanation that the lights remained on during the second half of the experiment sounds plausible; they were part of the automatic machinery which indicated when the tape recorder was turned on.

Second, in anticipation of this kind of criticism, Bem did interview his subjects in order to discover whether they had any "awareness" of the relationship between the amber and green lights and their own behavior during the test phases of the experiment. The "demand characteristics" or "active problem-solving behavior" interpretation would, of course, imply that the subjects were deliberately and consciously altering their responses by attending to both studies. Bem reports that the subjects failed to indicate any conscious awareness of any relationship between their own behavior in the test phase and the amber and green lights. Of course, subjects may have denied their awareness, but the interview data are better than nothing. Further criticism of Bem's model is presented in Chapter 5 where we discuss his analysis of dissonance experiments.

In summary, Bem reports two successful efforts to directly test basic postulates in his theory. Furthermore, it does not seem the case that any of the other theories discussed in this book could make these predictions in a simple and straightforward manner. Bem has made an extensive analysis of dissonance theory experiments within his Skinnerian framework. This theory and data on dissonance theory phenomena have been postponed until the section on forced compliance in Chapter 5.

Inoculation Theory (McGuire)

The general problem of inducing resistance to persuasion has been reviewed by McGuire (1964, 1967, pp. 501–502, 1968). McGuire (1964) notes that there are a number of contemporary approaches to the problem of inducing resistance to persuasion. The "behavioral commitment" approach, for instance, involves inducing the believer to take some more or less irrevocable steps which commit him to his belief. He might make a private decision, announce his decision publicly, engage in some sort of active participation on the basis of his belief, or become committed by some external agent such as fellow members of a group or an authority figure.

A second approach to inducing resistance to persuasion involves anchoring the belief to other cognitions. The present belief might be linked to accepted values, linked to other beliefs, linked to valenced sources and reference groups. McGuire suggests that inducing a resistant cognitive state is a third general category for inducing resistance to persuasion. A propagandist interested in limiting the effectiveness of counter-propaganda might induce anxiety about the issue, induce aggressiveness, raise self-esteem, or engage in ideological preconditioning.

PRIOR TRAINING

McGuire's (1964) fourth general category, into which he classifies his own inoculation theory, involves prior training in resisting persuasion attempts. Although one might think that training and general education produces resistance to persuasion, McGuire argues that intelligence and general education often increase receptivity to new arguments.

According to McGuire, the scope of his inquiry is "the uncovering of pre-treatments which, when applied to the person, make him less susceptible to persuasive messages than he is found to be without pre-treatments. Hence, studying resistance to persuasion is not simply the inverse of studying persuasion itself" (McGuire, 1964, p. 192). Thus it need not be the case that manipulations which produce the most attitude change to begin with (credible communicators, explicitly drawn conclusions, active participation, etc.) necessarily produce the most resistance to counterattack at a subsequent time. In fact, the opposite is sometimes the case; the techniques most effective in producing immediate change are sometimes least effective in immunizing against future attack (McGuire and Papageorgis, 1961).

McGuire often notes the relationship between his theory of inducing resistance to persuasion and the biological immunization process:

"In the biological situation, the person is typically made resistant to some attacking virus by pre-exposure to a weakened dose of the virus. This mild dose stimulates his defenses so that he will be better able to overcome any massive viral attack to which he is later exposed, but is not so strong that this pre-exposure will itself cause the disease" (McGuire, 1964, p. 200).

The postulates of McGuire's theory, however, can stand independent of the biological analogy; they can, for instance, also be derived from the selective exposure postulate:

"The hypotheses . . . derive from the 'selective exposure' postulate—that people tend to defend their beliefs by avoiding exposure to counterarguments rather than by developing positive supports for the beliefs. As a consequence of the ideological "aseptic" environment that results, the person tends to remain highly confident about his beliefs, but also highly vulnerable to strong counterarguments when forced exposure occurs" (McGuire, 1961b, p. 184).

BASIC POSTULATES

Following the analysis just presented, McGuire theorizes that persuasive attacks against truisms are effective because the individual cannot make the appropriate defensive responses. He is unable to muster the appropriate defenses because (1) he has never practiced them in the past and (2) since he thinks the beliefs are unassailable, he is unmotivated to undertake the necessary practice. Thus the two variables leading to the development of defenses—practice and motivation—are the two classical variables of most learning theories. Once the obstacles are defined, the requirements of an effective pretreatment to immunize against future attack follow directly.

1. A defensive pretreatment must motivate the believer to practice defensive responses.
2. It must insure that the believer has available the information, arguments, etc., so that he can construct an effective defense to practice.

McGuire's theory deals with beliefs "that have been maintained in a 'germ free' ideological environment, that is, beliefs that the person has seldom, if ever heard attacked" (1964, p. 200). In other words, it does not deal with controversial beliefs that have been subjected to frequent attack and counterattack. For this reason, McGuire chose to work with "cultural truisms," i.e., "beliefs that are so widely shared within the person's social melieu that he would not have heard them attacked, and indeed would doubt that an attack were possible." (1964, p. 201). After some pretesting, McGuire finally settled on health beliefs such as "It's a good idea to brush your teeth after every meal if at all possible"; "Mental illness is not contagious"; "The effects of penicillin have been, almost without exception, of great benefit to mankind."

HYPOTHESES

HYPOTHESIS 1.[5] SUPPORTIVE VERSUS REFUTATIONAL DEFENSES. A pretreatment that consists of arguments supporting the truism (*supportive defense*) is less effective than a pre-treatment which first attacks the belief and then refutes the attacks (*refutational defense*).

A supportive defense does provide the material and information so that the individual could construct and practice a defense if he were motivated, but unthreatened individuals will not be motivated to assimilate and practice the material since they believe that the truisms are unassailable. The refutational defense (attack and then defense of the truism), however, both motivates the individual by virtue of the threat contained in the attacking argument and also provides him with some material for practice when the attack is refuted.

This prediction has been verified in several of McGuire's series of experiments. We will describe McGuire and Papageorgis (1961) in some detail because the general experimental procedure is typical of that used in subsequent studies. Subjects were told that the experiment was a study of the relationship between reading and writing skills. In the first of the two, one-hour experimental sessions subjects were given various types of belief-immunizing treatments. In the second session two days later, subjects were exposed to strong counterargument messages attacking the beliefs. Of immediate relevance to hypothesis 1, two types of defensive material were employed. In one-half of the treatments, subjects were presented with arguments *supporting* cultural truisms; in the other half, subjects were exposed to arguments *against* the truism (i.e., a threat) together with refutations of these arguments (i.e., supporting material). This latter procedure is similar to biological inoculation.

The supportive defense produced *more* attitude change immediately following the defensive pretreatment than the refutational defense. In other words, the supportive defense had a direct impact on the attitude when no attack occurred. But when the antitruism attack did occur, it was the refutational defense which produced the most resistance. Antitruism attacks were *least* effective when preceded by a refutational defense. These results support hypothesis 1.

HYPOTHESIS: 2. IMPORTANCE OF THE MOTIVATING ASPECT OF THE REFUTATIONAL DEFENSE. The primary effectiveness of the refutational defense rests in its ability to motivate the individual to develop defenses.

---

[5] The present authors have organized McGuire's theory into a series of numbered hypotheses.

The success of the refutational defenses described in the paragraph above could result from two factors. (1) The threat created by the two antitruism arguments contained in the refutational defense could motivate the subject to develop generalized defenses against future attacks. Or (2) the individual may merely have assimilated the specific defenses provided by the supporting material provided in the counter-arguments to the attack. To test this hypothesis Papageorgis and McGuire (1961) followed the refutational defense pretreatments with two kinds of attacks. The *refutational-same* defensive procedure was followed by an attack which used the same arguments that had been previously refuted. The *refutational-different* defense pretreatment was followed by an attack utilizing novel arguments. If the immunity to persuasion produced by the refutational defense is produced by the specific defenses provided when the threat is refuted, the immunization should be ineffective against novel arguments.

As predicted, the resistance induced by the refutational defense is approximately the same for novel arguments as it is for the very same arguments which had been previously refuted. This confirms the importance of the motivating aspect of the threat in contrast to the information content of the supporting refutations.

HYPOTHESIS 3. ADDING THREAT TO THE SUPPORTIVE DEFENSE. Supportive defenses will be effective if combined with another defensive pretreatment which provides a motivation to construct a defense.

Consistent with results previously discussed, McGuire (1961b) reports that the supportive defense was relatively less effective than a refutational defense. But in support of the hypothesis, a double defense which combined the supportive and refutational was superior to the refutational defense alone. Moreover, the additional material provided in the supportive defense should be more useful when combined with the refutational-different than when combined with the refutational-same defense. This is because the refutational-different defense provides a threat but no specific material useful for a defense against the novel attack. The supportive defense would provide the information and the refutational-different defense would supply the motivating threat. The data (McGuire, 1961b) also confirm this second prediction.

HYPOTHESIS: 4. EXTRINSIC THREAT AND ASSURANCE. Immunization will be facilitated by extrinsic threat and inhibited by extrinsic assurance given to a truism.

One-half of the subjects in McGuire and Papageorgis (1962) were given the standard, "no-forewarning," introductory statements which describe the experiment as a verbal skills test dealing with health topics. The other half of the subjects were told that the experimenter was measuring how persuasible they were and that they would read communications attacking the truisms after they had read the supporting material. Since the truisms are threatened by the introduction to, or "cover story" for, the experiment and all subjects are motivated to develop defenses, a particular immunization or defense pretreatment need not, by itself, produce motivation. Thus the effects of forewarning should be greater for the supportive defenses (which do not themselves provide any motivation) than for the refutational defenses (which provide some motivation by virtue of the attack). Also, to the extent that the forewarning provides additional motivation above and beyond the threats in the defenses, the forewarning procedures should increase resistance to subsequent attacks. Both of these predictions are confirmed by McGuire and Papageorgis (1962). Furthermore, data from control conditions indicate that the impact of the forewarning was mediated through differential effectiveness of the immunizing defenses; the forewarning did not inhibit the impact of the antitruism attack.

In another study, Anderson and McGuire (1965) reassured one-half of their subjects by giving them feedback indicating that other subjects almost unanimously agreed that the truisms were true beyond a doubt. Several of the standard inoculation-defense pretreatments (supportive defensive, refutational-same defenses, and refutational-different defenses) were less effective in the reassured than in the nonreassured condition. The extrinsic reassurance in the truisms probability attenuated the motivating aspects of the antitruism attack.

HYPOTHESIS: 5. RETENTION. Persistence of induced resistance inferred by the motivation-stimulating threat may increase for a brief period of time following the threatening manipulation; but, since the resistance conferred by the actual communication of belief-bolstering material "is a direct function of the retention of bolstering material, we would expect it to decay following the ordinary forgetting curve" (McGuire, 1964, p. 222). See McGuire (1962, 1964) for further elaboration of these predictions.

Although the attack-threat increases motivation immediately, the believer must continue to accumulate additional material for a considerable time after being exposed to the threatening defense because "material relevant to these uncontroverted truisms is rather scarce in the ordinary, ideological environment" (1964, p. 222). Only after considerable time, when the threat has receded, will the induced motivation to accumulate material tend to decay.

This prediction is immediately relevant to a comparison to the refutational-same defense and the refutational-different defense. Both provide equal amounts of threat and motivation; but the refutational-different procedures do not provide specific material to construct a defense against the arguments in the impending attack. As predicted, the refutational-same defense is almost as effective against an attack two days later as it is against an immediate attack, but the refutational-different defense is even more effective against a delayed attack than it is against an immediate attack (McGuire, 1962). This latter finding presumably, can be traced to the motivated rehearsal of defenses during the two day separation between defense and attack.

HYPOTHESIS 6a. ORDER EFFECTS. Within a double defense which combines passive and active procedures, the passive-active sequences will be the most effective sequence if the attack is made up of the same arguments used in the defense; but the active-passive sequence will be the more effective sequence when the attack contains novel arguments (McGuire, 1961a). (Readers may want to recreate the reasoning behind this hypothesis before reading further; many of McGuire's hypotheses require extra assumptions and some clever deductions before they can be derived from the basic postulates.) According to McGuire, the active defense should be more effectively carried out if the subject can use the specific arguments of the passive defense; hence the passive-active sequence should be the more effective sequence against an attack including the same arguments used in the defense.

The predicted superiority of the active-passive sequence for an attack with *novel* arguments apparently rests on a new mechanism not used in the previous hypotheses. According to McGuire, the novel attack is effective partly because the subject is suddenly faced with apparently irrefutable arguments. The subject in the active-passive sequence, however, has already been through that experience—only to learn that the arguments could be refuted after all. The listed arguments of the active defense appeared unrefutable, but the subject soon discovered that they could be refuted easily when he read the passive defense. Thus the subject should be less influenced by the apparently unrefutable arguments in the novel attack. The data, however, fail to support either aspect of this interaction prediction; the two sequences were not significantly different for either the same or novel attacks.

HYPOTHESIS 6b. The threat-information sequence will be more effective than the information-threat sequence. Thus the refutational-supportive sequence will be more effective than the reverse. In all of the previous studies, the defense "pretreatments" have occurred prior to the attack. In line with hypothesis 6b, however, McGuire (1961b) predicts that the defense would be more effective if they followed the attack rather than preceded it. "Further, it was predicted that this superiority of restoration over immunization is greater with the supportive than with the refutational defense. Finally, it was predicted that the hypothesized superiority of the refutational-supportive defense sequence over the supportive-refutational sequence is more pronounced in the immunization than in the restoration procedure" (McGuire, 1961b, p. 185). Again, however, the data (McGuire, 1961b) fail to confirm any of these hypotheses.

Given the positive support for the other hypothesis, the negative data on these order hypotheses can probably be attributed to the additional assumptions required to make the order predictions rather than the basic postulates. Since all sequence data construct various sequences within the same experimental session, it is only necessary to assume that the subjects remember supporting material for an hour or so even if not motivated. If they can still remember the material when the motivation is created at a later time in the two-hour session, they will be stirred by the attacks to practice the supporting material and use it as a springboard or pump primer to develop additional defenses. The order hypotheses might well be supported in a study with a longer time delay between the various elements in the sequence.

SUMMARY AND EVALUATION

The data and hypotheses presented support the notion that cultural truisms, such as McGuire's health beliefs, are vulnerable to antitruism attacks because the individual is unmotivated to practice defenses until his belief in the unassailability is threatened. As we have argued, the negative evidence on order effects (hypotheses 6) can probably be traced to the incorrect additional assumptions necessary to make the prediction rather than the basic assumptions themselves. McGuire's theory is an excellent and thorough investigation of a relevant delimited problem. The overlapping studies both replicate previous work and extend on to new questions.

But just how "true" must a cultural truism be before an individual feels it is unassailable? McGuire deliberately chose the health issues because they best met his criterion of having been "raised" in an aseptic ideological environment where attack was unthinkable. Inoculation theory is explicitly limited to beliefs of this kind, but the empirical work has not been done to establish the limits of the theory.

Furthermore, there is no *direct* evidence that McGuire's manipulations affect the ability to counterargue. At present, the increased counterargument produced by threatening attacks is only an unmeasured hypothetical construct. McGuire's theory would be strengthened if it could be demonstrated that subjects could muster more counterarguments during a fixed period of time or that there is a shorter latency for counterarguments following a threatening attack. Similarly, it should be possible to find direct evidence of the "motivation to defend," which is, theoretically, induced when a cultural truism is subjected to antitruism propaganda.

Finally, there are alternatives to the "counterargument" explanation. We cannot, for instance, completely dismiss the argument that McGuire's defensive pretreatments affect the perceived persuasiveness of the subsequent antitruism attacks. The effect of the inoculation treatment might be that of telling subjects that the arguments against your belief (i.e., brushing your teeth three times a day is good) are typically weak arguments. In other words, the refutational inoculation introduces a set to judge all antitruism arguments as poor. When the second session presents more antitruism arguments, they are discredited because the subject judges them to be poor arguments—not because the subject has been motivated to produce refutations during the time between the two sessions.

McGuire himself has reasoned (hypothesis 6a) that the subject may learn something when the novel antitruism attacks are refuted in the refutational inoculation; he may learn that devastating *sounding* arguments on this topic are not so devasting after all. This line of reasoning would predict one of the central findings of McGuire's theory—that the refutational defense is superior to the supportive defense. The supportive defense merely provides supporting information; it does not discredit an antitruism communication. The "decreased perceived persuasiveness of the antitruism attack" argument, however, may not explain all McGuire's results. How this theory would make the extrinsic threat and assurance predictions (hypothesis 4) or the retention predictions (hypothesis 5) is not immediately obvious. If this set interpretation is correct, then breaking it just prior to the second session by warning the Ss that the antitruism attack arguments are going to be good, that the attacking source is a high credibility source, etc., should eliminate the McGuire effect. Similarly, the set explanation should operate even if the second session is contemporaneous with the first (inoculation) session, whereas the inoculation effect should *require* a temporal gap between the two sessions. Subjects would need time to develop their refutations.

The Awareness Problem

As indicated in the chapter on methodology, there are numerous ways in which experimenters themselves can unwittingly "produce" the results they wish to obtain. One source of artifact is the demand characteristics of the experimental design. Subjects often treat a social psychological experiment as a "problem" to be solved. They look for cues in the experimental procedure, for information about the "correct" solution. Thus social psychology needs to develop measures or techniques to detect suspicions that subjects may have while serving in experiments. Not measuring them does not eliminate the problems they may create.

These are problems that must be faced in all social psychological research. However, in the case of researchers who take a learning theory approach to the study of attitudes, there are added problems. The problems are twofold. On the one hand, the experimental hypotheses are often more direct, more obvious, or less complicated than those generated by other theoretical stands. As a consequence subjects may be able to detect what they "should do" more readily and more easily comply with the experimenter's wishes. On the other hand, there may be some added epistemological problems. For these reasons we have inserted a separate section in this chapter which considers in detail the problems that can arise when subjects in experiments concerned with conditioned attitudes are aware of the experimenter's hypothesis.

THE ADEQUACY OF A SIMPLE BEHAVIORISTIC MODEL

To what extent is a simple behavioristic model of human behavior adequate? Probably this question will typically focus on whether it is at least partly appropriate. (Not many would seriously say that it would suffice.) Clearly one does not merely wish to demonstrate that subjects are able to follow instructions (which is what an "experimenter demand" explanation of the results of experiments such as those of Staats, Lott, and others does in fact argue). One intends to show instead that the behavioristic model is indeed appropriate for describing the acquisition of attitudes. This programmatic intent is seen in the following quote from Staats, Staats, and Crawford (1962):

"A behavioristic approach to meaning, based on Hullian concepts, has been developed by Osgood (1953). This interpretation states that when a word is contiguously presented with a stimulus object, the conditionable components of the total response elicited by the object are conditioned to the word. A word thus comes to elicit part of the behavior elicited by the word it denotes. It has also been proposed that the meaning response elicited by a word is conditioned to other words with which it is contiguously paired (Mowrer, 1954). It has already been experimentally shown that word meaning will indeed condition to contiguously presented nonsense syllables (Staats and Staats, 1957), national and proper names (Staats, and Staats, 1958), and meaningful words (Staats, Staats, and Biggs, 1958). In addition, the intensity of conditioned meaning was shown to increase with an increased number of conditioning trials (Abstract, 1958). In each of these studies semantic differential scales were used to measure meaning (Osgood and Suci, 1955)" (Staats, Staats, and Crawford, 1962, p. 159).

This quote considers the acquisition of attitudes in the laboratory. We might also ask if the simplistic learning theory models are sufficient to account for the more complex attitude processes that occur in day-to-day life. Many of the theorists in this chapter have argued that attitude change and formation out in the "real world" are produced by the fundamental mechanism of classical conditioning. It may be that these naturalistic attitude processes, like the attitude change observed in some experiments, are produced by higher level cognitive processes. The investigator studying eyelid conditioning, for instance, must distinguish between the classically conditioned eyelid response and voluntary, or cognitively mediated, responses (Kimble, 1961). These investigators have been able to use the shape and timing of the eyelid response to distinguish voluntary and classically conditioned responses. Since this technique is not available in studies of verbal "classical" conditioning, it is possible to argue that the results in verbal studies are the result of some high level, cognitive process rather than fundamental classical conditioning.

Thus, for the social psychology of attitudes, accepting a simple behavioristic model implies that the learning of the attitudinal response is not mediated by other verbal or cognitive processes. Yet in discussing their data, most researchers who attempt to condition attitudes seem to deny or minimize the importance of whether their subjects were indeed aware of the true purpose of the experiment. From our own standpoint, however, the question of awareness could be a critical one. To the extent that subjects must be aware of the experimenter's intent in order to "become conditioned," a simplistic behavioristic model may not suffice. "Awareness" implies the presence of cognitive activities which conceivably may mediate the observed conditioning effect.[6]

ARE ATTITUDES ACQUIRED BY CLASSICAL CONDITIONING?

PSYCHOLOGICAL DATA. The second issue is whether or not the classical conditioning paradigm as opposed to the instrumental conditioning paradigm is indeed the correct one for research procedures such as those of Staats and Lott. The epistemological importance of definitively evaluating the appropriateness of the classical conditioning paradigm for these experiments partly lies in social psychologists' conceptualization of attitudes. Most social psychologists define attitude as having an emotional or affective component. Furthermore, most psychologists would argue that affective responses are largely learned by classical conditioning (e.g., Munn, 1961; Skinner, 1953). In spite of the commonality of references to the affective component of attitudes, relatively few studies attempt to obtain measures of the physiological processes which are assumed to be corollaries of emotional responding, though, of course, some exceptions can be found (Gerard, 1964; Zimbardo, 1966; Rankin and Campbell, 1955).

Few researchers in the verbal learning area explicitly accept the appropriateness of the classical conditioning paradigm. Yet psychologists who study the conditioning of attitudes use experimental procedures almost

---

[6] These criticisms apply in varying degree to the theories discussed in this chapter. Some investigators (Weiss, for instance) make it explicit that their theory of attitude change is only an analogy based on the simpler learning processes. They do not argue that the mechanisms of attitude change are identical to the simpler learning mechanisms. Similarly, the investigators in the "Yale approach" do not limit themselves to simple learning mechanisms. But other investigators, such as Doob and Staats, argue that the same mechanisms present in simple learning processes can be extended to attitude change processes.

identical to those used in verbal learning and do explicitly claim that the classical conditioning paradigm is indeed the appropriate one for their procedure and data. To the extent, however, that subjects are aware of what outcome the experimenter expects to find, the instrumental conditioning or selective learning paradigm may more accurately denote the learning process that did in fact operate. If true, such data can no longer effectively speak on whether the affective component of attitudes is classically conditioned. The researcher might just as well have given his subjects explicit verbal instructions and observed whether they obeyed and gave the correct responses. And if they did give correct responses, they can be considered as instrumental responding with the experimenter's approval serving as the reinforcement. For our purposes here, it is not important whether such instrumental responding is *exactly* what Orne (1962) had in mind when he spoke of the consequences of the demand characteristics of some experimental designs. Indeed, in terms of the language he used, it appears that Orne was thinking of highly cognitive problem-solving behavior, whereas the animal psychologists who study instrumental conditioning or selective learning can manage well without reference to cognitive concepts (perhaps largely because their subjects do not talk). At any rate, for our arguments here, we are treating the cognitive and noncognitive descriptions of "experimenter-pleasing behavior" as equivalent—that is, as referring to the same thing.

Hence the problem of "awareness"[7] is critical for both epistemological problems. (1) In the instrumental or selective learning situation, if "awareness" is necessary in order to obtain conditioning, then a simple behavioristic model may not suffice. Other, more cognitive activity may be a necessary mediating component. (2) But furthermore, if awareness exists in experiments such as those of Staats and Lott, severe doubt is cast on the appropriateness of the classical conditioning paradigm in preference to the simple instrumental response of trying to please the experimenter.

[7] In fairness, it is also possible that awareness is an epiphenomonon that has no functional role in acquisition of the learned response. In other words, subjects may be conscious of the experimental contingencies, but this awareness may just be a concomitant of the simple learning process (classical conditioning). Though present, the awareness may have no effect on the conditioning process. If this were indeed the case, its presence would in no sense impugn the importance of Staats' or Lott's findings.

In his early studies of the learning of paired associates through conditioning, Staats "handled" the awareness problem by eliminating from the data analyses the scores of those subjects who were classified as "aware" of the experimenter's intent by a postexperimental questionnaire in which subjects were asked to "write down anything they had thought about the experiment, especially the purpose of it, and so on, or anything they had thought of during the experiment" (Staats and Staats, 1957, p. 77). Later investigations into the awareness problem have indicated that this relatively low pressure request is not sufficient to properly separate the aware and unaware subjects. Speilberger, Levin, and Shepard (1962) note that

". . . absence of awareness in these studies [e.g., Verplanck, 1955; Greenspoon, 1955] is typically inferred on the basis of *Ss*' responses to brief and often superficial postexperimental interviews. When more extensive interviewing procedures have been utilized [Cushing, 1957; Krasner, Weiss, and Ullman, 1959; Kreickhaus and Eriksen, 1960; and Levin, 1961], more *Ss* are judged to be aware of correct contingencies (correlated hypotheses) which bring partial reinforcement" (Tatz, 1960).

In an experiment designed to directly examine the effects of a brief versus an extensive postexperimental questionnaire, Levin (1961, p. 73) provides further corroboration:

"The findings of the present experiment are consistent with those of previous verbal conditioning studies [e.g., Cohen et al., 1954; Tajfel, 1955] in that when a brief and general post-experimental interview was used to investigate *S*'s awareness of a correct contingency, there was evidence for conditioning without awareness. When a more extended and specific interview was employed, however, the evidence for conditioning without awareness was largely accounted for by *Ss* who had been aware but whose awareness was not revealed by the brief interview. . . . The importance of *S*'s awareness was further demonstrated by the finding that what *S* learned was a function of the nature of his awareness. The *Ss* who were aware of the reinforcement of only one of the reinforced pronouns [I or we] showed conditioning for that pronoun only" (Levin, 1961, p. 73).

Tatz's (1960) investigation discloses that subjects who achieve *partial solutions* without verbalizing the exactly correct verbalizations, will obtain significantly higher "conditionability" scores. Furthermore, he found that subjects may evolve "partial" solutions, even when they are not told that there is anything to solve. These partial solutions, which may not be verbalized on the completion of the study, may mediate a level of responding higher than that to be expected by chance. In summary, these results suggest that we should be very hesitant to conclude that a casual interview is sufficient to detect awareness.[8]

The issue of awareness was considered more than three decades ago by Thorndike and Rock (1934), who were attempting to support Thorndike's hypothesis that reward acts directly and automatically to strengthen stimulus-response connections. In spite of this early start, it should be clear that a resolution has not been found. By now the list of complicating factors that must be considered before verbal learning without awareness can be substantiated is long, indeed. Many of these problems have been summarized by Ericksen (1960):

"The most frequent definition of awareness and unawareness is in terms of verbal report. Awareness is equated with the ability to verbalize and unawareness with the inability or lack of verbalization . . . . We need to consider the adequacy of the questioning of the S, the motivation of the S to respond with the care and precision that is required, the care taken to assure that the S understands what is being asked him, consideration of the effects of the interrogation itself upon the delicate process of awareness, and most importantly an adequate scheme for classifying the S's verbalization along relevant dimensions . . . . A definition of awareness in terms of verbalization places a heavy burden upon the adequacy of language to reflect the richness of perceptual experiences and images" (p. 280).

Ericksen (1960, p. 281) raises the additional question of how the definition of awareness would handle other nonverbal voluntary responses.

---

[8] Of course one could assume that subjects' ability to diagnose the experiment is contingent upon sufficient cues from the experimenter when he interviews the subject at the end of the experiment. It is possible that a naive subject could do as well with these same cues even if he had not been in the experiment itself. Levin (1961) recognizes this possibility in his own experiment. "Whenever S's response to a post-experimental interview is employed as the basis for inferring the content of his awareness during the conditioning trials, as was the case in the present study, it can be argued that an S who verbalizes a correct contingency might have had the contingency *suggested* to him by some aspect of the interview and therefore might not have been aware of it during the conditioning trials." He points out that this form of suggestion could be eliminated by an experiment in which two Es were employed. Groups of Ss would be reinforced on different pronouns by one E and interviewed by another E who would not know on what pronoun S had been reinforced or whether or not he had conditioned.

That is, a subject may be at a loss to describe verbally the stimulus that has been presented to him, but perhaps he could choose the correct stimulus by means of another, nonverbalized response. In psychophysical experiments, for example, subjects who classified their responses to discriminations as "pure guesses" (thereby supposedly showing unawareness) revealed above chance discriminations. If awareness is equated with reportability, such subjects would have been categorized as aware on the basis of their discriminations taken alone (Adams, 1957).

In conclusion, Ericksen strongly challenges the belief that either instrumental or classical conditioning occurs without awareness of the experimental contingencies.

"From the evidence presented by Dulany (1962) and by Speilberger (1962) . . . , it seems quite clear that learning or behavior change as a function of these experimental conditions [as the Greenspoon "mmm-hmm" and "huh-uh" reinforcements] does not occur . . . in the absence of the subject's ability to verbalize mediational steps that occur between the stimulus conditions and changes in his behavior. . . . while we might firmly believe in the phenomena of classical conditioning this does not discharge an E from the duty of showing that his particular results are not attributable to the artifact of 'pseudo conditioning.' . . . It would seem that on the basis of the available evidence learning without awareness in human Ss is not adequately proven. A considerable research effort is needed not only to arrive at acceptable operational criteria of awareness but to thoroughly explore the different types of learning situations to determine what if any kind of learning can take place without awareness" (pp. 297–298).

The possibility that classical conditioning is a valid mechanism for developing attitudes is certainly interesting and clearly merits consideration. Until the awareness problem is adequately handled, however, the results of those researchers who study the classical conditioning of paired associates cannot be taken as providing definitive support for the contention that attitudes can be conditioned classically. Much of this type of attitude research has continually ignored the complicating factors cited by others as important in assessing whether a subject is aware of what's going on in the experiment. Even after Adams' (1957) and Krasner's (1958) comprehensive probes into the many subtleties of the awareness problem, this disregard continues to occur (Staats and Staats, 1958; Staats, Staats, Heard, and Nims, 1959; Staats, Staats, and Heard, 1962).

PHYSIOLOGICAL DATA. An alternative attack on the problem of empirically demonstrating the classically conditioned component of attitudes would examine subjects for signs of the type of autonomic arousal to the conditioned stimulus that is typically the concomitant of affective responding. Staats, Staats, and Crawford (1962) did conduct such an experiment. They conclude: "The results substantiated the theory that a word may gain its meaning according to the principles of classical conditioning, finally eliciting at least part of the response elicited by the stimulus object with which it has been habitually paired. In the same procedure in which a GSR was conditioned to a word, using aversive stimuli as UCS, a negative evaluative meaning was also conditioned to the word" (Staats, Staats, and Crawford, 1962, pp. 163–164).

The expected relationship between the intensity of the conditioned meaning response and the intensity of the conditioned GSR was also confirmed. "There was a significant tendency for Ss with more extreme conditioned GSR scores to the word LARGE also to display more intense negative evaluative meaning scores for the word" (p. 163). However, "neither the conditioned GSR nor the conditioned meaning response generalized to a synonym of the CS-word [BIG]" (p. 164).

Very possibly, however, GSRs were once again successfully "conditioned" to the word LARGE because of the high level of awareness among the subjects. Twenty-one out of twenty-eight subjects were aware that LARGE was often followed by noxious stimuli (although only two of these saw any connection between this and the semantic differential measurement of the words). This awareness was detected by Staats' usual brief and general postexperimental questionnaire; perhaps even more subjects could have been shown to be aware (especially of the connection between the noxiously reinforced word and the evaluative measurement scale) if a more sensitive and extensive questionnaire had been used. But the important point is that even if it were demonstrated that the subjects in Staats' experiment did show the physiological responses that are assumed to be the concomitants of affective arousal, this by itself would not unambiguously demonstrate the functional necessity of the classical conditioning process in producing the psychological outcomes they report.

As an example, suppose that the word (or thought) BAD elicits a GSR deflection. (Of course we are begging the question of how this GSR response initially got attached to the word BAD). Assume further that if the fictitious label GLUB were paired with the word STINK, subjects might reason to themselves that the experimenter is trying to tell them that GLUB should have negative connotations— that GLUB is "bad." When later asked to evaluate GLUB on the semantic differential, they would comply and rate it unfavorably while perhaps silently thinking of its "bad" qualities. If the experimenter also observed GSR deflections while GLUB was being rated, we could not unambiguously conclude that GSRs had been classically conditioned to GLUB. Instead, the deflections might simply be instances of the initially present GSR to the word (or thought) BAD which appear when the subject makes the instrumental response of trying to "do the right thing" or "please the experimenter" by rating GLUB negatively. They need not be interpreted as a newly acquired classically conditioned response to GLUB. It would be interesting to observe whether these GSRs occurred when subjects were specifically instructed to think neutral thoughts while GLUB was being presented. If they did, this might constitute stronger evidence of the acquisition of a classically conditioned attitude toward GLUB. In other words, it might still be the case that subjects' responses on the semantic differential were instrumental, but that words like "good" and "bad" through prior learning acquired physiological concomitants. Thus it is possible, as suggested by the fascinating research of Zimbardo et al. (1966), that subjects "produced" the physiological responses through cognitive mechanisms as a consequence of their awareness of the experimental contingencies. This does not necessarily mean that it is impossible to demonstrate the classically conditioned acquisition of attitudes. Just as voluntary and involuntary eyeblinks have been differentiated by topographical characteristics of the response, so, too, it may someday be possible to differentiate voluntary, cognitively produced GSRs from involuntary GSRs.

SOME RECOMMENDATIONS

If detecting "awareness" of "suspicion" is indeed an important consideration, what advice can we give to the practicing researcher? A number of precautions are available. Though they do not necessarily eliminate all interpretive problems, they certainly reduce them.

First, there is the standard procedure of presenting separate analyses for suspicious and unsuspicious subjects. Do those who can state the hypothesis or state that the experiment is a learning experiment give different results than those who are naive? In developing questionnaires to detect awareness, the obvious ordering of items would start with open-ended questions first and proceed to more specific, forced-choice items. After free responses have been elicited, subjects might be asked to list a number of specific possible experimental hypotheses and have subjects rank them in terms of the likelihood that each was indeed the experimenter's hypothesis.

As Levin (1961) suggested, the content of the postexperimental interview may provide sufficient clues to produce insight into the experimenter's hypothesis, even though such insight was absent during the experiment itself. This can partly be guarded against by using a separate interviewer who does not know the condition to which subjects were assigned. Control subjects for whom there were no reinforcing contingencies in the experiment proper provide a baseline for the extent to which the interview questions in combination with the experimental procedure produce awareness or insight. To evaluate the effect of the interview per se, one needs to apply the same interview to naive subjects who have not even participated in the experiment. If they were found to be "aware," their knowledge would clearly be due to the interview.

Another procedure for ascertaining what is learned is the transfer or generalization test (Campbell, 1954; Campbell, Miller, and Diamond, 1960; Miller, 1961). If, by means of a classical conditioning procedure, a previously neutral stimulus is given meaning or the power to elicit affect, the organism should be able to acquire a new instrumental response toward the stimulus with acquired meaning. Or, alternatively, the instrumental learning of a new response should be predictably facilitated or hindered by the presence of the stimulus with acquired meaning. Furthermore, the learned meaning should not be contingent on the presence of a particular experimenter. It should show up on tests separated in time and space from the original learning situation. The point here is that learning (or an attitude) is assumed to have some generality. If the response is situation-specific, if it only shows up in the laboratory with the experimenter present, the specter of "demand" is inevitably raised. Nearly all of the experiments reported in this book would be improved if the attitudes were tested in a different setting than that used for the manipulations. But, as we previously mentioned, behavioristic attitude change experiments are particularly susceptible to these demand characteristic explanations.

As part of every classical conditioning experiment, one needs controls for pseudoconditioning. Repetition of the unconditioned stimulus alone—without pairing of the conditioned and unconditioned stimuli—

can result in the evocation of a response to a conditioned stimulus that had previously been inadequate. Also, in verbal conditioning studies, interpretation is much cleaner if the words chosen as conditioned and unconditioned stimuli do not have previously established associative relations. The associations should be established in the laboratory.

If an experimenter purposefully displayed behaviors designed to antagonize subjects or motivate them to be uncooperative, the likelihood that results in support of the experimental hypothesis stem from subjects' motives to please the experimenter is remote. If identical outcomes are obtained when the design is replicated by a negative and a positive experimenter, the influence of subjects' motives toward the experimenter must be judged irrelevant.

Another procedure that can be applied with advantage in conditioning studies is standardly used by some experimental social psychologists. The experimenter provides the subjects with an erroneous experimental hypothesis. If data in support of this erroneous hypothesis would be opposed to the actual hypothesis, then attempts to please the experimenter would only interfere with support for the predicted outcome.

Chapter Summary

The theories grouped in this chapter share several characteristics. All share a Darwinian interest in the adaptive aspects of human behavior. Thus all place a great deal of emphasis on "objective" features of the environment and overt responses. Most behavioristic theories of attitude change are based on "generalizations" or "analogies" with learning theories supported by data from animal laboratories.

The first theory considered in this chapter was a paper published in 1947 by Leonard Doob. Attitudes are viewed as a mediating process. Objective stimulus → attitude learning bonds are developed according to the usual laws of learning. The attitude, which was a response to the objective stimulus, then takes on certain stimulus properties. An attitude stimulus → overt behavior bond is also learned. The attitude may be conditioned to a variety of objectively different stimuli. Thus, since these different stimuli are all attached to the same attitude, they may all produce the same overt response. A number of experiments by Staats and Staats and by the Lotts provide support for Doob's formulation. In general, these experiments demonstrate that the laws of attitude formation closely parallel the laws of classical and instrumental conditioning. But, perhaps more so than most of the other experiments reviewed in this book, these experiments are susceptible to a "demand characteristic" alternative interpretation. The typical classical conditioning procedures used make it quite obvious to the subject what the "correct" answer is.

The "Yale Approach" of Carl Hovland and his associates dominated research on attitude change throughout the 1950s. The first, and most influential, book in the series was *Communication and Persuasion* by Hovland, Janis, and Kelley (1953). The section on the Yale Approach began with a brief summary of the "working assumptions" spelled out in *Communication and Persuasion*. These "working assumptions" do not, however, constitute a formal theory. Consequently, the greatest portion of our section on the Yale Approach is devoted to a summary of the empirical investigations of attitude change. The Yale Approach is most important for the questions that it asked and for its stimulation of research interest in attitude change. This lack of a formal, systematizing theory has left the work bereft of elegance for some psychologists.

The next theory classified as behavioristic in this chapter was a rigorous application of Hull-Spence behavior theory in problems of attitude change by R. F. Weiss. Weiss notes that an opinion statement has many of the characteristics of a stimulus—it evokes a variety of responses in the individual. The argument, on the other hand, shares many of the characteristics of a reinforcer—it increases the probability of certain responses. Based on this analysis of the persuasive situation, Weis applied the principles of Hull-Spence with behavior theory to attitude formation. Weiss' paper may approximate the standards of a formal theory more closely than any other in this volume. But the theory is quite narrow in scope; Weiss' presentation has relatively little to say about most of the topics discussed elsewhere in this book.

The next section was an analysis of Bem's Skinnerian "radical behaviorism." Bem argues that an individual's attitude response is largely determined by the context in which the attitude statement is elicited. Through a Skinnerian analysis of verbal behavior, Bem argues that most of us depend on cues in the outside environment to tell us how we feel internally. Experiments in which context stimuli are "raised in the laboratory" support Bem's analysis. Most of Bem's effort was directed toward a Skinnerian analysis of cognitive dissonance phenomena; and so a major portion of our discussion of Bem is postponed until Chapter 5.

The final substantive section of this chapter was the presentation of McGuire's experiments on resistance to persuasion. Limiting himself to cultural truisms which are seldom attacked, McGuire argues that the individual is unable to muster the appropriate defenses because (1) he has never practiced them in the past and (2) he thinks the beliefs are unassailable and is thus unmotivated to develop defenses. A series of experiments support McGuire's argument that the most effective ways to induce resistance to persuasion include a threatening or motivating element. A final section discusses the "demand characteristics" or "awareness" problem.

As a result of classifying these theories together, the preceding chapter is more eclectic than any other in this volume. Although we have categorized the various theoretical papers as behavioristic theories of attitude change, the authors of the papers themselves might not agree. One thing is certain—they do not cite each other. Nonetheless, most share the characteristics outlined at the beginning of the chapter; they are, we felt, more usefully considered in a single chapter than separate chapters.

Chapter 4

Consistency Theories

Each of the theories to be discussed in this chapter makes a similar basic assumption. Each theory postulates a basic "need" for consistency. The focus of this striving for consistency varies somewhat from theorist to theorist. Some stress a basic "need" for everyone to be personally consistent (i.e., personality develops as a consistent whole); others emphasize the maintenance of consistency between attitudes, between behaviors, and among attitudes and behaviors; and still others emphasize the perception of the world in a consistent, unified manner. Usually, most of the theories further assume that the presence of inconsistency produces "psychological tension," or at least is uncomfortable, and in order to reduce this tension, one "re-arranges" his psychological world to produce consistency.

Examples of the consistency principle are innumerable: a factory owner who refuses to hire Negroes does not invite them home for dinner; a Communist Party member does not join the church; a member of the John Birch Society does not bring Christmas presents to a member of the Americans for Democratic Action, nor does he contribute campaign funds to an A. D. A.-approved political candidate. As Zajonc points out, "In this respect the concept of consistency underscores and presumes human *rationality*. It holds that behavior and attitudes are not only consistent to objective observers, but that individuals try to appear consistent to themselves" (1960, p. 280). But ". . . while the concept of consistency acknowledges man's rationality, observation of the means of its achievement simultaneously unveils his irrationality" (Zajonc, 1960, p. 281). The well-known and oft-quoted conversation reported

155

by Allport (1954, pp. 13–14) provides a beautiful example of the latter point:

Mr. X: The trouble with Jews is that they only take care of their own group.

Mr. Y: But the record of the Community Chest shows that they give more generously than non-Jews.

Mr. X: That shows that they are always trying to buy favor and intrude in Christian affairs. They think of nothing but money; that is why there are so many Jewish bankers.

Mr. Y: But a recent study shows that the per cent of Jews in banking is proportionately much smaller than the per cent of non-Jews.

Mr. Y: That's just it, they don't go in for respectable business. They would rather run night clubs.

Mr. Y maintains his attitudinal consistency in spite of information inconsistent with the attitude.

McGuire (1966) lists several ways in which inconsistency may be created within an individual who has a basic striving toward consistency. First, there are human logical shortcomings, which can lead to material fallacies, e.g., the ambiguous "some," or to formal fallacies, e.g., illicit process of the major premise (McGuire, 1960), although inconsistency theory today is based more on "psycho-logic" (Abelson and Rosenberg, 1958) rather than formal logic. Second, inconsistency may arise as a result of the person simultaneously occupying two conflicting social roles. The conflicting demands put upon the high school superintendent by the school board, the public, and the teachers (Gross et al., 1957) provide a neat example. Third, McGuire suggests that a person's environment may change, leaving him "encumbered with a conceptual baggage that no longer accords with reality." Fourth, a person may be pressured into behaving in ways inconsistent with his attitudes. Much of the dissonance theory research has been concerned with this type of situation. And finally, a person may be persuaded to change his attitude on some issue, only to have this new attitude be inconsistent with other attitudes he also holds. This list of sources of inconsistency is by no means exhaustive, but it does suggest that inconsistency occurs regularly and often in human life.

As indicated, the theme of a basic striving for consistency among attitudes commonly appears in psychological theorizing, and it is obvious that the concept has some face validity and some usefulness in organizing psychological data. Although much of the research based on consistency theories has occurred in the last decade or two, the idea is not new. Credit for the original idea is typically given to Heider (1944; 1946; 1958), although one sees occasional references to Lecky (1945), Franke (1931), or even Sumner (1907). More historically oriented readers should attend to the emphasis given to cognitive "wholes" by Lewin (1935, 1936, 1948), or the Gestalt influences in general (e.g., Wulf, 1922).

Setting aside the question of historical origin, this chapter describes and evaluates several recent theories of attitude change, each based primarily on the consistency principle. We will explore, in the following order, Heider's balance theory, along with three variations of and extrapolations from this model (Abelson and Rosenberg, 1958; Cartwright and Harary, 1956; Feather, 1964); Osgood's congruity theory (Osgood and Tannenbaum, 1955), which is really a special case of balance theory; and Newcomb's symmetry (1953) model. These models share an underlying assumption of "consistency," although they emphasize different sources of inconsistency. Since dissonance theory has generated considerably more experimental evidence than the others above, it will receive separate treatment in the following chapter.

The reader may discover an overabundance of concepts in the following discussion (e.g., balance, dissonance, congruity, symmetry). Keep in mind that the purpose of this chapter is twofold: one is to examine the concept of consistency and its usefulness in understanding attitude change; the other is to examine alternative theories that use the assumption of consistency as a basic premise. Several of the theories may seem to be saying the same thing in slightly different terms. However, each alternative theory is currently *used* to generate empirical predictions. We must therefore assess these alternative conceptualizations in some detail, elaborating on their similarities and differences. In the final analysis, however, it is the empirical usefulness of a theory that is important for scientific psychology.

HEIDER'S BALANCE THEORY

Heider's theory is concerned mainly with the relationships among three things in a given person's phenomenological world: the perceiver P; another person O; and some object X. There are two types of relations that may exist between each pair of this triumvirate: the liking relation; and the unit relation. Within each type of relation there are two subtypes, positive and negative.

The liking relation is simple. P either likes O (in Heider's notation, $P L O$), or P does not like O (P not $L O$), a convenient and easily understood dichotomy. The unit relation is less straightforward. Heider says, "Briefly, separate entities comprise a unit when they are perceived as belonging together. For example, members of a family are seen as a unit; a person and his deed belong together" (1958, p. 176). He further states:

". . . many of these conditions . . . that lead to unit formation . . . have been systematically investigated by the Gestalt psychologists who demonstrated that the formation of units is an important feature of cognitive organization. The Gestalt experiments often involved the perception of simple figures in the demonstration of such unit-forming factors at similarity, proximity, common fate, good continuation, set, and past experience" (1958, p. 177).

Thus things that are *perceived* as belonging together form a unit relation. In addition, whichever relationship is involved, Heider always emphasizes P's perception of the situation. As we shall see later, this is rather important from the theoretical point of view.

We have used in our example three things: two people and an object. Let us assume that there may be one and only one relation between each pair (for example, P likes O, or P does not like O). There are then eight (2^3) possible configurations among the three things. They are presented in Fig. 4.1. Each of these configurations may be regarded as a particular psychological state existing among the two people and an object, as perceived by one of the people. Heider's central theoretical concept, balance, is simple to define. He says that "the concept of balanced state designates a situation in which the perceived units and the experienced sentiments co-exist without stress" (1958, p. 176). Specifically, this means that if all three relationships are positive (P likes O, P likes X, O likes X), or if two of them are negative and one positive (P likes O, P dislikes X, O dislikes X), the state is referred to as balanced; all other combinations are *unbalanced*.[1] The balanced state is assumed to be a stable state, which resists influence from outside sources. The unbalanced state is assumed to be unstable and in addition to produce psychological tension within the individual that "becomes relieved only when change within the situation takes place in such a way that a state of balance is achieved" (1958,

[1] Heider and his associates sometimes refer to this state as unbalanced and sometimes as imbalanced. We shall arbitrarily refer to it as unbalanced throughout.

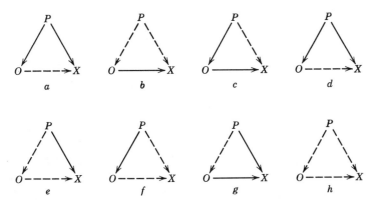

FIGURE 4.1. Schematic representation of balanced and unbalanced states. A positive relationship is indicated by an unbroken line; a negative relationship by a broken line. The direction of the relationship is indicated by the arrow. States *a, b, e,* and *f* are balanced states; states *c, d, g,* and *h* represent unbalanced states.

p. 180). This is the crux of the implications of the model for attitude change and resistance to change: balanced states are stable states and resist change; unbalanced states are unstable states and should change so that they produce balance. We shall say much more about this later. For now, the reader should note that in Fig. 4.1, states *a, b, e,* and *f* are balanced states and states *c, d, g,* and *h* are unbalanced states. The former (balanced triads) should therefore resist change and the latter (unbalanced triads) should not only change easily but also in a way that produces balance.

These figures all involve *triadic* situations—relationships among three things—which in our examples and in most of Heider's are two people and an object. Heider also discusses *dyadic* situations, relationships between two people or one person and an object. He mentions various statements one can make about these situations. For example, the state P likes O "induces" (produces a force toward or a tendency toward a particular state rather than actual production of the state) O likes P. P owns X (the unit relationship, designated by U) induces P likes X. If P likes O and O does not like P, a state of unbalance exists. Other things being equal, and assuming that O continues to dislike P, then P should come to dislike O.

The last sentence has implications important enough for us to pause briefly to discuss them. The point is that "other things being equal" is in this case an extremely important phrase. To some degree, Heider recognizes the complexity of the situation and discusses a relatively large number of possible liking and unit relationships that may exist between O and P. Heider discusses the triadic case as if all the relationships were unidirectional (e.g., from P to O, but not from O to P), with only one relationship existing between any two psychological objects. In the dyadic case though, relationships of both directions are assumed and there is at least some recognition of several possible relationships existing at the same time. This produces some confusion. There is little reason to assume that O's liking for P disappears merely because object X comes in the field. In the triadic case one should allow for bidirectional and multiple relationships, to assure a more complete, albeit more complex, analysis. To explore this avenue of thought let us assume that instead of the object X in the field there is a third person (Heider suggests using Q for this person) and examine some relationships that could exist at the same time in P's psychological world.

1. P is a neighbor of O; symbolized as $P\ U\ O$
2. P knows that O likes him $O\ L\ P$
3. However, P does not like O very much (one reason
   for 2 and 3 to exist at the same time could be, say,
   a marked difference in status between P and O) P not $L\ O$
4. O's brother-in-law lives with him $O\ U\ Q$
                                                                           $(Q\ U\ O)?$
5. O doesn't like his brother-in-law O not $L\ Q$
6. In fact, O despises his brother-in-law O not $L\ Q$
7. And O wishes he would move out of his house
   (even though O loves his wife, $O\ L\ W$, who adores
   her brother, $W\ L\ Q$) O not $L\ Q$
8. P finds O's brother-in-law rather amusing, even
   though, $P\ L\ Q$
9. naturally, O's brother-in-law does not live with P P not $U\ Q$
10. However, technically, Q is P's neighbor $P\ U\ Q$
                                                                           $(Q\ U\ P)?$

We ask simply: what does balance theory predict in the above example? Will P's attitude or attitudes change and, if so, in what direction? In the ten assertions above, one can abstract triads that are balanced and triads that are unbalanced. One could ask therefore if the whole structure is balanced or unbalanced. Heider says, "When *all* the sentiments toward that single entity are of like sign, balance obtains" (1958, p. 183; our italics). If we can assume that we should consider unit relationships along with sentiment (i.e., liking), then it is clear that the somewhat facetious example we have given is not balanced. But what will happen? Heider does not tell us. Others (e.g., Rosenberg and Abelson, 1960) have made the assumption that balance will be produced in the manner that is least effortful for P, which may in this case imply that P will move to a different house. The assumption of Rosenberg and Abelson is a very reasonable one and furthermore it is testable. It should be clear, however, that it is not an assumption that Heider makes and therefore constitutes an addition to the basic balance model. We are of course defining balance theory as "whatever Heider says it is," and from this starting point anything added to balance theory by others is a variation of the basic model. We will consider several of these variations later in this chapter. Before we attempt to critically assess the basic balance model let us inspect some research related to the model.

SUPPORTING DATA. In a dissertation supervised by Heider, Jordan (1953) tested the hypothesis that balanced situations are more pleasant than unbalanced situations. He gave each subject 64 hypothetical situations, of which half were balanced and half unbalanced. Each situation dealt with two people and an "impersonal entity." Jordan included all possible combinations of liking and unit relationships counterindexed with positive and negative relationships (i.e., $2^3 \times 2^3 = 64$). He instructed each subject to put himself in the place of P (i.e., each subject read "I" instead of P) and rate each situation on "Its inherent degree of pleasantness or unpleasantness" (p. 276).[2] An example of the situation for the subject would be, "I like another person; the other person likes an impersonal entity; I like the impersonal entity." The basic prediction was that balanced states would be regarded as more pleasant than unbalanced states. However, on the basis of pilot work, Jordan formulated three ad hoc hypotheses concerning "secondary preference determinants": (1) a positive relationship is pleasant and a negative relationship is unpleasant; (2) a liking relationship has a stronger effect than a unit relationship; (3) the relationship between P and O has a stronger effect than the relationship between P and X, and both of these have a stronger effect than the relationship between O and X. Adding to

---

[2] We comment later about the methodological drawbacks of such "role-playing."

these the assumption that balanced states are more pleasant than un-balanced states allowed Jordan to predict the rank order of the 64 hypothetical situations on pleasantness.

Jordan found that on the average, subjects rated balanced situations as more pleasant than unbalanced ones; but incidental findings necessitated several qualifications. For example, regardless of balance, situations containing component P DL O were rated as quite unpleasant. Moreover, unbalanced situations in which the lack of balance hinged partly upon a negative unit relationship were rated as mildly pleasant, inconsistent with the balance theory prediction.

The importance of these data stems partly from the way others interpret them. For instance, Heider cites the data as support for his theory. The objective observer would have to say that if they are support for the theory, then they are not strong support, since three ad hoc hypotheses and one theoretical qualification are necessary to account for the data. Jordan says the theory "emerges unscathed," but he mentions that the data necessitate a change in the theory from one of equating balance with pleasantness to equating it with "propriety."

Cartwright and Harary (1956) criticize Jordan's analysis on the grounds that Jordan made no distinction between the opposite of a relationship and the complement of a relationship (Heider does make the distinction at a later time; see Heider, 1958). They maintain that there is considerable ambiguity about the negative unit relationship and propose a distinction between the absence of the unit relationship (i.e., the complement of U) and a negative unit relationship (i.e., the opposite of U). For example, the triad P L O, P L X, O not-U X they call "vacuously balanced." That is, they propose that if "I like John" and "I like sports cars," the fact that "John does not own a sports car" should not theoretically produce imbalance. "Not own," they hypothesize, is not the opposite of "own," but rather the complement. This example would be labeled as vacuously balanced. As a test of this notion, they re-analyzed Jordan's data by simply ignoring the not-U relationship. They found that Jordan's vacuously balanced situations were rated as more pleasant than the unbalanced situations, but less pleasant than the balanced situations. They take this as support for their re-interpretation of Jordan's experiment, but they offer no reason, other than intuitive, why the vacuously balanced situations should be less pleasant than ordinary balanced situations. In sum, Jordan's experiment supports balance theory while suggesting a number of theoretical qualifications.

Despite the frequency with which Heider's theory is mentioned in the literature, few experiments directly explore the balance hypothesis. We shall briefly mention a few that do. In addition, we shall describe several other experiments concerned with some variation of balance theory when we discuss the particular theoretical variation.

Burdick and Burnes (1958) used a physiological measure (GSR) to test the hypothesis that imbalance creates tension. They found greater emotional reaction when the subject disagreed with a well-liked experimenter than when the subject agreed with him. These data support the basic balance hypothesis. However, a different outcome would not discredit the balance hypothesis. None of the consistency theorists strongly imply that "psychological tension" should be isomorphic with a measure of skin resistance. This notion demands an extra assumption about the relationship of *particular* psychological concepts to *particular* physiological measures. Of course, as McGuire (1966) has mentioned, physiological correlates do add a comforting "surplus meaning" to the concept of inconsistency.

In a second experiment in this paper, Burdick and Burnes found, as predicted by balance theory, that subjects who liked the experimenter changed their attitudes toward the position he "advocated," but subjects who disliked the experimenter changed their attitudes in the opposite direction. The latter finding is not clearly specified by balance theory. Thus, while supporting the assumption basic to balance theory (and all consistency theories), the experiment questions its complete adequacy.

Horowitz, Lyons, and Perlmutter (1951) sought information related to the balance hypothesis in a "natural" group discussion. They obtained sociometric indices of liking within the group. They also identified particular verbal events (i.e., important verbal behaviors that were somewhat controversial in the group) occurring in the discussion that were clearly produced by single people. Thus, having information about P's liking for O, and knowing that O produced event X, they made predictions about P's liking for event X. As Cartwright and Harary correctly comment on this experiment, "The data show a clear tendency for P to place a higher evaluation on Xs produced by more attractive Os. It is not clearly demonstrated that P likes Xs produced by liked Os and dislikes Xs produced by disliked Os" (1956, p. 278). It is a provocative, but nonetheless correlational, result.

Zajonc (1960) discusses an unpublished experiment by Harburg and Price at the University of Michigan:

"[S]tudents were asked to name two of their best friends. When those named were of opposite sexes, subjects reported they would feel uneasy if the two friends liked one another. In a subsequent experiment subjects were asked whether they desired their good friends to like, be neutral to, or dislike one of their strongly disliked acquaintances, and whether they desired the disliked acquaintances to like or dislike the friend. It will be recalled that in either case a balanced state obtains only if the two persons are negatively related to one another. However, Harburg and Price found that 39 per cent desired their friend to be liked by the disliked acquaintance, and only 24 per cent to be disliked. Morever, faced with the alternative that the disliked acquaintance dislikes their friend, 55 per cent as opposed to 25 per cent expressed uneasiness. These results are quite inconsistent with balance theory" (1960, p. 286).

Of course, one could offer several explanations for these data, but it is more important to note that balance theory does not completely account for them.

Another experiment by Price, Harburg, and Newcomb (1966) provides some further insight into the limitations of balance theory. They presented subjects with eight P-O-Q situations, involving same-sex peers that the subjects admitted liking or disliking. In each trial, the subjects' previous experience with O and Q dictated the P-to-O and P-to-Q relationships presented. The experimenters established the O-to-Q relationship. Price, Harburg, and Newcomb found ratings of pleasantness or uneasiness to follow the balance predictions only when the basic relationship between P and O was positive. For example, with the triad P L O, P not L Q, O not L Q, only 5% of the subjects indicated they would feel uneasy, and 89% said they would feel "pleasant." This example strongly supports the balance prediction. However, in the equally balanced triad P not L O, P L Q, O not L Q, 43% checked the uneasy side and only 35% checked the pleasant side of the attitude scale. Further, few subjects (17%) felt uneasy when all three relationships were negative—an unbalanced triad.

Price, Harburg, and Newcomb posit three parameters, other than striving for consistency, that arise when the P-to-O relationship is negative. First, when this relationship is negative, the person is *uncertain* whether O and Q reciprocate this attitude. Second, when this uncertainty exists, the person's feelings of *ambivalence* toward others becomes more salient. That is, the person becomes more aware of disliked aspects of the liked person and liked aspects of the disliked person. Third, when the person's feelings toward O or Q or both are negative, he tends to be indifferent to their attitudes toward each other, a lack of *engagement*. Several subjects apparently wrote "I dislike both of them and couldn't care less what they think" (p. 268). In summary, Price, Harburg, and Newcomb take a large step toward specifying the conditions under which balance theory does and does not predict adequately.

In an interesting series of studies, Gerard and Fleischer (1967) had subjects read eight short stories involving *P-O-X* relationships. They then asked subjects to recall the title of each story, the names of the characters, and details about the plots, and, in a second study, to rate the pleasantness of each story. As predicted, they found that the balanced story was rated more pleasant than the unbalanced only when the *P* to *O* relationship was positive. When the *P* to *O* relationship was negative, the unbalanced story was rated the more pleasant. Interestingly, Gerard and Fleischer also predicted and found the opposite relationship for recall. When the *P* to *O* relationship was positive, subjects recalled more about the story when it represented an unbalanced triad. When the relationship was negative, there was slightly less recall of the unbalanced story.

The recall data would seem to conflict with two studies by Zajonc and Burnstein (1965a, 1965b). Zajonc and Burnstein had subjects learn paired-associate triads and found that balanced triads were learned more easily (with fewer errors). In reconciling the disparity, Gerard and Fleischer postulate two distinct processes, both arising from the balance concept. In one process the subject assumes balance to exist, and indeed Zajonc and Burnstein did find errors in recall to be in the direction of producing balanced states. In the second process there is a tendency to remember structures that are in tension or lack a good Gestalt. It is this tension and uncertainty, Gerard and Fleischer say, that makes some stories more interesting and "difficult to put down" than others.

EVALUATION OF THE BASIC MODEL. These examples give the reader a flavor of the research explicitly generated by balance theory. Although the data often support the major balance hypothesis, other results are clearly contrary to some of the specific theoretical predictions. These exceptions deserve emphasis because of the frequent reference to balance theory in the psychological literature. Closer examination reveals that the typical reference appears in the discussion section of an experimental article, and states "These results are quite consistent with balance theory, since . . . ." Alternatively, when balance theory is used for *prediction* the results often do not conform completely to the theoretical expectations. The historical importance of the theory should not blind us to the fact that by today's more rigorous standards, the original formulation leaves many irregularities in the data unexplained. We turn to some conceptual criticisms of the theory in the unordered list that follows.

1. It is very unclear when a unit relationship exists and when it does not. Intuitively, one can say that a unit relationship exists when P perceives two things as "hanging together" phenomenologically. However, the specification usually takes place after the fact, and it is often difficult (although clearly not impossible) to specify *in advance* the existence of a unit relationship. Thus it has been difficult to use the unit relationship to *predict* psychological events, rather than just *explain* them. However in addition to more information from the individual subject, one might also use judges to select unit relationships for experimental purposes. In a given culture or society, those unit relationships most strongly formed, as estimated by judges, could be used in tests of the theory. This immediate but temporary solution would allow greater specificity in prediction.

2. Surprisingly enough, the liking relationship is unclear as well. Zajonc gives several examples that so vividly portray the unclarity that they are worth quoting: "Festinger once inquired in a jocular mood if it followed from balance theory that since he likes chicken, and since chickens like chicken feed, he must also like chicken feed or else experience the tension of imbalance" (1960, p. 285); "Two men vying for the hand of the same fair maiden might experience tension whether they are close friends or deadly enemies" (p. 286); "And no matter how much . . . (a child) . . . likes Popeye you can't make him like spinach, although according to balance theory he should." Although advertising psychologists might dispute the last assertion, further specification appears necessary, beyond just "liking," before any psychological implication is clear. We emphasize that the difficulty here is not necessarily in the theory, but rather in the ambiguity of the term liking. Indeed, it is not difficult to revise the theory so as to handle the examples above (see, for example, Abelson, 1968).

3. No distinction was originally made between the complement and the opposite of a relationship. However, Cartwright and Harary's reanalysis of Jordan's data prompted Heider to include this distinction in a later version (1958). Of course, the distinction is an integral part of the variation of balance theory that Cartwright and Harary present. In this sense, several of the criticisms of balance theory made below are obviated by one variation of balance theory or another. However,

none of the variations, including dissonance theory (Chapter 5), satisfy all of the criticisms.

4. It is unclear precisely what will occur when a state of unbalance exists. Granted a force will push toward a state of balance, but in any situation there are a number of alternative ways this could happen. McGuire (1966) has said in reference to all consistency theories that "The availability of these many alternative modes is quite convenient for the person confronted with an inconsistency among his cognitions, but it is an embarrassment for the theorist trying to predict what the person will do" (p. 13). Rosenberg and Abelson (1960) made a theoretical contribution by hypothesizing that the person will choose the least effortful way of reducing unbalance. Also, the dissonance theorists made a methodological contribution by suggesting that some of the avenues of unbalance reduction can be blocked off. However, the problem has received little direct attention.

5. There is no provision for *degree* of balance. A given state is either balanced or unbalanced. It is clear that there is an important difference between "P loves O madly, O dislikes P a little" and "P loves O madly, O can't stand the sight of P," although balance theory makes no distinction between the two situations.

6. The basic model pays little attention to the complexity of the individual case, whether this complexity is related to:

(a) multiple relationships within a triad;

(b) different types of relationships existing at the same time, e.g., $P \, L \, X, P$ not $U \, X$;

(c) the inclusion of other persons or objects in the psychological field, e.g., the inclusion of O's wife, who is obviously relevant for predictions about what is going to happen, in our previous example.

7. There is no provision for variation in intensity or extremeness of the relationship. The example given in paragraph 5 applies here as well.

8. There is a conceptual "looseness" about what unbalance is exactly. This "looseness" allowed Brown (1962), for example, to say, "It is very generally true that cognitive imbalance amounts to ambivalence" (p. 79). Of course, many would take issue with Brown's statement. If unbalance were equivalent to "ambivalence," then one could argue that the concept of unbalance would be redundant and superfluous. A second name for the same psychological event adds little clarification. A more clearly defined concept would not have produced such a misinterpretation.

9. There is no attention paid to the evaluation of the objects and people involved in the relationship other than liking or disliking. That is, an object may be inherently positive or negative aside from the relationships involved. The inherent evaluative aspect of the object could produce states of unbalance that would be balanced if only the liking relationships were considered. For example, the assertion "I love a whore and she loves me," if true, would probably make most people in the place of P uncomfortable, and lead them to view the dyad as unbalanced, because of the inherent social implications of the position of O. But Heider considers this a balanced situation (P L O, O L P), and ignores the inherently negative aspects of O. Osgood (1960, p. 349) points this out best when he asks, "But what if one of the elements is negative? Here we would have two 'good' people, both liking each other, but also liking an evil person, object or act (e.g., I love Mommy, Mommy loves a murderer, I love a murderer, etc.). If we agree that it is psychologically incongruent for a 'good' thing to be positively associated with a 'bad' thing, then the Cartwright-Harary model is untenable without elaboration." We merely add that this criticism applies as well to the basic balance model as it does to the Cartwright-Harary version of that model.

Before moving on to variations of balance theory, let us make a few concluding remarks about the theory qua theory. As mentioned, the model lacks much of the precision we have come to expect of a formal theory. Also, the model has not stimulated much research concerned with directly testing it as a theory, and this research, although sparse, has not supported the theory unequivocally. All of these are negative points about the model. The positive point, and perhaps the most important point, is that the theory has stimulated a great deal of thinking about cognition and cognitive consistency. In this sense the model has been important to psychology and to the study of attitude change.

Variations of the Basic Balance Model

All of the variations of balance theory represent attempts to increase the power of the theory by alleviating one or more of its conceptual inadequacies (although none eliminates all of the points mentioned above). Each variation in its own way represents an improvement on the basic model. We shall discuss only three variations here: Cartwright and Harary on what they refer to as "structural balance"; Abelson and Rosenberg's "cognitive balancing"; and Feather, who also refers to his variation as "structural balance."

CARTWRIGHT AND HARARY—STRUCTURAL BALANCE

Cartwright and Harary (1956) expended considerable effort in an attempt to formalize balance theory and to make it more general. In so doing they attempt to: (1) handle unsymmetric relationships (e.g., $P L O$; $O DL P$), which they feel Heider underemphasizes; (2) define balance for situation involving any number of entities; (3) distinguish between the complement of a relationship and its opposite (this distinction was discussed earlier); (4) handle different types of relationships at the same time (e.g., $P L X$; P not $U X$), as well as allow for other types of relationships besides the basic two Heider mentions; (5) take the notion of balance "out of the head" of P and apply it to ". . . cognitive units, social systems, or any configuration where both a relation and its opposite must be specified" (1956, p. 281); (6) define the degree of balance.

They introduce and utilize (signed-) digraph theory, as their descriptive tool (see Harary, Norman, and Cartwright, 1965). This mathematical system provides a graphic representation of relationships between entities, indicating both the direction of the relationships and the valence (positive or negative). The utilization of this particular mathematical model is an original and interesting approach.

The Cartwright and Harary revision and extension of balance theory is important for several reasons. It is clear that the model accomplishes what it intended to do. That is, it handles points 1 to 6 above quite well. Perhaps most important, Cartwright and Harary do not view balance as an either-or phenomenon. They define balance, with the aid of digraph theory, in such a way as to allow for and quantify degrees of balance. It should be emphasized, however, that all of the points covered by this model are accomplished by assumption or by definition. Thus the model raises empirical questions and its ultimate usefulness will be determined by empirical tests of these predictions. For example, the Cartwright and Harary model allows us to say by definition that situation A is more balanced than situation B. However, whether the two situations produce the predicted difference in psychological consequences is an empirical question. Unfortunately, the Cartwright and

Harary model has stimulated few direct tests of it. One exception is an experiment by Price, Harburg, and McLeod (1965). They utilized a sort of combination of the Cartwright-Harary model and the Newcomb model, and made approximations of the degree of balance based on the degree of discrepancy (between the attitude of P toward X and of O toward X) and the degree of "emotional involvement" between P and O. In a different vein, Morrissette (1958) presented subjects with some of the relationships in three- and four-person structures and asked subjects to predict the remaining relationships. For three-person structures, the theory was supported, although Morrissette found, as did Jordan (1953), that the theoretical predictions did not hold when negative relationships were involved. For four-person structures, however, the data were consistent with the theory only when the subject was one of the points in the three-person subsystems. These experiments provide steps in the right direction, but the lack of other data limits evaluation of the Cartwright-Harary model.

However, there is an interesting conceptual difference between Heider and Cartwright-Harary that should be clarified. Heider's theory is very phenomenological, and he emphasizes events and relationships as P perceives them, events in the life space of P. Cartwright and Harary want their model to have broader applicability and they take balance "out of the head" of P and make it a mathematical property, having reference to communication nets, sociometric matrices, or even neural networks. The Cartwright-Harary approach has the advantage of being more general, but there is a major disadvantage as well. It is often difficult to know whether their model calls for objective or phenomenal operational definitions. Let us take an example. Suppose we wish to ascertain the degree of balance in a sociometric matrix and we ask our subjects to list liked and disliked group members. For a given person, P, it is clear where we obtain his likes and dislikes: we ask him. But how about the reciprocal choices? Are we to ask P for his perception of who likes and dislikes him, or are we to ask the others in the group if each of them likes or dislikes P? Heider would clearly prefer the former, but the structural approach emphasizes the latter. To the extent that there is a difference between these two pieces of information (and there can be, especially with the unit relationship), the two approaches would produce different results. From the point of view of clarity, it is more important that Cartwright and Harary fluctuate between these two sources of information without appearing to recognize the variation in source or its importance. Thus their model has the drawback that the source of balance is not always clear.

ABELSON AND ROSENBERG—COGNITIVE BALANCING

This model deviates quite a bit from the basic balance model. Abelson and Rosenberg[3] (Abelson and Rosenberg, 1958; Rosenberg and Abelson, 1960) support their deviation by criticizing Heider's theory on three grounds. First, quite in line with the view expressed in this book, they contend that the Heiderian model generates no systematic research program. Second, they argue that Heider's model deals mainly with interpersonal perception, whereas they want to extend the model to "all cognitive processes in which the objects 'cognized' are of affective significance to the 'cognizer' " (Rosenberg and Abelson, 1960, p. 116). Heider does take most of his *examples* from the fields of interpersonal perception, but he seems to apply his theory beyond the boundaries of person perception. For example, one of his most referenced theoretical articles (Heider, 1946) has the word attitude in the title. In addition, the Cartwright and Harary work certainly represents at least one attempt to broaden the basic balance model. The structural model of Cartwright and Harary also obviates, at least to some extent, the third criticism of Abelson and Rosenberg, namely that the model has not been extended "beyond the P-O-X triad to parallel the complexities of structure found in real cognitive process" (Rosenberg and Abelson, 1960, p. 116). Partly because of these criticisms and partly because Abelson and Rosenberg try to derive a new model rather than merely an extension and revision of Heider's, their model assumes a somewhat different form than Heider's. Let us look at some of these differences.

First, and perhaps most important, Abelson and Rosenberg posit only one relationship between psychological objects (elements, as they call them), instead of Heider's two; and this relationship is affective. This affective relationship may be positive, negative, or "null." The last may be a neutral relationship between elements or simply the lack of a relationship. Conceptually, the null relation represents what Cartwright and Harary refer to as the complement of a relation. Seemingly, then, Abelson and Rosenberg discard the Heiderian unit relationship. It is more

---

[3] The model presented is somewhat different in the two articles. Where this variation exists, we shall assume that the last article represents the "latest word" and present it accordingly.

appropriate to say, however, that they merely subsume the unit relationship under the affective relationship. For instance, Abelson and Rosenberg give as examples such relationships as "possesses," "promotes," "is equivalent to," and "advocates." One would guess that Heider would label all of these unit relationships. Abelson and Rosenberg implicitly but parsimoniously assume that both of Heider's relationships act in psychologically equivalent ways. If the two relationships do act in equivalent ways, then only one concept name is needed. However, it is an empirical question whether only one relationship will account for all or a sufficient part of the data.

Abelson and Rosenberg emphasize that there are a number of possible alternative ways of restoring balance and suggest further that one may rank the alternative ways according to probability of outcome. They hypothesize that the probability of using a particular method of restoring balance is inversely related to the psychological effort necessary for the method. Necessary effort is operationally defined as the number of sign changes that the person must make to restore balance. Thus the more difficult it is for a subject to use a particular way of restoring balance, the less probable it is that he will do so. This assumption is very important because one simply cannot make specific predictions without it. We note in passing that Festinger (1957) also makes a similar assumption for his theory of cognitive dissonance.

Abelson and Rosenberg tested the hypothesis that balance is restored in the least effortful way in two different experiments. In these experiments subjects "played the role" of an owner of a department store. As a part of the content of this role, each subject was "assigned" a particular affective reaction toward each of three concepts: "high sales volume"; "modern art"; and Mr. Fenwick, the manager of the rug department. Each subject was further assigned relationships among the concepts, e.g., displays of modern art *reduce* (a negative relationship) sales volume; Fenwick *plans to mount* (a positive relationship) such a display in the rug department; Fenwick in his tenure as rug department manager *has increased* (positive) the volume of sales. These three specific relationships were assigned to all subjects. However, the affective reaction varied between experimental conditions. There were three experimental conditions, resulting in three "attitudinal structures." These three structures are represented in Fig. 4.2.

The reader should note several things immediately about Fig. 4.2. First, all of the structures are obviously unbalanced. Second, the graphic

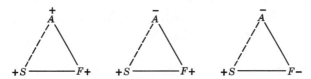

Figure 4.2. Three experimental structures (taken from Rosenberg and Abelson, 1960, p. 128). *S* denotes the concept "sales"; *A*, "modern art display"; and *F*, "Fenwick." Signs attached to these symbols indicate the initial valuations of the concepts by subjects assigned to the three structure groups. Broken lines indicate negative relations between concepts; solid lines, positive relations.

representation of the structures themselves varies from Heider's conceptualization. That is, *P* (the perceiver) is not represented. However, the signs attached to the concepts indicate the relationship of *P* to each of the "objects" in the field. Thus in Heider's terms this might be considered a *P-O-X-Q* system with unidirectional relationships existing between all possible pairs.

Each subject was subsequently presented with three communications. Each communication argued for a change in one of the relationships represented in Fig. 4.2 (e.g., one communication argued that modern art displays actually increase sales volume). "Thus, each subject was exposed to three communications any one of which, if accepted, could serve as the beginning of a process of cognitive change which would restore the total structure to balance; but accepting one of these three communications would involve only one sign change, while accepting the others would require two or three sign changes, depending upon the structure and the communication" (1960, p. 130).

Both studies used this basic procedure and their findings are quite interesting. The first study produced results quite consistent with the balance formulation. The second study indicated that the balance formulation was only part of the picture. First, apparently subjects in all groups were somewhat influenced by all three communications. Second, only in the groups where just one sign change was necessary to restore balance did any appreciable number of subjects achieve balance over the total structure. *"Apparently, it is difficult to elicit a strongly positive immediate reaction to communications which merely pave the way toward ultimate balance, instead of providing balancing material immediately"* (p. 140). Third, subjects tended to avoid the restoration of balance through disliking Fenwick, a finding reminiscent of Jordan's

(1953) data. Fourth, the sales relationship had a disproportionately large effect, leading Abelson and Rosenberg to postulate a *second* force (the first is the force toward cognitive balance) operating in the situation, i.e., a force toward the maximization of potential gain and the minimization of potential loss. The postulation of this second force led Abelson and Rosenberg to modify their model. That is, they end up saying that a balanced outcome will only be achieved when both forces operate in the same direction. When they do not, *"the typical outcome will not meet the requirements of a simple formal definition of cognitive balance"* (p. 145).

These two studies represent the main support for the Abelson and Rosenberg model. Consequently, we should note several methodological and empirical deficiencies in these experiments. First, the data were not perfectly ordered by the hypotheses and in fact the residual is statistically significant. Second, approximately one-third of the subjects were discarded from the analysis of each study, because they did not internalize the unbalance. Third, the basic data were ratings of the messages, including a question on their persuasiveness, and not actually measures of change produced. When measures of change were obtained, they were not significant.

The method of "role-playing" raises another methodological question.[4] Although there is some disagreement in the field on this point, the present authors are firmly convinced that "role-playing" is a rather weak method to use in attitude change experiments. There is evidence, derived within the framework of dissonance theory, that there can be a considerable difference between what a subject *says he would do* in a given situation and what he *will actually do*. To the extent that an experimenter can convince his audience that the two variables are isomorphic in his experiment, role-playing is an adequate method. However, if there is some doubt about this isomorphism, then role-playing is a weaker method than the experimental inducement of a psychological state. That is, the reader is less convinced that the results obtained by role-playing methods may generalize to psychologically more real situations. We feel that this is an important methodological point. It was mentioned before in Chapter 2 and it shall be mentioned again. In fairness, we repeat that others in the field disagree with us. However, when one runs an experiment

---

[4] Of course, this "act-as-if" procedure is only one of several definitions of the term, role-playing. We are only referring here to what might be called the weak end of the engagement dimension.

in which one experimentally induced a psychological state, the critic immediately wants to know if the subject was suspicious about the "true nature" of the experiment. The implication is that if the subject *knew* that you were interested in attitude change, he would behave differently than if he did not know. It seems to us that in experiments using a "role-playing" method, it is obvious to the subject that he is in an attitude change experiment, and the results thus obtained are therefore to be taken with at least a small grain of salt. The same criticism can be made of Jordan's (1953) ratings or any other totally "unreal" method.

In spite of the drawbacks to the two experiments, the model presented by Abelson and Rosenberg represents a considerable advance over the basic balance model of Heider. Let us recall the criticisms of the basic model to aid in evaluating the improvements of the present model. Initially Abelson and Rosenberg partially rid themselves of the criticisms of the unit relationship by discarding it altogether, although their model is still left with the ambiguities of the Heiderian liking relationship. They emphasize alternative ways of restoring balance, and hypothesize that the chosen way will be the least effortful one. Granted that the data do not provide unequivocal support for this hypothesis, the hypothesis and subsequent changes in the model represent a positive feature. The model also gives some necessary additional attention to the complex cognitive world of the subjects. In short, they offer us considerable improvement.

Lest we get carried away with praise, we will hurry to add that there are several important deficiencies in the model. First, like Heider, Abelson and Rosenberg do not provide for any variation in *degree* of balance. Second, there is no provision for either variation in intensity or extremeness of the relationship between two "concepts," or for variation in the intensity or extremeness of the attitude toward the object (concept). There are considerable data, more appropriately discussed in the next chapter under dissonance theory, indicating that all three of the preceding points are necessary to predict psychological events. The last criticism that we wish to make of this model is that although the authors postulate the existence of forces other than balance operating in their situation, they do not specify precisely enough how these forces interact and how they can be identified in advance so that one could make predictions. [See Abelson (1968) and Rosenberg (1968) for further discussion.]

FEATHER—A STRUCTURAL BALANCE MODEL. There are two main reasons why Feather's (1964; 1965) model is important in the present context: (1) it is specifically oriented toward communication effects and attitude change; and (2) it is a variation and improvement upon both the basic balance model and the Cartwright and Harary model.

Generally, Feather conceives of the source, the communication, the issue, and the receiver as "elements" of a "communication structure." That is, the source S delivers a communication C to a receiver R about some particular issue I. Unit and affective relationships are then posited among these elements and the result is analyzed according to Cartwright and Harary's version of balance theory.

Let us take an example. Figure 4.3 represents eight of Feather's balanced communication structures. Let us look at structure e and work through it as our example. We could verbalize that situation as follows: S does not like R and vice versa; in addition, they do not form a unit relationship; R likes the communication, which takes a negative position on an issue R feels negatively about, and in addition R has some sort of unit relationship with the communication; S feels positively about

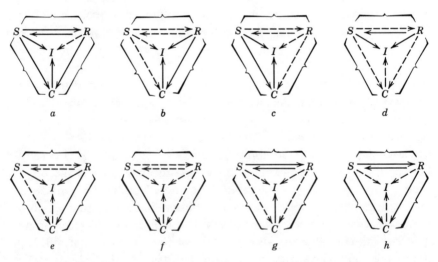

FIGURE 4.3. Eight balanced communications structures (from Feather, 1964). S indicates the source; R, the receiver; I, the issue; and C, the communication. Straight lines indicate the affective relationship; brackets indicate the unit relationship. Broken lines indicate a negative relationship; solid lines indicate a positive relationship.

the issue in question but gave a communication taking a negative position on the issue; S does not like the communication, and further is "unconnected" with it.

Let us draw some implications from this example of a communication structure. First, affective relationships (although not necessarily bidirectional) are represented between all possible pairs, but unit relations are not. Feather says he does not include a unit relationship between, for example, source and issue because he is not sure what it would mean. We agree, but we are also uncertain what it means for the remaining pairs (with the possible exception of a positive unit relationship between S and C). For example, what does a negative unit relationship between S and C mean? If this means that S and C are not connected in any way, then S, the source, will not be perceived as the source—in which case S is not S but someone else (0?). When S says he is forced to read the communication, e.g., "I don't like it any better than you do, but it is the law," does the subject then perceive an additional person to be part of the communication structure? If so, the relationships of this element to other elements in the structure would have to be specified before a prediction could be made.

Note also that the unit relationship always assumes the same sign as the affective relationship. This suggests, following the lead of Abelson and Rosenberg, that perhaps the unit relationship is redundant with the affective relationship and can be discarded. Again, however, this is an empirical question.

Several of the previously mentioned criticisms of the Cartwright and Harary model also apply to Feather's model. It is interesting to note that Feather anticipates our criticisms and mentions several ways in which his model could be developed and extended: (1) there is no provision for variation in the "strength" of a relationship; (2) the model does not take account of the importance of the issue for either the source or the receiver (we discuss later considerable evidence on "importance" as a variable in attitude change); (3) it is difficult to predict what the specific effects of unbalance will be; (4) the model does not take into account individual differences in the degree to which people are able to tolerate inconsistencies. The last, self-acknowledged deficiency of the model has not been previously discussed. We will talk about it in some detail later.

In spite of the drawbacks of the model, it does represent an improvement in balance theory in several respects. It is more specific than the basic model and therefore one feels more confident in accounting for data with it. It is specifically oriented toward attitude change and attempts to be precise even though the attempt is far from complete. [See Feather (1967) for presentation and discussion of several role-playing experiments.] However, the model does not specify how unbalance would be reduced. This is a major drawback. Without such specification, we cannot predict whether attitude change will occur or not. The model represents attitude change as the change from a negative relationship between R and C to a positive relationship between R and C. In any given situation, we cannot specify whether this relationship or some other will change in the communication structure to restore balance. One is left with the conclusion that the model could be a powerful tool with some revisions.

Our account of models we have classified as variations on the basic Heider model ends at this point. Next we consider the consistency models of Osgood and Newcomb. Both bear some resemblance to Heider's model, even though we are considering them in their own right and not as variations of the basic model.

Other Consistency Models

OSGOOD'S CONGRUITY MODEL

This model (Osgood and Tannenbaum, 1955; Osgood, Suci, and Tannenbaum, 1957; Osgood, 1960; Tannenbaum, 1967) appears to be a special case of balance theory. That is, it is similar to Heider's theory but deals specifically with the problem of the acceptance of a communication. It has the advantage that it makes explicit predictions about both the direction and the extent of attitude change. It is a special case, however, since it only attempts to deal with one particular situation. In this special situation there is a person (P), P's attitude toward another person $(S$—the source), who gives information pro or con about an object, matter, or other person (O) about which P also holds an attitude. A typical situation might be: P likes S, P likes O, S says something bad about O. Osgood represents the communication by what S says about O. He indicates attitude change by the changes in P's evaluation of both S and O as a result of this communication. Recall that in

Heider's system, if P likes O, and P likes S, and S says something good about O (indicating for Heider that S likes O), then a state of balance exists. Heider predicts a lack of pressure for any of the three relationships involved to change. Heider and Osgood diverge at this point. In Osgood's model, whether a state of congruity (Osgood's alternative to the term balance) exists depends on *how much* P likes O and S. If P likes O just a little bit and likes S a great deal, then incongruity exists and produces psychological pressure for P to change his attitudes toward *both* O and S.[5] This satisfies one criticism we had previously expressed about balance theory, but note that it does require an operational procedure for quantification of the affective relationships involved in a triad.

Osgood uses his semantic differential (cf. Osgood, Suci, and Tannenbaum, 1957) to quantify the relationships. Although the semantic differential is so well-known in psychology that we need not discuss it here, we may note that in attitude change research Osgood uses mainly the evaluative dimension.[6] This gives a seven-point scale (ranging from $+3$ to -3) measuring the affective nature of the relationships of P to O and P to S. There is no attempt at quantification of the affective nature of the communication S delivers about O, other than labeling it something good (an associative bond in Osgood's terms) or something bad (a dissociative bond).

Osgood formulates two important hypotheses regarding the prediction and measurement of attitude change. First, he hypothesizes that when incongruity exists, P's attitudes toward both O and S will change. Other consistency theorists typically expect only one of these relationships to change. Second, Osgood hypothesizes that the interacting elements (P's attitudes toward O and S) will be modified in inverse proportion to their intensity or polarization. That is, given that some incongruity exists in the situation, Osgood asserts that the more extreme P's attitude is toward one of the "objects," the less will that attitude change.

Suppose we know that our subject, P, likes President Johnson quite a bit, say $+2$ on our scale, but he dislikes Mao Tze Tung a great deal, say -3. Let us put aside all reality demands and assume further

[5] The elements also have to be in "cognitive interaction" for incongruity to exist. The bond provided by the communication usually forces this interaction, however.

[6] As the reader may recall, the other two main factors loading on the semantic differential are potency and activation.

that Mao says something good about President Johnson. In essence we
have a −3 source being associated through the communication with
a +2 object. For Osgood, the prediction of the resultant change in attitude toward President Johnson is given by the formula

$$\text{Change}_O = \frac{|S|}{|O| + |S|} P$$

Where $/S/$ and $/O/$ = the absolute degree of polarization of P's
attitude toward S and O, respectively (in this case $/S/ = 3$ and $/O/ =
2$); and P = the pressure toward congruity, i.e., the total amount of
change necessary for perfect congruity to exist.

The "pressure toward congruity" requires some explanation. When
two elements are associatively linked—e.g., S says something good about
O—the congruity model predicts that the person will develop an identical attitude toward S and O. The total amount of change necessary
for this to occur is equal to the pressure toward congruity. To accomplish
this, in the preceding example, Johnson could move to −3, Mao could
move to +2, or both could move to, say, −1. For associative bonds,
then, the pressure toward congruity equals the algebraic difference in
evaluation of S and O. Thus pressure toward congruity in the above
example is five, and the predicted change of P's attitude toward O
is:

$$\text{Change}_O = \frac{3}{2 + 3} 5 = 3$$

Thus Osgood would predict that if Mao said something good about
President Johnson, P's attitude toward President Johnson would change
three units, or from +2 to −1. On the other hand, the change in
P's attitude toward Mao would be:

$$\text{Change}_S = \frac{|O|}{|O| + |S|} P = \frac{2}{2 + 3} 5 = 2$$

Thus P's attitude toward Mao would change two units, or from −3
to −1. Note that Osgood makes two clear predictions for this example:

1. When there is incongruity as the result of S's saying something
good about O, P's final attitude toward the source of the communication
and the object will be the same (in this case, P's final attitude toward
each is quantified as −1).

2. The most polarized or extreme attitude changes the least as the result of incongruity.

In our example, P's attitude toward President Johnson was less extreme than his attitude toward Mao (3 versus 2), and therefore P's attitude toward Mao would theoretically change less than his attitude toward President Johnson (2 versus 3).

We have demonstrated an associative bond. One derives predictions in the same manner for dissociative bonds, but one computes the pressure toward congruity differently. With dissociative bonds the pressure toward congruity is equivalent to the amount of change necessary for P's attitude toward the source and the object to be equidistant from zero. Hence, if the example above read "Mao says something bad about President Johnson," the pressure toward congruity would have been one rather than five. In addition, as the reader may compute for himself, P's attitude toward President Johnson would have changed 0.6 units (to $+2.6$), and his attitude toward Mao would have changed 0.4 units (to -2.6). See Fig. 4.4 for a graphic representation of these two examples.

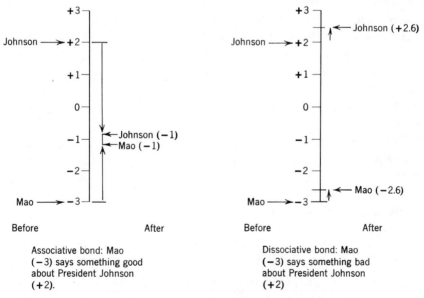

Associative bond: Mao (-3) says something good about President Johnson ($+2$).

Dissociative bond: Mao (-3) says something bad about President Johnson ($+2$)

FIGURE 4.4. Examples of theoretical attitude change as a result of associative and dissociative bonds. In both cases, President Johnson is assumed to have been rated $+2$ and Mao -3 prior to the communication (see text).

This is how one derives predictions from the model. It is a separate question, of course, about how accurate the predictions are. Osgood's predictions for attitude change have been directly tested only a few times [although see Tannenbaum (1967) for an excellent presentation of related literature]. Let us look at one or two of these experiments.

SUPPORTING DATA. In his dissertation, Tannenbaum (1953) first used the semantic differential to ascertain subjects' attitudes toward particular sources and objects. He later presented subjects with bogus newspaper articles in which pro or con statements were attributed to some of the sources about some of the objects. The sources he used were the *Chicago Tribune*, Senator Taft, and "labor leaders." The objects were abstract art, accelerated college programs, and legalized gambling. Later subjects rerated both the sources and the objects. Tannenbaum made predictions about changes in attitudes toward both the sources and objects by means of the congruity formulas we have just discussed. Tannenbaum found that the congruity model predicted quite well in this situation, but only if two "corrections" were made. Let us look at these corrections more closely.

First, the model implies that P changes his opinion equally about the source of the communication and the object of the communication. Tannenbaum found that this was not borne out by the data and that there was a consistent "directional shift." The change in the attitude toward the object or concept was consistently greater than the change in the attitude toward the source. This makes sense when one thinks of it in the following way: Suppose we hear person x say something about person y. What does this tell us about x and y? Unless what x has said is either an obvious lie or an obviously brilliant and original insight, we have probably learned much more about y from the communication than we have about x. If so, there is no reason to expect the attitude change toward x and y to be the same. If we add to this analysis the fact that y in Osgood's paradigm is often an object or a concept, then this merely strengthens our case for a difference in change toward x and y.[7]

More specifically, the magnitude of the respective shifts should depend upon how important x and y are to the subject. Indeed, Rokeach and Rothman (1965) found that predictions are significantly better when

---

[7] However, it is another question whether this directional shift has some constant value, as sometimes asserted in the literature.

one takes account of the importance of the separate items. The more important the subject thinks x is, say, the more it affects his evaluation of x and y in combination. Implicatively, the more important the source is to the subject, the greater the change in attitude about the object and the less about the source. The reverse would presumably be true, the more important the object.

In addition to the "directional shift" mentioned above, Tannenbaum found a second systematic error in the predictions of the model. For higher levels of "pressure toward congruity," subjects tended not to accept the assertion, but instead to reject it as false. Tannenbaum referred to this as the "correction for incredulity" and found that it was necessary to utilize this correction when the pressure was between three and six. Utilizing corrections for both directional shift and incredulity, Tannenbaum found a correlation of .91 between the predicted and obtained magnitude of the attitude change scores.

In another experiment (discussed in Osgood, 1960) Kerrick induced subjects to rate photographs and captions separately and then together. Using the ratings of the photographs and captions alone, he predicted, using the congruity model, how certain combinations of photographs and captions would be rated together. Kerrick found that if the captions and photographs originally had opposite signs, then congruity theory made adequate predictions (i.e., both became less extreme). However, if the picture and the caption had similar signs, Kerrick found that they *summated*, rather than being a compromise between the two ratings. For example, two things rated "good" alone were rated better in combination than either of them alone. The congruity model predicts that the rating of the combination would always be somewhere between the two individual ratings. Further corroboration of this finding in other areas has been provided by Fishbein and his associates (Fishbein, 1965; Fishbein and Hunter, 1964; Triandis and Fishbein, 1965). Evidence is now needed to decide when "summation" takes place and when congruity takes place. The reader is referred to Triandis and Fishbein for further details of this argument, and to Abelson (1968) for a Heiderian interpretation of summation.

The "correction for incredulity" raises another possible criticism of the model. The question is whether this correction is not throwing out a good deal of information that is useful and valuable for attitude research and theorizing. With a seven-point scale as Osgood uses, the total possible pressure toward congruity would be six. Osgood essentially eliminates from consideration all situations in which the pressure is between three and six. In other words, he disregards two-thirds of the measurement scale. He thinks that people simply do not believe assertions that are much different or discrepant from their own. The question then becomes "Is there something psychologically meaningful and lawful occurring in situations where there are assertions made that are quite discrepant from the subject's?" or is it simply that "Subjects don't believe assertions much different from their own"?

The evidence reviewed in the next two chapters suggests that the extent to which subjects "believe" the communication under these conditions may be manipulated and regulated in lawful ways. A detailed discussion of this point is better left to the next chapter. We may note for now that this is one criticism of the model.

Another criticism has to do with the quantification of incongruity. At present, the degree of incongruity, i.e., the pressure toward congruity, is merely a joint function of the evaluations of the source and object and whether the bond involved is associative or dissociative. This "bond" is really the communication, and as such deserves more attention than a two-category classification. Consider the following. Suppose Arthur Goldberg is $+2.0$ on Osgood's scale and Fidel Castro is -2.0. Suppose Castro makes some associative assertion about Goldberg. Ignoring the assertion constant, Osgood's prediction would seem to be that the subject's evaluation of each person would be zero (or if we corrected for incredulity, he would say that there probably would be no change). However, we are suggesting that our prediction should depend to some extent on how positive the assertion was.[8] It is an entirely different thing for Castro to say that Goldberg is the nicest person he has ever met than for him to say that Goldberg is not as bad as most people think. The latter assertion is perhaps more likely to produce attitude change toward Goldberg, Castro, or both than the former assertion. Plausible as this suggested revision is, the correlation of .91 reported by Tannenbaum indicates that Osgood's model accounts for much more of the variance than is typical for theories of attitude change.

In summary then we may say that although Osgood's model is very

[8] Actually, Osgood et al. (1957) did speculate that degree of incongruity might be related to the intensity of the assertion, but no attempt has been made to study this directly. Tannenbaum (1967) reports a study in which the argument of the communication is refuted, but this seems at best an indirect manipulation of intensity.

narrow in scope (i.e., as a special case of balance theory), it is well articulated and one can make very precisely quantified predictions. The work of Fishbein and Rokeach suggests some qualifications. In addition we have suggested that the necessity for the corrections for directional shift and incredulity may be masking real and important psychological processes. We need more data indicating the conditions under which attitudes toward the source will or will not change, and the incredulity correction may be throwing the baby out with the bath water. Also, the model fails to consider the strength or intensity of the bonding between elements. Other questions still remain, e.g., whether the assertion constant (directional shift) is really a constant and whether the probability of incredulity is an inverse function of the polarization of the elements involved. Further, Chapter 5 discusses data and theory related to a negative relationship between polarization of attitude and amount of change. The incongruity model will have to be reconciled with these data. In spite of these criticisms, considering the ambiguities and lack of precision in the usual "theory" of attitude change, Osgood's theory and theorizing provide a delightful change of pace.

NEWCOMB'S STRAIN TOWARD SYMMETRY

This discussion of Newcomb's model (1953; 1956; 1958; 1959; 1961) will be relatively short. This model is often mentioned in the literature as a "consistency" theory of attitude change. To some extent it is. But it is not so much a theory of attitude change as a theory of interpersonal attraction.

Newcomb's model deals with two people (A and B), their attitudes toward each other and an object (X). He assumes that A's "orientation" (attitude) toward B and toward X are interdependent, and that there is a "persistent strain toward symmetry" (i.e., balance) among the relationships involved. Although Newcomb (1953, p. 399) says that "The foregoing propositions represent only a slight extrapolation of Heider's general principle of balanced states," it is sometimes very difficult to tell whether the symmetry discussed at any given point is a phenomenological one in the life space of A (á la Heider) or a structural description imposed by the experimenter (á la Cartwright and Harary). It seems clear, however, that Newcomb intended his principle to apply to both phenomenological and structural events.

Given that A and B disagree about the worth of X, the amount of strain toward symmetry depends upon the intensity of A's attitude toward X and his attraction to B. Increasing the intensity of this attitude and attraction increases (1) the strain toward symmetry; (2) the likelihood of symmetry; and (3) the probability that A will communicate to B about X (in an attempt to persuade him, presumably). It is this "communicative act" from A to B about X (A to B re X, in Newcomb's terms) that should pique our interest here. Newcomb says that the "likelihood of a symmetry-directed A to B re X varies as a multiple function of the perceived discrepancy (i.e., inversely with perceived symmetry), with valence toward B and with valence toward X" (1953, p. 398).

Newcomb also directs himself to the question of why there should be a "persistent strain toward symmetry." A strain toward symmetry, he says, develops because communicative acts resulting in increased symmetry are likely to be rewarded and symmetry may thereby acquire secondary reward value. The authors are aware of no evidence on either point, but this does seem to be at some variance with other consistency theorists. Although the other theorists are not explicit on this point, they appear to assume that both the discomfort resulting from unbalance or dissonance and the desire to reduce unbalance or dissonance are developmental or maturational phenomena. Although we run the risk of either overinterpreting or misinterpreting other theorists (largely because they have not discussed the issue), there seems to be no indication in other models that this is learned. There is some evidence indicating that children have less "need" to be cognitively consistent, but this does not indicate whether this is a simple maturational variable or it is somehow learned. One of the main implications of this question is directed toward generalizing to other cultures. If it is a maturational variable, then one would expect that the "need to be cognitively consistent" would be rather invariant from culture to culture. If, however, it is learned, one would expect considerable differences between cultures depending on what children are taught and, perhaps, at what ages. We might expect some cultures to teach the value of inconsistency, for example. However, the question of the source of the basic motive postulated by consistency theorists remains an open but intriguing one.

To continue, Heider's model and that of Newcomb differ at several points. As we have mentioned, the present model does not clearly specify when the symmetry is phenomenological or structural. In addition, Newcomb places more emphasis on communication than does Heider. The greater the lack of symmetry, the greater the probability that A will communicate to B re X. This communication will not go on forever, however, as Schachter (1951) demonstrated in a well known experiment. Newcomb's emphasis on communication leads to differential predictions by the Heiderian model and the present one. For Heider, if A likes B and A likes X, but B does not like X, then either A comes to dislike B or he comes to dislike X. In this analysis B apparently may never know what went on. For Newcomb, if A likes B and X, but B does not like X, then the first thing to occur will be that A will communicate to B in an attempt to influence his feelings about X. However, Newcomb apparently does not rule out the possibility that A will come to dislike B or X with or without communication.

A more important question may be asked from the point of view of this book: Given that A communicates to B re X, is B going to change his attitude toward X? If so, why? Although we are interested in the question of attitude change, Newcomb's theory does not address itself directly to this question. For example, Newcomb's model predicts that people will associate or become friends with people with whom they agree. This conclusion is relevant to a study of attitude change only in the sense that a person will not change his attitude unless he comes into contact with people or information that is at variance with his present attitude. Newcomb also makes predictions about the relationship of interpersonal attraction to attitude change. The more A is attracted to B (or to a group), the greater the opinion change on the part of A toward the opinion held by B (or by the group). At the time that Newcomb published his theory, there already had been several experiments published showing a positive relationship between attraction and influence (e.g., Schachter, 1951; Back, 1951; Festinger, Schachter, and Back, 1950). Consequently these data do not provide a test of the Newcomb model since the theorizing came after the data had been obtained. In addition, now other data (Kiesler, 1963; Kiesler and Corbin, 1965; Kiesler, Zanna, and De Salvo, 1966) indicate that under some conditions at least there is a nonmonotonic relationship between attraction and ability to influence. That is, under some conditions (e.g., commitment to continue in the relationship), lowering the attraction between A and B may increase the influence of A over B.

In sum, the Newcomb model does not have a great deal to say about attitude change, although apparently (judging from the number of times it has been alluded to by others) many workers in the area of attitude change would disagree with this statement. In fairness to Newcomb, the model has been used mostly by him in the area of interpersonal attraction (who will like whom, and so forth). Readers interested in such an application of the model should read Newcomb's book on the topic (1961). Indeed, considering the application of Newcomb's model, some consider him to have put balance theory to its most severe test in terms of external validity.

Some Criticisms of Consistency Theories

We have discussed six variations of balance theory in this chapter. The basic model is Heider's. Others add to or subtract from the basic model, depending on their research strategies and interests. Cartwright and Harary try to quantify balance and also to apply it to groups. Abelson and Rosenberg simplify the basic model, but add predictive power by proposing how balance will be restored (i.e., by least effort). Feather takes detailed account of variables related to communication effects. Osgood also tries his hand at quantification, but limits his theoretical variation to the effects of communication in a particular setting. Newcomb appears less interested in the effects of communication than in precisely when the communication will occur and what its content will be. Despite the variations, we will discuss the consistency theories as a group. Criticisms of the theories are listed below, in no particular order. We have not yet discussed one consistency theory, dissonance theory, and the reader should not conclude that these criticisms also apply to dissonance theory necessarily. Some do apply and some do not.

1. As the reader may have guessed, our first criticism of consistency theories is that there are too many of them. When the theories are so similar in structure and purportedly deal with similar data and concepts, there is little advantage in this proliferation. More important, however, there is very little evidence either supporting an individual model or indicating its superiority over another model. The only consistency theory with much evidence related to it is dissonance theory. However, it is difficult to pit one model against another in an empirical test, because the separate theorists do not relate specific statements in their theories to theoretical statements the others make about the same phenomena.

2. There is a lack of precision in the predictions that the individual theories make. Except for Osgood perhaps, no one really says to himself, "The data must come out this way or the theory is obviously wrong." In addition to the equivocality about predictions, there is no real attempt to derive predictions that are theoretically unique. However, in the case where the theories simply do not predict well, we may decide against all of them.

3. There is little attention paid to quantifying the *degree* of inconsistency, again with Osgood (and his critics, Rokeach and Fishbein) being the obvious exception. Unless we may quantify and specify the degree of inconsistency, the predictions drawn will necessarily be somewhat loose.

4. As we tried to point out in our discussion of Heider's model, there is little attention paid to the complexity of the individual case. This applies equally well to the other models as well. However, our concern with this point would be lessened if the models predicted better.

5. McGuire (1966) notes that although consistency theorists hypothesize a basic need for consistency, others (e.g., Berlyne, 1960) are working on what appears to be a motive in the opposite direction. He says, "The . . . (consistent) . . . organism has a penchant for stability, redundancy, familiarity, confirmation of expectance, avoidance of the new, the unpredictable. Complexity theory's romantic organism works on a quite different economy. It has a stimulus hunger, an exploratory drive, a need curiosity. It takes pleasure in the unexpected . . . it finds novelty rewarding" (McGuire, 1966, p. 37). A note of theoretical challenge rings in the air. However, McGuire may have overstated the case. The desire to organize one's cognitive world into a good gestalt (the consistency principle) need not conflict with a desire to know or to explore. The fact that a child or a monkey will manipulate a complex latch or a toy for hours or that a person will look longer at an unusual picture (e.g., an elephant without a trunk) does not conflict with consistency theory necessarily. The integration of these two research areas should not be far off.

6. There has been little concern with the content of the communication and with degrees or kinds of reactions to sources of communication. Other research indicates that these are important variables to take into account.

We may add to this list of criticisms that in spite of everything consistency theories appear to be the most exciting development in attitude change research in the last ten years. However, the greatest amount of experimental research and most certainly the most ingenious experimental designs have come from the dissonance theory advocates. When we have looked more closely at dissonance theory and the experimental data associated with it, we may return to further and more particularistic criticisms of consistency theory in general. In addition, at that time, several of the theoretical issues in consistency theory that are currently being debated will be discussed.

Chapter 5

Dissonance Theory

ALTHOUGH dissonance theory is a type of consistency or balance theory, the large amount of data it has generated justifies a separate presentation. We should note that the theory is one of the most controversial in social psychology today. While controversy typically provokes emotional reactions, we hope to provide an exception. For other dispassionate criticisms, we refer the reader to Zajonc (1960), Brown (1962), and particularly Osgood (1960).

Since the theory has been revised somewhat by Brehm and Cohen (1962) and Aronson (1968), among others, we will try to indicate theoretical points which depart from the original version (Festinger, 1957). These revisions presumably allow more specific and unequivocal predictions. Other implicit revisions stem from individual experiments. In these experiments the specific predictions are derived from dissonance theory, but require at least one extra assumption. In some instances, such experiments are so well known that the additional assumptions can be treated as integral parts of the theory.

As indicated, the theory is a consistency theory. It is concerned with the relations among "cognitive elements" and the consequences when elements are inconsistent with one another. Cognitive elements are defined as bits of knowledge, or opinions or beliefs about oneself, about one's behavior, and about one's surroundings in the environment. Thus two cognitive elements may be: "The knowledge that I smoke heavily" and "The knowledge that smoking causes cancer."

In this theory, three possible relationships among elements are posited: (1) they may be irrelevant to one another (the knowledge that I smoke heavily, and the knowledge that it is raining in Algeria); (2) they may be consistent with one another (the knowledge that I smoke heavily and the knowledge that smokers are regarded as more masculine), referred to by Festinger as a *consonant* relationship; and (3) they may be inconsistent with one another (the knowledge that I smoke heavily and the knowledge that smoking causes cancer), referred to by Festinger as a *dissonant* relationship.

It is important to emphasize that the relationship between elements need not necessarily be *logically* consistent or inconsistent. It could be *psychological* as well. This should be obvious from example 2 above. More generally, dissonance is the consequence of "nonfitting" relations among cognitions. "Let us consider two elements which exist in a person's cognition and which are relevant to one another. The definition of dissonance will disregard the existence of all the other cognitive elements that are relevant to either or both of the two under consideration and simply deals with these two alone. *These two elements are in a dissonant relation if, considering these two alone, the obverse*[1] *of one element would follow from the other.* To state it a bit more formally, x and y are dissonant if not-x follows from y" (Festinger, 1957, p. 13). Festinger says that dissonance may arise from one or more of four different sources: logical inconsistency; cultural mores; one specific opinion being included, by definition, in a more general opinion (e.g., Republicans for Johnson); and past experience. Each of these potential "sources" of dissonance provides a somewhat different definition of "follows from" in the preceding definition of dissonance.

Clearly, then, logical inconsistency is not the only source of dissonance. To specify whether dissonance stems from some source other than logical inconsistency requires information about the person's previous experience, his cultural background, his present belief system, or his motivations in life. This definition of dissonance is both a strong and a weak point of the theory. It gives the theory breadth, but it sometimes makes it

[1] The word "obverse" is actually misused in dissonance theory. Indeed, the meaning of obverse is exactly opposite to what Festinger intended. The obverse of a proposition is a particular formulation that is logically equivalent to the original. It is a proposition inferred immediately from another by denying the opposite of that which the first proposition affirms. Thus the obverse of the proposition, "All A is B," is "No A is not-B." Although, strictly speaking, it is incorrect usage, we have used it in this chapter in deference to the original and subsequent formulations. However, the words "opposite" or "negation" would be more correct.

difficult to specify clearly the existence of dissonance in a given situation. For instance, take our example of the two cognitions, "the knowledge that I smoke heavily" and "the knowledge that smokers are regarded as more masculine." Though these two cognitions are likely to be consonant for a man, they are probably dissonant for a woman. In this case, one's view of oneself is the crucial variable. In other words, a third cognitive element is necessary to analyze most dissonance situations. This third element states a value or preference which implies the relation between the two other elements. It may be of the form "I am a masculine person" or "I am not the sort of person who lies or cheats" or "I am the sort of person who makes 'good' decisions." The above two cognitions then may be consonant for some men, dissonant for others, and even irrelevant for some, depending on the third cognitive element.

This ambiguity in translating the theory into experimentation can produce difficulties. For instance, we may usually make the assumption that people have a good opinion of themselves and desire to do well (e.g., on experimental tasks). But it is also obvious that not all people have this opinion of themselves and this may complicate matters in particular circumstances for some (or all) subjects. For example, Aronson and Carlsmith (1962b) have demonstrated that when one experimentally lowers a person's perception of his ability to perform a given task, doing well on the task at a later time creates dissonance. The knowledge that "I am terrible at this task" is dissonant with the knowledge that "I just performed well at it." In terms of translation from the theory, this means that if we attempt to manipulate dissonance by having people perform badly at a task, our success depends on their opinion of themselves. To the extent that a subject has a high opinion of himself, our manipulation creates dissonance. Our success in creating dissonance will vary according to the variation in self-esteem in our sample of subjects, leaving our experimental manipulation of dissonance somewhat less than perfect. The importance of this ambiguity would vary from experiment to experiment. In one, it might merely increase the variance of dissonance produced within conditions, but in another it could mean that no dissonance was produced at all.

To return to the theory itself, Festinger states that there are two basic hypotheses to his theory:

1. The existence of dissonance creates psychological tension or discomfort and will *motivate* the person to reduce the dissonance and achieve

consonance. This is very similar to the basic assumption of all of the consistency theories.

2. When dissonance exists, not only will the person attempt to reduce it, but he will actively attempt to avoid situations and information which would increase the dissonance.

Although Festinger refers to these as hypotheses, they might more properly be called postulates.

As we have said, the existence of dissonance produces pressures to reduce the dissonance. The greater the dissonance, the greater is the pressure. In turn, the magnitude of the dissonance is a function of two things: the importance of the elements and the weighted proportion of the elements that are in a dissonant relationship. The difficulty of specifying either or both of these properties is to some extent a rather weak point of the theory and requires discussion.

What is meant by the importance of the elements? This is never really made very clear in the theoretical expositions, but importance seems to be a two-pronged variable. For one thing it seems to mean how important the element qua element is for the person, though this too is often difficult to specify. For instance, how important is the element, "I smoke heavily"? The question does not seem to make much sense, especially in terms of quantification, except perhaps in the sense of asking "How addicted to cigarettes am I?" or "How difficult would it be for me to quit smoking?" The ambiguity is further heightened by the fact that for this theory the last two questions clearly refer to an element's resistance to change. An element's resistance to change and its importance are quite different theoretically. The concept of resistance to change tells us how dissonance will be reduced; the concept of importance tells us how much dissonance exists. The other aspect of the importance variable seems to be the implications of the element. The element "I am married" would seem to have great importance in terms of its *implications* (re correct behavior, cost of being divorced, and so forth), but does this mean that the element is thereby more important? The theory is unclear on this point. Thus, while importance is integral to the theory for specifying the magnitude of dissonance, we cannot readily compare or quantify the importance of different elements.

Specifying the magnitude of dissonance by means of the weighted proportion of the elements in a dissonant relationship is more difficult, and is for the most part ignored in the literature. The problem is this.

Most of the situational analyses by dissonance theorists are performed using a two-element simplification. Consider the case of the person who smokes heavily and who is presented with the Surgeon-General's report as a birthday present. Given that he reads the report (a problem we will ignore for the moment), theorists tend to analyze the situation in terms of these two elements: "the knowledge that I smoke heavily," and "the knowledge that smoking causes cancer." They make the two-element analysis for simplicity and ease of presentation (in an article, for instance), but it simply does not do justice to the complexity of the situation. There are really not two elements, but rather two *clusters* of elements that are relevant and that contribute to the degree of dissonance aroused. One cluster of elements consists of those that are consistent with smoking (masculinity, habit, addiction, fear of not being able to quit, etc.) and the other cluster is composed of elements that are inconsistent with smoking (disease, social disapproval, messiness, cost, fear of dying, etc.). One thing that contributes to the degree of dissonance then is the relative number of elements in each cluster: the more *equal* the number, the *greater* the dissonance. Further, each element contributes to the magnitude of dissonance in proportion to its importance. Dissonance is monotonically related to the number of dissonant elements, *each weighted for its importance.*

If one wished to quantify the importance of the separate elements more formally, then we suggest that the magnitude of dissonance should be equal to:

$$D = \frac{\Sigma K P_{1i}}{\Sigma K P_{2j}} = \frac{\sum_{i=1}^{i} P_{1i}}{\sum_{j=1}^{j} P_{2j}} = \frac{T_i}{T_j}$$

where

$$\begin{aligned} D &= \text{magnitude of dissonance} \\ P_{1i} &= \text{the importance of element } i \text{ in cluster 1} \\ P_{2j} &= \text{the importance of element } j \text{ in cluster 2} \\ K &= \text{a constant} \end{aligned}$$

and where

$$T_i \leq T_j$$

In other words, the largest number is made the denominator in the equation, giving a range of the possible magnitude of dissonance from 0 to 1.

After obtaining the data necessary for proper scaling one might find that a more elaborate system of constants would be necessary for precise quantification. In addition, Secord and Backman (1964) have pointed out that this type of formula for quantifying dissonance is in error for another reason. One can think of two situations where the cognitive elements involved in the dissonant relationships are of vastly different importance, but where the ratios would be the same for the two situations. The formula suggests equal dissonance for the two situations, but the theory maintains that the situation involving the more important cognitive elements would produce greater dissonance. Thus Secord and Backman suggest weighting the ratio by the mean importance of the elements entering into the dissonant relationship. The necessity of this addition, however, implies that "importance" is not a unitary variable in dissonance theory. Instead there appear to be two distinct types of importance, and both are necessary to specify the degree of dissonance. Also, the formula ignores the number and importance of consonant elements involved in the relationship. Nevertheless, this formula may be used for a rough estimate of the relative magnitude of dissonance.

This discussion illustrates the difficulty of quantifying dissonance. But it is an important problem and we shall return to it several times in this chapter. It has implications for methods of reducing dissonance and for manipulating the degree of dissonance. Attempts at quantification at this time have resulted only in a weak ordinal scale, and then only within experiments rather than across experiments. In terms of the research carried out to test this theory, this level of quantification has been sufficient. However, such a low level of quantification is not satisfactory for a theory of any (continuing) power, and for the theory to achieve precision, this problem will have to be solved.

As we have mentioned, the lack of effort in this direction is related to the fact that dissonance researchers have continued to find it useful to utilize a two-element simplification in their situational analyses. This simplification has misled several critics of the theory into thinking that Festinger and his associates do not recognize the complexity of the individual case. A typical example of this error is that of Chapanis and Chapanis (1964):

"Which brings us now to the crux of the matter: *is it really possible to reduce the essentials of a complex social situation to just two phrases?* Reluctantly we must say 'No.' To condense most complex social situations into two, and only two, simple dissonant statements represents so great a level of abstraction that the model no longer bears any reasonable resemblance to reality" (p. 21, their italics).

It is obvious that these critics mistake a simplification for the full theory. The theory seems to recognize individual complexity, but researchers thus far have found the two-element simplification useful for generating predictions in experimental settings. We may parenthetically note that all relevant clusters should be considered, and the number may be larger than two. In addition, Chapanis and Chapanis should recognize that one evaluates the usefulness of a theory on such grounds as the amount of data it accounts for and not necessarily on the basis of a semantic isomorphism with previous descriptions of "reality." As Hall and Lindzey (1957) have noted with regard to personality theories, it is ". . . high time the theorist was freed from obligation to justify theoretical formulations that depart from normative or customary views of behavior" (1957, p. 552, italics in original).

We have addressed ourselves to the definition of dissonance and its measurement. We may now ask the question: Given that dissonance (theoretically) exists between two clusters of cognitive elements, how may it be reduced? Festinger lists three theoretical ways of reducing dissonance. Each may have several behavioral manifestations.

1. The person may change a cognitive element related to his behavior. This could involve a change in the behavior or possibly a denial or distortion of the behavior. Consider the dissonance between "the knowledge that I smoke heavily" and "the knowledge that smoking causes cancer and related diseases" (we too will use the two-element case for the sake of simplicity). This dissonance can obviously be reduced by a change in the behavior associated with one of the dissonant elements, i.e., quit smoking. But some dissonance may still remain as a result of any one of several possible elements that may be dissonant with not smoking such as feelings of lessened masculinity or a feeling that because one smoked in the past one is therefore still susceptible to these diseases. Extrapolating from this we can see that to quit smoking would not necessarily even reduce dissonance for all people; it would, however, reduce dissonance for most. The denial or distortion of the behavior might also be difficult to maintain. For example, to distort the number of cigarettes smoked is one way to reduce the dissonance, but the pressures of reality might make it difficult to maintain this self-deceit.

2. The person may change a cognitive element related to his environment. This method of reducing dissonance presumably involves changing the environment in some way, whether this be the physical environment or the psychological environment. Obviously changing the physical environment is more difficult but still possible. If a person is very uncomfortable in cold weather but continues to live in the north, dissonance could be reduced by a physical move to a warmer climate. Alternatively, one could psychologically change the environment by asserting, for example, that the "dry" cold of Minnesota is not really that bad.

3. The third way that a person may reduce dissonance is to add new cognitive elements to one cluster or the other or both. Obviously, this method will not completely eliminate the dissonance but it will reduce it. This may be enough, however, and presumably would involve seeking out other information. If our cold-blooded person in the preceding example is a college professor, he may seek out information that tells him that the northern universities are of higher quality than the southern ones, and further that the professors in the northern universities are paid much more than their southern counterparts. Given that he feels that either or both of these items are important, they would reduce the dissonance he feels about continuing to live in the north.

These points state how a person may reduce or eliminate dissonance. But they do not tell us if a person who has dissonance will merely live with it, or if he will reduce it in some particular manner. There are really two basic questions here. First, how much dissonance can a person live with before some change occurs? And second, given that dissonance will be reduced in some manner, what changes in behavior or attitudes will occur? Both of these questions are basic to the theme of this book: when will attitude change occur and which attitudes will change?

Festinger answers the first question quite precisely. "The maximum dissonance that can possibly exist between any two elements is equal to the total resistance to change of the less resistant element. The magnitude of dissonance cannot exceed this amount because, at this point of maximum possible dissonance, the less resistant element would change, thus eliminating the dissonance" (1957, p. 28, all italics in original). Of course, he goes on to say that dissonance need not be at the maximum amount before some change occurs. At levels lower than this maximum, dissonance may be reduced by adding new cognitive elements. Probably this is the more typical case. So with extremely large amounts of dissonance, we may be reasonably certain that something will happen, that dissonance will be reduced. At lower levels of dissonance, we are less certain that dissonance will be reduced, but if it is reduced, the method of adding new cognitive elements will be preferred (over changing any of the elements involved in the dissonant relationship). Although this seems unclear for an individual subject, the theory does allow ordinal predictions between experimental conditions. If we can say that people in condition x have less dissonance than those in condition y, then the probability of each person in condition x reducing dissonance in some manner is less than the probability of each person in condition y doing so. We can then state quite explicitly that, as a group, people in condition x will show less *evidence* of dissonance reduction attempts than those in condition y. Thus, although the predictions may be unclear for any *individual,* they are quite explicit for comparisons between groups of individuals.

From Festinger's original presentation of dissonance theory, it is difficult to state precisely *how* dissonance will be reduced, e.g., which elements will be changed or which may be added. Brehm and Cohen (1962) argue that for dissonance theory to make unequivocal predictions concerning how dissonance will be reduced, one must introduce the variable of psychological commitment. They "assume that a person is committed . . . (if) . . . he has decided to do or not to do a certain thing, when he has chosen one (or more) alternatives and thereby rejected one (or more) alternatives, when he actively engages in a given behavior or has engaged in a given behavior" (1962, p. 7).

The addition of the commitment variable, they argue, allows one to do two things. First, it permits the specification of the existence of dissonance. That is, if one eats a vegetable that he dislikes, we are more confident that dissonance exists than if he merely agrees to eat the disliked vegetable (not that more dissonance necessarily exists, however). This makes it easier to put the theory "on the line" in tests against other theories, and increases the power of the theory to make predictions in individual cases. Second, it allows one to make more specific predictions about *how* dissonance will be reduced. Let us be more specific on this point. Theoretically, when one changes a cognitive element involved in a dissonant relationship, one always changes the less resistant element. Hence to derive predictions from the theory, we must be able to specify in advance which element is least resistant to change. Brehm and Cohen argue that commitment allows this specification, if one assumes that greater commitment to some behavior makes the cognitive element corresponding to that behavior more resistant to change.

Considerable evidence in a wide variety of situations has been accumulated by Festinger, his students, and associates concerning predictions derived by dissonance theory. In general, this evidence has supported the theory. However, recent evidence indicates some situational or other limitations of the model. We shall attempt to summarize some of the relevant experimental evidence, pro and con. Some of the evidence on both sides is solid and easily provides guideposts for future theorizing in attitude change.

To aid the reader we have attempted to categorize the wide diversity of situations and experimental paradigms in which dissonance theory has been applied. As examples, we have chosen two research areas, decision-making and forced compliance, for more detailed presentation. This chapter also contains brief summaries of research on several other topics. In addition, the topic of attitudinal discrepancy is discussed in depth in Chapter 6.

Dissonance and Decision-Making

Let us clarify the theoretical implications of dissonance theory about decision-making before proceeding to the evidence. First, the theory is relevant to the case where the person chooses among two or more alternatives, and by implication rejects the remaining alternatives. Thus Festinger maintains that merely stating *preferences* among alternatives does not in and of itself produce dissonance. Second, Festinger distinguishes between dissonance, a psychological process that occur after a decision, and conflict, presumably a process that occurs before a decision.

"The person is in a conflict situation before making the decision. After having made the decision he is no longer in conflict; he has made his choice; he has, so to speak, resolved the conflict. He is no longer being pushed in two or more directions simultaneously. He is now committed to the chosen course of action. It is only here that dissonance exists, and the pressure to reduce this dissonance is *not* pushing the person in two directions simultaneously" (Festinger, 1957, p. 39).

We will return to this point because of some theoretical disagreement about what goes on before and what after a decision.

Dissonance theory specifies four variables that affect the degree of dissonance following a decision.

1. The more important the decision, the greater the dissonance. Thus the prospective home owner deciding between two houses will have more dissonance (after the choice) than someone deciding between two brands of shaving cream.

2. The less attractive the chosen alternative (relative to the unchosen), the greater the dissonance.

3. The more attractive the unchosen alternative (relative to the chosen), the greater the dissonance.

We may state two and three more generally: any aspect of either alternative which, when considered alone, would lead to a different decision (i.e., choosing the other alternative) increases dissonance. Thus both negative aspects of the chosen alternative and positive aspects of the unchosen alternative have the effect of increasing the dissonance.

4. The greater the cognitive overlap (in general, read "similarity" for cognitive overlap) between alternatives, the less the dissonance. Presumably therefore a decision involving buying one of two cars would involve less dissonance than a decision between one car and a boat or a trip to Europe (other things being equal).

These are the general theoretical implications of dissonance theory for decision-making. Let us turn to some of the experimental evidence.

Brehm (1956) provided the first explicit test of dissonance predictions for decision-making. Briefly, each subject rated a series of objects, chose for herself one of two objects offered her, and then rerated the objects. To create a high dissonance condition, Brehm had some subjects choose between two objects quite close in attractiveness. Subjects in the low dissonance condition chose between two objects farther apart in attractiveness. Brehm predicted that subjects in the high dissonance condition would show greater evidence of dissonance reduction. That is, in comparison to their predecision ratings, they would exaggerate the attractiveness of the chosen alternative and underestimate the attractiveness of the unchosen alternative more than would subjects in the low dissonance condition. The prediction was generally confirmed. Since this experiment has become the prototype for applying dissonance theory to decision-making, it warrants detailed presentation and discussion.

Two hundred twenty-five female college students were told they were taking part in a market research study and that, as compensation, they would each be given a gift from one of the manufacturers participating in the study. Their first task was to rate each of eight similarly priced products (e.g., a toaster, a silk screen print) on a separate eight-point a priori rating scale. Thirty subjects were then "given" one of the products as their gift. This gift condition acted as a control condition to rule out possible explanations of the data based on such observations as "people tend to like what they own." By comparing this condition against the experimental conditions, one may test for the effects of choosing an alternative over and above that of merely owning it. The experimental subjects were told that they should have some degree of choice in the matter and were asked to choose which of two products they wished to have. Having chosen, they were given the product.

Each person was then asked to read bogus research reports on four of the products. Each of the reports discussed both good and bad aspects of one product. For half of the experimental subjects, these research reports dealt with products not involved in the choice. For the other half, two of the reports were about the products involved in the choice. Brehm expected that providing information on the choice objects would facilitate dissonance reduction. Each subject then rerated each of the eight objects. The excuse for this was that the first rating might be considered a first impression and that now the subjects had had more time to think about each product.

One final point should be made before we look at the data. The selection of the pairs of objects for choice was based on subjects' preratings. By manipulation, the attractiveness rating of the more attractive alternative (ultimately the chosen alternative[2]) was the same for all conditions. Thus the differential dissonance between conditions was due to the differential attractiveness of the less attractive alternative. The dependent variable was the change in perceived attractiveness of each

[2] There is an interesting experimental and theoretical point to be raised here. Actually, 48 of the subjects did *not* choose the object they had initially rated as the more attractive of the two. These subjects were discarded from the analysis, for which Brehm has been criticized (Chapanis and Chapanis, 1964). It is difficult to suggest what should be done with these subjects, partly because we do not know why they chose as they did. It might have been due to a change in opinion before the choice or, as Brehm suggests, due simply to the unreliability of the rating scale. It is quite clear, however, that had Brehm included them in his analysis, his results would have been statistically stronger, due to the obviously artifactual "dissonance reduction." We shall discuss some of the problems of discarding subjects later in the chapter.

alternative. There were presumably two main ways to reduce dissonance here: increasing the perceived attractiveness of the chosen alternative; and/or decreasing the perceived attractiveness of the unchosen alternative. Brehm predicted that the high dissonance subjects would do more of both (*both* methods of dissonance reduction considered together). A more conservative and stringent prediction is that the high dissonance subjects would do more of *each*.

The main data appear in Table 5.1. The first column contains the

TABLE 5.1. POSTDECISION CHANGES IN THE ATTRACTIVENESS OF ALTERNATIVES

	N	Initial Rating	Rating Change	Corrected Rating Change
No Research Reports				
Low dissonance	33			
Chosen		5.98	.33	.38[b]
Unchosen		3.54	−.14	−.24
Total change[a]			−.47	−.62[b]
High dissonance	27			
Chosen		6.19	.20	.26
Unchosen		5.23	−.66[c]	−.66[c]
Total			−.86[c]	−.92[c]
Research Reports				
Low dissonance	30			
Chosen		6.00	−.30	.11
Unchosen		3.47	.07	.00
Total			.37	.11
High dissonance	27			
Chosen		6.05	−.04	.38[b]
Unchosen		5.07	−.64[c]	−.41[b]
Total			−.60[b]	−.79[c]
Gift Only	30	5.19	−.40[c]	.00

From Brehm (1956).

[a] Total change in the direction of dissonance reduction. A minus sign under total change indicates a reduction in dissonance.

[b] Statistically significantly different from zero change ($p < .05$).

[c] Statistically significantly different from zero change ($p < .01$).

initial ratings of each alternative in each condition; the second column presents the average rating changes in attractiveness; the third column gives the "corrected" changes. Since the alternatives initially differed in attractiveness, one would expect differential statistical regression. Thus the "corrected rating change" represents the raw change score minus the mean change of items not involved in the choice but rated approximately the same on the initial rating.

Using Brehm's measure of total dissonance reduced (the decreased attractiveness of the unchosen alternative plus the increased attractiveness of the chosen alternative), there was a significant amount of dissonance reduced in three of the four conditions. More directly related to the hypothesis, with research reports, high-dissonance subjects showed significantly more evidence of dissonance reduction than low-dissonance subjects.[3] Without research reports, the trend is in the same direction but is not significant.

As indicated, Brehm's data support the predictions of dissonance theory, although there are several ambiguities. Let us list some questions left unanswered by Brehm's design and data and inspect other evidence related to these unclarities. Note that Brehm's experiment was not designed to answer all of these questions and we are merely using it as a springboard to discuss other related evidence on decision-making.

1. Does dissonance incurred as the result of a decision produce increased attractiveness of the chosen alternative and decreased attractiveness of the unchosen alternative? The principal change in Brehm's data was in the unchosen alternative, but the data about the chosen alternative were unclear. However, subsequent evidence indicates that change takes place in the chosen alternative as well (Walster, 1964; Brehm and Cohen, 1959a; Ehrlich, Guttman, Schonbach, and Mills, 1957; Deutsch, Krauss, and Rosenau, 1962), although change in the chosen alternative is often numerically, if not statistically, less than in the unchosen alternative. The evidence then seems to clearly show that making a decision produces dissonance and that as a result of attempts to reduce the dissonance, the attractiveness of the chosen alternative is psychologically increased and the attractiveness of the unchosen alternative is decreased.

---

[3] We might add that since the reports mentioned positive and negative aspects of both alternatives, it would be difficult to state precisely how the reports would affect the *degree* of dissonance (except that it should have no systematic effect between high and low dissonance conditions.)

However, apparently one must be *committed* to the decision; that is, the decision must imply the rejection of the unchosen alternative. If not, theoretically there is no dissonance, and the data collected in circumstances where commitment was not obtained indicate no evidence of dissonance reduction (Davidson and Kiesler, 1964; Jecker, 1964; Allen, 1964).

2. Does the similarity of the stimuli affect the degree of dissonance reduction? Recall that theoretically the "cognitive overlap" of the alternatives affects the degree of dissonance, and hence one should see greater evidence of dissonance reduction with less similar alternatives. The evidence indicates that the similarity of the stimuli does affect the degree of dissonance reduction in the expected fashion (Brehm and Cohen, 1959a; Brock, 1963).

Generally, the predictions of dissonance theory are supported by experimental data about decision-making. A host of unsolved problems remain. Festinger (1964) devoted a whole volume of experimental work by himself and his students to the problem of the process of decision-making and the application of dissonance theory to this process. Many of these problems are outside the boundaries of a book on attitude change, but the theory seems to be supported reasonably well by the experimental data in this area, although there are many unanswered questions. For further consideration of the data and theoretical implications of dissonance theory for decision-making, the reader is referred to Festinger (1964).

The postdecision process involves cognitive change not unlike that of attitude change; indeed the effects of this process may legitimately be referred to as attitude change. More important here, the theoretical predictions and data of dissonance theory on decision-making are very intimately related to the predictions and data in more traditional attitude change situations. This will become very apparent to the reader in the following discussion of the forced compliance situation.

The Forced Compliance Paradigm

This situation refers to the case where a person is induced to behave in a manner that is contrary to his beliefs or attitudes. The induction ordinarily takes place as a result of either promised reward for complying or threatened punishment for noncompliance. The case of a person performing some behavior that is inconsistent with his beliefs is not an unusual one. A casual inspection of the research literature on conformity (cf. Secord and Backman, 1964) reveals that very subtle group pressure induces people to behave in ways vastly inconsistent with their attitudes. Indeed, prior to his formulation of dissonance theory, Festinger (1953) published an article attempting to set forth the conditions under which one would or would not obtain *private attitude change* as a consequence of public compliance in a group (see Chapter 7 for a discussion of Kelman's interest in similar problems).

Festinger's (1957) theoretical formulation of the forced compliance situation is very simple. The person performs act x. This performance of the act is presumably inconsistent or dissonant with his attitudes Q, R, and N. The knowledge that he performed act x is dissonant with the knowledge that he believes Q, R, and N to be true. If the person cannot take back or deny act x (i.e., if the cognitive element representing the act is resistant to change), changing attitudes Q, R, and N so that they are consistent with act x is the only way to reduce dissonance.

In the forced compliance situation, any pressure (e.g., offered reward or threatened punishment) put upon the person to perform a discrepant act is consistent with performing that act. For instance, in the preceding example, paying our subject $100 to perform act x would provide an additional element consistent with x. The crucial theoretical statement applicable to the forced compliance situation, then, is: *the less the pressure (e.g., offered reward, threatened punishment, or greater choice) put upon the person to perform the act, the greater the dissonance.* Consequently, unless the person can reduce dissonance by distorting or denying his discrepant act, less pressure will result in greater attitude change toward consistency with the act. Thus the greatest attitude change will occur theoretically when the pressure is the minimal amount necessary to induce the subject to perform the act. Theoretically, any pressure greater than this minimal amount will result in less dissonance and less attitude change. This presumably occurs because anything consistent with performing the act will lessen the dissonance.

AN ILLUSTRATIVE EXAMPLE

Let us take as an example a well known experiment performed by Festinger and Carlsmith (1959). The subjects participated in the experiment as a regular part of their class activities. Their "experiment" involved doing an extremely dull task—putting spools on trays and turning pegs for one hour. At the end of the hour the subject was told that the experiment was really concerned with the effect of expectancy on performance. He was told that, whereas no expectancy had been created for him, some of the other subjects had been told that the experiment was enjoyable before beginning it. The experimental subjects were told that the research assistant who usually served as confederate was sick that day, and each subject was induced to tell the next "subject" (actually a confederate) that the experimental task was enjoyable and lots of fun. Half of the experimental subjects were paid $1 for doing this, and half were paid $20. (Presumably part of the payment was for being "on call" if needed). The subjects agreed to describe the task as enjoyable to the confederate, did so, and were dismissed (if a subject resisted, he was given special "encouragement"). The control subjects were not requested to perform the counterattitudinal act and were dismissed immediately after performing the experimental task. Next, all subjects took part in an "official" Psychology Department survey, given by an entirely different person in a different place. The survey asked about recent experiments that the person had taken part in and included were questions relevant to the task: how enjoyable he thought it was, how much he thought he had learned, how scientifically important he thought the experiment was, and to what extent he would be willing to participate in other similar experiments. Finally, subjects were questioned to ascertain if they were suspicious about anything in the experiment, and they were asked to return the money. Let us analyze the experiment from the theoretical point of view.

The task was designed so the person could not initially deny that it was dull. For each experimental subject, dissonance existed between two cognitions: "the task was extremely dull"; and "I told another person that it was enjoyable." Festinger and Carlsmith predicted that the smaller the payment offered the subject for performing the dissonant act, the *greater* the dissonance. How could the subject reduce this dissonance? He could deny that he had performed the act at all. This would reduce or eliminate the dissonance, but reality demands make this an unlikely method of reducing dissonance. He could try to convince himself that after all, he was forced to do it; that the experimenter did not seem to be willing to let him go unless he performed the act; or he could convince himself that the performance of the act was a trivial thing compared to the amount of money he received for performing the task. The last technique is clearly easier for the high-payment subjects than the low-payment subjects. However, central to the prediction, probably the easiest way to reduce dissonance in this situation is for one to convince himself that the dull task was not so "dull" after all. Most of the other avenues of dissonance reduction seem to be more or less "blocked off."

Parenthetically, in most dissonance situations there are several possible and plausible ways to reduce the dissonance. However, it is very difficult to test the effect of dissonance reduction when the dissonance is being reduced in a number of different ways. Only recently have we begun to understand how statistically to combine response measures in multivariate analysis. Also, long series of repeated measures on a single subject may distort the effect one is trying to measure. Therefore laboratory investigators typically make a conscious effort to "block off" all methods of dissonance reduction except one. The predictions and statistical tests are then made in terms of the one, presumably most likely, mode of dissonance reduction.

The technique of blocking off alternative avenues of dissonance reduction is typically an implicit, rather than explicit, feature of the experimental design. In the Festinger and Carlsmith experiment, for example, one possible mode of dissonance reduction would be for the subject to distort the situation and not perceive any inconsistency between the objective dullness of the task and his later positive description to the next subject. To rule out this possibility, it was necessary that the task clearly be dull and that the subject make an unequivocal and irrevocable statement that the task was fun. Then it would indeed be difficult to deny the "nonfittingness" of the knowledge about the task and the knowledge about what he has said. It may be that the explicitness of this "nonfittingness" is crucial for obtaining dissonance effects. With this in mind, let us return to the Festinger and Carlsmith experiment.

To review, Festinger and Carlsmith predicted that as a consequence of greater dissonance the $1 group would come to think that the dull task was more enjoyable than would the $20 group. The prediction was borne out by the data. The subjects in the $1 condition, when questioned later in the "official survey," indicated that they thought the initial task was more enjoyable than did either the $20 subjects or the control subjects. Hence this experiment provides clear support for a dissonance theory explanation of forced compliance effects.

Festinger and Carlsmith also presented evidence on an alternative but unlikely process that could have mediated the dissonance effect. The alternative is that $1 subjects in the process of giving their speech mentally rehearsed opposing arguments and thereby actually convinced themselves to a greater extent. The evidence, although not significant, was in the opposite direction: $20 subjects spent more time giving the speech; their speeches were rated by an observer (who did not know how much they had been paid) as being slightly more persuasive, given with greater conviction, and of slightly higher quality. We should note that these mental rehearsal and improvisation mechanisms have become the center of much controversy and will be discussed in detail later in the chapter.

The Festinger and Carlsmith study is an example of a particular kind of forced compliance situation often referred to as role-playing. A subject is induced to make an overt presentation inconsistent with his private attitudes. For example, he might be asked to say a dull task is interesting or to write an essay advocating an attitudinal position opposite to his own. Although the typical experimenter attempts to minimize variations in subjects' behavior, there is often considerable variation in the behavior actually performed by the subjects. Although dissonance theory does not make a clear distinction between role-playing and other types of forced compliance situations, nearly all of the theoretical controversy in the forced compliance literature has centered on those dissonance studies using the role-playing technique. In the following section we discuss forced compliance data which are uninvolved in this controversy because role playing is not a feature. Following this, we will discuss the role-playing controversy and the related evidence in some detail.

RELATED EVIDENCE

Recall the general theoretical notion that the less the pressure put upon the person to perform some counterattitudinal act, the greater should be the resulting attitude change. Brehm and Crocker (1962) asked hungry subjects to commit themselves to further food deprivation. Subjects paid nothing (versus those paid $5) said they were less hungry and ordered fewer items of food for later consumption. With thirsty subjects, Brehm (1962c) reports that male subjects paid $1 indicated less thirst than those paid $5 (but the result did not hold for females and there was no significant difference in the amount actually drunk for either sex). In a role-playing study Cohen (1962, pp. 73–78) used four levels of financial incentive ($.50, $1.00, $5.00, and $10.00) to induce undergraduates to write counterattitudinal essays on a local campus issue. The lower the inducement offered, the greater the attitude change. The theoretical prediction has also been supported in a study which varied the degree of justification given to the person for performing the act (Cohen, 1962, pp. 97–104). That is, with less justification for performing the discrepant act, there was greater subsequent attitude change toward a belief consonant with the act.

Another finding is that the more negative the character of the person or persons inducing the subject to perform the discrepant act, the greater the attitude change (Smith, 1961; Weick, 1964; Zimbardo, Weisenberg, Firestone, and Levy, 1965; Kiesler and De Salvo, 1967). It has also been found that the less "coerced" the subject is to perform the act, the greater the subsequent attitude change (Aronson and Carlsmith 1963; Brehm and Cohen, 1959b; Brehm, 1962b, pp. 84–88; Freedman, 1965).

The preceding findings are closely related to the effects of choice. In this case, "low-choice" subjects are essentially forced to perform a counterattitudinal act. They are led to believe that they have no alternative or volition in the matter, whereas "high-choice" subjects are told that they can leave if they wish. This method of manipulating choice is methodologically awkward. The more discrepant or dissonant the act, the larger the number of subjects who will wish to leave if offered the opportunity. Indeed, in one of the experiments reported in the previously cited article by Smith (1961), subjects were asked to eat a grasshopper; nearly half of the subjects refused and left. If the present authors had been in that experiment, three more subjects would have joined the mass exodus. The point is that with substantial differences in subject loss between conditions, theoretical conclusions are equivocal (see Chapter 2). For theoretical reasons then, we would want all subjects to actually perform the act, whatever it might be, but to manipulate experimentally the person's perceived choice in performing the act. Thus in the high-choice condition, the experimenter typically offers the choice to the subject rather blatantly. If the subject agrees, fine. If the experimenter thinks the subject is either wavering or going to refuse, then he quickly applies "subtle" pressures to induce the subject to perform the act. That is, he tells the subject, "It won't take long" or "please help me out with my research," and so forth. The intent of the experimenter is to apply just enough pressure to obtain acquiescence in performing the act, and still leave the subject with the feeling that the choice of staying was his.

There is no doubt that the effect of the experimental manipulation is to produce a difference between conditions in the degree of perceived choice. However, the procedure is somewhat ungainly in two respects. First, not all of the people in the high-choice condition receive the same manipulation; it varies somewhat from subject to subject. And second, this procedure probably produces greater variance in perceived choice in the high-choice condition than in the low-choice condition. As a result of the experimenter's variation in behavior in the high-choice condition, we do not know exactly which behavior produced the obtained effect.

The dissonance prediction obviously is that greater perceived choice in performing the discrepant act leads to greater dissonance and greater predicted attitude change toward consonance with the act. This prediction has been confirmed in a number of experiments (Brock, 1962; Brehm and Cohen, 1959b; Cohen and Latane, 1962, pp. 88–91; Davis and Jones, 1960; Brock and Buss, 1962; Hall, 1964). Taken together, these studies represent reasonable support for the dissonance theory predictions involving the choice variable.[4]

Lastly, dissonance theory makes a prediction concerning the dissonant behavior itself. That is, the greater the negative behavior that the person performs (Brehm and Cohen say "commits himself to"), or the more negative information about the dissonant situation, or the greater the amount of effort that the person must expend to perform the discrepant behavior, the greater the dissonance, and in each case the theory predicts greater attitude change toward consonance with the act. These predictions have been supported by several experiments (Aronson and Mills, 1959; Aronson, 1961; Brehm, 1960; Cohen and Zimbardo, 1962, pp. 143–151; Brehm and Cohen, 1959b; Gerard and Mathewson, 1966). Thus we may say that these three theoretical assertions have each received some empirical support, although the absolute number of confirming experiments is not large.

The Forced Compliance Controversy

We have discussed the forced compliance paradigm at some length and presented some of the data that dissonance theory has generated

---

[4] The authors are aware of only two experiments, both reported in Kiesler (1965), in which the opposite effect was obtained.

on this topic. However, as we have indicated, a lively theoretical discussion surrounds this topic.

The attack on the dissonance position comes from several different perspectives, but can be partitioned into two main streams of thought. One group of theorists has concentrated on the variable of incentive. This group appeared at first to offer alternative explanations for the dissonance studies using incentives, but now is concentrating on specifying the conditions under which "dissonance" results occur and those under which the opposite effects occur as a function of variations in incentives. Bem (e.g., 1964) provides a second stream of thought and suggests an alternative explanation of all of the dissonance experiments, based on Skinners learning theory. We next give an account of both of these disputes, respectively.

The first alternative might be phrased as "I have been paid well, therefore I believe." On this issue, both Janis (1959; Janis and Gilmore, 1965; Elms and Janis, 1965; Elms, 1967) and Rosenberg (1960a, 1965) have proposed theories of incentive effects with predictions opposite those of dissonance theory. Both focus on and are perhaps specific to role-playing, and both emphasize variables that presumably mediate attitude change in counterattitudinal role-playing.

Janis says that ". . . when a person accepts the task of improvising arguments in favor of a point of view at variance with his own personal convictions, he becomes temporarily motivated to think up all the good arguments he can, and at the same time suppresses thoughts about the negative arguments . . . . This 'biased scanning' increases the chances of acceptance of the new attitude position" (Janis and Gilmore, 1965, pp. 17–18). Presumably, a larger incentive increases the "biased scanning" and should therefore increase attitude change. Janis explains the opposite effect in the Festinger and Carlsmith experiment by suggesting that the $20 payment there acted as a negative incentive. The large payment, he says, might have produced suspicion, wariness about being exploited, and guilt about lying to a fellow student. Festinger says that the active process occurs in his $1 condition; that subjects in this condition, as the result of dissonance, changed their attitudes more than the control subjects. Janis emphasizes the incentive value of the $20. According to incentive theory, if a very large reward generates negative affect, it will tend to interfere with acceptance of the conclusions advocated in the role-playing performance; but if the monetary reward elicits positive feelings of gratitude and satisfaction, he would expect it to facilitate acceptance. Hence the possibility arises of an interaction between sponsorship and reward. "With positive sponsorship, the very large monetary reward would be expected to have a predominantly positive incentive effect and thus make for an increase in the amount of attitude change; whereas, with negative sponsorship a very large reward would be more likely to induce negative effects that would tend to make for less attitude change" (Janis and Gilmore, 1965, p. 26). Janis suggests limitations of generality of the dissonance effects, as well as suggesting an alternative explanation of the effects themselves. Unfortunately, the Janis and Gilmore data show no effects of incentive on role-playing and consequently leave this issue unresolved.[5]

On the other hand, Rosenberg (1965) suggests a methodological flaw in the dissonance experiments. He offers the concept of evaluation apprehension as the variable producing the dissonance results. Evaluation apprehension is ". . . any active, anxiety-toned concern that . . . (the subject) win a positive evaluation from the experimenter, or at least that he provide no grounds for a negative one" (Rosenberg, 1965, p. 29). Rosenberg's hypothetical subject develops hypotheses about how to win favorable evaluation by the experimenter, and in the dissonance experiments suspects that his honesty or his ability to resist a bribe are being tested. The subject given a larger payment for counterattitudinal behavior is less likely to show evidence of attitude change, Rosenberg says, because he does not want to show that he is the sort of person who can be bought off. Evaluation apprehension should be aroused any time that the posttest is not psychologically and physically separated from the rest of the experiment.

There are data relevant to the questions raised by both Janis and Rosenberg. The experiment of Cohen (1962, pp. 73–78) addresses itself to the question raised by Janis (a discussion relevant to the Rosenberg data is presented later). In this experiment variations in small payments produce the predicted dissonance effects. One would expect little differ-

---

[5] It is not altogether clear that dissonance theory and incentive theory make competing predictions. Certainly, the points of emphasis are different. Dissonance theory emphasizes the *act* of role-playing; incentive theory emphasizes the *process* of role-playing. When the process is allowed to vary between incentive conditions, dissonance theory loses its predictive value. When the process is not allowed to vary, incentive theory loses its predictive value. It seems clear that both the act and the process are important, but it is difficult to pit the theories against each other. One man's theory is another man's control group, so to speak.

ence in guilt and suspicion between subjects offered, say, $.50 and those offered $1.00; yet subjects offered $.50 change more. The alternative explanation of evaluation apprehension was ruled out in advance by the Festinger and Carlsmith experiment. They included in their design precisely what Rosenberg recommends: the posttest was given in a different place by a person presumably unconnected with the experiment (Rosenberg suggests that the degree of separation between manipulation and posttest may have been insufficient). Kiesler, Pallak, and Kanouse (1968) found dissonance results, although not strong, in a study in which the posttest was given in a different building by a person presumably from a different university.

Clearly, one cannot discard *all* of the dissonance data on methodological grounds. Does this mean that one always finds a negative relationship between incentive and attitude change? Not at all. Indeed, several experiments have produced a positive relationship between incentive and attitude. What is the resolution to this theoretical and empirical quandary? We wish to suggest two resolutions (without implying they exhaust the possibilities). One resolution focuses on other possible mediating variables systematically affected by degree of payment. The second points to possible limiting conditions for the arousal of dissonance.

One typical effect of greater payment is that people work harder. Dissonance theorists (e.g., Zimbardo, 1965) have derived a prediction for the effects of differential effort: the greater the effort expended in a counterattitudinal task, the greater the dissonance aroused. Note the clear implication here, however: dissonance theory loses its predictive power for the effects of incentives if degree of effort remains uncontrolled. If higher-payment subjects work harder at the task, the theoretical sources of dissonance compete with one another. Under these circumstances, the $20 subjects theoretically would have more dissonance than $1 subjects as a result of increased effort, but less dissonance as a function of payment itself. In some experiments (e.g., Festinger and Carlsmith), the differential effort between conditions is minimal, and the resulting dissonance is presumably due to differential payment. However, in other experiments, subjects receiving greater payment do work longer and harder, and one cannot clearly specify differential degrees of dissonance. We offer "the amount of effort expended" as one variable affecting the amount of attitude change produced as a function of incentive.

We hasten to add, however, that although degree of effort expended is an important theoretical construct, there is no evidence that it provides a powerful explanation of the data. In practice, typically, the experimenter tries to check on degree of effort expended after the experiment has been completed. In essay-writing, such a check might consist of judging the quality of the essays written or the absolute number of words written. While differences among conditions on these variables often turn out to be significant (Rosenberg, 1965; Janis and Gilmore, 1965; Elms and Janis, 1965), they still do not provide a neat explanation. In Rosenberg's experiment, for example, he found differences in essay "persuasiveness": "Six of the 20 subjects in the combined $.50 and $1 group had persuasiveness scores that were lower . . . than any that occurred in the $5 group" (1965, p. 40). Thus the $.50 and $1 groups apparently did not differ in the persuasiveness of their essay and did not differ in attitude. Combined, this low incentive group wrote less persuasive essays than did the $5 group and showed less attitude change. When Rosenberg tried to match the groups on persuasiveness by discarding subjects in the low incentive conditions who had extremely low persuasiveness scores, the high incentive group still showed greater attitude change. Although a covariance procedure would be a more powerful analysis, it is still unlikely that the difference between incentive conditions would become reversed to fit the dissonance prediction.[6]

Degree of effort, of course, is only one possible variable mediating the effects of incentives on role-playing. Hovland, Janis, and Kelley (1953) mention four others, all still relatively unexplored, that could serve as "mechanisms of internalization":

1. *Extraneous rewards.* It is possible that when an individual receives rewards following his overt statement, these reinforcements could

---

[6] However, while more words were written in the $1.00 condition than in the $.50 condition, there were no attitude change differences between these conditions. On the other hand, though there was greater attitude change in the $5.00 as opposed to the $1.00 condition, there was no parallel difference between these conditions in number of words written. Other studies also fail to uniformly show this relation between attitude change and effort across increasing levels of incentive (e.g., Janis and Gilmore, 1965; Elms and Janis, 1965; Carlsmith, Collins, and Helmreich, 1966; Collins and Helmreich, in press). Thus, while degree of effort may account for some instances in which higher incentives produce more attitude change, the circumstances in which this occurs are presently not well understood. Furthermore, it seems likely that other variables may prove to be more potent mediators of the positive relations between attitude and incentive that are currently found in the literature (Collins, 1968).

strengthen the ideas included in the overt statement, whether or not the subject believes what he is saying.

2. *Attention effects.* "The ego-involving task of verbalizing a communication to others probably induces greater attention to the content. . ." (Hovland, Janis, and Kelley, 1953, p. 230).

3. *Selective retention effects.* Since active practice has been shown to facilitate learning, it is possible that overt compliance facilitates the learning of the attitudes involved.

4. *Improvisation factors.* The reformulation of the message into the subject's own words "may give rise to a marked gain in comprehension of the content and thereby augment the chances that the persuasive communication will be influential" (Hovland, Janis, and Kelley, 1953, pp. 233–4).

Carlsmith, Collins, and Helmreich (1966) propose a slightly different resolution of the empirical and theoretical dilemmas in incentive research. They broach the notion that writing counterattitudinal essays does not in and of itself produce dissonance. "It is plausible that, especially among college students, the cognition that one is listing such arguments is not at all dissonant with the cognition that one believes the opposite. Rather, the ability intellectually to adopt such a position is the hallmark of the open-minded and intellectual" (Carlsmith, Collins, and Helmreich, 1966, p. 4). In this view, one must somehow be committed to the counterattitudinal act before dissonance is aroused.

In their experiment, Carlsmith, Collins, and Helmreich compared counterattitudinal, face-to-face role-playing with counterattitudinal, anonymous essay-writing. As predicted, they found a negative relationship between incentive and attitude change under the face-to-face condition, but a positive relationship under the anonymous condition. This experiment suggests limiting effects of the dissonance hypothesis, but does not indicate which of the several differences between conditions accounts for the positive or negative relationship.

Two experiments by Linder, Cooper, and Jones (1967) also point to limiting conditions of the dissonance hypothesis. They argue that dissonance results depend upon the freedom of the subject not to comply with the discrepant request. They argue, for example, that Rosenberg's subjects were effectively committed to the discrepant behavior prior to finding out about the incentives involved. In one experiment, Linder, Cooper, and Jones varied the degree of choice orthogonal to the amount of incentive. They found dissonance-like results only under the free-choice conditions. Under no choice conditions, the results were in the opposite direction (although not significant). In their second experiment they tried to replicate the Rosenberg procedure more closely. In these no-choice conditions, subjects were told, as were Rosenberg's, that they ". . . could participate in another little experiment that some graduate student in education is doing." In the high choice condition, the experimenter stressed that they had no obligation to participate and should "feel free to decide." This experiment is especially interesting since Rosenberg's data were replicated for the no choice conditions. Under the high choice conditions, however, the dissonance effect was produced. These two studies are at some variance with the Carlsmith et al. study as well. Both of the Linder et al. experiments used essay-writing to effect their manipulation, whereas Carlsmith et al. argue that essay-writing should not arouse dissonance.

In short, it seems reasonable to conclude that there are several sets of conditions under which the dissonance effect does not hold. These restricting conditions have not yet been exhaustively researched and remain a friutful line to follow up. If, however, one wishes to "sharpen" dissonance theory so that it can account easily for the conflicting data on incentives, then one must be careful to give due regard for other existing data. The Janis and King experiment comes immediately to mind. Their procedures produced neither the "social embarrassment" that was a prerequisite for dissonance results in Carlsmith et al. (1966; see also Aronson, 1966) nor the high choice necessary for dissonance results in the two studies by Linder et al.

An Alternative Explanation of Dissonance Phenomena

Janis and Rosenberg argue that the dissonance effect is not one of generality (with respect to incentives). Carlsmith et al. and Linder et al. offer data suggesting that dissonance may be aroused only under certain limiting conditions. Bem (1965; 1967) takes an entirely different tack on the problem. He assumes the dissonance results to be reliable, but offers a radically different mechanism for the effects.

Bem (1967; see also Chapter 3 for further discussion of Bem's model) argues that people learn to label verbally their own internal states and those of others by reference to overt behavior. The case of others seems quite clear. Consider the following contrast. Two different people kill their respective mothers, but one does it for a million dollars and the other for fifty cents. We as observers are much more likely to infer that the former person liked his mother than to infer that the latter did. We are more likely to assume, in Bem's terms, that the former's behavior was under control of external stimuli and the latter under internal stimuli. Bem makes the same statement for self: "The present analysis of dissonance phenomena, then, will rest upon the single empirical generalization that an individual's belief and attitude statements and the beliefs and attitudes that an outside observer would attribute to him are often functionally similar in that both sets of statements are partial 'inferences' from the same evidence . . ." (Bem, 1967, p. 186).

Bem carried out several studies concerned with the interpersonal aspects of the dissonance paradigm. Essentially, he gives his subjects (observers) information about *one* subject is a dissonance experiment (e.g., John did task X described, then was paid to tell another that the task was fun and interesting. What do you think John's opinion of the task was?). Bem's observers see the subject who was paid less as being more favorable toward the task. Why else, they wonder, would he have told someone else that the task was fun? Bem argues that the same process occurs for subjects in dissonance experiments: they think to themselves, "I did it for 50 cents, I guess I did like the task." This statement is not, Bem theorizes, the result of an aversive motivational state (dissonance), but rather a passive process by which the person infers his own attitudes from his behavior. This is a broad theoretical statement of some impact. Let us inspect his data and argument more closely.

Bem concentrates on two empirical topics which have been strongly influenced by cognitive dissonance theory: forced compliance and free-choice experiments. His alternative explanation and data on forced compliance studies are perhaps the more impressive:

"Consider the viewpoint of an outside observer who hears the individual making favorable statements about tasks to a fellow student, and who further knows that the individual was paid $1 ($20) to do so. This hypothetical observer is then asked to state the actual attitude of the individual he has heard. An outside observer would almost certainly judge the $20 communicator to be "manding" reinforcement (Skinner, 1957); that is, his behavior appears to be under the control of the reinforcement contingencies of the money and not at all under the discriminative control of the tasks he appears to be describing. The $20 communicator is not credible in that his statements cannot be used as a guide for inferring his actual attitudes . . . . Although the behavior of a $1 communicator also has some mand properties, an outside observer would be more likely to judge him to be expressing his actual attitudes and, hence, would infer the communicator's attitude from the content of the communication itself. He would thus judge this individual to be favorable toward the tasks" (Bem, 1967, p. 188).

In his 1965 article, Bem describes an interpersonal replication of the Cohen (Brehm and Cohen, 1962, p. 73) study. Each subject in Bem's "interpersonal replication" simply received a description of the situation faced by a single subject in the original Cohen study. He was thus told that in the spring of 1959, there was a "riot at Yale University in which the New Haven police incurred the wrath of the undergraduates." They were then told that an undergraduate had written an essay entitled "Why the New Haven Police Actions Were Justified," an essay which was to be clearly in favor of the police side of the riots. According to the description, "the decision to write such an essay or not was entirely up to the student, and he was told that he would be paid the sum of $.50 ($1.00) if he would be willing to do so. The student who was asked agreed to do so, and wrote such an essay" (p. 203). Bem's observers were asked to estimate the attitude toward the New Haven police of the subject described to them. Their estimates in the control, $.50, and $1.00 conditions were strikingly similar to the data actually obtained by Cohen. In his 1967 paper Bem reports a similar "interpersonal replication" of the Festinger and Carlsmith (1959) study. Again the results were quite similar to those reported by Festinger and Carlsmith. Similar results are also reported by Jones (1966) in a study in which subjects' attitudes and observers' judgments were compared directly in the same experiment.

Bem also reports an interpersonal replication of Brehm's (Brehm and Cohen, 1962, pp. 133–136) hunger study. Again, each of Bem's observers is given a description of the circumstances faced by one of Brehm's original subjects. Some observers were told about an undergraduate who volunteered to go an additional few hours without food for five dollars, while other of Bem's observers learned about an undergraduate who lived with his hunger without financial justification. When Bem's observers estimated the hunger ratings of the original Brehm subjects as described, their estimated ratings again correspond remarkably well to the ratings actually obtained in Brehm's original study.

In his final experiment in the forced compliance area, Bem attempted to replicate an interaction between length of counterattitudinal arguments and financial incentives found in the Festinger and Carlsmith experiment. Brehm and Cohen's (1962, p. 119) reanalysis of the Festinger and Carlsmith data indicated a negative correlation between the "number and variety of arguments and post-experimental attitudes in the $20 (low dissonance) condition and a positive correlation in the $1 (high dissonance) condition."

Using his interpersonal replication procedure, Bem described the plight of a subject in the original Festinger and Carlsmith experiment to one of his subjects. All observers actually heard a recording of the presumed counterattitudinal behavior. Half of the observers heard a recording of a "fairly imaginative and lengthy set of reasons as to why he had enjoyed the tasks" and other subjects heard another communication with "somewhat shorter and . . . comparatively unimaginative arguments."

Bem's observers' estimates of how the described subject would respond in the Festinger and Carlsmith situation replicated the original Festinger and Carlsmith results for the long communication—$1 subjects are more favorable than $20 subjects. For the short communication there is a nonsignificant result in the other direction—slightly more favorable attitudes in the $20 condition. If these results were analyzed within each of the incentive conditions, there would be a positive correlation between length of argument and attitude change in the $1 condition and a negative correlation between length of argument and attitude change in the $20 condition—a replication of the data from the original Festinger and Carlsmith experiment. The significance of this interpersonal replication, however, is clouded by the fact that the correlation between length of argument and attitude change has not been consistently replicated among the dissonance studies (Brehm and Cohen, 1962, p. 119; Collins and Helmreich, 1965).

Bem chooses the free choice experiments as his second effort to reinterpret dissonance findings in terms of his interpersonal or self-perception theory (Brehm, 1956; Brehm and Cohen, 1959b). In several of these studies, dissonance researchers had reported that when offered a choice among several desirable alternatives, subjects would increase their ratings of the chosen object and decrease their ratings of the unchosen object. This effect was greatest (1) when the alternatives were initially of approximately equal attractiveness, (2) if the alternatives were dissimilar, and (3) if the subject chose from among a larger number of alternatives.

For his interpersonal replication Bem described the following situation to his observers: "In a Psychology experiment, an 11-year-old boy was asked to rate how well he liked the toys that are typically popular with his age group. He was permitted to select one of these toys to keep for himself. We are interested in how well college students can estimate his ratings." Bem's observers were then told which toy the child had chosen and from which alternatives he was permitted to choose. The observers then made their own estimates of the child's ratings. The results matched three appropriate predictions from the dissonance studies: (1) the chosen alternative was rated higher than the unchosen alternative; (2) this effect was most pronounced for qualitatively dissimilar toys; and (3) the effect was greatest when there were four alternatives as opposed to two alternatives for choice.

The Bem description of the dissonance free choice studies, however, omitted an important characteristic of the original studies. The original studies used a pretest-posttest design, in which subjects typically chose among a range of objects which included the object they had previously rated as most desirable. In fact, a subject was discarded if he did not choose the same toy he had previously rated as most desirable (Brehm and Cohen, 1959b). We return to this point later.

However, Jones, Linder, Kiesler, Zanna, and Brehm (1968) criticize Bem's experiments and propose an alternative explanation of his data.

"Our alternative explanation of Bem's results proposes that an artifact in his descriptions of experimental conditions allowed a judgmental process quite different from that postulated by him. The descriptions used by Bem suggest that a typical subject would be quite unwilling to comply with the experimenter's request in the first place. However, the hypothetical subject in the description does perform the requested behavior. Observers should therefore infer that their subject was *atypical* and that he was initially more willing to comply than most subjects. Further, a subject who complied for a small incentive would be seen as more atypical than a subject who complied for a large incentive. Our alternative explanation asserts that Bem's observer-subjects were not behaving according to his hypothesis of self-perception, but rather that they merely judged differential hypothetical subject self-selection" (Jones et al., 1968, p. 249).

Jones et al. carried out a series of seven experiments designed to test their alternative hypothesis of differential subject self-selection. That is, Bem's observers may be thought of as ignoring possible systematic effects of the dissonant act itself and assuming that the positive attitude inferred in the low payment condition existed prior to payment or performance of the dissonant act. They found that they could replicate Bem's results with his procedures and that with smaller incentives, observers thought fewer subjects would agree to comply with the discrepant request. How-ever, when observers were provided with pretest scores (that is, initir attitudes of involved subjects), Bem's effect did not hold, and indeed it was reversed under some conditions. Observers who were aware of pretest scores predicted a positive relationship between incentives and attitude change for the typical forced compliance setting. In replications of the Brehm (1962a) hunger study, observers given pretest scores thought subjects would become hungrier over time, but not differentially as a function of incentives. Jones et al. also found that observers could not reproduce the effects obtained in the Linder, Cooper, and Jones (1967) study discussed earlier. Finally, in an "observer replication" of the original Brehm (1956) choice experiment, observers provided with prechoice ratings of the alternatives could not reproduce the dissonance effects. Indeed, there were trends in the opposite direction.

Jones et al. conclude that:

"Our interpersonal replications have strongly supported our criticisms of Bem's studies. However, these data do not completely refute Bem's the-oretical position. It may still be true that involved subjects do observe their own behavior and infer their attitudes (or feelings) from their be-havior, at least to some extent. What we have shown is that Bem's inter-personal replications cannot be used as the basis for such an argument. Our data refute Bem's claim that observers and involved subjects are inter-changeable . . . . To explore the processes by which the attitudinal re-sponses of involved subjects are determined it appears necessary to study involved subjects" (Jones et al., 1968, p. 267).

The major theoretical conclusion of Jones et al. is that Bem's experi-ments do not test his alternative explanation of dissonance phenomena (although Jones et al. do rule out the possibility of an isomorphism between observers and involved subjects). In this sense, Bem's alternative to dissonance theory remains untested. The question of "aversive motiva-tion" versus "passive process of attribution to self" remains unanswered. However, if one sets aside the question of observers, it is difficult to distinguish between Bem's interpretation and a dissonance interpretation of the forced compliance phenomenon. The major variable in Bem's inter-pretation—whether the statement is a "mand" or a "tact"—boils down to whether the subject is emitting the response as a result of environmental pressure or whether he has some "choice" as to whether or not he emits the behavior. And "choice" or "commitment" are two of the most fundamental and classic dissonance variables.

Other Research Topics Related to Dissonance Theory

Three books have been written and perhaps two hundred experiments have been carried out with dissonance theory as the central topic. It is very difficult to do justice to this amount of research in one chapter. We have picked out two subtopics—decision-making and the forced compliance paradigm—for rather detailed consideration. In addition, in the next chapter there is a detailed presentation of the dissonance theory predictions and data on the relationship of attitudinal discrepancy to attitude change. This should be enough to aid the reader's evaluation of the theory, but there are several other subtopics in which dissonance theory has been usefully applied. We indicate some of these below but omit the detailed presentation or comment which characterizes our treatment of previous topics.

THE AVOIDANCE OF DISSONANT INFORMATION

We have mentioned that one of the basic postulates of the theory is that a person will actively attempt to avoid situations and information that would increase dissonance.[7] However, the experimental data on the preference of consonant over dissonant information lack consistency (e.g., Cohen, Brehm, and Latane, 1959; Mills, Aronson, and Robinson, 1959; Rosen, 1961; Adams, 1961). In their summary, Brehm and Cohen (1962) conclude from these studies that ". . . while subjects sought out dissonance-reducing information, they did not necessarily

---

[7] The only theoretical exception to this presumably occurs with very high dissonance. One may attempt to increase the dissonance then. For example, suppose it becomes increasingly evident that one made a poor choice of automobiles, with repair bills piling up, and so forth. In that circumstance, the person may seek out other information inconsistent with his choice, with an eye to eventually undoing the choice and buying a different car (see Festinger, 1957, pp. 129–131, for a discussion of this point).

avoid dissonance-increasing information" (p. 93). One of the problems with each of these studies is that dissonant information was confounded with useful information. Usefulness and dissonance may well work in opposite directions in particular circumstances. That is, suppose a person were to elect to defend a particular position in a debate. Theoretically, having so elected, arguments favoring the opposite position should produce dissonance. However, knowing the arguments of the opposing debator is usually an advantage in a debate. Thus these arguments, although dissonant, are extremely useful.

Canon (1964) tried to resolve this issue by orthogonally manipulating both the usefulness of the information and the confidence of the subject in being able to handle dissonant information. He concluded that subjects generally prefer to read articles that support their decision. Decreasing the usefulness of the dissonant articles strengthened this tendency; also, decreasing a person's confidence in his ability to cope with the dissonant material increased his preference for consonant material. However, Freedman (1965) failed to replicate this finding, and the issue remains unclear. Two recent reviews draw opposite conclusions. On one side of the issue are Freedman and Sears (1965), who conclude people do not avoid dissonant information, and on the other side is Mills (1968), who concludes that at least under some circumstances they do. The hypothesis has clearly not received much support.

DISSONANCE AND PERSONALITY

In two interesting experiments, Bramel (1962; 1963) applied dissonance theory to the topic of defensive projection. He created an experimental setting in which he essentially "force-fed" male subjects the information that they had strong homosexual tendencies. This was presumably reflected on a dial that indicated the degree of arousal to pictures of males in varying states of undress. The subject was asked to mark down his own dial reading and also to guess the dial reading of another subject who was participating in the same task. He predicted that this information would produce more dissonance for subjects who had high self-esteem than for those who had low self-esteem. His predictions were confirmed: subjects with high self-esteem underrepresented the reading on their own dial and, in addition, attributed a higher reading (i.e., a greater homosexual reaction to the pictures) to the other subject (but only when they had a positive reaction to the other) than did subjects with low self-esteem. Kiesler and Singer (1963) report a similar out-come. In addition, Edlow and Kiesler (1966) show that, as one might expect, this effect only holds when the dissonant information is very difficult to deny. For a general discussion of the relationship of dissonance theory to personality variables, the reader is referred to Festinger and Bramel (1962).

The work of Bramel also draws attention to the importance of the concept of "self" in dissonance theory predictions. Typically, one assumes in dissonance experiments that the subject has a positive regard for himself. This assumption is necessary to make the derivation that some negative act like lying or cheating will produce dissonance. Bramel stresses that such a negative act would not be dissonant for anyone holding a very negative evaluation of himself (low self-esteem). It is probably true that most people hold at least a moderately positive view of themselves. Bramel's data therefore do not suggest a major overhaul of dissonance theory. They do indicate, however, how one may specify more clearly how to arouse dissonance for a given individual.

This raises a more important theoretical issue, that of psychological implication. For example, let us take the relation between self-esteem and the negative act of cheating. What are the implications for level of dissonance? Intuitively, it seems reasonable that cheating should pro-duce dissonance for someone very high in self-esteem and not produce it for someone very low in self-esteem. We are assuming that a high level of self-esteem psychologically implies not cheating and a low level of self-esteem implies cheating. There are two questions here. First, does low self-esteem really imply cheating? Or is there simply an absence of strict implication? Note the resemblance of this question to that raised by Cartwright and Harary (1956) concerning the complement of a relationship and its opposite in reference to Heider's theory. The second question is a related one and is oriented toward the necessary conditions for specifying psychological implication. That is, even granting that high self-esteem implies not cheating and low self-esteem implies cheating, what does a moderate level of self-esteem imply? These questions have not really been raised in reference to dissonance research. However, it may be that one of the crucial effects of such experimental procedures as the blocking of alternative modes of dissonance reduction and high commitment to the dissonant act is to explicitly force upon the subjects an implication of "nonfittingness" that might not otherwise exist.

DISSONANCE AND SELF-CONCEPT, A SELF-FULFILLING PROPHECY

Aronson and Carlsmith (1962) also performed an experiment related to the third cognition in any dissonant relationship, the concept of self. As we mentioned, although researchers sometimes experimentally manipulate the self-concept (Bramel, 1962), they most often simply assume that the subject has a good opinion of himself. In an extrapolation from dissonance theory, Aronson and Carlsmith maintain that if a person expects to do well on some task and does not, this creates dissonance. Perhaps less obviously, if the person expects to do poorly and actually does well, this also should create dissonance. In both cases, dissonance should produce subsequent cognitive or behavioral change. Thus, when a person expects to succeed and does poorly, he should take a preferred opportunity to "undo" the failure and turn it into a success. More interestingly, Aronson and Carlsmith also predicted that when a person expects to fail and actually succeeds, he will take the opportunity to change that success into a failure.

To test this hypothesis, Aronson and Carlsmith had subjects judge a series of photographs, the task supposedly representing a test of some personality attribute. Through manipulation, half of the subjects were led to believe that they were very bad at this task, and half were led to believe that they were very good. There were five sets of twenty pictures each in the task. The expectation of success or failure was built up on the first four sets. On the fifth set, half of the subjects had this expectation confirmed, half had it disconfirmed. Then, on a pretext, all subjects were allowed to rejudge the fifth set. The predictions were borne out by the data. The subjects who had their expectations confirmed did not change them on the rejudgment of the fifth set. Those subjects who had their expectations disconfirmed changed their judgments on the fifth set. The latter group includes those who had built up an expectation of failure through the first 80 trials, and who then succeeded on the first judgment of the fifth set of pictures. These people changed their judgments of the pictures on the second try, thereby insuring that they would fail. Hence the people expecting to fail insure their own failure; this is a self-fulfilling prophecy. This circular feedback system is analogous to that proposed by W. I. Thomas, who described the relation between sociological events in terms of the dynamics of a self-fulfilling prophecy.

This experiment has produced a rash of replications. The gist of these replications seems to be that (1) the effect will only hold if the person does not regard the task as something he can learn; and (2) the fewer the number of trials producing the initial expectation, the weaker the effect (cf. Brock, Edelman, Edwards, and Schuck, 1965). Thus the stronger the expectation of failure and the more the person regards the locus of failure as inherent in self (and hence presumably more resistant to change), the stronger the attempt to insure failure. We note, however, that not many of these replications have been successful (see Brock et al., 1965, for discussion).

DISSONANCE AND PHYSIOLOGICAL VARIABLES

Brehm performed two experiments (Brehm, 1962c; Brehm and Crocker, 1962) investigating the effects of dissonance on hunger and thirst. In both experiments, the subject is "deprived" all day. (In one experiment he is deprived of water; in the other, food). He is then induced to continue without food (or water) for the rest of the evening. The dependent variables are how hungry or thirsty he says he is, how much he "orders" from the experimenter to be consumed after the experiment is over, and (in the thirst experiment) how much he actually consumes. The dissonance manipulation is in the experimental induction. In one experiment subjects were differentially paid (nothing and $5) for committing themselves to further deprivation; in the other experiment they were differentially underpaid (subjects were told they would get nothing, but that other subjects received either $1 or $10, depending on condition). Generally, the results supported the hypothesis. High-dissonance subjects said they were less hungry and thirsty, ordered less for later consumption, and (in the thirst experiment) actually drank less than did low-dissonance subjects.

Brehm (1962c) cites an exploratory study by Back and Bogdonoff in which they performed a similar experiment but also took blood samples. They found that high-dissonance subjects actually had less mobilization of free fatty acids in the blood than did low-dissonance subjects, indicating that not only did the high-dissonance subjects *say* they were less hungry, but physiological variables corroborated their self-reports. However, other results (Brehm, Back, and Bogdonoff, 1964) are less clear. As a consequence, though the implications of this finding are fascinating, we must await further evidence.

A well-designed experiment by Zimbardo (1966) presents a demonstration of the suppression of physiological responding to match experimentally induced cognitive distortions. His subjects were tested individually in a two-phase experiment. In the first phase they memorized a practice word list, had their thresholds for painful shock determined, and then learned a list of nine words while simultaneously receiving two painful shocks per trial. Experimental subjects were then given either high or low justification for continuing in a second phase of the experiment where they were to learn another word list while receiving further shock. Zimbardo hypothesized that commitment to continue the shocks under low justification would produce dissonance and that this dissonance would be reduced by a re-evaluation of the painfulness of the shock.

As hypothesized, the high-dissonance subjects did perceive the shocks in the second phase as less painful than did low-dissonance subjects. From the present perspective it is more interesting that the galvanic skin response (GSR) to the painful stimulus was less for the high-dissonance subjects than the low, parallelling the self-report data. Furthermore, as one might expect if the high-dissonance condition did indeed produce a physiologically lower level of pain, that is, a lower level of drive, the high-dissonance subjects learned the last word list more quickly than the low-dissonance subjects. Zimbardo says that "The total process of dissonance-reduction may lead to an alteration of both the cognitive and non-cognitive components of any motivational state and thus the drive itself may be functionally lowered. If so, then various consummatory and physiological behaviors correlated with that motive, as well as subjective and instrumental reactions to it, should decrease" (1966, p. 217).

These results are intriguing and should arouse speculation and research on the parameters involved. For example, we know little of how such an effect might be mediated. Is the reduction in pain a direct consequence of the dissonance-arousing manipulation or does it depend upon an intervening cognitive change? Do situations exist that would produce cognitive or physiological change, but not both?

Dissonance has been defined as a motivating condition. In one sense, the Zimbardo-Brehm work may be viewed as showing how a decrease in one drive state (dissonance) produces a decrease in a coexisting drive state (e.g., hunger). If so, could the addition of hunger to an existing state of dissonance act as an irrelevant drive, in Hullian terms? Would more dissonance be reduced in a forced compliance setting if the subject were also hungry? All of these questions are of theoretical and empirical interest. Such questions impress upon us, however, the lack of straight-forward derivations from dissonance theory for physiological variables. The answers to such questions would add to the theory but not test it.

Summary and Conclusions

What can we conclude about the status of dissonance theory? The theory itself has been extraordinarily controversial. There are several reasons for this. First, the predictions are often reputed to be "nonobvious." The cuteness of the phrase has annoyed a number of researchers and theorists (cf. Weick, 1965, for a discussion of this and other points). But for a theory to be powerful, it must make predictions about events that other theories cannot handle. If one defines a nonobvious prediction as one that other theorists would not make *in advance* of the accumulation of the data, then it is certainly an advantage for a theory to make nonobvious predictions. The nonobviousness of the results of many of the dissonance experiments, however, may come about when experimenters make a conscious effort to rule out (at least important) alternative explanations of the data before carrying out the experiment. In this sense, predictions from dissonance theory are not more or less obvious than the predictions derivable from other theories. A well trained experimenter typically draws a "nonobvious" prediction from any theory that he is trying to test, as a result of ruling out alternative explanations by design.

Individual experiments in this field have been criticized for methodological and other reasons: differential dropping of subjects between conditions; weak results; lack of control groups that the critic would like to see; and, especially, alternative explanations of the results. However, these are not criticisms of the formal theory, but of the specific experiments testing the theory. Suppose a critic intends an alternative explanation of the results of an individual experiment to be a *theoretical* criticism. That is, the critic implies that the theory is not useful since he can supply an alternative explanation of a given experiment. It seems both reasonable and parsimonious that the critic should be prepared to offer the same or a similar explanation for other data accumulated by the theorist. At the very least, the critic should be expected to explain the other data in *some* way.

The theory has also been criticized for the complex methods and procedures that are utilized to test it. Aside from the fact that this again is not a criticism of the theory, we should like to point out that the behaviors which experimental social psychology wishes to study and explain and understand are complex themselves, or at least appear to be at this point in the history of social psychology. The complexity of an experimental procedure does not in and of itself reflect unfavorably upon the worth or validity of the data produced by that procedure.

There also seems to be almost as much concern with whether dissonance exists as a psychological variable as there is with the question of whether the theory predicts adequately about social phenomena. Take, for example, the case of a graduate student who says that subjects in a low-choice condition have more dissonance than those in a high-choice condition. When confronted with the fact that the theory specifies the opposite, he merely answers that he disagrees with the theory. He abstracts the concept from the theory and views it as having an existence independent of the theory. His position is basically unscientific. We regard it as our task here to make some statement about the theory as an axiomatic theory, rather than the reality of dissonance as a personality variable. These questions are best answered by the individual reader. Let us instead turn to a discussion of some of the positive and negative aspects of the theory, in that order.

It is obvious that the theory has been useful to social psychology and the study of attitude change. It has certainly generated more experimental work than any other theory of attitude change. Also, the theory has stimulated research in a surprisingly wide variety of topical areas. The breadth of situational application is one of the theory's more attractive features. Further, many of the data the theory's advocates have produced are not easily explained by other theories. Perhaps most important, future theory will have to account for many of these data in order to be judged minimally adequate.

Before criticizing the theory, let us pause to distinguish dissonance theory conceptually from other balance theories. How does dissonance theory differ from the basic Heiderian model? There are several points of departure, but Festinger's most important addition is perhaps his concept of psychological implication. With this idea we can conceptually differentiate dissonance from unbalance and point to situations that are unbalanced, but produce no dissonance. The triad "I own a tennis racket," "I love my wife," but "She does not own a tennis racket" is by definition unbalanced, but should produce no dissonance.[8] Festinger would assert that the first two statements do not psychologically imply the obverse of the third; in fact, they are unrelated to the third. This is a crucial point: although dissonance theory is a consistency theory, it does not define inconsistency identically to other consistency theories. In our experience, this has been a point of major confusion for undergraduates.

Another difference between dissonance theory and the basic balance model is that dissonance theory allows for varying magnitudes of dissonance to exist and specifies the theoretical factors affecting the magnitude of dissonance. The basic balance model does not allow for varying degrees of unbalance. The theoretical variations that do specify magnitude (e.g., Cartwright and Harary, 1956), define it differently than does dissonance theory.

The theoretical methods of reducing dissonance diverge from those that reduce unbalance. Unbalance is typically reduced by changing a relationship or an evaluation. Dissonance adds other modes of inconsistency reduction, e.g., adding cognitive elements or minimizing the importance of the dissonant elements.

The unit of theorizing and its location are different for balance theory and dissonance theory. For Heider, the statement "I like sports cars" is a relationship. Festinger always abstracts such a statement to make it a cognitive element, "The *knowledge* that I like sports cars." Liking sports cars and owning one are two different relationships for Heider; for Festinger they are simply two cognitions. Festinger thus avoids questions regarding affect and those regarding the relations among components of attitudes. Further, Heider might say that $P L X$ *induces* P owns (U) X. Festinger would view $P L X$ as an inert cognitive element; by itself, it would not *do* anything. In addition, the location of dissonance and unbalance can differ. In dissonance theory, dissonance is always an intrapersonal event. Loosely, it occurs in some individual's "head." Balance is sometimes intrapersonal, sometimes interpersonal. For example, Cartwright and Harary speak of unbalance in a group.

[8] This example of unbalance is intentionally a trivial one. No balance theorist would argue that it is intuitively unbalanced; it is only formally unbalanced. Further, it is an easy example to explain away by adding some aspect of psychological implication to balance theory (e.g., Abelson, 1968). Our only point is that the concept of psychological implication is not now an input to the formal balance theory.

Superficially, dissonance theory and balance theory appear quite similar. We have indicated several major differences between the two. Clearly, they do not make the same assumptions or the same predictions. We have already criticized balance theories as a group. We next add some specific criticisms of dissonance theory.

Some Criticisms of Dissonance Theory

1. It is extremely difficult, if not impossible, to make precise, quantitative measurements of the degree of dissonance. This has not been an important problem in the past. It has been possible to make a weak, ordinal representation of the degree of dissonance. That is, experimenters thus far have worked their way around this problem by producing such large differences in the degree of dissonance between conditions that there could be no doubt about a difference in dissonance. However, even in the present statement of the theory, it would take a tremendous amount of information about the cognitive world of a person to quantify his dissonance, including his cognitions before he arrives at the experiment (for each person), the importance of each of these cognitions, a little more information about what is and what is not a cognition, and, last, some idea of the relevance of each of these cognitions for the experimental situation. Fruitful information has been gained thus far without precise quantification of dissonance, but continued moderate precision would lessen the usefulness of the theory in the future.

2. How will dissonance be reduced? Researchers have attempted to get around this problem by experimentally blocking off alternative modes of dissonance reduction other than the one of main interest. However, this leaves unexplored the whole problem of what the person might have done had we not blocked off the alternative avenues of escape. That is, what variables control preferences for different dissonance reducing techniques? This question is not only of theoretical interest but of practical concern as well. The theory becomes ambiguous when the amount of experimental control lessens, and presumably one would like to generalize to situations where there is very little experimental control. For dissonance theory to have external validity, we need to know what modes of dissonance reduction are normative in particular situations. A further refinement would then consider individual differences within each of these settings. Unfortunately, there are no experimental data

on the first issue and only few that touch on the second (e.g., Steiner and Rogers, 1963; Steiner and Johnson, 1964).

3. As indicated, the question of individual differences requires further consideration. For example, the Aronson and Carlsmith (1962b) experiment suggests that the amount of dissonance that cognition x produces depends to a considerable extent, perhaps totally, on the cognitive world the person brings with him to the experimental setting. Although clear statistical differences may exist between conditions in the degree of dissonance produced, at the same time there may be huge individual differences within conditions. Thus one manipulation may indeed produce dissonance for every subject, but the between-condition comparison may not account for a great deal of the variance in dissonance produced. This does not amount to a criticism of the results of past research, but suggests instead that had there been greater control of this variance, statistical differences would have been stronger.

This is only one aspect of the problem of individual differences. People undoubtedly differ in the extent to which they can tolerate dissonance before being motivated to change. For example, the scientist presumably learns to suspend judgment until all of the evidence is in. This means learning to endure a great deal of dissonance. Before predictions can be made for individual subjects, a lot more must be known about this variable.

Some of the work by Harvey (1965) seems relevant here. He found reactions to a dissonant forced compliance situation to vary as a function of the subject's concreteness-abstractness (a dimension of cognitive structure; cf. Harvey, Hunt, and Schroeder, 1961). In Harvey's schema, greater concreteness implies a simple cognitive structure. He found, as he had predicted, greater dissonance reduction in the more "concrete" subjects. An interesting question is whether the concrete subjects changed more because they could tolerate less dissonance or whether a given dissonant act produced more dissonance for them. This could not be easily tested but nonetheless is of theoretical interest.

4. Precise predictions are impeded by the difficulty in measuring a cognitive element's resistance to change. The resistance of cognitions to change is an integral aspect of dissonance theory. If we do not know which of two dissonant cognitions is less resistant to change, we cannot specify in advance the direction of dissonance reduction. This we can refer to as the problem of *relative* resistance to change. Further, if we do not know the absolute level of resistance (of the less resistant cogni-

tion), we cannot say if a given degree of dissonance arousal will effect change.[9]

Intimately related to this point is some of the confusion regarding the term commitment. Kiesler (1968; Kiesler and Sakumura, 1966) argues that the terms commitment and dissonance are confused in the literature and points to three different emphases in discussions of the relationship between dissonance and commitment: (a) unless the subject is "committed," we cannot make an unequivocal prediction from dissonance theory; (b) unless the subject is committed, there may be no dissonance; and (c) the more the subject is committed, the greater the dissonance.

Kiesler argues that the most useful way to define commitment (at least with respect to dissonance theory predictions) is in terms of the relative resistance of cognitions to change. In this vein, he has investigated the effects of commitment to consonant behavior (where theoretically the cognition representing the consonant behavior is experimentally made more or less resistant to change) when the degree of subsequent dissonance arousal is kept constant (Kiesler and Sakumura, 1966; Kiesler and Mathog, 1968) or orthogonally varied (Kiesler, Pallak, and Kanouse, 1968). The point here is not to promulgate Kiesler's definition of commitment, but rather to suggest that the resistance to change of cognitions is an important but ambiguous part of dissonance theory—that resistance to change should be investigated directly.

5. How do we measure the importance of an element? We discussed the vagueness of this term before. As one of the few theoretical parameters that affect the degree of dissonance aroused, it is somewhat surprising that the ambiguity of the term has persisted.

6. Singer (1966) draws attention to the little-discussed problem of directly measuring the degree of dissonance. He acknowledges that investigators check the effectiveness of the manipulations (e.g., did you feel free to leave?), but that often the manipulations themselves and other situational variables suggest alternative explanations for a given experiment. Under these conditions, Singer suggests that an independent assessment of the existence or degree of dissonance arousal would clarify the conclusion to be drawn from the experiment. This is a worthwhile criticism, which Singer correctly applies to all consistency theories.

---

[9] This, of course, puts aside the question of other ways of reducing dissonance, such as adding consonant cognitions.

7. There is a question of the either-or nature of alternative modes of dissonance reduction. For example, consider the problem of attitudinal discrepancy, discussed in detail in the next chapter. There is a tendency for dissonance researchers to maintain that in response to a discrepant communication, a subject may either change his attitude in the direction advocated, *or* he may reject the communication (and derogate the communicator). Sherif has objected to this dichotomization, claiming that "attitude change, evaluation of communication, and subsequent lines of action are not alternatives. They constitute aspects of an interrelated pattern . . ." (Sherif, Sherif, and Nebergall, 1965, p. x). Although the evidence is not complete on this issue, we tend to agree with Sherif and suggest that attitude change, derogation, and distortion of the position of the communication may all be processes in reaction to a discrepant communication that go on simultaneously.

8. How may one specify when one cognition "psychologically implies the obverse" of the other? We raise questions with respect to the meaning of both terms, "psychological implication" and "obverse." We discussed the problem of psychological implication earlier, with respect to Bramel's suggestions. Aronson (1968) is also concerned with the same problem. He suggests that psychological implication is most precisely viewed in terms of the person's expectations about his world. Further, one may ascertain whether one cognition implies another by asking people, "Given that statement A (representing cognition a) is true, what is your expectation about the truth or validity of statement B (representing cognition b)?" This is an interesting method of specifying consonant or dissonant relationshisps in advance, especially, say, in another culture. However, one wonders whether the method holds in extreme cases. Suppose a person decides to walk down a particular street and is subsequently hit on the head by a falling brick. Assume that this was completely unexpected. If disconfirmed expectations produce dissonance, then the brick should produce dissonance (assuming our hypothetical subject lives through the experience). However, for Festinger, this event should not produce dissonance. The cognition "A brick will fall on my head" was not present at the time the decision was made to traverse the street. This is crucial for Festinger. Further, assuming that a falling brick is no more likely on this street than another, the two cognitions are irrelevant to one another. It seems that the Aronson approach may not add a great deal in terms of definitions of dissonance, but it may provide methodological assistance. In setting up an experiment where little is

known about the cognitive world of the subjects, Aronson's method of asking other people which cognitions "hang together" may still be useful in selecting an experimental situation in which to manipulate dissonance. In short, the Aronson suggestion may not represent a theoretical advance, but may be methodologically useful.

Brehm and Cohen (1962) take issue with Festinger about the use of the term "obverse." They argue that the statement "two cognitions are in a dissonant relationship when one implies the obverse of the other" places too many limitations on the theory. They suggest instead the substitution of the phrase, "In the direction of being obverse" for the word "obverse." In this sense, one can have degrees of "obverseness." Aside from the philosophical issues involved, the Brehm and Cohen suggestion does add breadth to the theory. Consider a question we asked before: Given that it creates dissonance for a person of high self-esteem to cheat or lie, does it also produce dissonance for a person of moderate self-esteem to do so? Strictly speaking, Festinger's original statement would imply that it does not (or perhaps that we cannot say whether it does or not). Now the Brehm and Cohen addition to the theory implies that it does produce dissonance for the person of moderate self-esteem, but less than for the person of high self-esteem.

9. Can dissonance theory be disproven? Several critics have complained that dissonance theory is almost Freudian in its ability to explain data, no matter how they come out. One wag maintains that all of the experiments mentioned in Brehm and Cohen's (1962) book could have come out the opposite way and the dissonance theorists would have been able to explain them. Of course, if the experiments had come out the opposite way, no one would have paid any attention to dissonance theory in the first place. It is true that the degree of "unequivocality" in dissonance theory predictions varies directly with the amount of information that the researcher has about the subject's cognitive world. It seems quite clear that one can make straightforward derivations from dissonance theory, and furthermore they can do so more readily than from many other theories.

We feel that the preceding criticisms of dissonance theory are important ones. Adequate solutions to these problems must be found or the usefulness of this theoretical orientation will be lessened in the future. In spite of these criticisms we also feel that the theory has been an extraordinarily useful tool for the study of attitude and cognitive change. It has produced substantial as well as provocative data. Future theorists must necessarily incorporate these data into their framework for looking at attitude change problems. In the final analysis, social psychology could use more theorizing of this sort. The field of social psychology has always lacked theories with power.

Chapter 6

Social Judgment Theory

In 1961, Muzafer Sherif and Carl Hovland's book *Social Judgment: Assimilation and Contrast Effects in Communication and Attitude Change* was published as Volume 4 in the series of "Yale Studies in Attitude and Communication." Whereas most of Hovland's leadership and effort in the study of attitudes had previously been of an empirical sort, this volume constitutes more of a theoretical statement. Yet, in proper modesty, Sherif and Hovland prefer to think of their work as more of an *approach* to the study of attitudes rather than a theory about attitude organization or attitude change. Nevertheless, for the purposes of this book we shall treat their monograph as a theoretical statement.

The method of theory construction is largely based on the use of analogy—extrapolations from principles of experimental psychology and psychophysics. This imperialistic exploitation of the findings of experimental psychology characterizes much of Hovland's previous work in attitude change and is natural in light of his training and long research experience with the classical problems and issues of experimental psychology. In the present instance, the analogizing is primarily from the fountainhead of the oldest careful scientific psychological research—the area of psychophysics. The collaborative effort gathers greater appropriateness when we recall Sherif's classic social psychological contribution in the area of judgment and social influence, *The Psychology of Social Norms* (Sherif, 1936).

Since the social judgment theory draws so clearly from the research

238

findings of another area, the problem of evaluating it is in one sense complicated. For one thing, researchers concerned with psychophysical judgment are not agreed on a single theory to represent their own data. In their discussion of anchoring effects in judgment, Bieri, Atkins, Briar, Leaman, Miller, and Tripodi (1966) distinguish two broad categories of anchoring theories—"centering" and "distance" theories. Furthermore, within each type they point to a variety of approaches that differ in the variables they regard as crucial. Thus when it comes to extrapolating to another area such as attitude organization and change there are several possibilities: the Sherif and Hovland model could be correct for psychophysical judgments but inappropriate for social-psychological judgments; it could be inappropriate or inadequate for psychophysics and nevertheless correct for social judgments; and finally, it could be right or wrong for both research areas. To simplify our task, this presentation will largely ignore the literature concerned with judgment of nonsocial objects and focus instead solely upon judgments and attitudes toward social stimuli.

In the following pages we present the data concerning the model, the empirical and theoretical problems it encounters, and its relation to other theoretical systems which comment on the same sets of data. We will draw from both of the major statements of the model, although there are slight differences between the initial (Sherif and Hovland, 1961) and later statement (Sherif, Sherif, and Nebergall, 1965). When dealing with points on which they differ we shall try to indicate which version is being considered. In instances where the theory is vague or simply omits discussion of an important theoretical point, we shall take an explicit theoretical stand so that specific predictions can be made. In such cases, we hopefully will make the same interpretation that Sherif and Hovland would make themselves, had they been asked. In doing so we recognize that while this procedure makes the theory more precise, it is perhaps unfair to the authors. They may well have chosen to avoid explicit pronouncement on some theoretical points because there was not sufficient data available to suggest the appropriate interpretation.

The organization will proceed as follows. We shall first present the central points of the theory, followed by the data that led to the development of the theory. This will be followed by a criticism of the theory and the data on which it is directly based. Two additional sections will discuss the more recent experimental literature on judgment and attitude change.

The Theoretical Propositions and Supporting Data

THE CENTRAL POINTS OF THE THEORY

Let us begin with an example uncontaminated by the complexities of the social situation. Consider one of the most common textbook and classroom demonstrations of *contrast* for introductory psychology students. The subject is asked to place one hand in a bucket of hot water and the other in a bucket of cold water. After a few minutes, both hands are simultaneously immersed in a third bucket with water of moderate temperature. The experience and judgment that the water in this third bucket is simultaneously hot and cold is ubiquitously compelling. The hand formerly in the hot water now feels cold, whereas the other hand, formerly in the cold water, now feels hot. Such "background effects" are readily observable in a variety of pedestrian examples. For instance, when the temperature rises up to 20 degrees from a long -15 to -20 degree spell, one can see the hometown men walking down the streets in Minneapolis with their coats unbuttoned enjoying the warmth, whereas the stranger who has just flown in from Southern California is clearly miserably cold in spite of his tightly buttoned garb.

These homey examples of contrast effects of course do not reflect the depth of research on judgmental processes. Furthermore, the social judgment theory of attitude change is concerned with assimilation effects as well as contrast effects.

The central contention of Sherif and Hovland's theory is that judgmental principles are central to an understanding of the organization of attitudes and the circumstances under which they can be changed. In our interpretation, the theory explicitly views attitude change as a two-stage process. First, one makes a judgment about the position of the persuasive communication relative to one's own position. Attitude change occurs after this categorization or judgment. The amount of attitude change depends on the judged discrepancy between the communication and the respondent's own position. Thus the essential assumptions and postulates of the theory are empirical generalizations about judgment, and these generalizations are derived largely from the psychophysical literature. They can be briefly summarized by paraphrasing Sherif and Hovland (1961, pp. 179–183 . To facilitate comprehension, each principle will be illustrated by an example. In preparation, assume that one is confronted with an array of 20 cubes identical in size, texture, material, odor, and all other dimensions except weight.

1. *When confronted with a series of stimuli, humans tend to order or arrange them on a psychological dimension even in the absence of explicit standards.* After lifting the cubes one at a time, one would think of them as ranging from heavy to light even without instructions to do so or information about the actual weight of any of the cubes.

2. *To the extent that explicit standards are absent, the ordering or judgments are less stable. This is particularly so for stimuli that are intermediate or between the extremes of a dimension.* In the typical demonstration of the development of a psychological scale without an explicit standard stimulus (e.g., Wever and Zener, 1928), the series of 20 weights would be lifted in random order with instructions to label them with numbers, ranging, for instance, from 1 (for the lightest) to 7 (for the heaviest). Obviously, on the first run through the series the labels selected would not order them very accurately, but with repeated rounds the numerical assignments to each cube would correspond fairly well to the actual weights and range of the cubes. The "accuracy" of the judgmental process would be improved if a cube of intermediate weight was designated beforehand as a 4 and one was allowed to lift this weight first. Without such a standard, cubes of intermediate weights would be labeled less accurately or reliably.

3. *Both internal factors (motivation, learning, attitude) and social factors (instructions, demand characteristics) influence judgments. This influence is greater when objective standards for judgment are lacking or when the set of stimuli do not form a well-ordered series.* Thus past experience would make a weightlifter more prone to use low numbers when judging the cubes (i.e., label the weights as "light"), whereas a watchmaker would be more prone to use high numbers (i.e., label the weights as "heavy"). Similarly, social factors such as listening to another person's judgment of each cube would be influential. This would be more true on early as opposed to late rounds of judgment; likewise it would be less true for our cubes than for a more ambiguously ordered or poorly graded set of stimuli such as statements about the European Common Market.

4. *The extreme or end stimuli serve as particularly potent reference points (anchors) when (a) a person has had little experience with an ordered stimulus series on a particular dimension, (b) the potential range*

of stimulus values is unknown, or (c) *no explicit standards for judgment are provided. "Anchors" are strong reference points.* Without an explicit standard, (such as a cube of intermediate weight among the 20 which was labeled 4), the heaviest and the lightest cubes would serve as reference points. Judgments of the relatively heavy and relatively light cubes among the set would be more reliable than judgment of intermediate cubes.

5. *Introducing an anchor at either end* (*or just beyond the end*) *of a prior series produces assimilation. Introducing a new anchor considerably distant from* (*beyond*) *the previous range of stimuli produces contrast.* In terms of our weight-judging task, suppose that after several rounds of judgments, in each of which the seven numbers were applied to the cubes, we now selected out the heaviest weight and told the judge to consider this as a standard. In other words, before starting in again, he is told that this is the heaviest cube, that it is to be labeled 7, and the other cubes are to be judged in comparison to this one. Thus before lifting and judging each of the others, he is to lift this "standard" or "reference" cube. One consequence of this procedure will be *assimilation*. Cubes will be assigned higher numbers on the average than would have been the case had we not introduced the standard (anchor). In other words, the entire distribution of judgments is shifted toward the anchor (*assimilation*). On the other hand, had we introduced an anchor that was considerably heavier than any of those in our initial set of cubes, judgments of the set would be displaced away from the anchor. For instance, a cube of middling weight which had previously been judged as 4 might now be judged a 3 or 2. Figure 6.1 (taken from Sherif, Taub, and Hovland, 1958) illustrates *assimilation* and *contrast* effects with judgments of a set of six weights ranging from 55 to 141 grams. The response scale has only six judgment categories instead of the seven used in the preceding examples. Each bar graph presents the pooled distribution of 300 judgments by each of six subjects. Figure 6.1*a* presents the distribution when judgments are made without an explicit anchor. In Fig. 6.1*b* an end stimulus (from the original set) was designated as an anchor and we see the characteristic assimilation effect. And in Fig. 6.1*c* an extreme external stimulus was introduced as an anchor and the characteristic contrast effect occurs.

These empirical generalizations derived from the literature on judgments of psychological attributes of physical stimuli form the foundation of the theory. Extrapolations to judgments about social stimuli are fairly direct. There are, however, two added assumptions.

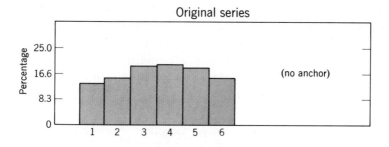

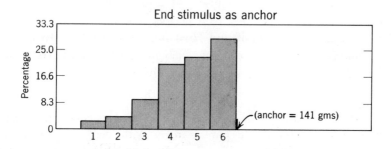

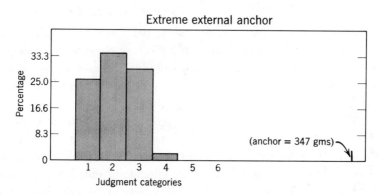

FIGURE 6.1. Distribution of judgments for series of weights without anchor (top) and with anchors at two distances above original series.

6. *The respondent's own stand on an issue serves as a strong reference point or internal anchor for judging attitude statements or persuasive communications.*

7. *When he is "involved" in the issue, his own stand produces even stronger anchoring effects.* Since the concept of "involvement" occupies

such a central position in the theory, it is important to define it. By "involvement" Sherif and Hovland seem primarily to refer to the intensity with which an attitude is held. But furthermore, when such attitudes are displayed, their expression is not primarily intended to be instrumental in procuring some immediate or situationally specific reward. Thus a position which is accepted or advocated solely in order to make another person respect or like one would not qualify. Ego-involving attitudes are related to ones "very conception of himself." In an earlier work (Sherif and Cantril, 1947, pp. 126–127) an ego-involved attitude is defined as a social value that the individual strongly identifies with and incorporates as part of himself. It is an attitude that is strongly rooted to a reference group—"to a person or group to whom the individual is committed" (Sherif and Hovland, 1961, p. 197). In his more recent statement (Sherif, Sherif, and Nebergall, 1965, pp. 64–65) Sherif emphasizes the *self-identity* aspect of involving attitudes. The involved person

". . . does not phrase his judgments as statements about the abstract attributes of the object. He phrases them with personal pronouns: '*I* think . . . ,' '*my* opinion . . . .' . . . when pressed for reasons, he frames them in personal terms: 'I am a member of the *X* family'; 'As a Negro, I feel . . .'; 'I am a Baptist' . . . ."

Yet note that even in these examples, the belief is tied to an important reference group; it is engaged with an entire value system. "Ego-involvement . . . is the arousal . . . of the individual's commitments or stands in the context of appropriate situations . . ." (Sherif, Sherif, and Nebergall, 1965, p. 65).

Given the above emphases in their conceptualization, it is perhaps easy to see why in terms of their research procedures Sherif and his co-workers have defined involvement as membership in a group with a known stand on an issue. Yet, as we later point out, if this particular operationalization of involvement is implemented by selecting subjects from natural, or existing groups, clear-cut interpretation of the data is ambiguous. It is of course conceivable that randomly assigned subjects could be experimentally induced to join or not join particular groups, thereby eliminating criticism stemming from nonrandom assignment. Offhand, however, this does not appear to be an easy solution. Other operationalizations of involvement are perhaps more feasible. For instance, any of the various operationalizations of committment might also be considered synonymous with involvement. Similarly, procedures which experimentally increase the intensity of subjects' attitudes might do. However, Sherif would not feel comfortable with an operationalization that focuses solely on intensity or certainty of belief. He considers ego-involvement in an attitude as more than a matter of intensity or strength. It is the importance of an attitude relative to or in comparison with other attitude dimensions. Operationally, this requires experimental alteration of the subject's ranking of the importance of one attitude dimension relative to others. Of course it remains to be seen whether or to what extent these various operationalizations are independent of one another.

Returning again to a consideration of the addition of these assumptions about the effect of "own-position" and "involvement," we can now apply the judgment principles to judgments about social objects. Hence in judging the position of an attitudinal statement, respondents who strongly favor a pro position themselves will displace intermediate items toward the con end of the dimension, whereas strongly con respondents will displace these same items in the opposite direction. Middling items are presumably most vulnerable to distortion since they are most distant from any external or internal anchor. Likewise, respondents with a strong or ego-involving attitude are most likely to distort judgments about the position of middling items.

In extending the judgment principles to include judgments about persuasive communications, Sherif has distinguished three important theoretical regions along an attitude dimension—the *latitude of acceptance,* the *latitude of rejection,* and, separating the two, the *latitude of noncommitment* (Sherif, Sherif, and Nebergall, 1965).[1] The latitude of acceptance constitutes the band of positions around one's own which one evaluates or judges as acceptable or tolerable; the latitude of rejection is that band of positions which one judges to be intolerable or unacceptable. In terms of experimental operations, Sherif defines latitude of acceptance as those statements which the respondent is willing to agree with or endorse; he defines latitude of rejection as those statements which the respondent marks as objectionable. The latitude of noncommitment is a residual category. It is defined as those positions not cate-

---

[1] This latter region, though mentioned in the first book (Sherif and Hovland, 1961), only receives empirical elaboration in the later volume (Sherif, Sherif, and Nebergall, 1965).

gorized as either acceptable or objectionable. Category boundaries are presumably determined by the degree to which a person is involved in the issue.

These three conceptual areas of an attitude dimension direct attention to the individuals attitude structure. For those with extreme positions, they typically divide the attitude dimension into three regions—a region of acceptable stands, a region of objectionable stands, and, separating the two, a band of intermediate or neutrally evaluated positions. However, for those with moderate positions, the attitude dimension may be further subdivided; for such persons there may be two distinct latitudes of rejection—one at each extreme. Each latitude of rejection would be separated from the latitude of acceptance (located at the middle of the dimension) by a latitude of noncommitment.

In summary, the theory points to a number of variables which, when present, allow distortion to intrude into the judgment process: an extreme stimulus (external anchor); ambiguous items, an ambiguous communication, or a poorly graded series of items or attitude positions; little past experience with the stimuli; situational factors which do not induce the respondent to discriminate between items; and a strong position or deep involvement in one's position on an issue. The breadth of this list of variables that control the judgment process will somewhat mislead the reader, however, in that Sherif's own recent work focuses primarily on the effects of involvement. This concentration of effort suggests, if only indirectly, that involvement exerts a greater effect on social judgments than any of the other factors save perhaps item position or communication position per se. Therefore we shall present the effects of involvement on judgment in fuller detail.

For the subject highly involved in his position on an attitude dimension, his position serves as a strong anchor; the consequence of this ego-involvement in one's position is a broader latitude of rejection. Initially (Sherif and Hovland, 1961) a narrower latitude of acceptance was also predicted as a consequence of involvement, but this has not turned out consistently to be the case (Sherif, Sherif, and Nebergall, 1965). Necessarily, then, to the extent that latitudes of acceptance remain unaffected, changes in the latitude of noncommitment inversely reflect changes in the latitude of rejection.

Figure 6.2 presents our interpretation of the theoretical distortion of item (or communication) position as a function of its true discrepancy from the respondent's own stand for each of three levels of involvement

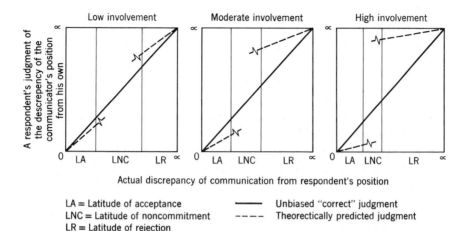

FIGURE 6.2. Theoretically predicted distortions in judgments of the communicator's position and shifts in the latitudes of noncommitment and rejection under three levels of involvement.

with a position on the attitude dimension. It shows that (1) within the latitude of acceptance, "true" discrepancy is underestimated as an increasing function of discrepancy, (2) within the latitude of rejection, true discrepancy is overestimated as a decreasing function of distance, (3) both of these effects are more exaggerated by the highly involved respondent and minimized by the uninvolved respondent, (4) for all involvement levels, the shift in direction of distortion presumably occurs within the latitude of noncommitment but close to the latitude of rejection,[2] and (5) for all levels of involvement the latitude of acceptance is approximately equal in size.

The seven enumerated judgment principles presented earlier probably seem sufficiently compelling to those of us who are not scholars of the psychophysical literature. Furthermore, the implications derived for judgments about social stimuli probably also seem straightforward. The less wary student may be quite satisfied with the precision of the predictions that can be made from these few simple principles. At this juncture, however, he may still wonder what the theory has to do with attitude

[2] Sherif never precisely states where along these three theoretical regions the shift occurs. In the absence of contradictory data this seems like the most reasonable supposition.

change. This puzzlement can be quickly quieted by reiterating the central assumption of the theory—that judgmental effects mediate attitude change. "The effects of a communication . . . depend upon the manner in which it is categorized by the individual." As we shall detail, according to the theory, if one knows how a communication is judged by the respondent, one can predict its persuasive effect. Thus, as previously indicated, the theory clearly implies a two-stage process—judgment, then attitude change (or stability).

Let us turn now to the problem of predicting attitude change. Sherif and Hovland present several propositions which presumably are consequences of the judgmental effects discussed above.

1. When persuasive attempts fall within his latitude of acceptance, an individual's opinion changes.

2. When they fall within his latitude of rejection he does not change his opinion. Indeed, Sherif and Hovland contend that communications falling within this region are likely to "reinforce the respondent's initial stand" or perhaps even produce boomerang effects.

3. As discrepancy between the respondent's own stand and the position advocated by the communication increases, there will be greater opinion change provided that the advocated stand does not fall within the latitude of rejection.[3]

4. For communications which advocate positions within the latitude of rejection, increased discrepancy produces less opinion change. Thus some point presumably close to the boundary between the latitude of noncommitment and the latitude of rejection defines the inflection point in the curvilinear function relating discrepancy to opinion change.[4]

Clearly then, the respondent's categorization is indeed central for predicting attitude change effects. Therefore all variables that control the judgment process become the essential predictive variables in the theory.

---

[3] This prediction may not appear to be explicitly derivable from the theory. For instance, in at least one place Sherif and Hovland (1961, p. 157) suggest a simple inverse linear relation. However, we interpret their hypothetical curves (1961, p. 49) as generally implying a curvilinear function. Furthermore, they do discuss (1961, p. 159) the curvilinear function described by Carlson (1956). Other presentations by those sympathetic to the Sherif and Hovland position have also interpreted the function as curvilinear (e.g., Whittaker, 1963).

[4] A more detailed discussion of these predictions and their derivation from the judgmental effects will be presented in a later section of the chapter entitled "Criticism."

SUPPORTING DATA COLLECTED BY SHERIF AND HOVLAND

We now consider how Sherif and Hovland were initially led to this particular emphasis in the study of attitude change. L. L. Thurstone, who was one of the major creative contributors to modern psychometrics, combined the methods that were currently in use for judging psychophysical stimuli with some assumptions from normal probability statistics to develop procedures for scaling social attitudes. Thurstone hoped to offer a rational basis for quantifying things that could not be independently related to measurable physical dimensions.

Among the various methods for judging stimuli, the method of equal appearing intervals is most widely used. Other techniques such as paired comparisons are particularly cumbersome because they require such a huge number of judgments. The method of equal appearing intervals simply requires that judges sort attitude statements into a given number of piles so that the statements in each pile are equally distant from those in adjacent piles. Thurstone was aware of the possibility that when a judge orders attitude statements he may be indicating his own position on the attitude dimension as well as providing scale values for particular attitude statements. "If the scale is to be regarded as valid, the scale values of the statements should not be affected by the opinions of the people who help construct it. This may turn out to be a severe test in practice, but the scaling method must stand such a test before it can be accepted as being more than a description of the people who construct the scale" (Thurstone and Chave, 1929, p. 92). Thus, in proposing his methods of attitude scale construction, Thurstone assumed that the scale values that were assigned to items would not depend in any way on the particular beliefs or attitudes of those who had served as judges.

Subsequently, several persons empirically tested this assumption and confirmed it. In reviewing these studies, however, Sherif and Hovland felt that the tests were not sufficiently sensitive and that they contained methodological problems which biased the results in a direction supporting the Thurstone assumption of independence between a judge's own attitude and his sorting of attitude statements. For instance, in the first test of this assumption (Hinckley, 1932), judges who lumped into a single pile as many as 30 statements out of 114 were assumed to have been careless and therefore were discarded as "poor judges." In some of the other studies Sherif and Hovland suspected that none of the judges held particularly strong or extreme stands on the issue under study. Therefore, even though "judges' own attitude" might indeed be a variable that influences judgments, the curtailment in the positions actually held by the judges in these studies would not allow the effect of "own attitude" to appear; i.e., the judges did not differ much.

To test this basic assumption in the Thurstone scaling procedure, Hovland and Sherif (1952) replicated Hinckley's experiment on attitude toward Negroes. They used Hinckley's original 114 statements but made certain that persons who were highly involved in the attitude issue were included among their judges. The distributions of the statements by judges with different initial positions can now be found in introductory textbooks. The Hinckley criterion for discarding judges would have eliminated three-fourths of Hovland and Sherif's Negro judges and two-thirds of their pro-Negro white judges. These judges with strong pro-Negro attitudes tended to lump the anti-Negro statements together. Furthermore, the item scale values generated by Negro judges, pro-Negro white judges, anti-Negro white judges, and white judges who meet the Hinckley criterion regarding "carelessness" differed from the original Hinckley values. Judges with extreme positions tended to displace neutral items away from their own positions, thereby generating a "piling up" of items distant from the judge's own position. To ascertain more definitively that these results were not due to "carelessness," Hovland and Sherif asked their judges to estimate the proportions of pro- and anti-Negro statements. They found that the estimated proportions of unfavorable statements coincided with the actual number of placements in unfavorable categories. In other words, judges did know what they had done during the judgment task. Although they may have indeed distorted the degree to which particular statements were pro or con, they knew how many they placed on each side of the midpoint. Had they been careless, as Hinckley maintained, these latter estimates would have been off.

It is easy to see how these findings relating judge's own attitude to the perception and differentiation among attitude items put Hovland and Sherif on the track of other judgmental effects in attitude research.

Let us turn now to some of the data that appear in support of both the initial and subsequent statements of the theory. Two field studies are described in the first presentation of the theory—the "prohibition study" and the "election study." For illustrative purposes we shall focus on the prohibition study (Hovland, Harvey, and Sherif, 1957). The study was carried out in Oklahoma shortly after a referendum which favored prohibition by a small margin. It is highly similar to both the 1956 election study and the 1960 studies which comprise *Attitude and Attitude Change* (Sherif, Sherif, and Nebergall, 1965).

Respondents participated in two sessions. In the first, latitudes of acceptance and rejection were determined by asking respondents to place each of nine statements on the issue into one of the three categories (latitude of acceptance, latitude of rejection, and latitude of noncommitment) and, in addition, to indicate his most and least preferred position. The nine statements presumably formed a Guttman-like scale[5] in which items could be ordered on the dimension, though no assumptions were made about the intervals between items. The theoretical importance of involvement required subjects who were likely to be deeply involved in the issue. Thus 183 subjects were sought from Women's Christian Temperance Union groups, the Salvation Army, and strict denominational colleges to represent the extremes on the dry side. Extremely wet stands were represented by 25 acquaintances of the experimenters. An additional group of 290 subjects had moderate stands.

One to three weeks after administration of initial measures, subjects were exposed to a tape recording of one of three communications from an unspecified source. Each was 15 minutes long and addressed the different considerations in the same sequence (e.g., the religious aspect, health considerations, financial considerations). A moderately wet communication was presented to wet, dry, and unselected subjects. A wet communication was presented to extremely dry subjects and a dry communication was presented to both wet and unselected subjects. Three types of dependent measures were obtained: (1) an estimate of the position of the communication; (2) the favorability of subjects' reactions to the communicator in terms of fairness and impartiality; and (3) a remeasure of their most preferred position and their latitudes of acceptance and rejection.[6]

Since the responses to all three of these dependent measures are theoretically determined by the respondent's prior judgmental response,

[5] Sherif et al. seem to believe that not all attitudes on social dimensions will form a Guttman scale (Sherif, Sherif, and Nebergall, 1965, p. 10); however, this seems to be a necessary requirement if the theory is to make predictions.

[6] Thus they employed an unbalanced design in which the dependent measures were confounded with any order effects due to position of a response measure among the three.

and since his judgmental response depends on his internalized reference scale or anchor, it is theoretically important to look first at the latitudes of acceptance and rejection of the different subject groups. Comparison of extreme and moderate subjects on the prohibition issue shows that those with extreme positions use broader categories for rejection than for acceptance and that their category for rejection is wider than the rejection category of more moderate subjects. The subjects in the election study also displayed this same tendency. In this later study, for the majority of those with extreme positions, latitudes of rejection were broader than latitudes of acceptance. On the other hand, for more than half the moderate subjects the width of their latitudes of acceptance exceeded the width of their latitudes of rejection. Hence moderate and extreme subjects have quite different reference scales for placing or ordering statements.

Sherif and Hovland next consider the implications of these differences for the three dependent measures—judging a speaker's position, evaluating him, and changing one's own attitude. In general, the expectations for judgments were obtained. Those with extremely wet stands judged that the moderately wet communication advocated a drier position than it did, whereas those with extremely dry stands judged this same communication as advocating a much wetter position than it did. These judgment effects are contrast errors. Presumably for both groups the communication was within the latitude of rejection, though more clearly so for the extremely dry subjects. Furthermore, as one might expect, the dry subjects show stronger contrast than the extremely wet subjects. On the other hand, those whose own position was close to that advocated by the communication judged it more accurately. They saw it as indeed advocating a slightly wet position.

These findings carried over into ratings of favorability. As seen in Fig. 6.3, the closer the communication to the respondent's own position, the more likely he is to favorably evaluate the communication. The wet communication was favorable to an increasingly smaller percent of subjects holding positions at each more distant point on the dimension. The same was true for those exposed to the extreme dry communication. In the case of those exposed to the moderately wet communication, the percent of favorable evaluations decreased with added distance on either side of the communication.

The attitude change results also depended on the position of the respondent. Among those exposed to the wet communication, the net per-

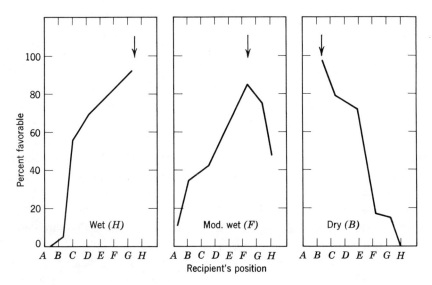

FIGURE 6.3. Percentage of favorable evaluations of wet, moderately wet, and dry communications by subjects holding various positions on prohibition. The arrow (and letter in parenthesis) indicates the approximate position of the communication.

cent of change in the direction advocated was $+4.3\%$ for the extremely dry subjects versus 28.3% for the unselected subjects. For those exposed to the dry communication, the net percentages of change were $+4.0\%$ for the extremely wet subjects versus $+13.8\%$ for the unselected subjects. In each case, compared to the moderate subjects, approximately twice as many extreme subjects remained unchanged by the communication.

Similar figures were obtained in another field study of political attitudes prior to the 1960 presidential election. The percentage of change among those taking a moderate position was almost twice as frequent as those with extreme stands (Sherif, Sherif, and Nebergall, 1965, p. 175).

CRITICISM

The theory can be criticized from two standpoints—empirical and logical. The empirical considerations concern the extent to which Sherif and Hovland's own data as well as others' support their theoretical predictions. Logical questions concern the extent to which the predictions of the theory do indeed follow from the basic premises. We now critically examine only the prohibition and election studies. In addition, we shall consider some logical aspects of the theory. A fuller treatment of the literature associated with each segment of the theory will appear in later sections.

THE PROHIBITION AND ELECTION STUDIES. The major methodological criticism of the prohibition and election studies is that the groups are not randomly selected and assigned to conditions. Neglecting this essential feature of the experimental method necessarily creates ambiguity regarding the causal antecedents of observed effects. The consequence is that any observed differences between the subject groups can as readily be attributed to group differences on other dimensions besides the crucial dimension of involvement. This criticism strikes at all three of the dependent effects that are of interest: judging either attitude statements or the position of communications; evaluating the favorability or fairness of the communicator; and accepting the position advocated by the communication.

The problem faced by Sherif and Hovland was how to demonstrate the powerful effects of involvement. Apparently, they questioned whether one could *experimentally* induce such differences. Thus they chose as subjects natural groups who were deeply committed to a strong stand on an issue and compared them to other groups who were less strongly committed. They, of course, were cognizant of the problem this created but felt impelled to insure a high level of involvement. Though their data do in large part show the effects predicted by differences in involvement, there are nevertheless numerable plausible rival hypotheses to explain their obtained outcomes.

It is very possible to argue that the "involvement" groups also differed in intelligence, open-mindedness, education, age, and a variety of other characteristics besides the one to which they wish to point. Let us spell out how these variables may account for the attitude change effects obtained in the prohibition study without reference to group differences in involvement. For instance, studies show that one important factor governing attitude change is comprehension of the message. Intelligent, well educated subjects may be expected to show more change in that they are more likely to comprehend a complex auditory presentation. Thus it should not be surprising if moderate subjects—the college students—show more change than Salvation Army Women and WTCU members. It is quite plausible that these more extreme groups are indeed less intelligent and less well educated than the college students. Thistlethwaite, de Haan, and Kamenetsky (1955) have shown that comprehension of the intended conclusion was positively related to the respondent's intellectual ability. Furthermore, under some conditions, those with superior comprehension of a communicator's conclusion tend to be influenced more (Thistlethwaite and Kamenetsky, 1955).

We may also expect age and open-mindedness to generate the same predicted outcome. The type of person attracted to such extreme groups as the WCTU may very well be more dogmatic, rigid, or closed-minded than the average person. This closed-mindedness could produce errors in judgment as well as greater resistance to persuasive attempts. Rokeach (1960) has pointed out that dogmatic people have greater difficulty in problem solving. In analyzing these differences, he finds that they are not due to a lack of analytical ability. Rather, the dogmatic person tends to be deficient in synthesizing new information with old knowledge. This would seem to be precisely the deficiency that would lead to decreased persuasion among extreme groups such as the Salvation Army or the WCTU. Being unable to assimilate and synthesize the elements of the communication with their prior belief system, they remain unchanged. Similarly, older people are usually more fixed and intractable in their attitudes. On this dimension, too, the groups differed in a direction which would allow this variable by itself to account for the obtained outcome.

Another aspect of the subject selection problem concerns the difference in the extremity of respondents' positions; in Sherif and Hovland's research, differences in involvement were correlated with differences in extremity. This is, of course, expected. The U-shaped function relating extremity of position and intensity of belief is a common finding (Suchman, 1950). In terms of the theoretical predictions, it is important to isolate the effects of the two variables. According to Sherif and Hovland, the resistance to persuasion found in "involved" subjects is presumably due to their involvement and not to the extremity of their position.[7]

---

[7] Differences in initial extremity also raise the issue of regression. Given the assumption of a normal distribution of initial positions, in the absence of any experimental treatment those classified as extreme are likely to appear more middling on a second measurement. On the other hand, those with middling initial positions are more likely to remain stable. These artifactual differences run counter to Sherif and Hovland's theoretical expectations for these groups and therefore do not constitute a rival explanation of their effect.

Sherif and Hovland would argue that both extremity and involvement were instrumental. In principle the involvement effects do not depend on endorsement of an extreme position. Hence, were middle-of-the-roaders highly involved in their position, they too would exhibit greater assimilation and contrast effects and consequently less attitude change than uninvolved middle-of-the-roaders, simply because of the anchoring effects of involvement. While ordinarily one does not think of people who endorse the middle of a position as ego-involved with their stand, one can imagine this happening. For instance, a ward heeler for the Democratic Party in Chicago holds a very middling democratic position—in contrast to A.D.A. or more liberal type democrats. Nevertheless, a person such as the ward heeler may be much more involved in his stand than many of those who espouse more liberal positions. Interestingly, in the more recent presentation (Sherif, Sherif, and Nebergall, 1965) Sherif reports that ego-involved subjects can be identified by a narrow latitude of noncommitment and that, furthermore, when identified as "involved," middle-of-the-roaders do indeed show the predicted effects.

Other differences between the extreme and moderate groups emerge if we try to define more narrowly the boundaries of "involvement" or separate the concept into component parts. For example, commitment provides another dimension of difference between the extreme and the moderate groups. While strong commitment to a position often characterizes those who are deeply involved in an issue, it is clear that in other instances people become committed to a stand without any deep involvement with the issue. Kelman (1958) has labeled such instances "compliance." In the present case, the highly involved groups probably did feel much more commitment to their stand—though we could undoubtedly imagine circumstances where persons deeply involved in a stand on an issue felt less commitment than others who cared little about the issue.[8]

Ambiguity can also stem from a variety of "past history" differences between the two type of subjects. Those involved in the issue may have frequently practiced applying negative labels to positions antagonistic to their own.

Other problems may stem from the motivational underpinnings of

---

[8] Likewise, taking Sherif and Hovland's definition of involvement—membership in a group with a known stand—there are undoubtedly numerous instances in which appearing on a membership list *does not* imply commitment.

the initial attitude held by the different groups. One important contribution of the functional approach to the study of attitudes (Sarnoff and Katz, 1954; Katz and Stotland, 1959; and Smith, Bruner, and White, 1956) is the emphasis that the same attitude can be held by different persons for different reasons. Furthermore, they argue that when the motivational basis for the attitude differs, the techniques for changing the attitude must also differ. In the case of the prohibition study this may be particularly true (Zimbardo, 1961). Among those who actively join groups organized to promote legal sanctions against drinking, their antiliquor attitudes may serve important ego-defensive functions. Liquor may represent loss of self-control, licentiousness, concupiscence, and sin. Promulgation of their own view may be important for defense, suppression, and masking of their impulses in this direction. For attitudes held in support of such ego-defensive functions, persuasive attempts that rely on informational input and cognitive restructuring may hardly touch the respondent. Such people may be particularly resistant to that brand of persuasion. Instead, self-insight procedures (McClintock, 1958) or the provision of other social-emotional supports for their fears may be the key to persuasion. On the other hand, for those who held more moderate positions, their position may have been less intimately tied to their central value system. For them, the possibility of altering their stand may not imply a risk of exposing themselves to motives in themselves that they would find difficult to confront with equanimity. For the wet subjects with extreme views, a different set of motives may have been tied to their attitudinal position. For some of these persons, retaining a wet position may have been motivated by the instrumental value of liquor. They may have been store owners who made money through the sale of liquor.

This discussion of the causal antecedents of these obtained effects raises a related question concerning the central assumption of the theory—do judgmental processes really mediate attitude change results? The fact that they are observed to covary (show the predicted correlations) obviously does not by itself establish that the attitude change effects are indeed due to the temporally prior judgments of the position advocated by the communicator or evaluation of the communicator's trustworthiness. In the prohibition and election studies, the fact that the judgmental responses were measured prior to respondents' statement of attitude does not help. Both processes may be simultaneous or concomitant. Or, on the contrary, the judgmental response may be a consequence of the amount of attitude change.

How can one ascertain the causal relation between judgment and attitude change? It does not appear as though there is any easy solution. Certainly, negative instances in which the expected judgment effects were not in accord with the obtained attitude change would cause doubt, particularly if the instrument on which no effect was obtained was known to be a reliable measure and the sample size provided substantial power. In other words, if an experimental treatment which produced attitude change was shown to have no effect whatsoever on the judgmental responses of a separate, independent group, it would be difficult to argue that judgmental changes had produced or mediated the observed attitude change. This type of attack on the problem, of course, amounts to trying to prove the null hypothesis. Although statistical propriety prohibits such folly, lack of better solutions may provide some justification. As indicated, one would insist in such instances upon statistical tests which have great power. It would also be better to test the judgmental effect on an independent group rather than the same group that will be measured for attitude change. When the same group is used, complications inevitably make causal inference murky. If the judgmental effects are assessed after the attitude measurement, they may represent balancing or consistency operations in which the subject attempts to adjust his judgments so that they are in tune with his present attitudinal position. If judgments precede the measurement of attitude, there is perhaps less danger, but then too we run the risk of assuming that the underlying causal relations conform to the particular temporal arrangement we have chosen for our response measures. Thus the causal connection may still be reversed; the treatment may essentially provoke only attitude change occurring during (or after) the treatment and not necessarily at the precise time we measure it. Therefore the fact that we measure it after measuring judgmental responses does not preclude the possibility that the judgmental changes still represent efforts to retain balance or consistency among one's cognitions.

Of course the preceding considerations apply as cogently to the case where the judgmental response is measured in a separate independent group. There, too, if judgment effects are found, they may be a *consequence* of attitude change, even though attitude change remained unmeasured.[9]

[9] To add further to this causal puzzle Sherif and Hovland's own work may mislead the unwary about their stand. They firmly argue in both books that the judgmental response mediates attitude change or influence processes. Judgment

ASSIMILATION AND CONTRAST EFFECTS. Although it sometimes appears as if the principles Sherif and Hovland presented for attitude change were logically deduced from the judgment principles, this is probably not the case. It is more probably true that both sets of principles represent empirical inductions. Furthermore, it appears that the judgmental principles rest heavily on the outcome of a single study (Sherif, Taub, and Hovland, 1958). Since in many instances they fail to state either the principles themselves or their logical connections in a detailed or precise form, closer examination of some of them may be fruitful. How are assimilation and contrast effects affected by extremity? The basic outcomes are straightforward: assimilation occurs provided the communication is within the latitude of acceptance, and contrast occurs when it falls within the latitude of rejection.[10] But within either of these regions, is the magnitude of assimilation (or contrast) constant or, as we have interpreted it in Fig. 6.2, does it vary as some function of discrepancy? Presumably the scale end points must necessarily restrict the amount of assimilation (or contrast) that could occur, but apart from modifications imposed by scale restriction, a constant distortion effect could conceivably occur over most discrepancy levels. It seems as if Sherif and Hovland imply that this is not the case. Instead, they seem to suggest that within the latitude of acceptance, the greater the actual discrepancy between respondent's and communicator's stand, the more assimilation occurs; whereas in the latitude of rejection, greater discrepancy produces less contrast. This implies that both the greatest assimilation and the greatest contrast occur for positions of "moderate"

---

is conceptualized as the independent (or mediating) variable and attitude change the dependent variable. However, their earlier research on scaling problems superficially implies an opposite position in that in these studies they were concerned with the possibility that a judge's own attitude influences the way he judges opinion statements. Thus in these studies attitude was the independent variable and judgment the dependent variable. Any apparent contradiction between the two types of research disappears when we simply note that they enter the sequence of events at different points in time. This becomes clear when we merely list the elements of the chain in their proper temporal sequence: (1) the subjects own prior attitude (anchor); (2) his judgment about the attitudinal or persuasive materials; and (3) his subsequent attitudinal position.

[10] As previously indicated, the more recent statement (Sherif, Sherif, and Nebergall, 1965) emphasizes and empirically explores the latitude of noncommitment as well.

discrepancy falling somewhere within the latitude of noncommitment—that area separating the rejection and acceptance regions.[11]

Deep involvement in the issue does two things: it presumably increases the magnitude of both contrast and assimilation effects, and it produces a shift in the range of scale positions within which each of the two processes occur. But, if so, are the increments in assimilation and contrast constant or do they interact with discrepancy? Once again, Sherif and Hovland appear to imply that the increase in contrast or assimilation that occurs with greater involvement is not a constant but depends on the degree of discrepancy.

ATTITUDE CHANGE EFFECTS. Regardless of which of the preceding alternatives accurately represents the correct social judgment view, either will effectively generate the obtained empirical outcome of less attitude change for persons highly ego-involved in the issue. For communications within (or close to) the latitude of acceptance, the involved respondent will assimilate the communicator's position toward his own much more than the uninvolved respondent and as a consequence will perceive the communicator as advocating less change. Being thus subject to less pressure toward change, his original position will remain less influenced than that of the uninvolved respondent. If we consider the analogous effects for these two types of respondents when they receive instead a communication in their latitude of rejection, the predictions are perhaps less clear. However, if we argue analogously, the involved respondent by virtue of greater displacement of the communication away from his own position will find it less tolerable, more incredible, and less persuasive. This analysis leads to the outcome of less attitude change for highly involved subjects under all levels of discrepancy.

The problem of deriving boomerang effects still remains. Sherif and Hovland contend that boomerang effects should be manifested most

---

[11] Ward's interpretation of the effect of discrepancy within the latitude of rejection is directly opposite to our own (Ward, personal communication, 1968). He sees the model as predicting *increasing* contrast within the latitude of rejection. (For the latitude of acceptances, his interpretation concurs with our own.) He further suggests that in attempting to supply these principles to predictions for attitude change, it may be useful to distinguish absolute change and relative change (the percentage of possible change). While some studies indicate that discrepancy is directly related to absolute change, Fisher and Lubin (1958) show it to be inversely related to relative change.

often by highly involved subjects, particularly after exposure to a highly discrepant communication. This prediction was apparently empirically derived. Our own logical analysis of the theory leads to an exactly opposite conclusion. In analyzing this situation it is important to consider two things. First, we must keep in mind the temporal assumption of the theory—judgment occurs first and attitude change follows. The second thing that bears attention is a consideration of the function or purpose of a boomerang response. One possible interpretation is that they occur as an attempt by the respondent to differentiate his own position from that of the communicator. If so, however, note the implication when we add to this the temporal assertion of the theory. First, we attribute to the highly involved subject *less* need for a boomerang response. Since according to assimilation and contrast principles he will display more contrast and displace the discrepant communicator's stand further away from his own than the uninvolved subject, he should have less residual need to dissociate his own position from that of the communicator. And therefore he should be less likely to show a boomerang response. Note that if we removed the temporal restriction imposed by the theory and assumed instead that judgment of the communicator's stand and statements of one's own opinion reflect a simultaneous hydraulic process, the typical empirical outcome of greater boomerang for involved subjects would be understandable.[12]

How can Sherif and Hovland rescue themselves from this derivation which contradicts their empirically derived expectations? Several possibilities could impugn the preceding argument. For the highly involved subject there always may be stronger *residual or extraneous* motivation to differentiate himself from an unacceptable communicator which still remains after the operation of any judgmental distortions. Additionally, for the highly involved subject scale restriction (due to the use of fewer judgment categories) seems more likely to disallow differentiation by contrast. Since all the "necessary" differentiation cannot be achieved by contrasting the communication, shifting his own position away from the communicator remains as the only alternative. This would imply

---

[12] It is important to note that this same line of reasoning would hold even if other interpretations of why boomerang effects occur were true. For instance, if people boomerang to "psychologically increase" their certainty in their own belief, the argument above would still apply.

that when presented a highly discrepant communication, those highly involved in a moderate position should display larger boomerang effects than those involved in an extreme position because they have more room to shift their own position (in terms of scale space). This could be tested by manipulating whether subjects were given a nonanchored scale on which they were allowed to assign whatever scale values (numbers) they chose to described positions on the dimension.

OTHER CHARACTERISTICS OF THE THEORY. A few metatheoretical aspects of the theory also warrant comment. Sherif strongly asserts that knowledge of how a person categorizes things is essential for predicting attitude change effects. A person's involvement with the issue provides one key for predicting his categorizing behavior. In their discussions of theory, psychologists (e.g., Spence, 1952) have differentiated those whose laws are primarily R-R laws from those who focus on the development of S-R laws. As almost all introductory texts point out, both laws allow prediction, but only S-R laws permit control. Being ahistorical, a theory comprised of relationships among responses does not contain information on the antecedent conditions that promote the development or acquisition of those responses.

To the extent that the principles emphasizing the necessity of knowing a person's categorizing or judgment indeed represent the thrust of social judgment theory, the theory loses power in the sense of control of human behavior. One must know one set of a person's responses in order to know another set. This emphasis on individual differences in attitude structure along with the reliance upon data collected in the field seem particularly distant from Hovland's previous experimental emphasis and achievement. The central role of individual differences is additionally paradoxical in light of Sherif's criticisms of dissonance theory for the eventual likelihood that it will have to make explanations in terms of individual differences. He characterizes dissonance theory as inadequate in that it fails to provide rules that specify which dissonance-reducing alternative a person will choose and argues that as a consequence it cannot make precise predictions. He foresees that dissonance theory will eventually have to explain the choice among the several dissonance-reducing alternatives "in terms of unidentified individual differences in coping with discrepant confrontations" (Sherif, Sherif, and Nebergall, 1965, p. xi). ". . . The option of one or another of the alternatives has been stated so generally . . . . as to become a matter of individual differences in psychodynamic mechanisms" (Sherif, Sherif, and Nebergall, 1965, p. 217). Improvement "would require that a new personality typology be devised with all the attendant methodological complications" (Sherif, Sherif, and Nebergall, 1965, p. xi). Although dissonance theory researchers may strongly disagree with Sherif's evaluation, the important point here is that social judgment theory itself is in one sense an individual difference theory.

Sherif is undoubtedly aware of this, but he believes that there would be great methodological problems in developing new measures of personality typologies to identify individual differences in preference among modes of dissonance reduction, whereas individual differences in persons' categorization of communications "can be computed precisely" (Sherif, Sherif, and Nebergall, 1965, p. xi). Furthermore, and perhaps of greater importance, to the extent that specifiable antecedent stimulus conditions can be shown to control judgmental responses, the criticisms that stem from the R-R relation between judgment and attitude simply vanish.

Most social-psychological theorizing employs cognitive concepts. It can be argued, for instance, that dissonance theory at least as initially presented (Festinger, 1957) is concerned solely with the cognitive consequences when cognitive elements stand in dissonant relation to one another. The rules for translating these mental events into behavioral acts is left unspecified by the theory. This is not to say that no such rules exist. Obviously those trained in the dissonance tradition have learned many rules for applying the theory in experimental settings, and perhaps many failures to replicate dissonance experiments can be traced to ignorance of them. The point, however, is that the "formal statement" of the theory does not contain them. The social judgment theory in contrast is much more closely tied to specific measurement methods (e.g., the techniques for measuring latitudes of acceptance, rejection, and noncommitment). To this extent, the theory is more behavioral than others. At the same time, however, it is clear that the processes with which the theory is concerned are largely cognitive.

The last significant consideration is the extent to which the theory was developed inductively as opposed to deductively. It should be apparent that the important theoretical assumptions were empirically derived and that the theory was developed inductively. Our previous discussion of the logical derivation of some predictions emphasizes this point.

Recent Experimental Literature

JUDGMENT EFFECTS

The work on the judgment or scaling of attitude items falls into two groups, which essentially attack the same issue from different sides. One approach considers the extent to which incorrect scale values are generated by Thurstone scaling procedures when the judgments of certain classes of judges are excluded. The other (and larger) body of research focuses on the extent and direction of influence exerted by the judge's own attitude. Social judgment theory is concerned more directly with the second focus.[13] However, both sets of literature are obviously relevant to the judgment phase of social judgment theory. They focus on the antecedent stimulus characteristics as well as the intrapsychic characteristics of the judge as determinants of the judgmental response.

THE ACCURACY OF THURSTONE SCALE VALUES. As previously noted, the study that most directly stimulated the work by Sherif and Hovland on the effect of the judges' own attitudes was performed by Hinckley in the 1930s. In a recent replication of his original study, Hinckley (1963) used the same attitude items. However, contrary to the earlier procedure whereby subjects who placed more than 30 out of the 114 statements into a single pile were discarded, no subjects were discarded. Further differences between the replication and the original study included a more careful premeasure of the judges' own position and a smaller sample of judges. Hinckley reports a correlation of .94 as compared to the original correlation of .98 between the median scale values assigned by pro- and anti-Negro groups. Furthermore, he notes that there is no tendency for particular categories of statements, neutral or otherwise, to be judged more extreme by either group. Pointing to the comparability of the two correlations, he concludes that the measuring function of a scale constructed by the Thurstone method will not be affected by the judges' own position.

His data, of course, do confirm the similarity in the ratings of judges who differ in attitude. However, the crucial question is whether the

---

[13] Since the studies in this second group do not attempt to separate the effects of the judges' involvement in the issue and the extremity of his position, a separate discussion of each variable is unnecessary.

direction and nature of the small differences can be explained by the theory. As Granneberg (1955), Hovland and Sherif (1952), and Kelley, Hovland, Schwartz, and Abelson (1955) point out, the correlation is a poor measure of the similarity between ratings. Whereas the correlation is relatively sensitive to agreement in rank orderings, it is relatively insensitive to *perceived differences* between attitudes that are similarly ranked. (For instance, note that the correlation between x and x^2 for the integers 1 to 20 is .975). Thus, even though judges may rank items similarly, it is still quite possible that judges with different attitudes will assign different magnitudes of scale values to those items.

Upshaw (1965) used a restricted set of items which included only those with minimal ambiguity, and he confirmed the findings of the two Hinckley studies. Judges with different attitudes produced almost perfectly correlated ratings. Two additional outcomes, however, supported the Hovland and Sherif position: judges' attitudes and the item judgments were negatively related, and the pro-judges evaluated the most pro-items as more favorable and the most anti-items as more unfavorable than did the other judges. However, Upshaw rejects the contrast and assimilation processes that Hovland and Sherif invoke as explanatory mechanisms. He attributes the negative relation between attitude and scale value to differences in "origin" rather than to a process called "contrast." Likewise, he views the tendency of pro-judges to rate pro-items more favorably than other judges as a manifestation of differences in the "judgmental unit" rather than a consequence of an "assimilation" process. He argues that judges do not differ in the astuteness of their discriminative abilities, but rather that they only differ in their judgmental language. He believes that Sherif and Hovland should have emphasized both the origin and unit aspects of the judgmental language instead of invoking such dynamic processes as "assimilation" and "contrast." He concludes that the final scale values that are assigned by judges can be expected to differ from one another in terms of an additive constant which corresponds to the origin of the scale and a multiplicative constant corresponding to the unit of the scale, and goes on to note that this is all that is demanded from an interval scale (which is what the Thurstone and Hinckley scales are designed to be).

At first thought, one might judge that Upshaw's conclusions do not leave us any better off than we were initially in that for every scale that is constructed we would need to know the additive and multiplicative constants for that set of judges. Perhaps, too, we need to know these same constants for the respondent when we attempt to measure his attitude. However, as Upshaw (personal communication, January, 1968) points out, in defining an interval scale as one that is invariant with transformations of origin and unit, one implicitly declares that *for purposes of measurement,* neither the origin nor the unit conveys any information. Therefore these two parameters can be ignored in that their values are always arbitrary. Taking the average value is as defensible as any other method of generating a scale of arbitrary origin and unit.

Since Upshaw believes that the Hovland and Sherif data (1952) can be accounted for entirely by origin and unit, he feels they have no implication whatsoever for Thurstone scaling. He would not say that judgmental displacements are uninteresting psychologically, but, rather, that they should be viewed as linguistic phenomena until someone provides data that clearly force a perceptual interpretation.[14]

THE EFFECT OF JUDGE'S OWN ATTITUDE. As indicated, social judgment theory is more directly concerned with the biasing effect of one's own attitude on objective judgments of the appropriate scale values for attitude items. Segall (1959) examined the effect of the judge's own attitude under two judgment tasks, absolute judgments and judgments relative to one's own position. He found that in the absolute judgment task the judge's own attitude had little influence, whereas in the relative judgment task his own attitude was indeed important. This latter finding, however, is less striking than one might first expect since it essentially amounts to the judge's ability to obey instructions (i.e., judge the items relative to their own position). The more important finding of Segall's study is the "order effect."

When judges are presented attitude statements that cover only parts of the total stimulus dimension, absolute judgments of the entire set of statements are biased. Segall handles these findings in terms of adaptation level theory but notes that the "residual factors"—the judge's own attitude—*did not* have a strong effect. Noting three possible interpretations of his data, Segall favors a modification of adaptation level theory such that it takes into account the differential contributions of the serially

---

[14] "A perceptual interpretation of a 'constant error' would need to be supported by ratio scale data, along the lines of that supplied by Hicks and Campbell (1965). However, our ratio scaling theories are so fragile that almost any demonstration of constant errors with such scales are likely to result in a challenge to the scaling model . . ." (Upshaw, personal communication, January, 1968).

arranged stimuli. He suggests temporal weighting of stimuli so that those which occur earlier in a contiguous series contribute more heavily to the adaptation level. This amounts to a within-session primacy effect. When he couples this with a between-session recency effect he can account for all the facets of his data on absolute judgment. Thus his findings are consistent with adaptation level theory provided that experiences are weighted differentially according to their degree of remoteness in time and the nature of the judgment task.

A major finding of Hovland and Sherif was that subjects at one end of attitude continuum overloaded extreme categories at the opposite end of the continuum with items. In terms of Segall's study, this would have amounted to an interaction between item position and judge's own attitude on a response measure concerned with the number of items placed in each category. Segall does not present data analyses that would explicitly test this hypothesis. He did find that subjects who were first exposed to pro-statements exhibited contrast and judged anti-statements as more anti than did subjects who were not first exposed to pro-statements. Converse findings were obtained for the judgments of pro-statements by people who had or had not previously been exposed to anti-statements.

Berkowitz and Goranson (1964) show that regardless of the actual discrepancy between a judge's own attitude and his partner's view, when a judge was previously induced to like her partner they minimized the difference between themselves and the partner's position. On the other hand, when the judge was induced to dislike her partner, regardless of the objective discrepancy between herself and the partner, she overestimated the difference between their scale positions.

Upshaw (1962) distinguished four models to explain judgment behavior. The first he called perceptual vigilance. According to this model, the more extreme the judge's own attitude (and the greater his personal involvement), the more likely he is to be threatened by the judgment task. As a consequence, judges displace items in a direction opposite to their own position. Neutral judges, on the other hand, being less involved in the task, give more accurate judgments than the extreme judges. In other words, according to this model, only contrast effects of varying sizes would be found. A second model, the assimilation-contrast formulation, presumably engages two processes: assimilation of items close to one's own position, and contrast of items distant from one's own position. Presumably, the Sherif and Hovland theory is some sort of amalgamation of the assimilation-contrast model and the perceptual vigilance model.

In Upshaw's interpretation, manipulation of the item series in terms of its range or in terms of constriction at one or the other end of the entire attitudinal dimension should have no effect according to either the vigilance or the assimilation-contrast model. Furthermore, he states that manipulation of the item series should not interact with the judge's attitude. It is the characteristics of the judge (not the items) that are crucial. Actually, however, it is not perfectly clear that his interpretation is necessarily correct. For instance, it is quite conceivable that an extremely pro-judge who is presented a set of items to scale which only cover the con end of the dimension will experience much more threat from those items than, for instance, a judge with the same attitude who is given a broader range of items, some of which match his own position. The same sort of exaggeration may occur in the assimilation-contrast model as well for item series with different ranges.

The third model, the adaptation level model, appears to make more complex predictions than either of the other two in that it includes more variables, namely, both the judge's own attitude and the item series to be judged. The two factors should interact or combine to affect the scale positions assigned to items. The judge's attitude contributes to the "residual effect" and serves as an anchor, but, in addition, the item series as a whole also represents a background or context within which or against which individual items are judged.[15]

The fourth model is the variable series model. Its critical feature is whether or not the item series includes the judge's own position. Unlike adaptation level theory, in which the entire set of attitude items determines the adaptation level for the next item, the variable series model predicts an interaction between "own-position" and "item series."[16] It

---

[15] Adaptation level theory assumes that the individual uses the entire range of experienced stimuli plus his own attitude—which is a residual factor—in forming the adaptation level. Helson does not provide any precise information regarding how the residual stimuli should be weighted in combination with the context or background stimuli. Furthermore, as already indicated, Helson provides no cues regarding temporal weighting. It is conceivable that all three of these factors interact in some complex manner.

[16] It should be noted that adaptation level theory also includes own-position as part of the residual factors which go into the determination of the adaptation level.

treats the question of whether or not the judge's own position is within or outside of the item series as a dichotomous or noncontinuous variable; gradations of the judge's position within these two categories are presumably irrelevant.

Upshaw concludes from his data that the variable series model receives the most support. He argues that the Sherif and Hovland criticism and research which cast doubt on the assumptions and data of Hinckley and Thurstone (that judges' own attitudes are irrelevant) are due to the fact that Hovland and Sherif used judges whose own attitudes were beyond the range represented by Hinckley's items.[17] Upshaw's careful analysis of scaling problems using the Thurstone technique is clearly more ambitious than the preceding work. His experimental design, at least in part, allows differential predictions for the different interpretations of bias in the scaling data. That is, the different theoretical interpretations which are available to explain these effects have at least been partially put to competing tests.

Manis (1960) found a U-shaped curve relating the standard deviation of the judgments of a set of items to the judges' attitudes. The significance of this finding is its apparent support for the Hovland-Sherif model. In other words, for a total set of judges, there is more dispersion in the scale values assigned to items which appear at the extremes of the item series. In effect, this could be produced by assimilation and contrast tendencies of the judges within the total pool who have their own attitudes at either the pro or con end of the dimension. Thus the pro-judges are biasing their estimate of the con-items downward in the con-direction, whereas the con-judges would be biasing the same items in the opposite direction. In considering Upshaw's research, Manis notes that Upshaw's data can be used in support of his own finding. Upshaw found that the standard deviation of item values increased with pro-ness of attitude. Manis argues that because the anti-judges in Upshaw's experiment held positions near the middle of the series used, that this relation between pro-ness and the standard deviation can be considered as a replication of part of the U- relation which he found.

Ostrom (1966), continuing the line of investigation initiated by Up-

---

[17] On the other hand, as will be subsequently discussed, the recent work by Cook and his co-workers would suggest that this is not the case in that Cook has found the type of displacements that Sherif and Hovland point to occurring in all of his judgment groups, not just those with very extreme positions.

shaw, studied the effect of the judge's perspective (the range of stimuli taken into account by the judge) for two levels of judge involvement. He manipulated ego involvement in the same manner in which Hovland and Sherif did, namely, by selecting different natural groups. Curiously, Ostrom reports data that differ from the Hovland and Sherif (1952) outcome. Furthermore, the data differed most on the portion of his experiment that was a replication of the Hovland and Sherif study. Hovland and Sherif found that Negro judges displaced attitude items away from their own position and toward the anti-Negro end of the scale, a finding that was replicated by Ward (1962), who compared pro-Negro Civil Rights pickets in terms of judgments of items concerned with attitude toward the Negro. Curiously, Ostrom's data are exactly opposite.

Ostrom attempts to reconcile his own findings on the effect of involvement with those of Hovland and Sherif and Ward, by pointing to possible changes in perspective that have occurred since those studies were performed. He suggests that the race difference observed by Hovland and Sherif has reversed itself during the 15-year time span. However, if this were the case, the temporal shifts occurred not over 15 years, but rather during the 4 years that gap Ostrom's and Ward's studies.

Zavalloni and Cook (1965) replicated Sherif and Hovland's initial exploration of the influence of judges' attitudes on ratings of favorableness of statements about a social group. They posed two questions. (1) Is the displacement effect limited solely to subjects with extreme positions and strong involvements? (2) What particular types of items (in terms of content structure or degree of favorability) are likely to show the greatest or most consistent differences in ratings by subjects who themselves possess different attitudes? They used the same items as those originally used by Hinckley in constructing his scale of attitude toward the Negro and subsequently used by Hovland and Sherif (1952), Hinckley (1963), and Upshaw (1962). They selected groups of judges in terms of membership in specific organizations and on the basis of replies to a self-report inventory of attitude toward Negroes. All told, they had five groups of judges which, although they did not hold attitudes toward the Negro that were equally spaced along the attitude continuum, nevertheless did represent five distinct points on the dimension.

The most central contention of Sherif and Hovland—that ratings of item favorability are influenced by the rater's own attitude—was strongly confirmed by Zavalloni and Cook's replication. However, some of the more specific hypotheses advanced by Sherif and Hovland concerning the characteristics of subjects who displace items, the nature of the items that are susceptible to displacement, and the ratings of items at the opposite end of the continuum were not supported.

1. Whereas Hovland and Sherif suggested that ratings are influenced by the judge's own attitude only in the case of those judges who have extreme positions or strong involvement in the issue, Zavalloni and Cook showed that ratings of both intermediate and negative items were in the predicted order for all five of their groups of judges, at least two of which can be assumed to be not strongly involved in the issue of race and probably moderate in their own positions. This confirms earlier findings by Upshaw (1962). As Zavalloni and Cook point out, Hovland and Sherif's view that ratings are influenced only in the case of subjects with extreme positions and strong involvement is simply an assumption and not explicitly required by their theoretical position.[18] In addition, it makes more sense to think of displacement as a continuous function of the *degree* of extremity or involvement of the judges.

A comparison of the five groups in terms of the number of statements that were assigned extremely unfavorable scale values showed a linear decrease from the most favorable group to the least favorable group. However, the effect for the number of items assigned unfavorable scale values is consonant with the notion that all groups will show the displacement effect and that its occurrence is simply a matter of degree of involvement or position extremity of the judge. On the other hand, while the opposite direction of effect should be expected for the favorable items, that was not in fact found. If anything, the direction of difference was opposite to that which would have been expected.

2. Whereas Sherif and Hovland reported that neutral items would be most subject to displacement and therefore most sensitive as indicators of the respondent's own attitude when the respondent is asked to judge these items, Zavalloni and Cook qualify these findings. They suggest that those items which include both positive and negative elements are most susceptible to displacement. What this implies is that bias occurs when subjects ignore one portion of an item and overemphasize another

[18] In his more recent statement (Sherif, Sherif, and Nebergall, 1965), Sherif asserts that high involvement itself is a sufficient condition for creating biased ratings.

portion. Sherif and Hovland may have been led to their position by their review of the psychophysical literature in which the neutral, unstructured, and ambiguous stimuli do show the greatest displacement, an outcome consistent with adaptation level theory (Helson, 1948; Helson, 1959) and with anchoring theory (Rogers, 1941; Volkman, 1951). However, as Zavalloni and Cook point out, this is not the case with neutral statements on social issues. There are references to show that context (Fehrer, 1952) or judges' attitudes (Weiss, 1959) do not affect clearly neutral statements on social issues. It is possible that judges may legitimately regard "truly" neutral items as irrelevant. As argued by Campbell, Lewis, and Hunt (1958), whether or not there is a qualitative shift at the midpoint or whether the continuum is simply one of more or less (for example, light-heavy or short-long) may be crucial. If there is a qualitative shift at the midpoint, then the midpoint represents an automatic internal anchor. For such dimensions displacement effects for midpoint items should be minimal.

3. The last point on which Zavalloni and Cook fail to confirm a Sherif and Hovland hypothesis concerns the ratings of items at opposite ends of the scale. Sherif and Hovland predict that extreme judges at either end of the scale tend to make fine discriminations among the items at the end that corresponds to their own position and conversely to lump together items at the opposite end of the scale. In reviewing other studies by Prothro (1955 and 1957) and Upshaw (1962) as well as the original Hovland and Sherif (1952), Zavalloni and Cook point out that no study of social judgments seems to yield results completely consistent with this prediction. The general finding has been that subjects favorable to the issue place more items in the extreme categories at both ends of the scale than do subjects unfavorable to the issue. Their own data confirm this generalization. Zavalloni and Cook present several hypotheses that may account for this effect. The suggestion that handles the most data with the least number of problems is that subjects who agree with an item tend to rate it as more favorable than those who disagree with it, whatever it's general location is on the scale.

A simple assumption that subjects who agree with a statement tend to see it as more favorable than those who disagree with it leads to the prediction that unfavorable subjects, who agree with unfavorable statements, will rate the statements as more favorable than will pro-subjects, who disagree with the statements; at the other end of the scale, this assumption leads to the prediction that favorable subjects, who agree with the favorable items, will rate them as more favorable than the anti-subjects, who disagree with them (Zavalloni and Cook, 1965, p. 54).

In a subsequent paper Selltiz, Edrich, and Cook (1965) confirm some of the findings of Zavalloni and Cook. "Subjects with differing attitudes differed systematically in their ratings of *unfavorable* and *intermediate* items" (p. 415). Consistent with Hovland and Sherif's (1952) predictions pro-Negro subjects rated these items as more unfavorable than anti-Negro subjects rated them. However, as found in the earlier paper, significant differences were found between mean ratings of groups that were both on the same side of an attitude continuum—white subjects who were active members of a pro-integration organization and white subjects who were taking elective courses in intergroup relations but who did not belong to a pro-integration organization. They assumed that the mean position of these two groups differed, even though both were on the pro-Negro side of dimension. Thus, again, it was not just the groups with very extreme positions and high issue-involvement at opposite ends of the scale who differed from one another, but, as indicated, groups with different mean positions on the same side of the neutral point also differed from each other. This was also confirmed when subjects were classified on the basis of a self-report inventory. The earlier findings regarding displacement of favorable and unfavorable items were also replicated in this study.

In a third study (Waly and Cook, 1965), the effects of own attitude on judgments of *plausibility* were examined. Presumably judgments of plausibility, though different or separate from those of favorableness, should nevertheless show the same displacement effects as a consequence of the judge's own attitude. This in fact turned out to be true. Subjects who agreed with the position which the item supported judged that statement to be a more plausible or effective argument than those who disagreed with the position advocated by the item. (In some senses this is similar to studies which regard the evaluation of the communicator as a measure of dissonance reduction). The findings of this study suggest that plausibility ratings as well as tasks requiring the placement or scaling of items can be used as a disguised or indirect measure of attitude. Waly and Cook provide a good criterion for measuring or evaluating the adequacy of an indirect attitude measure. They suggest that a good indirect measure would correlate more highly with a self-report measure for those subjects who are immune to social desirability influences on the attitude in question. Immune and susceptible comparison groups could be defined by scores on tests such as the Marlow-Crowne "Need for Approval" scale or by situational manipulations which make the achievement of some personal goal like obtaining a job contingent or not contingent on reflecting a particular position on an attitude scale.

Ward (1966) correctly notes the confound between involvement and extremity of attitude position in the Hovland and Sherif (1952) study. In a previous study (Ward, 1965), all the subjects were extremely pro-Negro white students who were equated for extremity of attitude on the race issue but who differed in personal involvement by experimental manipulation and by subject selection. The subject selection consisted of two groups: members of a voluntary organization which had picketed segregated movie theaters and subjects who were not members. Involvement was experimentally manipulated within the picket group by stressing the importance of picketing for some of these subjects just prior to the experimental task. Ward found that the more highly involved the subjects were, the more they displaced the position of attitude statements. In a gross sense, then, this provides support for the notion that involvement will produce the sort of contrast effects that Hovland and Sherif suspected. Contrary to their model, however, the difference between the involvement conditions was not greater for the mid-range items than for the "less ambiguous" items at the extremes. Ward interpreted these effects by applying Helson's adaptation level model. He extended the application of the model by assuming that involvement represents the saliency of the judge's attitude. In other words, when involvement is high, own attitude (the residual) must be weighted more heavily. Therefore, as a consequence of high involvement, items are displaced more toward the opposite end of the scale.

Ward's second study (1966) examined involvement, own attitude, and item position in a factorial design. The dependent measure was the judgment of attitude statements. His general procedure was to use a three-part questionnaire. The first part contained statements of varying degrees of favorability, which the subject judged on favorability. The second part contained statements which the subject either endorsed or rejected to provide a measure of his own attitude. The third part contained three Likert-type questions concerning the subject's involvement. The first pertained to the intensity with which the subject's attitude was held, the second to the subject's degree of personal involvement in the issue, and the third to the subject's perception of how much the issue could personally affect him. Ward found that as the judge's involvement in the issue increased, his mean judgment of the statements moved further from his own position. The same effect was found as a function of the extremity of the judge's own attitude. No interactions were significant in the variety of tests. Ward again concluded that the adaptation level interpretation of involvement effects is the most appropriate one.

The attack by Kelley et al. (1955) on the question of how an individual's own attitude affects his judgments of the favorability of other attitudes showed that groups whose own attitudes differed did not differ in their judgments when they scaled items by the method of paired comparison. They did differ when they used the method of successive intervals. But the largest differences between the groups were obtained when the items were scaled according to the method of equal appearing intervals. Probably on this basis, Edwards (1957) argued that the displacement effect "is primarily a function of the method by which the judgments were obtained, that is, the method of equal appearing intervals" (p. 116).

In a more recent article, Ager and Dawes (1965) search for some sort of conclusion about the nature of the judgment process that would explain why displacement effects occur with the method of equal appearing intervals but not with the method of paired comparisons. They note the potential importance of Coombs' (1964) distinction between intraset comparisons and interset comparisons. The methods of equal appearing intervals and successive intervals involve comparing an attitude statement with a category boundary, that is, an interset comparison. On the other hand, the method of paired comparisons involves comparing attitude statements with other attitude statements, which is an intraset comparison of attitude statements. Since the data of Kelley et al. show that a judge's own attitude does not affect the attitude-attitude comparison but does affect the attitude-category boundary comparison, Ager and Dawes point out the possibility that an individual's attitude may only affect his use of category boundaries. In other words, it is possible that a person's own attitude does *not* affect his basic discriminal abilities. In support of this view Upshaw (1962) observes that when an individual's own attitude lies outside the range of stimuli that he is categorizing, he "spreads" his category scale so that it will include his own attitude. Consequently, he locates the judgmental stimuli in fewer categories than he would if his own attitude were within the range of these stimuli.

Thus Upshaw's data imply that a judge's own attitude only affects his use of categories. In other words, it suggests that the discriminative process itself is not affected and presumably other judgmental processes may not be affected.

However, Ager and Dawes (1965) stand in opposition to this possibility and argue that "when a right winger says he sees no difference among varieties of left wingers this implies an inability to *discriminate* among them *over and above* a preference for categorizing them together" (p. 535). Recognizing the problem of simply looking at the correlation between the judgments of judges with different attitudes, they focus instead on the pattern of errors made by judges with differing attitudes. In other words, they do not simply consider whether two different groups order statements in a similar manner but rather whether their pattern of errors is similar. They define error as deviation from consensus judgments. Using a paired comparison task (requiring discrimination between attitude statements), they demonstrate that displacement effects can indeed be obtained.

Contrary to the findings of Cook and his collaborators, Ager and Dawes report no difference between unfavorable and favorable judges. Of course, the implication is that the paired comparison task is least susceptible to item displacement and that a difference between judges might have been obtained had they used a different type of judgment procedure. The more important conclusion from the Ager and Dawes study, however, is that attitude-attitude comparisons are not qualitatively different from attitude-category boundary comparisons. In other words, they conclude that categorization and discrimination are *both* subject to displacement effects as a consequence of the judge's own attitude.

There is yet another important point to consider—the extent to which judges believe that social consequences will ensue as a function of how one judges things. Thus the involved Bircher may indeed be able to discriminate among types of liberals and radicals but may still tend to place them in one major category because of his concern about social outcomes. There seems to be little doubt that those subjects selected for inclusion in the Ager and Dawes study did have very extreme attitudes and consequently might have been highly involved in their position on the issue (favorability toward science). However, there is no simple way to evaluate whether a possible concern about social outcomes affected the way they judged statements in the paired-comparison task without replicating the study under conditions in which judges are explicitly instructed to ignore or consider the possible social consequences of recognizing and emphasizing differences between positions toward science.

Atkins (1966) examined the effect of own attitude and subject's ability to discriminate among attitudinal stimuli on judgments of moderate items concerning fraternities. The items were presented in either extremely profraternity or extremely antifraternity contexts. Initially, own attitudes exerted the strongest source of bias for distortion. Subsequent judgments showed assimilation trends in the direction of the context anchors and the effects of own attitude diminished. Atkins expected that subjects who were poor in their ability to discriminate among statements would show greater susceptibility to anchoring effects. On the other hand, just the opposite prediction could conceivably be made. For instance, since the subjects who are poor in discriminant ability would tend to use fewer categories, there is less room for them to show any kind of distortion effect, whether assimilation or contrast. In other words, they run out of room on the scale. At any rate, in his analysis of subjects who differ in ability to discriminate, Atkins found no differences.[19]

A recent study on clinical judgments by Bieri, Orcutt, and Leaman (1963) can be taken as supporting the Sherif and Hovland notion that assimilation affects are more likely to occur with ambiguous stimulus series.

SUMMARY. In summary, the recent experimental work on judgment or scaling of items raises a number of issues which bear further consideration and suggest that some of the predictions stemming from social judgment require modification. Questions have been raised concerning whether the observed displacement effects reflect discrimination or categorization processes. Similarly, the importance of the response language has been noted. Midscale displacements are more complicated than initially thought. For some dimensions where there is a qualitative shift

---

[19] There are two things to consider about this failure to find differences between high and low discriminators. First, the hypothesis may in fact be wrong. Low discriminators may not be more subject to anchoring effects. Another alternative however, is that being classified as a low discriminator reflects not only a *cognitive* process which leaves a person more susceptible to external anchors, but additionally, a low motivational or attention level. If so, the impact or salience of the anchor would be reduced, thereby counteracting any cognitive effects of greater susceptibility to anchors.

at the midpoint there may be strong midscale anchor effects. The characteristics of midscale items has also been more carefully examined in order to isolate the specific characteristic that make items "ambiguous." Displacement effects have been shown to be continuous rather than restricted to certain portions of the response dimension. Furthermore, at least for scales concerned with attitudes toward the Negro, there appears to be a special effect for pro-items.

THE INVOLVEMENT-DISCREPANCY CONTROVERSY

As indicated, social judgment theory comments most thoroughly about two independent variables: the respondent's issue involvement and the extremity of his own position. These independent variables affect attitude change, though of course other stimulus variables which affect judgment also have an important position in the theory. Similar variables also appear in dissonance theory as important determinants of attitude change (see Chapter 4). In dissonance theory, however, they are more likely to be labeled "importance" and "discrepancy." Since the two theories at least appear to make competing predictions for both variables, we will review the conceptual and empirical conflicts surrounding each variable separately.

CONCEPTUAL PROBLEMS WITH INVOLVEMENT. Sherif and Hovland make clear-cut predictions of decreased persuasion as involvement with a stand becomes more intense. They initially defined involvement in terms of group membership. Without pointing to a specific crucial differentiating feature, we can all agree that in some way the WCTU and Salvation Army women were more "involved" than the moderates. But when we try to isolate the specific crucial difference, what guides do we use? Is the essential feature group membership, a public stand, or strong affect? Perhaps all three together, or perhaps still others? Sherif (Sherif, Sherif, and Nebergall, 1965) converts some of his empirical outcomes into an approach to the direct measurement of involvement. He states that "the degree of involvement and personal commitment on the . . . issue . . . can be determined operationally by comparing the sizes of . . . the latitudes of acceptance, rejection, and non-commitment." This apparent step toward precision is deceptive, however, in that it still does not permit independent specification of the variable (involvement) by the experimenter—a basic requisite in the mature sciences.

Involvement has been defined above as a response-defined subject variable and we still remain ignorant of the antecedent conditions that produce it. Thus the conceptual analysis of involvement remains unsatisfying from the standpoint of science's basic aim of analysis, partition, and delineation of gross variables into more atomistic ones. As they use the term, it appears as a potpourri concept which may have several independent elements. Earlier in our discussion of the prohibition study, hints at some of the conceptual problems with involvement emerged from considerations of the potential confounds which plague a manipulation consisting of subject selection. In other words, one cannot tell what produced their effects. This raises the issue of convergent and discriminant validity (Campbell, 1960; Campbell and Fiske, 1959; Chronbach and Meehl, 1955). Consideration of discriminant validity argues that some potential differences between WCTU women (extremes) and college students (moderates) would not be classified as components of issue involvement (e.g., differences in intelligence, education). However, other differences such as "salience," "commitment," "emotional arousal," "social support," and "cognitive support" may stand as good candidates. How is involvement related to "certainty" or "depth of conviction"? Perhaps too we should consider lack of "evaluation apprehension" (Rosenberg, 1965) and "extremity."

As noted, Sherif and Hovland confounded issue involvement with position extremity in their own research because they felt that the effects of deep involvement could only be studied by selecting subjects with extreme stands. Though involvement and discrepancy generate similar attitude change predictions in social judgment theory, they are conceptually distinct. Therefore their joint manipulation is unsatisfactory. Furthermore, contrary to Sherif and Hovland's arguments, locating moderate groups with deep position involvement and more extreme groups with only minimal involvement seems feasible. Consider the political dimension. As previously suggested, many of those who participate in ward work for the Democratic party undoubtedly feel greater commitment and involvement with their stand than some of those who espouse much more liberal positions but do relatively little behaviorally to support their beliefs. It would be important to show that the predicted effects for involvement are not specific to positions located at the extremes of the response dimension. Deep involvement in a moderate position should also act as an anchor. It should increase the breadth of positions at the extremes which fall into the latitudes of rejection, and it should reduce the likelihood of attitude change.

Whereas Sherif and Hovland effectively emphasize the importance of a respondent's involvement in an issue, they do not consider the effects of involvement with the communicator. When the respondent merely reads a persuasive communication from an unspecified source, interaction between the respondent and another person—the unknown communicator—is masked. It lacks potency. Nevertheless, even in these cases, there is an implicit interaction. Beiri et al. (1966) point to this other potentially important consideration. They speak of two dimensions along which a person's involvement in an interaction situation can vary. One dimension is the intensity of involvement, the other is its attribute properties—the trait dimensions or sentiments along which an interaction can be characterized. Foa (1961) and Leary (1957) focus on how to depict an interaction in terms of types of traits and order the problem by suggesting two orthogonal axes of dominance-submission and love-hate. At any rate, one's latitude of acceptance and rejection for a particular issue may undergo considerable situational variation depending upon the person who presents the counterpersuasive message. The *degree* and *type* of involvement with him may appreciably alter the judgment process or set one applies to the topic under discussion.

Our emphasis on convergent and discriminant validity impels us to search for the extent to which we can obtain results that contradict our theoretical expectations for involvement by manipulating any of these components. Data forced the early Italian physicists who sat atop their separate hills arguing over the real definition of "force" to develop three separate concepts: "force," "kinetic energy," and "momentum." So too, data may restrict the breadth of involvement. But the by-product will be increased precision in prediction.

Research on involvement. In this section we shall omit all of the naturalistic studies on involvement which comprise the empirical basis of the two books on social judgment theory. The essential conclusions of those studies as well as their methodological and conceptual problems have already been summarized and need no further reiteration here.

Zimbardo (1960) experimentally manipulated involvement by telling subjects that their attitudes—judgments about a juvenile delinquency case—did or did not provide "a good indication of their basic social values, their personalities and their outlook on life problems" (Zimbardo, 1960, p. 88). More change occurred under high involvement. This outcome appears to support dissonance theory, which predicts more change under high importance (involvement), and to counter social judgment theory, which predicts reduced change under high involvement. Although a theory is rarely dealt a death blow by a single disconfirmation, if one is intent upon "saving" social judgment theory, detailed consideration of Zimbardo's procedure does suggest several "explanations."

First, Zimbardo himself pointed to the difference between issue involvement and response involvement. If the mere presentation of the issue is sufficient to elicit concern and interest, issue involvement has been engaged. On the other hand, response involvement denotes an instrumental relation between espousing a given position and obtaining a particular goal. In response involvement, the emphasis is not on the attitudinal position but rather on some *other* desired goal. His involvement manipulation undoubtedly induced the other goal—the subject became concerned with how she might appear to the world, to her friend, or to the experimenter. In style with the more recent phrase of Rosenberg (1965), greater evaluation apprehension was induced in the highly involved subjects. Under such circumstances the subject looks around for cues that will enable him to respond so as to put himself in a good light. In the Zimbardo experiment this may well have meant agreeing with the persuasive communication, the position supposedly advocated by one's friend. In contrast, in the Sherif and Hovland comparison between highly involved and uninvolved subjects, concern with the importance of their stand on the issue characterizes the highly involved person. Considerations such as "what position should I take to create a good impression or please the experimenter?" remain irrelevant. If we had to guess at which group in the prohibition study had higher *response* involvement, it would have been the more moderate college subjects. In other words, to the extent that the Zimbardo and Sherif and Hovland studies are indeed comparable, they support one another on the effect of *response* involvement.

Another consideration is the source of the communication in the two studies. In the Zimbardo study the communicator was a close personal friend, whereas in the prohibition study the communicator was a stranger. Consider the repercussions of opinion change versus opinion stability in the two studies. For Zimbardo's involved subjects, lack of agreement with the communication implied a basic dissimilarity between the communicator and the subject in terms of fundamental values, personality, and life outlook—a possibility that would appear to test the solidarity of any close friendship. Essentially, then, lack of agreement risked loss of a close personal friend. In our previous discussion of the prohibition study, exactly the opposite function of agreement was cited. For WCTU women, lack of agreement (attitude stability) would help maintain one's close friendships.

Zimbardo alluded to still another basic difference. For his subjects the communication provided normative information from a valued reference group, whereas the prohibition study exposed subjects to informational influence from a source outside of one's reference group. Thus, even apart from the different meanings (operationalizations) of involvement in the two studies, the different outcomes may be attributable to the discrepancy between influence attempts.

Still another difference between the two studies stems from the perception of manipulative intent. This factor too may interact with involvement. If so, even if high involvement meant the same thing in the two studies, opposite outcomes could have obtained. In the prohibition study, the intent to persuade was patently obvious; in the Zimbardo study, though the subject received information on her friend's point of view and her friend likewise learned of the subject's own point of view, there was no overt persuasive intent. Thus perception of intent to persuade drastically differed in the two studies.

The last difference is pointed out by Sherif and Hovland. They argue that laboratory manipulations aimed at creating high involvement may never approach the high level of involvement exemplified by their own selection of naturally involved subjects. For this argument to help them, they must further argue that the effects of involvement are really curvilinear with both low and high levels curtailing change and only moderate levels promoting it. To do this they depict the two conditions of the Zimbardo study as low and moderate involvement and the two groups in their own study as moderate and high. Although this explanation of the different outcomes hardly seems convincing, we shall return to their curvilinear expectations for involvement later.

Miller (1964) attempted to demonstrate that experimentally oriented social psychologists can indeed infuse extremely high levels of issue involvement into their artificial and temporally curtailed experimental treatments. Miller tried experimentally to induce some of the characteristics which separated the extreme WCTU women from the moderate college students in the Sherif and Hovland prohibition study. Picking fluoridation as an issue which a priori seemed relatively remote from the important concerns of his high school subjects, he involved half of them with their position on this issue by increasing the salience of the issue, providing social support for the subject's position, inducing the subject to muster cognitive support for his position, and committing the subject to future action in support of his own position. The other half was similarly involved in an irrelevant issue. All the subjects were then induced to unwittingly expose themselves to a counterpersuasive communication. Then, those who had been involved in their position on fluoridation were compared with those who had been similarly involved in the irrelevent issue. As Sherif and Hovland might have predicted, the subjects involved in the fluoridation issue were less influenced by the countercommunication.

Two problems present interpretive difficulty. First, latitudes of acceptance and rejection, as measured after the experimental treatment with an instrument similar to that used initially by Sherif and Hovland, remained unaffected by the experimentally induced involvement. Though experimental involvement produced the attitude change effects predicted by social judgment theory, there was no evidence that these effects were mediated by the judgment processes which, according to the theory, cause them. One can readily attribute such failures to poor measures, but this possibility should be overcome to the extent that the mediating event (judgment) should be more powerful that its consequence (attitude change). In fairness, however, we note, that considerations of instrument reliability (number of items) would support an interpretation for lack of effect which points to poor measurement, particularly since all Ns were small. Additionally, the instrument did not allow subjects to indicate their latitude of noncommitment. This might further curtail sensitivity.

The second interpretive problem concerns the effect of induced involvement on the respondents' position. Examination of subjects' positions on the irrelevant issue (on which they received no communication) showed that experimentally induced involvement increased extremity. Thus it is safe to assume that even though random assignment normally guarantees groups with similar initial mean positions, when implementation of involvement was completed, the involved group had a more extreme stand. This means that we cannot state whether the effects are due to involvement per se or whether instead they depend on differences in extremity of position (or distance between respondent's own view and that advocated by the communicator).

A personality interpretation of the prohibition study—one that explains the outcome by pointing to personality differences between the experimental groups—has already been discussed. Miller (1964) partially examined this possibility by selecting subjects from the extremes on Rokeach's (1960) dogmatism scale. Although there was a slight tendency for more dogmatic subjects to resist persuasion, this effect was not strong ($p < .10$) nor did dogmatism interact with other treatment differences.

Pursuing a personality interpretation of involvement effects, Miller and Devine (1968) directly explored the effects of broad and narrow latitudes of rejection as a personality trait. Latitudes of acceptance and rejection were measured for approximately 30 attitude dimensions and subjects were dichotomized in terms of the number of issues on which their latitude of rejection was larger than the mean for that issue. Hence the two groups of subjects differed in the extent to which they typically (across many issues) had a broad latitude of rejection. At a later time, each type of subject received persuasive communications both on issues on which his latitude of rejection was narrow and issues on which his latitude of rejection was broad. According to social judgment theory, subjects should change more on issues on which they had a narrow latitude of rejection. Contrary to theory, however, the manipulation had no effect. This remained equally true when discrepancy of the two types of communication was controlled. On the other hand, the two types of subjects did respond differently to the persuasive appeals. Those with typically broad latitudes of rejection more strongly resisted persuasion. Though not precluding other interpretations as well, this outcome does support a personality interpretation of the prohibition study and other similar studies. It suggests that persons with characteristically broad latitudes of rejection may be overrepresented in extreme groups and that whether or not these people were involved in the specific issue under question may not be crucial. Zimbardo (1960) also provides support for this same conclusion. Those with broader initial latitudes of acceptance and smaller latitudes of rejection more readily accepted their friend's position.

In a correlational study Powell (1966) provides still further support for a personality interpretation of Sherif and Hovland's involvement effects. Dogmatism (Troldahl and Powell, 1965) was positively correlated with position extremity in each of three studies. Furthermore, those high in dogmatism displayed broader latitudes of rejection, and for two of three tests they also displayed narrower latitudes of noncommitment.

In another study (Miller and Zimbardo, 1964) involvement was defined by subjects' self-report. Again, two types of subjects were selected—those who reported involvement in many issues and those who reported involvement in few. All subjects read persuasive communications on two types of issues—those they had personally reported as involving and those in which they were uninvolved. Issues for each subject were selected so that the subject's premeasured extremity was equal on the two types of communications. Moreover, mean extremity for the two types of subject group was also controlled. In this study the two subject groups did not differ in attitude change. This may not be particularly surprising. Conceptually, the meaning of a difference in number of issues one cites as involving remains unclear. In large part, it simply may reflect differences in need to present oneself to the experimenter as vital and interested in many things. On the other hand, whether the particular issue was involving or uninvolving did matter. Subjects changed *more* on involving issues. This outcome seems counter to the social judgment prediction. As noted earlier, however, Sherif and Hovland suspected that persuasion might be curvilinearly related to involvement. "If only small degrees of change (in involvement) are provided through manipulation, we may primarily be seeing the effects of heightened interest and of increased attention to the communication and these may produce greater opinion change. Only when powerful modifications are made will the predicted resistance to change and "boomerang" effects become apparent" (Sherif and Hovland, 1961, p. 197).

Miller and Zimbardo analyze the details of their procedure and conclude that their subjects were unmotivated to carefully read and assimilate the persuasive communications. They read them in individual rooms, unsupervised, self-paced, with the promise of a detailed clinical diagnosis and write-up of their personality as soon as they finished. These would be the precise circumstances where communications on *involving* topics are more likely to evoke "interest and increased attention." Indeed, a follow-up study confirmed this interpretation in that subjects who were not promised personality feedback spent more time reading the communications and did not recall less information from the communications on uninvolving topics

These findings point to the importance of involvement for the "input" side of persuasion. Attitudes cannot be changed if people do not expose themselves to the stimuli which can change them. Involvement, to some extent, directs or focuses attention and interest toward new inputs of information on the topic. It may also cause this information to be rejected, and misjudged, but these are separate processes. Thus this experiment can be interpreted as providing support for Sherif and Hovland's expectation that involvement is curvilinearly related to attitude change. But it is important to note that this is an extratheoretical point which does not stem from the judgmental principles on which the theory is based. Furthermore, it runs counter to the expectation derived strictly from the judgment principles. According to the judgment principles, the persons who change their opinion after hearing a persuasive communication are those for whom the communication falls within their latitude of acceptance. To the extent that these subjects are uninvolved in the issue, they will display less assimilation. Hence these uninvolved subjects will perceive the communication as *advocating* more (though "reasonable") change and theoretically should end up changing their opinions *more*.

Freedman (1964) studied involvement with a concept formation task. He told the high involvement group that their performance on the first concept formation task was an indication of their intelligence and perceptiveness; the low involvement group was told that the first task was relatively unimportant, implying that the second test was important. After subjects performed the first concept formation task, they were asked for a description of *alpha,* the concept they were to induce (e.g., alpha is a triangle in the first spatial position). Then subjects were given a 12-item identification test consisting of instances to be labeled *alpha* or *not alpha.* Following this they were told they would be given some additional instances of *alpha* and were given 16 instances labeled *alpha* or *not alpha.* Five of these instances were discrepant from the old concept (their first description of alpha). (Discrepancy of the new conception of alpha from the old conception was also manipulated by varying the number of elements common to the new and old concepts). After these 16 additional instances, subjects were asked for a "final" description of *alpha.* Concept change was scored by counting the number of elements that were added or subtracted to subjects' second descriptions of alpha.

Freedman's involvement manipulation superficially seems to be closer to what Zimbardo has characterized as response involvement in contrast to issue involvement. Like Zimbardo, Freedman emphasizes the salience of the subjects' response in determining the experimenter's evaluation of the subjects' character. Nevertheless, he obtains involvement effects quite opposite to those of Zimbardo—high involvement caused *less* change. The crucial difference between the two experiments is that Zimbardo's response involvement manipulation is induced for the subject's *new* response, whereas Freedman response-involved the subject in his *initial* response. Thus the experimental group which Freedman labels as his low involvement group—those who were led to believe that their second description of the concept was crucial for tipping off their true intelligence to the experimenter—was equivalent to the group which Zimbardo labeled as the high involvement group! In this light, the two studies confirm one another. By response-involving subjects in the meaning of their response to some new information (the 16 additional instances of alpha) one makes that information more influential.[20]

Role-playing experiments (Janis and King, 1954; King and Janis, 1956; Elms, 1966) are also relevant to the involvement issue. When the subject is induced to role-play a new position counter to his original attitude, he is involved in a *new* position. To the extent that involvement in one's original stand inhibits change toward a new position, involvement in a new stand should promote change toward that new position. Although role-playing effects are subject to exception (Stanley and Klausmeier, 1957), the more general finding is increased persuasion. If measures of latitudes of acceptance, rejection, and noncommitment were obtained, they should show the predicted changes in the role-players. Furthermore, if role-playing is indeed an "involvement" manipulation, the role-players should display narrower latitudes of noncommitment.[21]

Miller and Levy (1967) examined emotional arousal as a component

[20] This interpretation of the Freedman involvement manipulation is one-sided; it overemphasizes the meaning of the treatment for the uninvolved group while tending to ignore the "committing aspects" of the high involvement treatment. An additional control group which receives no involvement instructions might have helped to clarify which involvement treatment produced the effect or whether both contributed.

[21] The role-playing experiments have been interpreted in a variety of other ways. Festinger (1957) has emphasized a forced compliance interpretation. An effort explanation, however, is equally compatible with a dissonance interpretation. Those who improvise from a skeleton outline presumably expend more effort than the less active "listeners." Still another dimension of difference separating the role-players and nonrole-players is the awareness of the experimenter's intent to persuade. The nonrole-players clearly know that someone is trying to alter their beliefs, whereas the role-player may be unaware that in having him role-play, the experimenter is trying to alter the subjects' own beliefs.

of involvement. In their procedure, they aroused overweight women by insulting them about their obesity. The arousal was ostensibly inadvertent and was not connected to the topic on which they later received a persuasive communication. This situation differs from the usual circumstances in which we consider emotional arousal to be a component of involvement. Typically, the aroused state is tied to the cognitive elements that are under attack. In this experiment the two were unconnected. If emotional arousal per se is a component of involvement, its effects should generalize to any temporally contiguous persuasive attack. The results did not support this view. Rather, they were more in line with the previous findings of Schachter and Singer (1962). The insulted women were *more* vulnerable to persuasion. Of course, this outcome does not exclude the possibility that when the emotional arousal is specifically tied to the cognitions under persuasive attack, persuasion will be reduced.

In conclusion, to what extent do the data on involvement support or refute social judgment theory? How do they speak on dissonance theory, which seemingly appears to predict an opposite outcome for involvement (importance)? According to dissonance theory, the more important the initial cognition (attitude), the more dissonance is generated by exposure to an opposite position and the more consequent pressure to reduce dissonance (and change one's attitude). Can the apparent incompatibility of dissonance theory and social judgment theory be resolved? We shall treat these questions in order.

There is some evidence that one component of "involvement" can be conceptualized as a subject variable. This is not unreasonable. We may expect persons to differ in the ways that they habitually judge objects. Correlated directions of difference may likewise be found on such dimensions as "category-width" (Pettigrew, 1958; Rosen, 1961; Steiner and Johnson, 1965; Mercado, Guerrero, and Gardner, 1963), "dogmatism" (Rokeach, 1960; Powell, 1966; and Foulkes and Foulkes, 1965), "assimilation-contrast" (Berkowitz, 1960), and "size of latitude of rejection" (Miller and Devine, 1967).

It may also be informative to examine differences in self-esteem. Persons with little self-esteem may be expected to have broader latitudes of acceptance. Similarly, we may find that persons separated in terms of how much contrast they display on a typical perceptual judgment task also systematically differ in the amount of contrast they show in attitude change studies. Whether these potential subject differences reflect a unifactored trait awaits empirical testing. Furthermore, to whatever extent there are subject differences which could account for Sherif and Hovland's involvement effects, there may nevertheless be residual involvement effects of the sort that they thought they were in fact studying.

The data on experimentally manipulated involvement becomes much more consistent when one examines the involvement manipulation in closer detail. Whenever the subject is involved in a second or potentially new position, (e.g., Zimbardo, 1960; Freedman, 1964; Janis and King, 1954; King and Janis, 1956; Elms, 1966) he is more likely to change toward the new position. This can be interpreted as an incentive effect— the instrumental value of changing one's opinion under "response involvement" conditions. The subject modifies his belief to obtain his friend's approval, to appear intelligent to the experimenter, to hold beliefs more closely aligned with those he thinks the experimenter espouses. This is *not* the kind of manipulation Festinger had in mind for "importance." For Festinger, importance is defined in terms of cognitions which support, confirm, or buttress the *original* belief—not a new position that someone advocates.[22]

When subjects are induced to feel that their initial position is more important (Miller, 1965; Freedman, 1964; Greenwald, 1966) they typically show less attitude change. This outcome is in accord with social judgment theory. But if we include the extratheoretical assumption of the theory—low involvement produces input or attention problems and therefore the function relating involvement to persuasion is curvilinear— these studies are difficult to interpret because they employ only two levels of involvement. In other words, they are supportive only to the extent that one can intuitively or on a priori grounds locate the two levels of involvement on the entire involvement dimension. In all of them, this seems quite easy to do and the consequent interpretation of the outcomes support the social judgment approach. Nevertheless, a parametric manipulation of involvement would be more satisfying.

Taken as a whole, these data on first glance appear to challenge the dissonance theory prediction. But, as is obvious to any student of dissonance theory, attitude change is not the only avenue for dissonance reduction. All that dissonance theory stipulates is that increased impor-

---

[22] See the chapter on dissonance theory for a more thorough discussion of "importance" in dissonance theory.

tance will lead to greater dissonance. What the subject does with his dissonance depends on characteristics of the situation. This points to an obvious resolution of the apparent conflict. As importance (involvement) increases, attitude change may move downward in the heirarchy of preferred modes of dissonance reduction. Other alternative modes may take over—defaming the source, seeking or planning to seek new information supporting one's initial view, distorting the speaker's position.

The last interpretation receives some support from a recent experiment by Eagly and Manis (1966). They manipulated involvement by issue selection and studied its effect on source and message evaluations. Male and female subjects responded to each of two communications. One was relevant for males only; the other was relevant for females only. They report subjects' evaluations of the communication and the communicator for both communications (though they apparently measured attitude change as well). The expectation of harsher evaluations from issue involved subjects generates the prediction of an interaction between issue and sex. In an analysis of covariance which controlled initial attitude extremity, this prediction was confirmed for message evaluation (fair and well written). On the other hand, they obtained no clear differences in source evaluation or attitude change. These data provide some support for the notion that people react more negatively to a counterattitudinal communication when they are involved in the issue. Indeed, Sherif and Hovland show in their own data that the "highly involved" subjects who resisted change described the communicator in much more disparaging terms. Thus the apparent theoretical contradiction may vanish when actually put to test.

CONCEPTUAL PROBLEMS WITH DISCREPANCY. Just as there were conceptual problems with involvement, so too discrepancy needs closer scrutiny as an independent variable. Do those who use it operationalize it the same way? Is it in fact a unitary concept? Must communicator-respondent discrepancy necessarily be confounded with the extremity of the respondent's position?

Social judgment theory predicts that those with extreme stands are always less likely than moderates to change their attitude simply because of the well-known correlation between extremity and involvement. But is this necessarily the case? As indicated, it is conceivable that one can find people who are as involved in their middle-of-the-road position as are others with more extreme views. If we assume that we are indeed able to control the issue involvement of people occupying different stands, would discrepancy have equivalent effects on both groups?

Assuming we could conquer the problem of constructing an equal interval discrepancy scale so that "high" and "moderate" meant the same thing to those in both groups, social judgment theory would nevertheless predict that for any level of discrepancy, moderates have a greater probability of attitude change. This prediction stems from the added considerations regarding the degree to which positions at different points along a scale are anchored. Involvement considerations aside, extreme positions are more firmly anchored, less ambiguous, and subject to less self-deception as to where one really stands on the issue.[23]

The problem we are facing here is twofold: the difficulty of creating equal discrepancy manipulations for persons with different initial positions, and the fact that even if we could, the inevitable difference in "anchoredness" of positions at different scale points would yield different functions for discrepancy. So far, our discussion assumed or implied that we selected for comparison two different types of subjects—extremes and moderates. At this point, the reader may wish to echo the entire host of other problems created when subject selection is substituted for experimental manipulation. Let us assume instead, however, that we can experimentally induce different extremities in randomly selected groups and then expose them to persuasive communications. This still does not solve the problem of the differential anchoring of middle positions and extreme ones. Nor does it guarantee that issue involvement will be equal for the two groups. Just as a manipulation of involvement changed subjects' extremity, so too manipulating the extremity of initial positions may produce differences in involvement.

A second consideration is the unidimensionality of discrepancy. Most discussions (and experimental operations) simply consider the discrepancy between the positions advocated by the communicator and the respondent. But there are other potential dimensions of discrepancy or difference between the communicator and respondent—other attitude dimensions and values; social class, prestige, and power; age and sex; group membership, interests, and activities—all of which the theory

---

[23] The way in which this theoretically stems from anchoring effects is as follows. "Own position" serves as an anchor. However, end scale values also serve as anchors. Presumably, then, if one holds a very extreme position, the consequential anchoring effects should be particularly strong.

clearly neglects. While social judgment theory attends to the respondent's distortion of message position, the research in this tradition has perhaps purposefully left the characteristics of the communicator ambiguous. Thus these other dimensions of similarity or dissimilarity to the source (discrepancy) cannot intrude into the results or, perhaps more accurately, to whatever extent they do, they cannot be analyzed. Nevertheless, it is hard to imagine that when known by the respondent, they would not affect assimilation and contrast effects. From the respondent's viewpoint, all of them can be converted into a good-bad evaluation. To the extent that the overall evaluation of the source is positive, assimilation tendencies should be increased; likewise, to the extent that they are unfavorable, contrast effects should be exaggerated (or superimposed). These considerations would incorporate into the social judgment model the communicator credibility characteristics emphasized by Aronson, Turner, and Carlsmith (1963) as well as a number of other source attributes.

RESEARCH ON DISCREPANCY. As Sherif and Hovland note, research on discrepancy has yielded conflicting outcomes. Whereas a variety of studies show increased persuasion with increases in discrepancy (Cohen, 1959; Bergin, 1962; Freedman, 1964; Goldberg, 1954; Greenwald, 1966; Hovland and Pritzker, 1957; Bochner and Insko, 1966; Zimbardo, 1960), evidence for decreased change with larger discrepancies is also available (Cohen, 1959; Fisher and Lubin, 1958; Greenwald, 1966; Hovland, Harvey, and Sherif, 1957; Miller and Levy, 1967; Whittaker, 1963).

Since social judgment theory predicts a curvilinear relation between attitude change and discrepancy, it is crucial that experimental tests employ multiple levels of discrepancy. If not, any direction of outcome other than "no effect" can be interpreted as supporting or refuting the social judgment outcome. Even with multiple levels of discrepancy, however, the only outcome that cannot be interpreted as supporting social judgment theory is a U-shaped function with *least* change for moderate levels of discrepancy. With simply an increasing function, one may only be at the low end of the curve; with a decreasing function, one may only be at the high end of the curve. To date, with one possible exception (Bochner and Insko, 1966) there is no study that unequivocally disconfirms the social judgment theory prediction for discrepancy.

Dissonance theory appears to predict an outcome counter to that of social judgment theory. Greater discrepancy between one's own stand

and that of another credible source will generate more dissonance. Thus, when attitude change is the chosen technique for reducing dissonance, change should be an increasing function of discrepancy.

Within the dissonance framework, Bergin (1962) and Aronson, Turner, and Carlsmith (1963) have attempted to spell out the circumstances under which one may obtain decreases in persuasion as a function of increased discrepancy. According to their formulation, communicator credibility controls the effect of discrepancy. When credibility cannot be assailed, the only response alternative is attitude change. As credibility decreases, however, derogation replaces attitude change as the preferred mode of dissonance reduction, particularly if discrepancy is great. If so, a person can reduce dissonance much more easily by derogating the communicator (Aronson, Turner, and Carlsmith, 1963, p. 33). This elaboration does not alter the basic supposition of dissonance theory— that greater discrepancy induces greater dissonance. Rather, it qualifies the details of how the dissonance will be reduced.

Other aspects of their theoretical analysis are also noteworthy. Since high communicator credibility creates more dissonance, at any level of discrepancy a more credible communicator should produce more attitude change than a less credible source. But as discrepancy increases, derogation will replace attitude change as the preferred method of dissonance reduction. In addition, they assume that with extreme use of either mode of dissonance reduction, the two dissonance reduction techniques become clear-cut alternatives, whereas when either is used more moderately, dissonance may be reduced by a combination of both processes.

Although the theoretical analysis of Aronson, Turner, and Carlsmith (1963) is compelling, their data fail to support it in detail. The predicted effects for attitude change were obtained. A highly credible source produced more change than a mildly credible source. Furthermore, with the highly credible source greater discrepancy produced more change. In the case of the less credible source, change was curvilinearly related to discrepancy—an outcome consonant with the social judgment model. Their derogation data, however, are less satisfying. Within each level of communicator credibility, derogation was unrelated to discrepancy. According to prediction, the mildly credible communication should have provoked increasing amounts of derogation as a function of the discrepancy of its stand. In fact, they obtained a nonsignificant trend in the opposite direction.

There are other implications of their theoretical analysis that warrant further comments. The general dissonance theory proposition regarding magnitude of dissonance is that the total amount of dissonance generated by a manipulation would be reflected in the sum of all response measures which reflect dissonance reduction. In the experiment by Aronson et al., assuming they have successfully blocked alternative dissonance reduction techniques, and assuming that apples and shoestrings could be added, the sum of their two response measures should always be higher for the highly credible communicator. (A discrepant communication should create more dissonance when presented by a more credible source.) Similarly, within each credibility level, the sum should increase as a function of discrepancy. Obviously, however, the technical problems involved in this type of approach are not very easily surmounted.

Another consideration is the correlations between derogation and attitude change. Their theoretical analysis suggests that within each discrepancy level, pooling the data from both credibility levels, the correlation between derogation and attitude change should become increasingly negative as a function of discrepancy:

". . . it seems reasonable to assume that at the extremes, opinion changes and derogation of the communicator are clear alternatives. A person is not likely to change his opinion in the direction of a communicator whom he has sharply derogated; similarly, he is not likely to derogate a communicator who had induced a major change in his opinion. This is true *only* at the extremes. Theoretically, if neither opinion change nor derogation is extreme, dissonance may be reduced by a combination of both processes" (Aronson et al., 1963, p. 32).

Unfortunately, they do not present the correlations for each of the discrepancy levels.

Since the attitude change data are compatible with social judgment theory, since the derogation data fail to show the predicted effect with increasing discrepancy—particularly with a mildly credible communicator—and since the correlations between the two response measures are not even reported, the data cannot be viewed as either a refutation of social judgment theory or a confirmation of dissonance theory. On the other hand, the obtained interaction points to the importance of variables not really considered by social judgment theory—particularly source credibility. Manipulation of the same levels of discrepancy yielded different outcomes under different levels of credibility. This seems to be more of an omission than a contradiction of social judgment theory.

As indicated in a previous section, social judgment theory has tended to ignore communicator characteristics. One previously discussed possibility is that with each added positive attribute, a communicator broadens a respondent's latitude of acceptance. This simply implies that the inflection point in the function relating attitude change to discrepancy is shifted to higher levels of discrepancy as positive attributes of the source are increased. Nevertheless, if discrepancy is great enough, an inflection point will be found.

Aronson et al. argue that in the hypothetical case of the prefectly credible communicator—one who cannot be derogated—persuasion will be an increasing function of discrepancy. It is interesting to note, however, that for Job, even God's credibility faltered when he thought his demands were too extreme. This raises another important theoretical consideration: Can credibility be treated as a stable, fixed, attribute of a person? That is, does T. S. Eliot's stature remain equally impeccable regardless of the extremity of his critical stance? It seems likely that such information is processed along with other prior knowledge so that in some cases a highly credible source who takes an extreme stand is in fact less credible than a mildly credible source who takes a more intermediate position.

Bergin (1962) reports a study quite similar to that of Aronson et al. The results focus on changes in self-evaluation on the masculinity-femininity dimension (i.e., attitudes toward the self). Three levels of discrepancy and two levels of credibility were factorially manipulated. Discrepancy was defined in terms of subjects' latitudes of acceptance and rejection. Since the extreme discrepancy level was clearly within the subjects' latitude of rejection, the monotonic increase in attitude change found for increasing levels of discrepancy under the high credibility condition seems to refute the social judgment position. Apart from our prior comments on the similar outcome reported by Aronson et al., there are more specific criticisms of the Bergin results.

Perhaps the most compelling alternative is the demand interpretation. When the psychiatrist tells the subject that he is less masculine than he thinks and then asks the subject to rate himself again on the masculinity-femininity dimension, the second self-rating may soley reflect tendencies to follow instructions. Who can impugn a psychiatrist? "He's telling me what I should write down, so that's what I'll write." One could test the correctness of the demand interpretation by eliminating attitude change as a potential source of dissonance reduction and allowing the subject to reduce dissonance only by minimizing the "importance" of the issue. If he judged the issue as more important under higher levels of discrepancy, it would support the demand interpretation. If, instead, he judged the issue as less important with higher discrepancies, the dissonance interpretation would be supported.

In the previously mentioned experiment by Miller and Levy (1967) discrepancy was also manipulated. The data provide partial support for the social judgment model. Women in shopping plazas showed decreasing agreement with the supporting arguments of a communication as a function of increased extremity of the advocated position. In an after-only design, a mildly credible communicator urged lower salaries for elementary teachers as a means of improving education. The communications contained identical arguments and only differed in terms of the extremity of the proposed solution—lower salaries a bit, cut salaries in half, or eliminate salaries altogether. In support of the expectations of Aronson et al., while persuasion decreased over extremity levels, defamation of the source increased. This finding, of course, is also consistent with Sherif and Hovland's prohibition data in which negative evaluations of the communicator covaried with stability of attitudes.

In a most elaborate joint manipulation of discrepancy and source credibility, Bochner and Insko (1966) tried to thoroughly explore the discrepancy dimension. The communicators, a Nobel Prize winner and a YMCA director, advocated one of nine levels of sleep per night (eight to zero hours). The persuasion curves for both sources over levels of discrepancy have significant nonlinear components. Inspection reveals an increase in persuasion from low to moderate levels of discrepancy and a decline at extreme discrepancy levels. For the less credible source the decline appears at a lower discrepancy level (reflected in a source $\times$ discrepancy interaction). Though the quadratic componant is not significant for the high credibility source, it is noteworthy and perhaps not too surprising that even Sir John Eccles, notable physiologist and winner of the Nobel Prize, produces substantially less persuasion when he advocates no sleep as opposed to one hour per night.

Bochner and Insko separate source disparagement from communication disparagement. While these two response measures can obviously be operationally distinguished, the conceptual meaning of the distinction may not be as clear. Nevertheless, Bochner and Insko argue from the potency of their obtained effects that source disparagement is the more important determinant of opinion change. (Obviously, however, the direction of causal relation between opinion change and disparagement is sheer speculation.) In general, their data show that a more highly credible source receives less disparagement. But, curiously, higher discrepancy only increased disparagement of the communication; it did not affect the source. In a subsequent study on discrepancy, Insko, Murashima, and Saiyadain (1966) obtained a clear curvilinear effect as a function of increasing discrepancy.

In sum, how does social judgment theory fare on the question of the effects of discrepancy? As with involvement, due to the curvilinear expectations, experiments with only two levels cannot be decisive. Since the more striking predictions of the model are those indicating decreased attitude change under high discrepancy levels, any studies showing such a direction of effect have been taken as supporting the theory. As emphasized earlier, however, such findings are equally consonant with dissonance theory provided that other responses besides attitude change are taken into account. Nevertheless, there is one study that provides support for social judgment theory and does appear troublesome for dissonance theory. This is the previously cited study by Freedman. Under the condition where subjects were told that their first concept was important, discrepancy had a curvilinear effect upon influence. This outcome, of course, supports the social judgment theory analysis for the effect of discrepancy, yet it presents difficulty to dissonance theory in that for this study a shift to source disparagement is not a viable explanation of the drop-off in concept change under the highest discrepancy level.[24] While dissonance theory does specify a variety of other modes of dissonance reduction besides attitude change and disparagement of the source, it is not readily apparent that any of the other dissonance reduction techniques could easily be invoked to explain the discrepancy effect in Freedman's study.

Conclusion

It seems appropriate here to review the characteristics of the model and summarize its strengths and weaknesses. Obviously, the model serves an organizational function by accounting for an array of data concerned with the effects of discrepancy and involvement upon attitude change.

[24] Note that it is the discrepancy effect, not the involvement effect, which is being stressed.

Moreover, it incorporates a substantial literature concerned with the judgment of attitude items. The conceptualization of attitude in terms of latitudes of acceptance, noncommittal, and rejection, along with the development of measurement techniques to assess them, appears to have distinct advantages. It focuses attention more directly upon the organization of an attitude and argues that attitude is not just a single point on a dimension. Concomitant with this stress on attitude organization or structure is an emphasis on function. Sherif and Hovland point out that the judgment processes they describe have the functional value of maintaining personal integration by fostering disassociation from negatively valued positions or persons and exaggerating the self-similarity or congruence of acceptable positions or persons.

In addition, their approach has led to some other important developments in the area of attitude measurement. The recent focus on the subtle features of the experimental situation which produce unintended pressure on subjects to want to behave in particular ways (demand characteristics) and the subtle sources of experimenter error which unobtrusively enter into many laboratory settings have focused attention on the need for more new, indirect measures of attitude (e.g., Webb, Campbell et al., 1966). The social judgment approach has seemingly produced three new indirect measurement techniques.

The objective task of judging attitude statements can be used as a measure of attitude. Presumably, the stronger the judges' attitude, the more one will observe a "piling up" of statements in an end category. However, the recent work of Zavalloni and Cook (1965) and Selltiz, Edrich, and Cook (1965) suggest some modifications of Sherif and Hovland's outcomes.

The "own categories technique" can also be used to indicate attitudes. Subjects are given the objective task of judging or sorting statements, but instead of requiring them to use a fixed number of categories, they are free to determine the appropriate number of categories themselves. Sherif and Hovland maintain that those with stronger (more extreme) attitudes use fewer categories. Carolyn Sherif (1963) shows that the technique can be used to indicate differences between cultures as well as differences between an individual and his culture. Glixman (1965) provides another source of confirmation by showing that for dimensions presumably producing low involvement and generally moderate positions subjects use fewer categories (in contrast to dimensions about the self for which involvement is presumably high).

Third, Sherif, Sherif, and Nebergall (1965) suggest that involvement can be indirectly measured by examining the size of the latitude of noncommitment. Those with a narrow latitude of noncommittal are presumably more deeply involved in the issue. It remains to be seen, however, whether these indirect measures will ultimately prove useful.

Those who are familiar with the development of social psychology over the last three decades have long associated Sherif with an interest in field studies and naturalistic experiments—an insistence on developing a social psychology of the real world rather than just the experimental laboratory. His work on the social judgment approach with Hovland, Nebergall, and his other students and associates perpetuates this lifelong characterization of his interests and work. There is, of course, a gratifying degree of reassurance when principles extrapolated from the rarified atmosphere of the experimental laboratory find verification in more natural settings. In view of the difficulty of implementing research in the field, Sherif's constant efforts in these directions are admirable.

We must note once again that one of the important dimensions on which theories are evaluated is the degree to which they stimulate new research. While not matching the explosive thrust of dissonance theory on space allocations in current social-psychological journals, research stimulated by social judgment theory has nevertheless captured a fair share of current journal space. It has raised new issues for experimentation and, like dissonance theory, produced its own coterie of loyal but "unbiased" experimenters. Perhaps also like dissonance theory, it owes part of its success in stimulating research activity to the looseness of its theoretical structure. While lack of precision in the formulation and derivation of theoretical principles irritates the logical analysist, it protects the theory from an embarrassing accumulation of disconfirmations and allows room for imaginative additions, amplifications, and experimental implementations by others.

Although numerous positive aspects have been mentioned in the preceding paragraphs, most of them are "side effects." They are points that are irrelevant to the major consideration—an assessment of how adequately the theory predicts attitude change. The data on attitude change do seem to largely support the predictions of the theory. However, that by itself does not allow us to say "proven correct." The reason for this is that the theory also specifies the process by which change does or does not occur. And to date, there are no data which unequivocably show that the theoretically specified judgment process does account for the observed attitude change effects. Thus a basic difficulty is the central proposition of the theory: judgmental responses mediate attitude change. The difficulty of establishing empirical support for the temporal ordering implicit in this proposition has already been mentioned. Perhaps it must remain an assumption.[25]

Some of the very aspects that have been cited as advantages of the theory can at the same time be considered pitfalls. The obvious hazards of attempting to make causal assertions on the basis of experiments in which subjects are not randomly assigned to conditions warrant little further comment. The emphasis on individual difference variables turns the problem of explanation back another cycle and, as Sherif himself has noted, focuses attention on the need for a technology to adequately measure them. Furthermore, we must discover what manipulations produce the observed differences between individuals.

Although the lack of precision in the theory may have certain heuristic advantages, one would like to know precisely what the theory predicts. This lack of precision and unclarity about the logical relation between the judgment principles and the attitude change predictions may reflect the fact that the theory consists largely of empirical inductions. In other words, for Sherif, further precision awaits additional experimentation. In one sense the theory is quite narrowly focused. When concerned with attitude change it attends mainly to two independent variables, involvement and discrepancy. Relatively little has been done with some of the other stimulus variables which are potentially important in terms of the theory's basic assumptions. A variety of other stimulus attributes of a persuasive communication [e.g., context (Miller, 1966) and ambiguity] have not been experimentally explored.

Finally, there are numerous basic questions about anchoring effects which remain unanswered. Do anchors affect the basic discriminal process or do they merely impose alterations upon the response language?

---

[25] We have clearly taken the position that the theory unequivocally postulates that attitude change effects are mediated by judgment processes and that any mediating process must temporally occur prior to the effect it mediates. However, in a recent private communication, Sherif has not been willing to take this strong position about the temporal relation between judgment and attitude change. We understand his reluctance. Our own suspicions are that this temporal sequence does not empirically occur—that judgmental distortion and attitude change are simultaneous or temporally interchangeable processes. Nevertheless, we interpret the published versions of the theory as being emphatic on this point and have therefore retained it in our presentation.

What is the effect of temporal factors on anchoring effects? How do situational factors (Brown, 1953) intrude? Do other seemingly effective techniques such as "forewarning" alter latitudes of acceptance, rejection, and noncommitment? Does perception of an intent to persuade increase the vividness or definiteness of the boundaries between the different latitudes? What meanings do people subjectively ascribe to the latitudes of acceptance, rejection, and noncommitment? Do changes in their boundaries actually imply future behavioral changes as well, or are they merely shifts in the use of one's response language?

When we look at social judgment and try to portray its central thrust, it becomes evident that Sherif was struck by the contrast between laboratory studies of attitude which almost ubiquitously show some net positive change—even when a low prestige communicator delivers a ten-minute speech (Hovland and Weiss, 1951)—and our everyday observations which show people to remain remarkably fixed in their beliefs and habitually resist persuasion. These differences between the laboratory setting and data collected in the field have been noted and commented upon before (Hovland, 1959; Hyman and Sheatsley, 1947). Nevertheless, in partnership with this emphasis on resistance to persuasion Sherif presents the key to overcoming it. Persuasion will succeed when it proceeds by small steps. To be successful, each persuasive attempt must be modest. Presumably, when successful, the respondent's latitude of acceptance has been broadened. The astute social engineer exposes his target to repeated coercion, which gradually but eventually argues for a stand which the respondent initially would have patently rejected. The successive shifts in the respondent's latitude of acceptance seem to take time. How tightly can the persuasive efforts be packed on the time dimension? Perhaps, too, other social supports, cognitive supports, commitments, and behaviors must be coordinated with these shifts in judgmental behavior. The research on the implications of social judgment theory for behavioral modification or social engineering largely awaits implementation.

Chapter 7

Functional Theories of Attitude

"OF what use to a man are his opinions?" (Smith, Bruner, and White, 1956). This opening question epitomizes the central focus of three clusters of theoretical papers which we have classified as functional theories of attitude change. Two of these theories are similar enough to be presented jointly. One, by M. Brewster Smith, Jerome S. Bruner, and Robert W. White, (1956), is presented in a book entitled *Opinions and Personality*. This theoretical statement was presumably derived inductively from the detailed clinical case histories which provide the empirical foundation for the theory. The other theory, by Daniel Katz and his colleagues, is primarily presented in three papers (Sarnoff and Katz, 1954; Katz and Stotland, 1959; Katz, 1960). A third related approach by Herbert C. Kelman is best discussed in a separate section.

Two Functional Theories: Smith, Bruner, and White and Katz

Given the nature of contemporary American psychology, it is perhaps not surprising that the most likely answer to the question "Of what use to a man are his opinions?" takes the form of a list of needs or functions that are likely to be met or served by an opinion. At first glance such an approach seems susceptible to an unending eclecticism. For any opinion which does not fit into the current list of functions, the theorist can simply invent a new function—much in the fashion that psychologists added "needs" such as curiosity, exploration, and gregariousness in an attempt to "explain" behavior which could not be reduced to a striving for basic physiological deficiencies in the body.

In spite of the obvious explanatory folly of an unending list of social instincts, such as those McDougall (1917) posited to explain every discrete social act, there are two senses in which a functional approach may be useful. First, a functional theory of attitude change does take a position on the relationship between attitudes and other facets of human behavior. It construes man as an organism striving after certain goals and analyzes opinions in terms of the extent to which they facilitate obtaining these goals—goals that are evident from behavior and other facets of personality. Second, a list of goals is both a method of description and perhaps a powerful empirical predictor too. When combined with information on how an individual realizes his goals, we have a useful description of that person. To the extent that some of these goals and techniques are shared by mankind—or even subgroups of man such as southerners, liberals, union men—the attitude theorist is provided with potentially useful data about the subjects of his theory. Furthermore, as Katz argues in some detail, knowledge of the functions that support an opinion can determine the most effective strategy for modifying that opinion, illuminate the reasons why it is currently held, and suggest reasons why it has changed in the past.

Katz (1960, p. 167) lists three advantages to a functional theory of attitude change. Though not everyone would agree that all three are truly advantages, they help give the flavor of Katz's orientation.

1. The functional theory is a step in the direction of a more phenomonological approach: "Many previous studies of attitude change have dealt with factors which are not genuine psychological variables, for example . . . the exposure of a group of subjects to a communication in the mass media. . . . Merely knowing that people have seen a movie or watched a television program tells us nothing about the personal values engaged or not engaged by the presentation" (Katz, 1960, p. 167). Smith, Bruner, and White also agree that a stimulus (communication, group contact, etc.) can be understood only in the rich and idiosyncratic context provided by each individual's own personality.

"Behavior occurs as an interaction between striving organism and environment. What of the environment? Clearly it exists as *environment* only in relation to some organism . . . . Each [person], through his needs, interests, and aversions defines what for him constitutes the *effective* environment" (Smith, Bruner, and White, 1956, p. 30).

2. "By concerning ourselves with the different functions attitudes can perform we can avoid the great error of oversimplication—the error of attributing a single cause to given types of attitudes" (Katz, 1960, p. 167).

3. "Recognition of the complex motivational sources of behavior can · help to remedy the neglect in general theories which lack specification of conditions under which given types of attitude will change" (Katz, 1960, p. 168).

Both Smith-Bruner-White and Katz list four functions[1] which an opinion may serve. To a large extent, the functions are similar. The parallel functions from each set are presented in Table 7.1. Although the two

TABLE 7.1.   THE FUNCTIONS OF OPINIONS

Katz	Smith, Bruner, and White
1. Instrumental, adjustive, utilitarian	Social adjustment
2. Ego defensive	Externalization
3. Knowledge	Object appraisal
4. Value-expressive	Quality of expressiveness

sets do overlap considerably, there are some respects in which the correspondence breaks down. These differences between the two theories may at times be confusing to the reader. However, if presented separately, the differences might well be ignored. For instance, the two functional theories often disagree significantly on how attitudes are to be categorized. This lack of agreement on category boundaries illustrates the arbitrary nature of the functional categories. The lack of convergence

[1] In an initial theoretical paper (Sarnoff and Katz, 1954) only three major motivational determinants of attitudes were cited: (1) reality testing or knowledge function; (2) reward and punishment; and (3) ego defense. A second paper (Katz and Stotland, 1959) delineates five types of attitudes which differ according to the relative importance of the three components of attitude—affect, cognition, and behavior. For instance, affective associations (which are classically conditioned) have minimal cognitive structure, whereas intellectualized attitudes have substantial cognitive structure but little behavioral structure.

on a single set of functional categories reflects gaps in our knowledge and therefore is a serious criticism of the functional theories. The problem undoubtedly stems from the lack of empirical research stimulated by the theorist; empirical data would presumably provide insight into the most appropriate category boundaries. On the other hand, it could be argued that the entire taxonomic problem is entirely arbitrary and not dependent on empirical studies.

After discussing the meaning of each of the four functions, we shall consider the similarities and differences between the two approaches. In general, our presentation will deal more thoroughly with the Katz formulation. There are two reasons for this. Katz articulates his position with greater detail, and he has stimulated more research in connection with his theoretical position. We primarily emphasize his most recent statement (Katz, 1960).

THE INSTRUMENTAL, ADJUSTIVE, OR UTILITARIAN FUNCTION

Katz.

"This function recognizes the fact that 'people strive to maximize the rewards in their external environment and to minimize the penalties.' The child develops favorable attitudes towards the objects in his world which are associated with the satisfactions of his needs and unfavorable attitudes toward objects which thwart him or punish him" (Katz, 1960, p. 171).

It is the objects which are utilitarian, not the attitudes about the objects. As an individual moves through life, striving to obtain certain outcomes and avoid others, many objects in his environment are associated with success and failure. As a result of this reality-based experience with objects in the environment—foods, oil furnaces, electric toasters, other individuals, organizations, political parties, abstract concepts and symbols, etc.—some are associated with successful achievement of positively valued goals and others with avoidance of undesired events. According to Katz, an individual develops a positive attitude, while developing an "approach habit," toward objects which serve this utilitarian function; likewise, he develops negative attitudes toward objects that thwart his needs. The learned responses toward the positive or aversive objects presumably obey the laws of behavioristic learning theory. Katz considers these learned responses as attitudes. But, additionally, he considers the evaluative affect toward the objects as an attitude. The mechanism by which these affects are acquired remains unspecified. But taking our key from Katz and simply applying the behavioristic model in straightforward fashion, we can assume that the mechanism is "respondent" or "classical" conditioning (e.g., Skinner, 1953).

Since the experience with the attitude object is founded in reality, attitudes about the objects are relatively difficult to manipulate directly through verbal appeals.

"[Although] the need state may not be under the control of the propagandist, he can exaggerate or minimize its importance. In addition to playing upon states of need, the propagandist can make perceptible the old cues associated with the attitude he is trying to elicit . . . .

"Two . . . conditions, then, for the *arousal* of existing attitudes are (1) the activation of their relevant need states, and (2) the perception of appropriate cues associated with the content of the attitude" (Katz, 1960, p. 177).

The conditions for the *change* of attitudes about utilitarian objects are similar to the conditions of arousal.

1. Threat or deprivation of the need which the object serves.

2. The creation of new needs and/or new levels of aspiration.

3. Shifting the contingency of rewards and punishments. Objects which have, in the past, been utilitarian in the prediction of needs can be rendered useless in the goal-striving process, and new objects can be given instrumental value for need reduction.

4. The propagandist can emphasize new and better paths for need satisfaction.

"The area of freedom for changing utilitarian attitudes is of course much greater in dealing with methods of satisfying needs than with the needs themselves. Needs change more slowly than the means for gratifying them, even though one role of the advertiser is to create new needs. Change in attitudes occurs more readily when people perceive that they can accomplish their objectives through revising existing attitudes" (Katz, 1960, p. 178).

SMITH, BRUNER, and WHITE. We can best present this formulation of the social adjustment function in an extended quote from the authors. Their emphasis is somewhat different from that of Katz. Smith, Bruner, and White stress the usefulness of the attitude itself in establishing a social relationship. One relates to reference groups by holding the opinions which are expressed by one's idols, and the expression of opinions has many implications for our relationship with those persons with whom we directly interact. This emphasis on the utilitarian function of the attitude per se contrasts with Katz's focus on the utilitarian function served by the object of the attitude. In other words, while Katz included all needs which an object might serve, Smith, Bruner, and White focused on the social functions served by the attitude. The quotation is also important because it illustrates the way in which Smith, Bruner, and White rely on illustrative examples from their case studies to support their theory.

"Opinions can play another role; that of facilitating disrupting, or simply maintaining an individual's relations with other individuals. It is in this realm particularly that one must take care to distinguish the functions served by holding an opinion and by expressing it, for the strategy of expression is of particular importance in maintaining or cementing one's relationship with what may be called "membership groups"—the individuals which whom one is in direct contact . . . .

"The function of social adjustment served by holding an opinion is at once more subtle and more complex. For it is by holding certain views that one identifies with, or, indeed, differentiates oneself from various "reference groups" within the population. By reference groups we mean here those groups in terms of whose standards the individual judges himself and with which he identifies or feels kinship . . . . Representative of reference groups are such symbols as "intellectuals," "average middle-class Americans," "decent girls," and so on. The act of holding certain opinions . . . is an act of affiliation with reference groups. It is a means of saying, 'I am like them.'

"Reference groups, we shall see, may also play a negative role in opinion functioning. There are groups with which one seeks to reject kinship or identification. Thus, one of our subjects sought as hard to dissociate himself from the bourgeoisie as he sought to associate himself with the *avant garde* left. When rebelliousness and rejection are prominent features in a man's adjustment, we may expect negative reference groups to play a prominent role in his opinion formation.

"Two rather unique kinds of social adjustment can also be achieved by holding opinions of a certain kind. First, one may develop opinions as the expression of a need to be autonomous from others. Such declarations of autonomy—and we must distinguish the term from rebellion—are in a curious backhand way still another mode of identifying oneself with various reference groups. Thus one of our subjects showed a strong need for working out his opinions independently, unswayed by prevailing points of view. This procedure was for him a way of expressing his lack of dependence on others; but it was also a way of identifying with that nebulous category known as "independent and liberal thinkers." And second, it is sometimes convenient to indulge hostility toward others by holding opinions that are at odds with prevailing beliefs. If such an adjustment be neurotic in origin, it is nonetheless a form of negativism one occasionally encounters" (Smith, Bruner, and White, 1956, p. 41–43).

THE EGO-DEFENSIVE OR EXTERNALIZATION FUNCTION

KATZ (EGO-DEFENSIVE). Among the various functions served by an attitude, quite clearly the ego-defensive function is the one most closely related to psychoanalytic thinking. "The person protects himself from acknowledging the basic truths about himself or the harsh realities in his external world. Freudian psychology and neo-Freudian thinking have been preoccupied with this type of motivation and its outcomes" (Katz, 1960, p. 170). Thus this subsection of "functional theory" could also be labeled the psychoanalytic theory of attitudes. While its theoretical origin can be clearly traced to Freud, its social-psychological elaboration is primarily found in the literature on prejudice toward national, racial, and religious outgroups. Katz suggests that attitudes toward these targets, as well as those toward certain political issues, are largely traceable to the operation of defense mechanisms.

"[Defense mechanisms] stem basically from internal conflict with its resulting insecurities . . . . They proceed from within the person, and the objects and situation to which they are attached are merely convenient outlets for their expression . . . . The point is that the attitude is not created by the target but by the individual's emotional conflicts . . . . Moreover, though people are ordinarily unaware of their defense mechanisms . . . they differ with respect to the amount of insight they may show at some later time about their use of defenses" (Katz, 1960, pp. 172–173).

SARNOFF (PSYCHOANALYTIC THEORY). Sarnoff, initally in collaboration with Katz and McClintock and subsequently in collaboration with others, has most intensively extended the research concerned with the ego-defensive bases of social attitudes. Let us review here Sarnoff's theoretical statement of the relation between social attitudes and psychoanalytic theory (Sarnoff, 1960).

Sarnoff defines attitude similarly to the definitions of Campbell and Green quoted in Chapter 1. He says an attitude is a disposition to react favorably or unfavorably to a class of objects. Attitudes are inferred from overt responses. Since overt responses are made to reduce the tension generated by motives, Sarnoff assumes that the attitudes are developed while the person is making tension reducing responses to various classes of objects. "An individual's attitude toward a class of objects is determined by the particular role those objects have come to play in facilitating responses which reduce the tension of particular motives and which resolve particular conflicts among motives." (A motive is defined as "an internally operative tension-producing stimulus which provokes the individual to act in such a way as to reduce the tension generated by it and which is capable of being consciously experienced.") In line with functional theory, Sarnoff acknowledges that the divergent attitudes held by different persons toward the same class of objects may reflect different ways in which persons have learned to reduce the tension generated by the same motive. Conversely, identical attitudes may aid the reduction or mediate the reduction of quite different motives much in the same manner that the response of smiling could be an index of such diverse motives as love, anxiety, or hatred.

The crucial problem from the standpoint of psychoanalytic theory of attitude change and development is the degree to which attitudes and motives are congruent or discrepant. If a person (1) has high achievement motivation and (2) consciously accepts this motive, he should have a variety of specific attitudes consistent with his motivation. He will have favorable attitudes toward those conditions of work that permit him to achieve concrete objects which connote achievement such as prizes or certificates. Likewise, he will have favorable attitudes toward persons who can reduce the tension generated by his achievement motive. Conversely, this same person will have unfavorable attitudes toward conditions that preclude or interfere with achievement. Additionally, he will have negative attitudes toward objects that connote failure or persons who impede his own achievement. Thus, for motives which are consciously acceptable, the related attitudes should be determined by the role objects play in reducing the tension generated by the motives.

To take one of Sarnoff's examples, if an individual has an aggressive motive which he *can* consciously accept, he will develop favorable attitudes toward those objects which facilitate reduction of this aggressive motive. Thus Sarnoff argues that during World War II, white troops in integrated units came to develop more positive attitudes toward Negroes because they observed Negroes reducing a strong motive which they shared with them, namely, hatred of the enemy. In other words, the aggressive motive to demolish the enemy was partly satisfied by observation of Negroes engaging in behavior instrumental to that end; therefore more positive attitudes toward Negroes were developed.

The previous statements suggest little that is new. It is when motives are not consciously acceptable that psychoanalytic theory brings its contribution to bear. *For consciously unacceptable motives, attitudes facilitate occluding the perception of the motive.* In addition, they facilitate overt responses which enable the individual to reduce the tension produced by these unacceptable motives. Thus an "attitude," as ostensibly revealed by standard measurement techniques, will accurately reflect the relevant unconscious motive.

Further complications are introduced because there may be other conscious motives for which the ego-defensive attitude *is* functional for direct tension reduction. For instance, a person may display anti-Negro attitudes because such behavior may promote approval by his neighbors. This in turn may make them more likely to patronize his store and thereby satisfy his motive to make money—a motive which may be high in his motivational hierarchy. At the same time, however, he may have an aggressive motive which he cannot consciously accept. His anti-Negro behavior may help reduce the tension generated by that motive, but at the same time he can deny that he is being aggressive and tell himself that he simply has to behave that way toward Negroes or else he won't be able to survive economically. Furthermore, he may engage in another ego-defensive process—projection—and attribute to Negroes the aggressive motive which he himself possesses. Thus he may tell himself that those Negroes deserve to be excluded from his store.

Sarnoff distinguishes two main types of attitudes that serve ego-defensive motives: (1) attitudes which facilitate the perceptual obliteration of threatening external stimuli and (2) those which facilitate the perceptual obliteration of threatening internal stimuli. Particular defense mechanisms are associated with each type. For the first he lists attitudes which facilitate denial and identification with the aggressor. And for the second he lists attitudes which facilitate repression, projection, and reaction formation. As a third class he considers attitudes which facilitate overt symptomatic responses to the tensions of consciously unacceptable motives. Under this category he considers rationalization. The first group—denial, avoidance, and identification—is generally considered more socially handicapping than the other two (Miller and Swanson, 1960, pp. 194–288).

Still other more magical or mysterious Freudian treatments of attitudes can be found in works such as those of Janowitz and Bettleheim (1950). Some of these analyses attempt to account for the specific targets for different systems of repressed motives by appealing to archetypical association patterns. Hence attitudes related to repressed "id" motives (e.g. sex, aggression) steming from the deepest recesses of the personality will most readily be held toward dark or black outgroup targets (Negroes), whereas "superego" motives (e.g., cleanliness, industriousness) will more readily be held toward fair outgroup targets (e.g., Jews).

Katz (ego-defensive function continued). In his discussion of how ego-defenses support attitudes, Katz summarizes four techniques for arousing ego-defensive attitudes and three techniques for changing them.

1. "Attitudes which help to protect the individual from internally induced anxieties or from facing up to external dangers are readily elicited by a form of threat to the ego" (Katz, 1960, p. 180).

2. Many ego-defensive attitudes are elicited and strengthened by the social support that they receive. Although there is nothing intrinsic in the theory of ego-defensive attitudes which specifies that they are dependent on social support, Katz feels that the prejudice literatures demonstrates the descriptive fact. Pettigrew (1961) has argued in favor of this same point. However, whereas Katz feels that many prejudicial attitudes serve two functions simultaneously—ego-defense and social adjustment—Pettigrew implies that an ego-defensive function is irrelevant in most cases.

3. "A third condition for the arousal of ego-defensive attitudes is the appeal to authority. The insecurity of the defensive person makes him particularly susceptible to authoritarian suggestion" (Katz, 1960, p. 180).

4. "A fourth condition for defensive arousal is the building up over time of inhibited drives in the individual, for example, repressed sex impulses . . . . The drive strength for defensive reactions can be increased by situational frustration . . . . Frustration in areas unrelated to the attitude will increase the strength of the prejudice" (Katz, 1960, p. 181).

This fourth arousal mechanism is quite similar to the Freudian displacement mechanism. For instance, an early, elegant statement relating prejudicial attitudes to repressed energies from other motivational systems was presented by Dollard (1938). To this, however, he added the important theoretical notion of "triggering instances"—behavior by the target which is the eliciting cue for the expression of the negative attitude (or its behavioral component). As Dollard emphasized, the cue function was indeed just that and no more in that it rarely fully "justifies" the behavior it produces. In other words, stored motive strength by itself is not a sufficient condition for eliciting the attitude. Some legitimizing eliciting behavior from the target must also be present.

Katz completes his discussion of this topic with a list of three techniques to change ego-defensive attitudes.

1. Since ego-defensive attitudes are elicited by threats to the ego, the removal of threat is a necessary, though not a sufficient, condition. And, since threats to the attitude (both relevant and irrelevant) serve to entrench it, the propagandist (therapist, social worker) must strive to eliminate *all* threatening features of the communication situation.

2. "In the second place, catharsis or the ventilation of feelings can help to set the stage for attitude change . . . . Catharsis may function at two levels. It can operate to release or drain off energy of the moment . . . . It can also serve to bring to the surface something of the nature of the conflict affecting the individual" (p. 183). Katz does mention one qualification of the use of catharsis. For example, in a group discussion designed to alter unfavorable attitudes toward the draft, emotional antidraft outbursts by various group members may reinforce other members' existing attitudes. Unless there are positive features of the catharsis session which lead to a constructive consideration of the problem, the session could have the effect of entrenching, rather than changing, ego-defensive attitudes. One technique is to make sure that the session is long enough "for the malcontents to get talked out so that more sober voices can be heard."

3. "In the third place, ego-defensive behavior can be altered as the individual acquires insight into his own mechanisms of defense" (Katz, 1960, p. 183).

SMITH, BRUNER, AND WHITE (EXTERNALIZATION). Again a quotation will best present Smith, Bruner, and White's treatment of the role of inner motives and conflict. Since our presentation of their theory includes no separate section on supporting data, a few examples of the type of data they muster are also included. As mentioned before, the empirical support stems from their ten detailed case studies.

"We speak of externalization when the evidence shows that a person has *responded to an external event in a way that is colored by unresolved inner problems*. Outside events are treated as if they were analogous to inner ones, and the attitude taken toward them corresponds in some way to the attitude that is taken toward the inner struggle . . . .

"1. Covert strivings influence selectivity in the perception of objects. The presence of a covert striving, whether repressed or merely suppressed, creates a predisposition to perceive this striving in the object . . . .

"2. Attitudes toward objects are influenced by attitudes toward covert strivings. For the most part our men were disposed to condemn the behavior of the Russians that corresponded to their own covert strivings. They externalized the conflict . . . .

"In some cases, however, the subject tended to sympathize with a perceived tendency in Russia that was denied satisfaction in himself. This was true of Chatwell, for example, who frankly admired Russian industrial productivity while lamenting the lack of productivity in his own highly verbal occupation . . . .

"3. Attitudes toward objects are further influenced by preferred adjustive strategies. Sometimes our subjects' opinions, and especially their suggestions as regards policy, seemed to be influenced by satisfaction with an adjustive strategy that had worked well in their personal lives. Lanlin, for example, who had found happiness in salesmanship, proposed to ease the international situation by letting the Russian people know what we had to offer, whereas Upjohn, who had gradually achieved a good capacity for firm decisiveness, especially during his military service, advocated a strong policy line toward Russia even if it should result in war . . . .

"In other cases an adjustive strategy was externalized which represented the most that a person dared to do in his personal life. Kleinfeld offered a case in point when he declared that the Russians must be appeased lest they break out in open aggression, thus advocating a strategy he had found necessary in order to exist as a small shopkeeper and as a Jew . . . .

"4. The amount and importance of externalization differs greatly in different cases . . . ."

THE KNOWLEDGE FUNCTION OR OBJECT APPRAISAL

KATZ (KNOWLEDGE FUNCTION).

"Individuals not only acquire beliefs in the interest of satisfying various specific needs, they also seek knowledge to give meaning to what would otherwise be an unorganized chaotic universe. People need standards or frames of reference for understanding their world, and attitudes help to supply such standards . . . . People are not avid seekers after knowledge as judged by what the educator or social reformer would desire. But they do want to understand the events which impinge directly on their own life" (Katz, 1960, pp. 175–176).

Presumably attitudes acquired in an effort to understand and structure the environment will generally be elicited when some problem arises which cannot be solved without the information associated with the attitude.

"The factors which are productive of change of attitudes of this character are inadequacies of the existing attitudes to deal with new and changing situations . . . . Any situation, then, which is ambiguous for the individual is likely to produce attitude change. His need for cognitive structure is such that he will either modify his beliefs to impose structure or accept some new formula presented by others" (pp. 190–91).

Katz's formulation of the knowledge function is less detailed than his analysis of the ego-defensive function. Furthermore, unlike the discussions of some of the other functions, he presents few data. Compared to the well formulated theories discussed in the chapters on dissonance and cognitive consistency, the knowledge function is the weakest aspect of Katz's functional theory. The feature of functional theories which elevates them above "mere eclecticism" is the ability to make statements about the differential conditions for the arousal and change of attitudes which have differing functional foundations. Differential predictions are particularly sparse for the knowledge function.

SMITH, BRUNER, AND WHITE (OBJECT APPRAISAL). Whereas Katz stresses the tendency for individuals to impose a consistent structure on their environment, a principle central to dissonance and cognitive consistency theories, Smith, Bruner, and White focus on the adaptive function which attitudes serve in meeting the problems of day-to-day life.

". . . The holding of an attitude provides a ready aid in 'sizing up' objects and events in the environment from the point of view of one's major interests and going concerns . . . . Presented with an object or event, he may categorize it in some class of objects and events for which a predisposition to action and experience exists. Once thus categorized, it becomes the focus of an already-established repertory of reactions and feelings, and the person is saved the energy-consuming and sometimes painful process of figuring out *de novo* how he shall relate himself to it. If the environmental fact either defies categorization or is categorized in such a way as to bring harmful consequences to the person, new attitudes may be developed or shifts in categorization may occur. In sum, then, attitudes aid us in classifying for action the objects of the environment, and they make appropriate response tendencies available for copying with these objects" (Smith, Bruner, and White, 1956, p. 41).

In many ways the Smith-Bruner-White formulation of object appraisal is more like Katz's utilitarian function than his knowledge function. Utilitarian attitudes, according to Katz, reflect an individual's past experience with objects in reality, and utilitarian attitudes are aroused and changed in the context of dealing with new problems in the environment. Similarly, the Smith-Bruner-White formulation of the object appraisal function stresses the role that gathering information plays in the day-to-day adaptive activities of the individual. However, both the knowledge function and object appraisal are closely related to behavior theory's concept of stimulus generalization. As previously indicated, the lack of agreement about how attitudes are to be categorized into functions is a criticism of the functional approach. It indicates a lack of theoretical or empirical consensus on the functions that attitudes serve.

VALUE-EXPRESSION

Katz (value-expression function). Katz's value-expressive function reflects the emphasis of "ego psychology" in current psychoanalytic thought (e.g., Hartmann, 1964). Katz describes three related aspects of the value-expressive function. First, while ego-defensive attitudes have the function of obscuring a person's true nature from himself, other attitudes have the function of giving positive expression to an individual's central values and his self-concept. Second, Katz indicates that the expression of attitudes helps the individual define his self-concept. He uses the example of a teenager who adopts the dress and speech habits of his peers in order to clearly establish his status as a teenager and demonstrate his independence from the adult world. Finally, Katz notes that "when individuals enter a new group or organization, . . . [they] will often take over and internalize the values of the group" (Katz, 1960, p. 174).

However, the main theme of the section on value-expressive attitudes is found in the first part of the preceding paragraph—the satisfaction an individual gains from expressing himself. "Satisfactions . . . accrue to the person from the expression of attitudes which reflect his cherished beliefs and his self-image." The second and third aspects of the expressive function are similar to Smith, Bruner, and White's social adjustment function. An individual can express an attitude as a means of relating to other people, and he can incorporate the attitudes of reference groups in order to "become like" or "be one of" the respected reference group. Again there is a lack of consensus about how attitudes are to be categorized into functions.

Since the self-concept of the adult is molded by social forces—childhood socialization, identification with reference groups, or conformity to the norms of his face-to-face groups—the propagandist must understand these social antecedents to the self-concept in order to modify attitudes which reflect a person's self concept.

There are two situations that are likely to arouse a value-expressive attitude. "The first is the occurrence of the cue in the stimulus situation which has been associated with the attitude." Something in the current stimulus situation must key the individual off to the fact that some aspect of his self-image is relevant. The second condition is basically a deprivation state. There must be "some degree of thwarting of the individual's expressive behavior in the immediate past. The housewife occupied with the routine care of the home and children during the day may seek opportunities to express her views to other women at the first social gathering she attends" (Katz, 1960, p. 187).

The two conditions for changing value-expressive attitudes are quite similar and closely related to the conditions for arousing them. (1) "Some degree of dissatisfaction with one's self-concept or its associated values is the opening wedge for fundamental change . . . . (2) Dissatisfaction with old attitudes as inappropriate to one's values can also lead to change. In fact, people are much less likely to find their values uncongenial than they are to find some of their attitudes inappropriate to their values . . . . The influences exerted upon people are often in the direction of showing the inappropriateness of their present ways of expressing their values" (Katz, 1960, p. 189). We interpret the first point to mean that a manipulation threatening self-esteem (or chronically low self-esteem) makes all value-expressive attitudes, no matter what their content, vulnerable to change. The second point seems to stress that specific value-expressive attitudes can be changed by showing that that specific attitude is inconsistent with a more basic value.

SMITH, BRUNER, AND WHITE. When he states that "Satisfactions . . . accrue to the person from the expression of attitudes," Katz apparently commits himself to a need for self-expression. Smith, Bruner, and White, on the other hand, diverge from a strictly functional perspective of the *expression* of attitudes in that they discuss the expressive *nature* (not function) of opinions.

"Opinions, like any other form of complex behavior, are involved in . . . a pattern of consistency. They reflect the man's style of operating. When we speak of the "expressive nature of opinions" we refer *not to any need for expression* [emphasis ours], but rather to the simple fact that a man's opinions reflect the deeper-lying pattern of his life—who he has become by virtue of facing a particular kind of world with a particular kind of constitution" (Smith, Bruner, and White, 1956, p. 38).

Thus Smith, Bruner, and White's formulation of the expressive *nature* of opinions bears little resemblance to Katz's expressive *function*. Not only do Smith, Bruner, and White specifically reject the notion of an expressive need, they argue that the expressive aspects of an opinion do not serve a function for the rest of the personality. Opinions are just consistent with the other information we know about an individual. An intelligent man does not deal in abstractions to meet his needs for abstraction. Rather, the abstractions in his opinions are simply another symptom of his intelligence.

EXPERIMENTAL SUPPORT

KATZ. Relatively few data have been gathered specifically as a test of Katz's functional theory of attitude change. Katz and his colleagues (Wagman, 1955; Katz, Sarnoff, and McClintock, 1956; Culbertson, 1957; Katz, McClintock, and Sarnoff, 1957; McClintock, 1958; Stotland, Katz, and Patchen, 1959) have, however, reported a series of interrelated studies dealing with some of the hypotheses discussed in Katz's paper. Most of the research centers around explorations of the ego-defensive function.

The authors of *The Authoritarian Personality* (Adorno et al., 1950) suggested that a bigoted attitude could be based either on conformity to social norms or on the dynamics of ego-defense. As these authors suggested, and as Katz spells out, the most effective techniques of attitude change are unlikely to be the same for ego-defensive prejudice as they are for prejudice based on conformity to social norms. In particular, therapeutic techniques such as catharsis and insight are likely to be effective against prejudice based on ego-defense—but not for prejudice serving other functions. And "reality oriented" techniques, such as threat or promise of social approval, should be ineffective against any prejudiced attitude tied up in the dynamics of ego-defense.

The most straightforward test of these notions would be to preselect persons whose attitudes are based on ego-defense, for instance, and then to try to change the attitude by various techniques. Theoretically, for subjects whose attitudes rest on ego-defense, insight or catharsis should be more effective than informational appeals, threats, social pressure, etc. The research described below, however, has not concentrated on evaluating the relative effectiveness of various persuasive techniques. However, even if one took this approach, the meaning of the results would probably be ambiguous. The problem is that whatever interpretational appeal was used (an appeal aimed at providing insight into the ego-defensive function that the attitude serves) it would not necessarily be typical of all interpretational appeals. If a particular interpretational approach proves more effective than a particular informational approach in one experiment, that does not mean that all interpretational appeals, or interpretational appeals in general, are superior to all informational appeals for those whose attitude rests upon some ego-defensive function. The crucial problem is equating the two persuasive attempts on other irrelevant dimensions—an almost insoluble task. The alternative and more feasible approach is to select two groups, both of which have the same attitude. However, for one their attitude must serve a knowledge function, whereas for the other it must serve an ego-defensive function. Now, if half of each group is given each type of persuasive appeal, functional theory predicts an interaction which reflects the match between type of appeal and functional underpinning of the attitude. Theoretically, the interaction would show up over and above and main affects due to the fact that one type of appeal may have inadvertently been constructed so as to be generally more persuasive than the other.

The researchers who have experimentally attempted to test functional theory typically have chosen to assign intact groups to each of the persuasive techniques. One change manipulation will be given to a class or intact group, and the other persuasive techniques are typically given to other classes. This means that the experimental groups differ not only in the persuasive techniques used, but also in the kinds of subjects selected. In one case (McClintock, 1958) two of the persuasive techniques were administered to females in a local college while the third technique was administered to students in E's own class in a different school.

The consequence of these considerations is that experimenters have shied away from statements about the relative effectiveness of persuasive appeals. Rather, experimenters have tested a closely related hypothesis. For instance, these authors argue that, among subjects receiving an *interpretational* appeal, it will be those with attitudes based on ego defense who will show the most attitude change. To further strengthen the hypothesis, it has been suggested that among subjects receiving an *informational* appeal, the extent to which the attitudes are based on ego defensiveness makes no difference. (For them, all that should be relevant is the extent to which their attitudes serve a knowledge function.) In other words, rather than tailor the persuasion to the personality of the recipient, the experimenters have examined what happens when the listener's personality happens to be tailored to the persuasion.

McClintock (1958) utilized three types of persuasive communications: (1) an informational message (the cultural relativism argument was used to introduce information which should lead to less prejudice); (2) an interpretational message (a case study and consequent analysis were designed to cast light on the unhealthy dynamics which can lead to prejudice); and (3) an ethnocentric message—a message that implied that the subjects should become more prejudiced. McClintock also obtained measures of personality predispositions to conformity and ego defensiveness. Both were measured by subscales from the California F scale.

Let us look first at those subjects who read the antiprejudice *informational* message (see Table 7.2). Subjects who were high on conformity

TABLE 7.2. Informational influence, sessions 1 to 3

Conformity (Other-directedness)			Ego-Defense		
Low	Medium	High	Low	Medium	High
29%	55%	67%	47%	49%	4 %
		p level			*p* level
Low–Medium	.04		Low–Medium	ns	
Low–High	.003		Low–High	ns	
Medium–High	ns		Medium–High	ns	

Note: Percent of subjects showing positive change.

showed more attitude change in response to this message than those who were low in conformity. However, the informational message was equally effective for subjects who differed in ego-defensiveness. On the other hand, the ego-defensiveness of subjects who received the *interpretational* approach did make a difference in attitude change (see Table 7.3). Subjects who were moderate on the ego-defensiveness scale showed more attitude change than those who were low or high on the ego-defensiveness scale.

Thus, as predicted by Katz's formulation, personality traits do appear to be relevant to the effectiveness of a communication. The stronger support for the theory, however, lies in the fact that a personality trait is related to attitude change *only when the persuasive communication is tailored for that particular personality trait.* Conformity makes a difference for an authoritative appeal but not for an interpretational appeal; ego-defensiveness makes a difference for interpretational appeals but not for an authoritative appeal.

There is one disconcerting aspect of the data on ego-defensiveness, however. At first glance, it would seem that Katz's theory should predict a linear relationship between ego-defensiveness and attitude change; high ego-defensive subjects should show the most change, medium subjects the next most, and low subjects the least. Inspection of Table 7.3, how-

TABLE 7.3. INTERPRETATIONAL INFLUENCE, SESSIONS 1 TO 3

Conformity			Ego-Defense		
Low	Medium	High	Low	Medium	High
82%	57%	73%	75%	95%	53%
		p level			p level
Low–Medium	ns		Low–Medium	.015	
Low–High	ns		Low–High	.08	
Medium–High	ns		Medium–High	.0003	

Note: Percent of subjects showing positive change.

ever, reveals that the data do not support this prediction. To handle this point, Katz argues that the defenses of highly defensive people are so rigid and well prepared that they would reject any attack on these defenses no matter how powerful or subtle. Thus Katz contends that the crucial comparison is between the moderate and low ego-defensive subjects. He suggests that subjects moderate in defensiveness should be flexible enough to accept attitude change, and their attitudes should be somewhat involved in the defense mechanisms. On the other hand, while subjects low in ego-defense should be more flexible or open to an attack on whatever defenses they do have, their prejudice is unlikely to be founded on their meager ego-defenses. Hence, for these low defensive subjects, the interpretational appeal should have little or no persuasive impact.

Given this line of reasoning, Katz's theory must at least predict that moderate ego-defenders will show more attitude change than low ego-defenders. McClintock confirmed this hypothesis when the attitude was measured five weeks after the interpretational message had been read; when the attitude change was measured immediately after the message, however, the difference was far from significant. The fact that this differential effect does not show up immediately is taken as additional support for the theory. It suggests that some sort of relatively fundamental personality change is mediating the attitude change—a change which takes time to develop. This pattern has also been found by Katz, McClintock, and Sarnoff (1957) for two of their four measures of ego-defensiveness.

The fact that defensiveness has no moderating effect on attitude change in response to an informational appeal—defensiveness affects attitude change only in response to an interpretational appeal—lends support to the idea that prejudicial attitudes can stem from defenses that are part of the personality system. Further support for the role of ego-defense in prejudice is provided by the fact that, although highly defensive subjects regularly show the *least* attitude change in response to an antiprejudice appeal, they show the *most* attitude change in response to an ethnocentric appeal (McClintock, 1958). Studies by Culbertson (1957) and Wagman (1955) lend further support to the general relevance of ego-defense in prejudicial attitudes.

To confuse the picture, however, Katz, Sarnoff, and McClintock (1956) found a nonsignificant trend ($p < .10$) for moderately defensive subjects to change *less* than low defensive subjects. Stotland, Katz, and Patchen (1959) also report a trend for the most attitude change with low ego-defenders. The only safe generalization that can be made appears to be that low and moderate defensive Ss change more than high in response to an interpretational appeal. This conclusion does not provide strong support for functional theories; in fact, it may even be opposite to the functional predictions.

To add further to the problems in interpreting these studies, it should be noted that the measures of defensiveness are closely related to prejudice. In the preceding studies, defensiveness was often measured with subscales of the F scale and the F scale itself was specifically developed to correlate with prejudice. As a consequence, the different subject groups not only differ in personality but must necessarily differ in prejudice as well. Perhaps the differences in attitude change can most easily be explained in terms of the discrepancy between the advocated position and the subject's own position.

These data do not provide much of an empirical foundation for a functional theory of attitude change. This is because, first, only a very small portion of the theory has been subjected to an empirical test. Second, the hypotheses that have been tested are not unique to a functional theory of attitude change. The notion of conformity and ego-defensive bases for prejudice, as well as the suggestion that insight materials would be effective for prejudice based on personality dynamics and not for prejudice based on conformity to group norms, has long been a part of the prejudice literature (Adorno, Frenkel-Brunswik, Levinson, and Sanford, 1950). Finally, the prediction that moderate ego-defenders should be most influenced by an interpretational appeal is not unequivocally supported by the data. The research itself has produced several interesting findings in the area of prejudice, but it cannot be claimed yet that we have much empirical data attesting to the usefulness of Katz's broadly ranged functional approach to the study of attitude change.

SARNOFF. Sarnoff (1965), working more closely with concepts and hypotheses derived from Freudian psychology, has added substantially to the literature supporting the relation between ego-defenses and attitudes. He notes that in his previous research with Katz there may have been severe deficiencies in the measurement of ego-defense. One of their techniques was to code subjects' responses to TAT cards into three categories of ego-defense against aggression. The three categories were projection, extrapunitiveness, and denial. They used the sum of the separate scores as the measure of their predicted variable. Sarnoff notes that *post hoc* analysis suggested that this approach was fallacious in that, of the three categories, only projection yielded significant predictions for the attitudinal criterion. One problem in using TAT-type cards to define the presence or absence of particular defense mechanisms is that subjects are prone to give stories of finite length to each stimulus. Therefore, to the extent that one motive or type of defense appears within a story, there is no room left for other motives to show. A subject who is highly defensive and uses all three mechanisms extensively, when compared to a generally undefensive subject who does occasionally use projection, may nevertheless end up with a lower score on projection. The ceiling imposed by story length can mask the difference between these two types of persons. If one then uses a summary score, he has restricted his chances of finding big differences among subjects in their use of ego-defenses. A more sensitive procedure would be to use cards that tap particular defense processes. One would then look at cards which are prone to elicit a particular defense and segregate subjects in terms of whether or not they responded to that stimulus.

In his later experiments, Sarnoff attempted to sort out more distinctly the theoretical relationship between the defense in question and the motive presumably being defended against. Thus, in examining the ego-defensive basis of the social attitude of cynicism, he considered the defense mechanism of reaction formation as particularly salient. Furthermore, he argued that in the case of cynicism, reaction formation was linked to a particular repressed motive, namely, affection toward others. Hence the specific hypothesis that Sarnoff tested in this experiment was that after being exposed to an affection-arousing stimulus, persons high in reaction formation against affection would show increased cynicism, whereas those low in reaction formation would not.

Reaction formation was measured by use of the Blacky test. Associated with each picture were three summary statements designed to represent a different defense mechanism for guarding against affectionate feelings. One of these defenses was reaction formation; the other two were projection and regression. These same three defenses were always represented by the three statements which subjects ranked for each picture. (The specific content of the statements varied according to the picture theme and the order of the three statements was counterbalanced across pictures.) At the same time that reaction formation was measured, cynicism was also measured. A set of 10 items was imbedded within a 20-item questionnaire designed to measure "attitudes toward life." Several weeks later subjects were exposed to one of two conditions designed to arouse affection. The high arousal condition was a dramatic presentation of an excerpt adapted from William Saroyan's play *Hello Out There*. The low arousal group listened to a tape recording of the same excerpt. After exposure to these experimental manipulations, subjects retook the original cynicism scale items.

Although the effect of the experimental manipulation was to make all subjects less cynical, the results show that those subjects who were high in reaction formation on the premeasure were more resistant to the experimental induction of high arousal of affection.

In another experiment, Sarnoff (Sarnoff and Corwin, 1959) examined the relation between castration anxiety and the fear of death. The specific hypothesis was that individuals who are high in castration anxiety will show a greater fear of death after sexual arousal than those who are low in castration anxiety. Clearly, this hypothesis is derived from psychoanalytic thinking which posits strong castration fears prior to the resolution of the oedipal conflict. In the psychoanalytic formulation, the castration fears are acquired as a consequence of strong feelings of affection toward the mother and desire to possess her. After the resolution of the oedipal conflict and the repression of castration anxieties, unconscious castration anxiety may still be manifested in conscious fears of bodily injury or other mishaps. But, since there is no consciously logical connection between sexual arousal and fear of death, most other theories in this volume would have difficulty making his prediction.

On first consideration, the relation of this research to social attitudes seems remote. However, in an important sense, this is not the case at all. Rather, the fear of death can be considered as representative of a fairly general syndrome of attitudes which has greater breadth than the usual attitudinal or opinion topic employed in most experimental studies of attitude change. What Sarnoff is dealing with here are attitudes toward mishap, illness, misfortune, or, more generally, the lack of internal control over one's fate.

Again, the usual before-after design was used, subjects completed a scale measuring fear of death and a measure of castration anxiety again based on the Blacky test before being exposed to one of two levels of sexual arousal—pictures of nude women or pictures of fashion models. The results clearly confirmed Sarnoff's hypothesis. Provided they were exposed to the highly arousing sexual stimuli, those subjects who were initially high in castration anxiety showed a greater increase in fear of death between the premeasure and postmeasure than did those who were low in castration anxiety. Among those merely exposed to the pictures of fashion models there was no difference in the pre-post scores of high and low castration anxiety subjects.

In another study performed by one of Sarnoff's students (Bishop, 1967) the study by Festinger and Carlsmith (1959) reported in the chapter on dissonance theory was replicated under slightly modified conditions.

In the original version subjects were first exposed to a boring task for a considerable length of time. They were then asked to volunteer to tell other subjects who were about to participate in the experiment that the task they had just performed was extremely interesting and not boring. In one experimental condition, subjects were promised $20.00 for relating this information to subjects who were waiting for the experiment to begin. In the other condition they were offered only $1.00 for conveying this same information to waiting subjects. A subsequent measurement of their own attitudes toward the boring task showed that, as predicted from dissonance theory, subjects who were induced to lie to their peers for a low reward had more favorable terminal attitudes toward the task than those who had been offered the high reward for lying.

Bishop (1967) thought that this relation between incentive and attitude change would not be found uniformly among all subjects. More specifically, she hypothesized that subjects whose personality conformed to Freud's conception of the anal character would respond quite differently to privation than those low in anality. Thus in her version of the Festinger and Carlsmith procedure it was important to manipulate "degree of privation." This was achieved by inducing subjects to anticipate winning a $20.00 reward for their participation in the experiment. However, whereas all subjects anticipated winning $20.00, some in fact only won $1.00, whereas others won $19.00. This manipulation of privation was accomplished by having the experimenter make a drawing from a punchboard to determine the subject's winnings. As expected, she found an interaction between the personality measure of anality and the manipulated variable of privation. Under low privation (subjects win $19.00 instead of $20.00) highly anal subjects were more favorable in their evaluation of the extremely boring task which they had volunteered to describe as interesting to potential subjects. Conversely, however, under high privation ($1.00 instead of $20.00) the highly anal subjects were subsequently more negative toward the task.

In summary, then, the research of Sarnoff and his colleagues shows an often ingenious application of Freudian principles to the prediction of differences in attitude for subjects with different basic personalities or subjects who differ in their dependence upon particular ego-defense mechanisms.

SMITH, BRUNER, AND WHITE. In the case of Smith, Bruner, and White's theory, there is little to report in terms of quantitative data. The support for their theoretical speculations consists of a detailed, extensive, clinical probing into the personality functioning of ten men. As such, their theoretical formulation is an inductively derived system which does not rest upon quantitative experimentation. This was, of course, their choice. But, when judged by the criteria used to evaluate the other theories in this volume, the supporting data are weak indeed.

Criticism of the Functional Theories

KATZ AND SMITH, BRUNER AND WHITE

Our critical comments, though generally applicable in principle to both the Katz and the Smith, Bruner, and White formulations, will focus on the Katz version of functional theory. This is not meant to imply that of the two, Katz's theory stands on more treacherous ground. On the contrary, Katz's theory is spelled out in greater detail, and makes specific predictions for quantitative studies of attitude change. For these reasons, it is both easier and more instructive to criticize than the less structured book by Smith, Bruner, and White.

Perhaps a good starting point for a discussion or criticism of the functional theories of attitude change is to ask what one would do if one were to set about trying to change a person's attitudes. The functional theories tell us that one cannot answer that question without knowing what function the particular attitude in question serves. That by itself is not a stopping point, however, because one quickly realizes that it is essentially an individual difference theory, that is, the same attitude can serve different functions for different persons. The implication of this is that one would not know right off hand what kind of persuasive appeal or what kind of procedure to use unless one knew the individual in question. Knowing the individual and knowing his attitude on the particular issue would still not help. We need to know what function the attitude served for that individual. Whereas other theories also focus on individual differences (for instance, the social judgment theory is clearly such a theory), nevertheless, the other theories still predict main effects. They contain variables that allow us to predict group differences or the effects of stimulus treatments over and above variation among individuals. The functional theories, however, leave us powerless to predict unless we have accurate measures of individual characteristics. Thus its foremost requirement and most striking present lack is a technology for assessing the function of attitudes. The functional theorists have made little headway in providing such a technology and, furthermore, have invested relatively little effort into the problem. (One exception perhaps is the work on the F scale by Adorno et al. Another is the systematic work of Sarnoff and his colleagues. However, both research efforts are entirely specific to the ego-defensiveness function of attitudes.)

On the other hand, it may be too much to ask that Katz be able to develop the instruments needed to identify the function served by any particular attitude. His own research demonstrates that, by dividing subjects into groups that are generally high or low on ego-defensiveness, he can increase our predictive power. He succeeds in spite of the fact that he has not demonstrated that any particular attitude for any particular individual serves the ego-defensive function. Of course, if the measures of defensiveness and conformity are correlated with the attitude—as they are when subscales of the F-scale are used to measure defensiveness and conformity and the attitude is prejudiced—then we cannot be sure that that measure of defensiveness or conformity would identify ego-defensive attitudes in other topic areas.

There remains another, somewhat less important criticism. A propagandist or laboratory scientist must administer a personality test, score it, and then sort his audience into separate subgroups before he can tailor his speech to the audience. This is a cumbersome aspect of Katz's individual differences theory and presents problems both to the applied propagandist and the laboratory scientist. In other words, the operational procedures are more complicated than they would be for other theories. This is, of course, a practical consideration and not a logical flaw in the content of theory itself.

Considering the breadth of the theory, one notes that different aspects have been subject to more detailed treatment by other theorists. Thus, for instance, one may say that the consideration of the instrumental function has been dealt with by the stimulus response or behavioristic theories of attitude and that the knowledge function has been handled by the theory of cognitive dissonance or other consistency theories. As previously indicated, the ego-defensiveness function is the one area of functional theory for which those intimately associated with the theory have initiated some research. Although the value-expressiveness function is a somewhat novel idea, it has generated almost no experimental research. It is not even empirically established whether or not depriving people opportunity for expression produces stronger motivation to display value-expressive attitudes. At any rate, given this eclectic nature of the theory, it is not likely that future evaluations of the theory will yield many predictions that are distinct from other current theories reviewed in this volume. Thus, while theories are ordinarily evaluated partly in terms of their ability to make predictions not made by other theories, the very aim of Katz's functional theory—the development of a broad, systematic account of attitude development and change—tends to preclude the derivation of hypotheses not found in other "middle range" theories.

Another criterion on which theories can be evaluated (other than *new* hypotheses) is the extent to which the hypotheses they do present are specific or clearly testable. Most of the more unusual as well as specific predictions are associated with the psychoanalytic thinking behind the ego-defensive function. The data are not unequivocally supportive of the theory, but most other theories would have trouble predicting these data. However, when one does look for specific hypotheses to be tested within the other three functions, relatively few are found. Furthermore, when one is found, one can often think of data which contradict it. Consider the following statement: ". . . Those objects in the environment which aid in understanding the world would be evaluated highly . . . . [I]f the object itself is clearly understood, it will be evaluated more highly than if it is understood . . . vaguely" (Katz and Stotland, 1959, p. 438). In considering this statement the first thing that comes to mind is data from another research tradition on the effects of distraction which tend to show just the opposite. Namely, when subjects are distracted, that is, when they are not able to clearly comprehend the content of the communication, they are better persuaded (Allyn and Festinger, 1961; Festinger and Maccoby, 1964). What are the specific circumstances under which one or the other of these two possibilities apply? Katz cites a paper by Cohen, Stotland, and Wolfe which purportedly shows that subjects liked clearly written stories better than ambiguously written stories as evidence in support of the functional hypothesis. However, it is easy to interpret that research in terms of demand characteristics (Chapter 2) or simply in terms of a manifestation of aesthetic principles.

Some hypotheses appear to be tautologies. For instance, consider the following statement: "Attitudes based on the need to understand will often have well differentiated cognitive components, since this gives the individual a more adequate basis for understanding his world" (Katz and Stotland, 1959, p. 438). How would one diagnose whether an attitude is based on a "need to understand" separately from measurements of the extent to which it has "differentiated cognitive components?" Still other hypotheses for the three nonego-defense functions are so general, that empirical tests are difficult. For instance, consider the following: "Key factors in attitude change are not the situational forces or the amount and types of information to which the individual is exposed, but the relation of these factors to the individual's motive patterns" (Katz and Stotland, 1959, p. 456). This quote underlines the individual difference emphasis of their theory, and it makes a testable point, namely, that individual differences can contribute more variance to an outcome than other environmental or situational factors. Psychology has tussled with these kinds of propositions before as, for example, with the heredity-environment controversy (nativism versus empiricism). The task of exploring which of the two factors can potentially contribute greater variance is probably a fruitless question.[2] Yet, this hoary issue—whether one system of variables is more potent or controls more variance than another—relates to one of the central propositions that Katz makes when he argues that need systems fall into a specific rank order in terms of their urgency.

The generality of Katz's theoretical statements is a pervasive characteristic of the several statements of functional theory. As previously indicated, it often appears as if he is attempting to coalesce or subsume all other theories under a single title. If this is indeed the intent, then it is essentially a translation exercise in which the work of others is incorporated into a single linguistic system. Recognition of this ambitious characteristic of Katz's theory simultaneously explains its disappointing qualities. While emphasizing that attitudes exist in a completely interdependent system, that they can be either independent or dependent variables, that they interact with perception, motivation, and cognition, Katz and his colleagues have succeeded in applying psychological concepts to a wide range of social phenomena. But, with the exception of the ego-defensive function, they have not delineated the conceptional bound-

---

[2] It may be more reasonable to pick a single culture or society and evaluate the relative contributions of these two factors as their effects are observed to occur within that culture, rather than look at their relative contributions "in principle."

aries of their theoretical terms, nor have they provided guidelines for how to operationalize their theoretical terms. Thus, for instance, let us reconsider a quotation which describes the instrumental or utilitarian function:

"People strive to maximize the rewards in their external environment and to minimize the penalties. The child develops favorable attitudes towards the objects in his world which are associated with the satisfactions of his needs and unfavorable attitudes toward objects which thwart him or punish him" (Katz, 1960, p. 171).

As used here, is "attitude" different from "learning"? If not, why confuse the issue by using two different terms? If so, wherein lies the difference? How does the statement quoted above fit with those instances reported by clinicians in which people also learn to like things that thwart their needs or are aversive? Presumably when such instances occur it is because other motives have been engaged. But where is the predictive value of the theory? How do we assess the presence or absence of such non-adaptive or nonhedonistic motives independently from the responses that we wish to explain? Furthermore, what is the mechanism by which the evaluative response gets attached to objects which elicit approach and avoidance habits? What laws govern the acquisition of these evaluations? These are indeed difficult problems. That others besides Katz have not solved them does not improve the predictive validity of functional theory. Perhaps both the strength and weakness of the theory rests in its ambitious aim.

Compliance, Identification, and Internalization: Three Processes of Attitude Change (Kelman)

Kelman's theory of attitude change differs somewhat in general approach from the explicitly functional theories discussed previously. For one thing, Kelman builds his theory on the processes of attitude *change;* the two previous theories were theories about attitudes but contained relatively little focus on change per se. Smith, Bruner, and White base their theory on the detailed clinical examination of ten men. They examine the role of attitudes in maintaining the stability of individuals' personality. Katz too, makes statements about change as deductions from a theory about the functions which the attitudes (not attitude change) might serve. He places his formulation on a foundation constructed in part from survey research and a concern with such "real life" attitudes as prejudice, voting, and political attitudes. Kelman, on the other hand, forges his theory out of an intellectual tradition which has depended on controlled laboratory experiments for most of its hypotheses and data.[3]

Kelman's theory is also less functional than the two previously discussed; he does not talk about "needs" that are satisfied or "functions" that attitudes, or attitude change, might serve. But we have included his paper in this chapter because it shares one important goal with the other theories. Kelman's theory clearly implies that knowledge of how an attitude was acquired is the key to knowing how to change it effectively. The same attitude may have developed in two different persons by different processes. Therefore the procedures by which they can best be altered would not be the same.

COMPLIANCE

"Compliance can be said to occur when an individual accepts influence because he hopes to achieve a favorable reaction from another person or group. He adopts the induced behavior—not because he believes its content—but because he expects to gain specific rewards or approval and avoid specific punishments or disapproval by conforming. Thus the satisfaction derived from compliance is due to the *social effect* of accepting influence" (Kelman, 1958, p. 53).

An attitude internalized through the process of compliance would, in Smith, Bruner, and White's terms, serve the social adjustment function.

ANTECEDENT CONDITIONS. The amount of attitude change produced by compliance depends on the relative importance of the effect which is anticipated from the compliant act. In other words, compliance is most likely to be a process of attitude change in situations where the power of the influencing agent is based on control of rewards and punishments.

CONSEQUENT CONDITIONS. "When an individual adopts an induced

[3] See the discussion on Hovland (1959) in Chapter 2 for some of the conflicting conclusions implied by these two sources of data. One of these conflicting conclusions particularly relevant here is that laboratory experiments typically are able to demonstrate that the subjects are influenced by the persuasive manipulations, whereas field studies find attitudes relatively entrenched and typically are unable to demonstrate that the persuasive event had any impact on the audience.

response through compliance, he tends to perform it only under conditions of surveillance by the influencing agent" (Kelman, 1958, p. 54).

IDENTIFICATION

"Identification can be said to occur when an individual accepts influence because he wants to establish or maintain a satisfying self-defining relationship to another person or a group. This relationship may take the form of classical identification in which the individual takes over the role of the other, or it may take the form of a reciprocal role relationship. The individual actually believes in the responses which he adopts through identification, but their specific content is more or less irrelevant. He adopts the induced behavior because it is associated with the desired relationship. Thus the satisfaction derived from identification is due to the *act* of conforming as such" (Kelman, 1958, p. 53).

ANTECEDENT CONDITIONS. The amount of attitude change produced by identification depends on the "influencing agent." In other words, identification is most likely to be a process of attitude change in situations where the power of the influencing agent is based on his *attractiveness* to the individual.

As first consideration, the antecedent conditions of the identification process do not appear to be independent of the antecedent conditions of the compliance process. According to Kelman, compliance depends on the communicator's "control of rewards and punishments"; identification depends on the communicator's "power." However, many psychologists have defined power as the ability to control the rewards and punishments others receive (Skinner, 1953; Thibaut and Kelley, 1959; Stogdill, 1959; Butler and Miller, 1965; Collins and Guetzkow, 1964). How then does identification differ from compliance? Kelman is not clear on this issue. It could be that Kelman would want to argue that identification is based on total attractiveness from all sources of power. While those who have been concerned with "identification theory" have separated out various dimensions which might control identification—status envy (Whiting, 1960), control over resources (Bandura, Ross, and Ross, 1963), similarity, etc.—we can think of these components as additive. The person whose attractiveness rests on all three components may indeed be more attractive to a subject even though circumstances may be such that in this particular instance he cannot actually control the subject's receipt of rewards and punishments. On the other hand, however, Kelman may explicitly wish to exclude *any* component of attractiveness which stems from control over rewards and punishments. In fact, Kelman (1958) has spoken of three distinct sources of power—means control, attractiveness, and credibility—each of which form the antecedent conditions for a *different* attitude change process.

Consequent conditions. "When an individual adopts an induced response through identification, he tends to perform it only under conditions of salience of his relationship to the agent" (Kelman, 1958, p. 54). Presumably, any attitude change that occurs is largely dependent on maintaining the social relationship.

Compliance and identification are quite similar to the two mechanisms Smith, Bruner, and White subsume under their social adjustment function. Smith, Bruner, and White stress the role that conformity plays in gaining acceptance in "membership groups" or one's immediate circle of acquaintances. Where Smith, Bruner, and White discuss only *opinion conformity* as a compliant act, and *group acceptance* as the only social effect, Kelman broadens the compliance process to include any compliant act and any social reinforcer.

As their second of the two submechanisms of social adjustment, Smith, Bruner, and White note that internalizing the values of a reference group functions to define an individual's relationship to his social context. In discussing the value-expressive function, Katz notes the social origins of the self-concept. Kelman's identification process has commonality with both of these positions. A compliant act is induced through the process of identification because the act defines, strengthens, or consummates an important *relationship* to an important other person.

INTERNALIZATION

"Internalization can be said to occur when an individual accepts influence because the content of the induced behavior—the ideas and actions of which it is composed—is intrinsically rewarding. He adopts the induced behavior because it is congruent with his value system. He may consider it useful for the solution of a problem or find it congenial to his needs. Behavior adopted in this fashion tends to be integrated with the individual's existing values. Thus the satisfaction derived from internalization is due to the *content* of the behavior" (Kelman, 1958, p. 53).

The process of internalization has some similarities to the object appraisal function of Smith, Bruner, and White and also to the utilitarian function as presented by Katz. The formulations of both Katz and Smith, Bruner, and White deal primarily with attitudes that were acquired out in the day-to-day life of the "real world." Perhaps for this reason both theories emphasize the manner in which an individual can test an opinion about an object against the "truth" or the reality of the object. Subjects who have been corraled into a laboratory for controlled experimentation, however, must evaluate any information they receive against their current stock of information. It would be an unusual experiment which gave the subjects the opportunity to test the validity of the content in the persuasive communication against some objective criterion before administering the posttest. Perhaps this limitation of the laboratory situation is one of the reasons why Kelman discusses only the possibility that the subject might *consider* (rather than discover, as Katz might put it in his utilitarian function) a piece of information useful for the solution of a problem. Situations where an individual cannot (or does not) test information against reality are common outside, as well as inside, the laboratory. In fact, survey research usually reveals that it is the unusual citizen who gathers factual material to support his political opinions or who bothers to subject them to reality testing (Freedman and Sears, 1966). It is probably quite typical for an individual to accept the factual validity of a communication if it is "congruent with his value system."

Antecedent conditions. The amount of attitude change produced by internalization depends on the prepotency of the response which is advocated.

Consequent conditions. "When an individual adopts an induced response through internalization, he tends to perform it under conditions of relevance of the issue, regardless of surveillance or salience" (Kelman, 1958, p. 54).

SUPPORTING DATA (KELMAN)

In his 1958 paper, Kelman reports the results of a study specifically designed to test his theory about three processes in attitude change. The study took place in early 1954, just before the announcement of the Supreme Court decision on desegregation, and it used Negro college freshmen as subjects. The communications were tape recorded interviews between a moderator and a guest which argued that it would be desirable to maintain some of the *private* Negro colleges as all-Negro institutions in order to preserve Negro culture, history, and traditions—even if the Supreme Court declared segregation unconstitutional. While the content of the communication messages was kept constant, the source and the degree of the communicator's persuasive power were manipulated. A communication specially designed to maximize each of the three processes of attitude change was presented to a separate group of subjects. These communications manipulated the variables which Kelman discusses in his antecedent conditions section of the theory. All subjects then answered three questionnaires, each designed to maximize the variables which Kelman discusses under consequent conditions.

1. THE COMPLIANCE COMMUNICATION. Every attempt was made to make the communicator appear as though he possessed means of *control.* "He was introduced as the president of the National Foundation of Negro Colleges . . . . It became evident that his foundation had been supporting the college in which the study was being conducted . . . . He made it clear that he would withdraw foundation grants from any college in which the students took a position on the issue in question, which was at variance with his own position" (Kelman, 1958, p. 55).

2. THE IDENTIFICATION COMMUNICATION. This interview was structured in such a way that the communicator would have high attractiveness. "He was introduced as a senior and president of the Student Council of a leading Negro university . . . . He presented the same message as the first communicator, but he made it clear that he was presenting not only his own opinions but the overwhelming consensus of opinion of the college students represented in an opinion poll which he had just conducted among Negro college seniors" (Kelman, 1958, p. 55).

3. THE INTERNALIZATION COMMUNICATION. This interview was constructed in such a way as to give the communicator high credibility. "He was introduced as professor of history of one of the country's leading universities. In the course of the interview it became evident that he was one of the top experts on the history and problems of minority groups; that he was highly respected by both his colleagues and by members of minority groups; and that he had a fond concern for the welfare of the American Negro community. He presented the same position as the other speakers, but he made it clear that his position was based on his research and on the evidence of history" (Kelman, 1958, p. 55).

Since all subjects answered three questionnaires, they were given the opportunity to express their opinions in three separate circumstances. One questionnaire was completed under conditions of *salience* and *sur-*

veillance. Salience was maximized by administering the questionnaire immediately after the communication. Surveillance was maximized by emphasizing that the questionnaire was being administered at the communicator's request, and that he would see each subject's answers. In addition, the subjects signed their names and gave other identifying information. A second questionnaire was completed under conditions of *salience* and *nonsurveillance.* Salience was again maximized by administering the questionnaire immediately after the first questionnaire, in other words, very shortly after the end of the speech. However, the questionnaire was anonymous, and subjects were assured that their responses would be seen only by the research staff and would *not* be seen by the communicator. The third questionnaire provided an opportunity to express one's opinion under conditions of *nonsalience* and *nonsurveillance.* Salience was lessened by administering the questionnaire from one to two weeks after the communications session, in a different setting, under different auspices, and by a different experimenter. The questions were imbedded in a large number of other attitudinal items and no mention of the communication was made. As was the case with the second questionnaire, subjects were assured that their answers would remain anonymous.

Since this experiment was specifically designed to test Kelman's theory, the predictions are relatively straightforward. If we assume that the attitude change produced by the communicator with means-control is produced by a compliance process, then that attitude change should be manifested only under conditions of surveillance. Indeed, the data do indicate that subjects who heard the compliance communication showed significantly more attitude change when told that the communicator would see their answers than they did with either of the other two anonymous questionnaires.

If the attitude change produced by the speaker with high attractiveness takes place through an identification mechanism, Kelman argues that the attitude change should be manifested only under conditions of salience. Again under high salience (the questionnaires administered immediately after the communication) attitude change was significantly greater than that found on the nonsalient (delayed) questionnaire. Finally, if the attitude change produced by the speaker with high credibility is produced by an internalization mechanism, then the change should manifest itself under all conditions of testing. An analysis of variance indicates that there were no significant differences among the three questionnaires for the subjects receiving the internalization communication. Thus the data in general confirm the predictions from Kelman's study.

As is the case with any single study, however, the results are not totally unambiguous. The study used a repeated-measures design; in other words, all subjects answered all three questionnaires. It is a fairly common finding in studies of this kind that the amount of attitude change discovered decreases as the length of time between the persuasive manipulation and the posttest increases. This "decay" of attitude change operates in the same direction as some, though not all, of Kelman's hypotheses. Furthermore, as Kelman points out, the drop from Questionnaire 1 to Questionnaire 2 is almost as large in the identification group where there should be no difference as it is in the means-control group where the theory calls for a difference. Kelman does report a subanalysis in which he considers only subjects who were relatively favorable toward the position advocated by the communicator. This group probably contains a larger percentage of people who were influenced by the communication. In this subsample the difference between the surveillance and the nonsurveillance questionnaires (1 and 2) is much larger for the means-control group than for the credibility group.

Finally, other differences which theoretically should have been expected were not tested. For instance, on the third questionnaire subjects in the internalization condition should show more agreement than those in the compliance and identification conditions. Likewise, on the second questionnaire, subjects in the identification condition should show more change than those in the compliance condition. Although no test of these differences is reported, inspection of the means suggests that they would not be supported.

Insofar as any single study constitutes proof for a theory, these data are on the whole quite supportive of Kelman's formulation. Encouraging as these data from a single study may be, in number they stand in vivid contrast to the mass of studies which support some of the theories presented in other chapters of this book.

CRITICISM

The first thing that we might ask about Kelman's theory is in what sense is it a theory? He speaks of three processes of attitude change: compliance, identification, and internalization. These terms could easily be considered three chapter headings or labels for social psychological research. One could study each of them as either an independent or a dependent variable. It is not even clear that they all directly refer to attitude change. For instance, others who have written about attitude change would not consider the compliant act itself a form of attitude change. It can better be considered "conformity" or a consequence of social influence in that we typically consider an attitude as stable or extended in time. And, as Kelman predicted and confirmed, the change produced by compliance was short-lived.

Kelman initially labeled his article "three processes of attitude change." Subsequently (Kelman, 1961) he spoke of "processes of opinion change." But still later, in a reprint of this same article (Kelman, 1963), he referred to his initial classificatory effort of differentiating the three processes as "a framework for the analysis of social influence." It would seem that here he is standing on much firmer ground in that in the broad sense, attitude change does constitute one form of social influence, though of course there are others. In other words, the term "social influence" is broader and encompasses more than the term "attitude change."

Another consideration is that Kelman's treatment of compliance is not comprehensive. Although the complying act by itself is not attitude change, sometimes at some later point subsequent to the compliant act, attitudes do change in a direction congruent with the compliant act. This is demonstrated in the forced compliance literature. Finally, the fact that compliance is not a sufficient condition for attitude change requires further theoretical consideration. Kelman states that compliance requires surveillance. However, compliance can sometimes be induced without surveillance.

In attempting to evaluate Kelman's work as a theory, it is important to consider how his three processes should be conceptualized. There are three possible alternatives. We could consider the three as definitions of three types of theoretical terms (concepts, constructs). If so, we could then study them as either independent variables or dependent variables. Alternatively, we could consider them as labels for three general classes of psychological laws. In terms of these possibilities, the theory at best is a set of three laws; at worst, it is a set of three definitions!

In what sense can the three processes be considered as definitions of concepts. As Hemple (1952), Bergmann (1957), and others have pointed out, dispositional constructs (concepts) such as elasticity or magnetism are often defined with a special type of definition—a definition which is stated in the "if-then" form and uses the subjunctive tense.

In other words, it is a definition which requires the scientist do something and then make an observation before he can state that x is or is not elastic. Hemple terms this procedure an operational definition—a definition which has superficial similarity to a law because of its "if-then" form. To be specific, what one means by "elastic" is "*if* I stretched it and let it go, *then* it would return to its original size." But note that one never knows whether x is elastic until one performs the test. If one wished to study whether magnetized metals are more resistant to corrosion, one would have to know which metals were or were not magnetized. That is, one needs a definition of magnetic. A procedure such as sprinkling iron filings on a sheet of paper placed on top of the metal and observing whether a certain effect occurred would "define" whether or not a particular metal was magnetic.

Kelman's three processes can be conceptualized as dispositional concepts similar in principle to magnetism or elasticity. Thus one could study the relation of any of the three types of attitudes—compliance attitudes, identification attitudes, and internalized attitudes—to other social psychological variables. In doing so, one could consider Kelman's efforts as having provided the operational definitions for the three types of attitudes. For example, if one wishes to compare the resistance of "compliance attitudes" to fear-arousing counterpropaganda, one must first know in which of the three categories a particular attitude falls. Taking a key from Kelman's work, if an attitude is adopted because a group or another individual offers a favorable reaction for displaying the attitude and then the attitude is not expressed when surveillance is absent, it is a *compliance attitude*. Being thus able to define the three types of attitudes, we then go on to discover how these three theoretical constructs (concepts) are functionally related to other variables (concepts). If we find that the three were indeed differently resistant to fear-arousing counterpropaganda, we have discovered a law. However, if we treat the three processes in this way—as three definitions—we can hardly categorize Kelman's work as a theory.

On the other hand, we could consider the three processes as a set of three laws. Then, to the extent that the laws have some generality, Kelman's work can pass muster as a theory, though, admittedly, it would be a theory of somewhat smaller than optimal scope. Taking the stand that these three processes are "laws," we can construct some good arguments for considering them as such. Kelman speaks of the antecedents of the "three processes" and their "consequents." Among the antecedents he considers are "the basis for the importance of the induction" (of influence), the "source of power of the influencing agent," and "the manner of achieving pre-potency of the induced response." For each of these three there are three possible techniques. Presumably depending on which technique is used, there will be a different consequent and therefore a different one of Kelman's three labels—compliance, identification, or internalization—would be applied to the attitude that is produced. Quite obviously, where one is talking about antecedents and consequents, one must be talking about laws; and what Kelman has done for us is to provide a label for some laws.

Table 7.4 shows Kelman's summary of the distinctions between the three processes. One question that arises is whether it is possible for any one of the three antecedents to produce all of the consequents. Are these antecedents and their respective consequents mutually exclusive? In other words, if one of the antecedents listed under compliance obtains, is it necessarily the case that none of the consequents listed under the other processes (identification and internalization) can in fact occur? For instance, if the source of power of the influencing agent is attractiveness, a source presumably serving as an antecedent for the identification process, is it inconceivable that a response induced on the basis of attractiveness could not become imbedded in the person's value system? If it did turn out to appear imbedded in the person's value system, would Kelman then turn around and say that the source of influence also had high credibility (an aspect of the communicator when the internalization process occurs)? Or, to consider another aspect of this same problem, is high source credibility the sole means of producing attitude change which is congruent with and can be incorporated into one's prior value system? Other questions concern the relative resistance to counterpropaganda of attitudes acquired via the three processes. Also, are different types of counterappeals differentially effective for attitudes formed via the different processes?

Are there any experiments which are suggested or need to be done after Kelman's one experiment? As indicated above, his theory could conceivably generate a variety of hypotheses. In a later paper (Kelman, 1962) Kelman does present some new hypotheses. For instance, he proposes that induction of action is more likely to lead to attitude change if the approach component of the person's relationship to the object is based on identification rather than internalization. He also hypothesizes that induction of action is more likely to revert to the original belief

Table 7.4. Summary of the distinctions between the three processes

	Compliance	Identification	Internalization
Antecedents			
1. Basis for the *importance of the induction*	Concern with social effect of behavior	Concern with social anchorage of behavior	Concern with value congruence of behavior
2. Source of *power of the influencing agent*	Means control	Attractiveness	Credibility
3. Manner of achieving *prepotency of the induced response*	Limitation of choice behavior	Delineation of role requirements	Reorganization of means-ends framework
Consequents			
1. Conditions of performance of induced response	Surveillance by influencing agent	Salience of relationship to agent	Relevance of values to issues
2. Conditions of change and extinction of induced response	Change perception of conditions for social rewards	Changed perception of conditions for satisfying self-defining relationships	Changed perception of conditions for value maximization
3. Type of behavior system in which induced response is embedded	External demands of a specific setting	Expectations defining a specific role	Person's value system

From Kelman, 1961, p. 67. (This table also appears in Kelman, 1963.)

level and less likely to lead to attitude change when the avoidance component of the person's relationship to the object is based on identification rather than internalization. In other words, induced action is more likely to be effective in consequently producing attitude change when approach tendencies are in the domain of role considerations rather than value considerations; it is less likely when the opposite is the case. One problem in testing these hypotheses, however, is the question of how one ascertains whether the person's relationship to the object is based upon identification or internalization. Presumably, self-report would not be an effective method because Kelman states that these effects would be particularly marked if the roles in question are relatively latent or unconscious in the person's current life space. In a more recent paper, Kelman (1963) extends his thinking to the psychotherapeutic situation. He draws out of his theory a variety of implications for successfully implementing change during therapy.

In conclusion, Kelman's theory seems to be a fairly compelling analysis of attitudes as far as it goes. It recognizes that the same attitude can be expressed for a variety of reasons. In many senses Kelman's theory is much more specific than the other functional theories, which makes it easier to draw new hypotheses from it. Yet Kelman himself has not extensively followed up the initial presentation with research. And though he has occasionally presented new ideas to be tested, he has not systematically spelled out the kinds of hypotheses that can be derived from his theory. Thus its true value can only be judged at a later time following the accumulation of additional research specifically generated by the theory.

Chapter 8

Epilogue

WE have critically reviewed a number of theoretical approaches to attitude change in the preceding chapters. We hope our readers have not thought us unduly harsh in our criticism. However, for the most part theorizing in this area is still at a relatively low level: assumptions are not made explicit; relations between theoretical constructs are not spelled out; and the details necessary for precise predictions are often missing. Consequently, we feel that detailed criticism is necessary and desirable at this stage in the study of attitude change. However, in making responses specific to given theories, we have avoided several more general questions. This short chapter addresses itself to these issues.

The problem of comparing various theoretical orientations is particularly difficult. In the original theoretical and empirical writings, we found little evidence of confrontation among the various theories. Although there are exceptions—such as the discrepancy-attitude change controversy between dissonance and social judgment theory (Chapter 6)— most theoretical and empirical work tends to ignore the rest. We were shocked, for instance, to find that many of the theorists in the S-R chapter (Chapter 3) did not even refer to each other, much less other theoretical orientations. One of our purposes has been to stimulate comparisons of the various theories of attitude change. We kept our chapter topics as broad as possible in order to bring several different theories into juxtaposition within each chapter. We also made a deliberate effort to overrepresent those empirical studies which overlap two theories. It is probably the case that too few experiments have been designed specifically to test conflicting predictions made by different theories. On the other hand, it is also probably the case that important similarities have been overlooked in the ethnocentric enthusiasm of a theoretician and his graduate students. Campbell (Chapter 2), for instance, has argued that the difference between behavioristic and cognitive theories of attitude change is inappropriately magnified by differences in connotation in the theoretical language. It is as important to understand the similarities between two different theoretical terms—such as importance and involvment—as it is to understand the differences.

One major obstacle to the comparison of the theories is created by the experimenter's choice of dependent variables. The behavioristic or cognitive theorist is entirely justified in designing a dependent variable to meet the exacting terms of his theory. However, we are critical of the tendency to use only one dependent variable (especially in comparative tests of theories) and to exclude the sort of dependent variables that would have been used by other theoreticians.

The problem is not limited to a contrast between cognitive and behavioristic theories. Even within the consistency theories, for example, a contrast between Osgood's theory and the others is made difficult because Osgood uses the semantic differential as his only dependent variable and few of the other theorists have utilized this well-established attitude measurement technique—even as a second or third dependent variable. We strongly recommend that researchers in the field of attitude change include a wider spectrum of dependent variables when possible. Furthermore, studies specifically designed to examine the relationship among various dependent variables are badly needed.

The problem is not completely methodological. Many theories of attitude change are concerned with relatively limited sets of inputs and outcomes. They do not concentrate on the same problems. It often requires more than a little ingenuity to design an experiment which meets the requirements of both theories. Since a comparative test is likely to be at the frontier of both theories, the experiment may fail because the design does not include all the necessary theoretical prerequisites.

We must therefore use a little ingenuity in constructing our experiment so that it does provide us with a valid test of each theory. On the other hand, occasionally the theory is simply untestable. In that case, we must force the theory to be explicit before we can test it.

A comparative test of a theory, of course, is unlikely to lead us to discard either theory under test. Often perhaps, the attempt to contrast the theories generates new issues. The present attention to the distinction between response-involvement and issue-involvement (Chapter 6) may be viewed as one instance of this.

A theoretical comparison usually requires an experimental design with great precision and control. Consequently, this research is conducted in the laboratory. Whatever the advantages to be gained in the laboratory, we also need information concerning the relative power of our theoretical variables to influence behavior when other sources of variance are not so well controlled. For instance, the great predictive power of dissonance theory in the laboratory disappears in the natural setting, partly because we lack information on the normative use of various dissonance-reducing alternatives in real-life situations. Similarly, we need information about the ecological generality of results discovered in the laboratory. A particular laboratory finding, for instance, might be found only in a type of situation which occurs very infrequently out in the "real world." Furthermore, the few field studies we do have usually differ from laboratory studies on substantive as well as methodological grounds (Hovland, 1959, Chapter 2). For these reasons and many more, we need more field research on attitude change. There are many who would say that a theory does not have to predict attitude change in natural settings; but there should be none who says that he does not even want to know whether his theory can predict in a natural setting.

With the possible exception of the functional and behavioristic theories, most theorists have paid relatively little attention to attitude formation (as opposed to attitude change). Some would say, of course, that the process of attitude formation is identical to that of attitude change. In the former case, the argument goes, one is changing the attitude from neutral to one of some valence; in the latter case, one is changing the attitude from one valence to another. However, others might argue that many attitudes are formed on the basis of simple conditioning, and that the more cognitive decorations to attitudes come later in the process. Such a view might imply that attitude change is a cognitive process and attitude formation a simple conditioning process. A more functionally oriented theorist would say that both processes occur in formation and change, and that such a distinction merely illustrates the different motivational bases of attitudes. From present knowledge, we have little basis to choose among these alternatives however.

A major portion of the experimental research on attitude change has been conceived within the confines of the consistency assumption. As we have discussed at some length, this assumption states that people strive to maintain a consistent relationship among certain elements of their cognitive world. Nonetheless, it seems quite clear that a theory based on such an assumption cannot account for all of the data on attitude change. McGuire (1966), for example, discusses research results quite inconsistent with the consistency assumption. He cites work on curiosity or the exploratory drive as a prime example. If we may allow anecdotal evidence, then attitude formation and change in children seems quite irrelevant to notions of consistency. The powerful effects of conditioning seem especially apparent there.

Among the various theories of attitude change, the consistency theories are on the whole more precise and have provided us with many interesting data. Our only point is that they may not justify such an imbalance in empirical work. We enter a special plea for experimental effort on theoretical models which are not founded on the consistency assumption. But, as McGuire (1966) has noted, the pendulum seems to be swinging back, and perhaps the emphasis is already shifting. We hope that this book, through its critical analyses of the several theories, will provoke more research on this as well as other issues.

References

Abelson, R. P. Psychological implication. In R. P. Abelson, E. Aronson, W. J. Mc-
Guire, T. M. Newcomb, M. J. Rosenberg, and P. H. Tannenbaum (Eds,),
Theories of cognitive consistency: a sourcebook. Skokie, Ill.: Rand-McNally,
1968.

Abelson, R. P., and Rosenberg, M. J. Symbolic psycho-logic: a model of attitudinal
cognition. *Behavioral Science,* 1958, **3,** 1–13.

Adams, J. Laboratory studies of behavior without awareness. *Psychological
Bulletin,* 1957, **54,** 383–405.

Adams, J. S. Reduction of cognitive dissonance by seeking consonant information.
Journal of Abnormal and Social Psychology, 1961, **62,** 74–78.

Adorno, T. W., Frenkel-Brunswik, E., Levinson, D. J., and Sanford, R. N. *The
authoritarian personality.* New York: Harper, 1950.

Ager, J. W., and Dawes, R. M. The effects of judges' attitudes on judgment.
Journal of Personality and Social Psychology, 1965, **1,** 533–538.

Allen, V. Uncertainty of outcome and post-decision dissonance. In L. Festinger,
Conflict, decision, and dissonance. Stanford, Calif.: Stanford University
Press, 1964. Pp. 34–42.

Allport, F. H. *Social psychology.* Cambridge, Mass.: Houghton Mifflin, 1924.

Allport, F. H., and Hartman, D. A. The measurement and motivation of atypical
opinion in a certain group. *American Political Science Review,* 1925, **19,**
735–760.

Allport, G. W. Attitudes. In C. Murchison (Ed.), *Handbook of social psychology.*
Worcester, Mass.: Clark University Press, 1935. Pp. 798–884.

Allport, G. W. *The nature of prejudice.* Cambridge, Mass.: Addison-Wesley, 1954.

Allyn, J., and Festinger, L. The effectiveness of unanticipated persuasive communication. *Journal of Abnormal and Social Psychology,* 1961, **62,** 35–40.

Anderson, L. R., and McGuire, W. J. Prior reassurance of group consensus as a
factor in producing resistance to persuasion. *Sociometry,* 1965, **28,** 44–56.

Aronson, E. The cognitive and behavioral consequences of confirmation and disconfirmation of expectancies. National Science Foundation Research Proposal,
Harvard University, 1960.

Aronson, E. Dissonance theory: progress and problems. In R. P. Abelson, E. Aronson, W. J. McGuire, P. M. Newcomb, M. J. Rosenberg, and P. H. Tannenbaum (Eds.), *Theories of cognitive consistency: a sourcebook.* Skokie, Ill.: Rand-McNally, 1968.

Aronson, E. The effect of effort on the attractiveness of rewarded and unrewarded stimuli. *Journal of Abnormal and Social Psychology,* 1961, **63**(2), 375–380.

Aronson, E. The psychology of insufficient justification: an analysis of some conflicting data. In S. Feldman (Ed.), *Cognitive consistency.* New York: Academic Press, 1966.

Aronson, E., and Carlsmith, J. M. Effect of the severity of threat on the devaluation of forbidden behavior. *Journal of Abnormal and Social Psychology,* 1963, **66**, 584–588.

Aronson, E., and Carlsmith, J. M. Experimentation in social psychology. In G. Lindzey and E. Aronson (Eds.), *Handbook of social psychology.* Reading, Mass: Addison-Wesley, 1968.

Aronson, E., and Carlsmith, J. M. Performance expectancy as a determinant of actual performance. *Journal of Abnormal and Social Psychology,* 1962, **65**(3), 178–182.

Aronson, E., and Mills, J. The effect of severity of initiation on liking for a group. *Journal of Abnormal and Social Psychology,* 1959, **59**, 177–181.

Aronson, E., Turner, J. A., and Carlsmith, J. M. Communicator credibility and communicator discrepancy as determinants of opinion change. *Journal of Abnormal and Social Psychology,* 1963, **67**, 31–37.

Asch, S. E. The doctrine of suggestion, prestige and imitation in social psychology. *Psychological Review,* 1948, **55**, 250–276.

Asch, S. E. *Social psychology.* Englewood Cliffs, N.J.: Prentice-Hall, 1952.

Asch, S. E. Studies in the principles of judgments and attitudes: II. Determination of judgments by group and by ego standards. *Journal of Social Psychology,* 1940, **12**, 433–465.

Asch, S. E. Studies of independence and conformity: a minority of one against a unanimous majority. *Psychological Monographs,* 1956, **70**, 9, (Whole No. 416).

Athey, K. R., Coleman, J. E., Reitman, A. P., and Tang, J. Two experiments showing the effect of the interviewer's racial background on responses to questionnaires concerning racial issues. *Journal of Applied Psychology,* 1960, **44**, 244–246.

Atkins, A. L. Own attitude and discriminability in relation to anchoring effects in judgment. *Journal of Personality and Social Psychology,* 1966, **4**, 497–507.

Back, K. W. Influence through social communication. *Journal of Abnormal and Social Psychology,* 1951, **46**, 9–23.

Bain, R. An attitude on attitude research. *American Journal of Sociology,* 1928, **33**, 940–957.

Bales, R. F. *Interaction process analysis; a method for the study of small groups.* Cambridge, Mass.: Addison-Wesley, 1950.

Bandura, A., Ross, D., and Ross, S. A comparative test of the status envy, social power and the secondary reinforcement theories of identificatory learning. *Journal of Abnormal and Social Psychology,* 1963, **67,** 527–534.

Bem, D. J. An experimental analysis of self-persuasion. *Journal of Experimental Social Psychology,* 1965, **1,** 199–218.

Bem, D. J. Inducing belief in false confessions. *Journal of Personality and Social Psychology,* 1966, **3,** 707–710.

Bem, D. J. Self-perception: an alternative interpretation of cognitive dissonance phenomena. *Psychological Review,* 1967, **74,** 183–200.

Benney, M., Riesman, D., and Star, S. Age and sex in the interview. *American Journal of Sociology,* 1956, **62,** 143–152.

Bergin, A. E. The effect of dissonant persuasive communications upon changes in a self-referring attitude. *Journal of Personality,* 1962, **30,** 423–438.

Bergmann, G. *Philosophy of science.* Madison, Wisc.: University of Wisconsin Press, 1957.

Berkowitz, L. The judgmental process in personality functioning. *Psychological Review,* 1960, **67,** 130–142.

Berkowitz, L., and Goranson, R. E. Motivational and judgmental determinants of social perception. *Journal of Abnormal and Social Psychology,* 1964, **69,** 296–302.

Berlyne, D. E. *Conflict, arousal, and curiosity,* New York: McGraw-Hill, 1960.

Bieri, J., Atkins, A. L., Briar, S., Leaman, R. L., Miller, H., and Tripodi T. *Clinical and social judgment: the discrimination of behavioral information.* New York: John Wiley and Sons, 1966.

Bieri, J., Orcutt, B. A., and Leaman, R. Anchoring effects in sequential clinical judgments. *Journal of Abnormal and Social Psychology,* 1963, **67,** 616–623.

Bishop, F. The anal character: a rebel in the dissonance family. *Journal of Personality and Social Psychology,* 1967, **6,** 23–36.

Blake, R. R., and Mouton, J. S. The dynamics of influence and coercion. *International Journal of Social Psychiatry,* 1957, **2,** 263–305.

Blumer, H. *Critiques of research in the social sciences: I. An appraisal of Thomas and Znaniecki's "The Polish peasant in Europe and America."* New York: Social Science Research Council, 1939 (Bulletin 44).

Bochner, S., and Insko, C. A. Communicator discrepancy, source credibility, and opinion change. *Journal of Personality and Social Psychology,* 1966, **4**(6), 614–621.

Bock, R. D. Multivariate analysis of variance of repeated measurements. In C. W. Harris (Ed.), *Problems in measuring change.* Madison, Wisc.: University of Wisconsin Press, 1963. Pp. 85–103.

Bogardus, E. S. Measuring social distance. *Journal of Applied Sociology,* 1925, **9,** 299–308.

Braithwaite, R. B. *Scientific explanation.* Cambridge, England: Cambridge University Press, 1953.

Bramel, D. A. A dissonance theory approach to defensive projection. *Journal of Abnormal and Social Psychology,* 1962, **64,** 121–129.

Bramel, D. A. Selection of a target for defensive projection. *Journal of Abnormal and Social Psychology,* 1963, **66,** 318–324.

Brehm, J. W. Attitudinal consequences of commitment to unpleasant behavior. *Journal of Abnormal and Social Psychology,* 1960, **60,** 379–383.

Brehm, J. W. An experiment on coercion and attitude change. In J. W. Brehm and A. R. Cohen, *Explorations in cognitive dissonance.* New York: John Wiley and Sons, 1962. Pp. 84–88.

Brehm, J. W. An experiment on thirst. In J. W. Brehm and A. R. Cohen, *Explorations in cognitive dissonance.* New York: John Wiley and Sons, 1962. Pp. 137–143.

Brehm, J. W. Motivational effects of cognitive dissonance. In M. R. Jones (Ed.), *Nebraska symposium on motivation.* Lincoln, Neb.: University of Nebraska Press, 1962a.

Brehm, J. W. Post-decision changes in the desirability of alternatives. *Journal of Abnormal and Social Psychology,* 1956, **52,** 384–389.

Brehm, J. W. *A theory of psychological reactance.* New York: Academic Press, 1966.

Brehm, M. L., Back, K. W., and Bogdanoff, M. D. A physiological effect of cognitive dissonance under stress and deprivation. *Journal of Abnormal and Social Psychology,* 1964, **69**(3), 303–310.

Brehm, J. W., and Cohen, A. R. Choice and chance relative deprivation as determinants of cognitive dissonance. *Journal of Abnormal and Social Psychology,* 1959b, **58,** 383–387.

Brehm, J. W., and Cohen, A. R. *Explorations in cognitive dissonance.* New York: John Wiley and Sons, 1962.

Brehm, J. W., and Cohen, A. R. Re-evaluation of choice alternatives as a function of their number and qualitative similarity. *Journal of Abnormal and Social Psychology,* 1959a, **58,** 373–378.

Brehm, J. W., and Crocker, J. C. An experiment on hunger. In J. W. Brehm and A. R. Cohen, *Explorations in cognitive dissonance.* New York: John Wiley and Sons, 1962. Pp. 133–136.

Brock, T. C. Cognitive restructuring and attitude change. *Journal of Abnormal and Social Psychology,* 1962, **64**(4), 264–271.

Brock, T. C. Communication discrepancy and intent to persuade as determinants of counterargument production. *Journal of Experimental Social Psychology,* 1967, **3**(3), 296–309.

Brock, T. C. Communicator-recipient similarity and decision change. *Journal of Personality and Social Psychology,* 1965, **1,** 650–654.

Brock, T. C. Effects of prior dishonesty on post-decision dissonance. *Journal of Abnormal and Social Psychology,* 1963, **66,** 325–331.

Brock, T. C., and Buss, A. H. Dissonance, aggression, and evaluation of pain. *Journal of Abnormal and Social Psychology,* 1962, **65**(3), 197–202.

Brock, T. C., Edelman, S. K., Edwards, D. C., and Schuck, J. R. Seven studies of performance expectancy as a determinant of actual performance. Unpublished manuscript, 1965.

Brown, D. R. Stimulus similarity and the anchoring of subjective scales. *American Journal of Psychology,* 1953, **66,** 199–214.

Brown, R. Models of attitude change. In *New directions in psychology.* New York: Holt, Rinehart, and Winston, 1962. Pp. 1–85.

Brown, R. *Social psychology.* New York: Free Press, 1965.

Brown, W. Auditory and visual cues in maze learning. *Public Psychology,* 1932, **5,** 115–122.

Burdick, H. A., and Burnes, A. J. A test of "strain towards Symmetry" theories. *Journal of Abnormal and Social Psychology,* 1958, **57,** 367–370.

Butler, D., and Miller, N. Power to reward and punish in social interaction. *Journal of Experimental Social Psychology,* 1965, **1,** 311–322.

Caldwell, O., and Lumdeen, G. E. Changing unfounded beliefs—a unit in biology. *School Science and Mathematics,* 1933, **33,** 394–413.

Campbell, D. T. Conformity in psychology's theories of acquired behavioral dispositions. In I. A. Berg and B. M. Bass (Eds.), *Conformity and deviation.* New York: Harper, 1961.

Campbell, D. T. Factors relevant to the validity of experiments in social settings. *Psychological Bulletin,* 1957, **54,** 297–312.

Campbell, D. T. The indirect assessment of social attitudes. *Psychological Bulletin,* 1950, **47,** 15–38.

Campbell, D. T. Operational delineation of "what is learned" via the transposition experiment. *Psychological Review,* 1954, **61,** 167–174.

Campbell, D. T. Perception as substitute trial and error. *Psychological Review,* 1956, **63,** 330–342.

Campbell, D. T. Recommendations for APA test standards regarding construct, trait, or discriminant validity. *American Psychologist,* 1960, **15,** 546–553.

Campbell, D. T. Social attitudes and other acquired behavioral dispositions. In S. Koch (Ed.), *Psychology: a study of a science.* New York: McGraw-Hill, 1963. Pp. 94–172.

Campbell, D. T., and Fiske, D. W. Convergent and discriminant validation by the multitrait-multimethod matrix. *Psychological Bulletin,* 1959, **56,** 81–105.

Campbell, D. T., Lewis Nan A., and Hunt, W. A. Context affects with judgmental language that is absolute, extensive and extra-experimentally anchored. *Journal of Experimental Psychology,* 1958, **55,** 222–228.

Campbell, D. T., Miller, N., and Diamond, A. L. Predisposition to identify instigating and guiding stimulus as revealed in transfer. *Journal of General Psychology,* 1960, **63,** 69–74.

Campbell, D. T., and Stanley, J. C. Experimental and quasi-experimental designs for research on teaching. In N. L. Gage (Ed.), *Handbook of research on teaching.* Chicago, Ill.: Rand-McNally, 1963. Pp. 171–246.

Campbell, N. R. *Physics: the elements.* Cambridge, England: Cambridge University Press, 1920.

Canon, L. K. Self-confidence and selective exposure to information. In L. Festinger, *Conflict, decision, and dissonance.* Stanford, Calif.: Stanford University Press, 1964, Pp. 83–95.

Cantril, H. *Gauging public opinion.* Princeton. N.J.: Princeton University Press, 1944.

Carlsmith, J. M. Varieties of counterattitudinal behavior. In R. P. Abelson, E. Aronson, W. J. McGuire, T. M. Newcomb, M. J. Rosenberg, and P. H. Tannenbaum (Eds.), *Theories of cognitive consistency: a sourcebook.* Skokie, Ill.: Rand-McNally, 1968.

Carlsmith, J. M., Collins, B. E., and Helmreich, R. L. Studies on forced compliance: I. The effect of pressure for compliance on attitude change produced by face-to-face role-playing and anonymous essay writing. *Journal of Personality and Social Psychology,* 1966, **4,** 1–13.

Cartwright. D., and Harary, F. Structural balance: a generalization of Heider's Theory. *Psychological Review,* 1956, **63,** 277–293.

Chapanis, Natalia P., and Chapanis, A. Cognitive dissonance: five years later. *Psychological Bulletin,* 1964, **61,** 1–22.

Chein, I. Behavior theory and the behavior of attitudes: some critical comments. *Psychological Review,* 1948, **55,** 175–188.

Christie, R., and Geis, F. (Eds.), *Studies in Machiavellianism.* New York: Academic Press, 1968.

Cohen, A. R. Communication discrepancy and attitude change: a dissonance theory approach. *Journal of Personality,* 1959, **27,** 386–396.

Cohen, A. R. An experiment on small rewards for discrepant compliance and attitude change. In J. W. Brehm and A. R. Cohen, *Explorations in cognitive dissonance.* New York: John Wiley and Sons, 1962. Pp. 73–78.

Cohen, A. R. A "forced-compliance" experiment on repeated dissonances. In J. W. Brehm and A. R. Cohen, *Explorations in cognitive dissonance.* New York: John Wiley and Sons, 1962. Pp. 97–104.

Cohen, A. R., Brehm, J. W., and Latane, B. Choice of strategy and voluntary exposure to information under public and private conditions. *Journal of Personality,* 1959, **27,** 63–73.

Cohen, A. R., and Latané, B. An experiment on choice in commitment to counter-attitudinal behavior. In J. W. Brehm and A. R. Cohen, *Explorations in cognitive dissonance.* New York: John Wiley and Sons, 1962. Pp. 88–91.

Cohen, A. R., and Zimbardo, P. G. An experiment on avoidance motivation. In J. W. Brehm and A. R. Cohen, *Explorations in cognitive dissonance.* New York: John Wiley and Sons, 1962, Pp. 143–151.

Cohen, B. D., Kalish, H. I., Thurstone, J. R., and Cohen, E. Experimental manipulation of verbal behavior. *Journal of Experimental Psychology,* 1954, **47,** 106–110.

Collins, B. E. Counterattitudinal behavior. In R. P. Abelson, E. Aronson, W. J. McGuire, T. M. Newcomb, M. J. Rosenberg, and P. H. Tannenbaum (Eds.), *Theories of cognitive consistency: a sourcebook.* Skokie, Ill.: Rand-McNally, 1968.

Collins, B. E., Ellsworth, P. C., and Helmreich, R. L. Correlations between pupil size and the semantic differential: an experimental paradigm and pilot study. *Psychonomic Science,* 1967, **9**(12), 627–628.

Collins, B. E., and Helmreich, R. L. Studies in forced compliance. II. Contrasting mechanisms of attitude change produced by public-persuasive and private-true essays. A version read at Eastern Psychological Association, 1965.

Cook, S. W., and Selltiz, C. A multiple-indicator approach to attitude measurement. *Psychological Bulletin,* 1964, **62,** 36–55.

Coombs, C. A. *A theory of data.* New York: John Wiley and Sons, 1964.

Couch, A., and Keniston, K. Agreeing response set and social desirability. *Journal of Abnormal and Social Psychology,* 1961, **62,** 175–179.

Couch, A., and Keniston, K. Yeasayers and naysayers: agreeing response set as a personality variable. *Journal of Abnormal and Social Psychology,* 1960, 60, 151–174.

Cronbach, L. J. An experimental comparison of the multiple true-false and multiple-choice tests. *Journal of Educational Psychology,* 1941, **32,** 533–543.

Cronbach, L. J. Further evidence on response sets and test design. *Educational and Psychological Measurement,* 1950, **10,** 3–31.

Cronbach, L. J. Response sets and test validity. *Educational and Psychological Measurement,* 1946, **6,** 475–494.

Cronbach, L. J. Studies of acquiescence as a factor in the true-false test. *Journal of Educational Psychology,* 1942, **33,** 401–415.

Cronbach, L. J., and Meehl, P. E. Construct validity in psychological tests. *Psychological Bulletin,* 1955, **52,** 281–302.

Crowne, D. P., and Marlowe, D. *The approval motive; studies in evaluative dependence.* New York: John Wiley and Sons, 1964.

Culbertson, F. The modification of an emotionally held attitude through role playing. *Journal of Abnormal and Social Psychology,* 1957, **54,** 230–233.

Cushing, M. C. Affective components of the response class as a factor in verbal conditioning. *Dissertation Abstracts,* 1957, **17,** 2313.

Dabbs, J. M., Jr., and Leventhal, H. Effects of varying the recommendations in a fear-arousing communication. *Journal of Personality and Social Psychology,* 1966, **4**(5), 525–531.

Dahlke, A. E. The effects of reinforcement and punishment on attitude change. Unpublished doctoral dissertation, University of Minnesota, 1963.

Davidson, J., and Kiesler, S. Cognitive behavior before and after decisions. In L. Festinger, *Conflict, decision, and dissonance.* Stanford, Calif.: Stanford University Press, 1964. Pp. 10–19.

Davis, K. E., and Jones, E. E. Changes in interpersonal perception as a means of reducing cognitive dissonance. *Journal of Abnormal and Social Psychology,* 1960, **61,** 402–410.

DeFleur, M. L., and Westie, F. R. Verbal attitudes and overt acts: An experiment on the salience of attitudes. *American Sociological Review,* 1958, **23,** 667–673.

Deutsch, M., and Krauss, R. M. *Theories in social psychology.* New York: Basic Books, 1965.

Deutsch, M., Krauss, R. M., and Rosenau, Norah. Dissonance or defensiveness? *Journal of Personality,* 1962, **30**(1), 16–28.

Dickson, H., and McGinnies, E. Affectivity in the arousal of attitudes as measured by galvanic skin response. *The American Journal of Psychology,* 1966, **79,** 584–589.

Dollard, J. Hostility and fear in social life. *Social Forces,* 1938, **17,** 15–26.

Dollard, J., and Miller, N. E. *Personality and psychotherapy.* New York: McGraw-Hill, 1950.

Doob, L. W. The behavior of attitudes. *Psychological Review,* 1947, **54,** 135–156.

Dulany, D. E. The place of hypotheses and intentions: an analysis of verbal control in verbal conditioning. In C. W. Ericksen (Ed.), *Behavior and awareness.* Durham, N.C.: Duke University Press, 1962. Pp. 102–129.

Eagly, A. H., and Manis, M. Evaluation of message and communicator as a function of involvement. *Journal of Personality and Social Psychology,* 1966, **3**(4), 483–485.

Edlow, D. W., and Kiesler, C. A. Ease of denial and defensive projection. *Journal of Experimental Social Psychology,* 1966, **2,** 56–69.

Edwards, A. L. *Techniques of attitude scale construction.* New York: Appleton-Century-Crofts, 1957.

Edwards, A. L., and Walker, J. N. A note on the Couch and Keniston measure of agreement response set. *Journal of Abnormal and Social Psychology,* 1961, **62,** 173–174.

Ehrlich, D., Guttman, I., Schönbach, P., and Mills, J. Post-decision exposure to relevant information. *Journal of Abnormal and Social Psychology,* 1957, 54, 98–102.

Eisman, B. S. Attitude formation: the development of a color-preference response through mediated generalization. *Journal of Abnormal and Social Psychology,* 1955, **50,** 321–326.

Elms, A. C. Influence of fantasy ability on attitude change through role-playing. *Journal of Personality and Social Psychology,* 1966, **4**(1), 36–43.

Elms, A. C. Role playing, incentive, and dissonance. *Psychological Bulletin,* 1967, **68,** 132–148.

Elms, A. C., and Janis, I. L. Counter-norm attitudes induced by consonant versus dissonant conditions of role playing. *Journal of Experimental Research in Personality,* 1965, I, 50–60.

Entwisle, D. R. Interactive effects of pretesting. *Educational and Psychological Measurement,* 1961, **21,** 607–620.

Ericksen, C. W. Discrimination and learning without awareness: a methodological survey and evaluation. *Psychological Review,* 1960, **67,** 279–300.

Ewing, T. N. A study of certain factors involved in changes of opinion. *Journal of Social Psychology,* 1942, **16,** 63–88.

Eysenck, H. J., and Crown, S. An experimental study in opinion-attitude methodology. *International Journal of Opinion and Attitude Research,* 1949, **3,** 47–86.

Faris, E. The concept of social attitudes. *Journal of Applied Sociology,* 1925, **9,** 404–409. Also in K. Young (Ed.), *Social Attitudes.* New York: Holt, 1931.

Feather, N. T. A structural balance analysis of evaluative behavior. *Human Relations,* 1965, **18,** 171–185.

Feather, N. T. A structural balance approach to the analysis of communication effects. In L. Berkowitz (Ed.), *Advances in experimental social psychology,* Vol. 3. New York: Academic Press, 1967. Pp. 100–166.

Feather, N. T. A structural balance model of communication effects. *Psychological Review,* 1964, **71,** 291–313.

Fehrer, Elizabeth. Shifts in scale values of attitude statements as a function of the composition of the scale. *Journal of Experimental Psychology,* 1952, **44,** 179–188.

Festinger, L. Behavioral support for opinion change. *Public Opinion Quarterly,* 1964, 28, 404–417.

Festinger, L. *Conflict, decision, and dissonance.* Stanford, Calif.: Stanford University Press, 1964.

Festinger, L. Social psychology and group processes. *Annual Review of Psychology,* 1955, **6,** 187–216.

Festinger, L. *A theory of cognitive dissonance.* Stanford, Calif.: Stanford University Press, 1957.

Festinger, L. A theory of social comparison processes. *Human Relations,* 1954, **7,** 117–140.

Festinger, L., and Bramel, D. The reactions of humans to cognitive dissonance. In A. J. Bachrach (Ed.), *Experimental foundations of clinical psychology.* New York: Basic Books, 1962.

Festinger, L., and Carlsmith, J. M. Cognitive consequences of forced compliance. *Journal of Abnormal and Social Psychology,* 1959, **58,** 203–210.

Festinger, L., and Maccoby, N. On resistance to persuasive communications. *Journal of Abnormal and Social Psychology,* 1964, **68,** 359–366.

Festinger, L., Schachter, S., and Back, K. *Social pressures in informal groups; a study of human factors in housing.* New York: Harper, 1950.

Finley, J. R., and Staats, W. W. Evaluative meaning words as reinforcing stimuli. *Journal of Verbal Learning and Verbal Behavior,* 1967, **6,** 193–197.

Fishbein, M. The relationships between beliefs, attitudes and behavior. Paper presented at a conference, "Prospects and problems in the psychology of knowledge," at the University of Pennsylvania, 1965.

Fishbein, M., and Hunter, R. Summation versus balance in attitude organization and change. *Journal of Abnormal and Social Psychology,* 1964, **69,** 505–510.

Fisher, S., and Lubin, A. Distance as a determinant of influence in a two-person social interaction situation. *Journal of Abnormal and Social Psychology,* 1958, **56,** 230–238.

Fleishmann, E., Harris, E., and Burtt, H. *Leadership and supervision in industry: an evaluation of a supervisory training program.* Columbus, Ohio: Ohio State University, Bureau of Educational Research, 1955 (cited in Festinger, 1964).

Foa, U. G. Convergences in the analysis of the structure of interpersonal behavior. *Psychological Review,* 1961, **68,** 341–353.

Foulkes, D., and Foulkes, S. H. Self-concept, dogmatism, and tolerance of trait inconsistency. *Journal of Personality and Social Psychology,* 1965, **2**(1), 104–110.

Franke, R. Gang und Character. *Beihefts, Zeitschrift für angewandte Psychologie,* 1931, No. 58 (cited by Zajonc, 1960).

Freedman, J. L. Involvement, discrepancy, and change. *Journal of Abnormal and Social Psychology,* 1964, **69,** 290–295.

Freedman, J. L. Long-term behavioral effects of cognitive dissonance. *Journal of Experimental Social Psychology,* 1965, I(2), 145–155.

Freedman, J. L., and Sears, D. Selective exposure. In L. Berkowitz (Ed.), *Advances in experimental social psychology.* New York: Academic Press, 1966.

Gerard, H. B. Physiological measurement in social psychological research. In P. H. Leiderman and D. Shapiro (Eds.), *Psychobiological approaches to social behavior.* Stanford, Calif.: Stanford University Press, 1964.

Gerard, H. B., and Fleischer, L. Recall and pleasantness of balanced and unbalanced cognitive structures. *Journal of Personality and Social Psychology,* 1967, **7,** 332–337.

Gerard, H. B., and Mathewson, G. C. The effect of severity of initiation on liking for a group: a replication. *Journal of Experimental Social Psychology,* 1966, **2**(3), 278–287.

Glixman, A. F. Categorizing behavior as a function of meaning domain. *Journal of Personality and Social Psychology,* 1965, **2**(3), 370–377.

Goffman, E. On face-work. *Psychiatry,* 1955, **18**, 213–231.

Goldberg, S. C. Three situational determinants of conformity to social norms. *Journal of Abnormal and Social Psychology,* 1954, **49**, 325–329.

Goldstein, M. J. The relationship between coping and avoiding behavior in response to fear-arousing propaganda. *Journal of Abnormal and Social Psychology,* 1959, **58**, 247–252.

Granneberg, R. T. The influence of individual attitude and attitude-intelligence upon scale values of attitude items. *American Psychologist,* 1955, **10**, 330–331. (Abstract)

Green, B. F. Attitude measurement. In G. Lindzey (Ed.), *Handbook of social psychology,* Vol. 1. Reading, Mass.: Addison-Wesley, 1954. Pp. 335–369.

Greenspoon, J. The reinforcing effect of two spoken sounds on the frequency of two responses. *American Journal of Psychology,* 1955, **68**, 409–416.

Greenwald, A. G. Behavior change following a persuasive communication. *Journal of Personality,* 1965, **33**, 370–391.

Greenwald, A. G. Effects of prior commitment on behavior change after a persuasive communication. *Public Opinion Quarterly,* 1966, **29**(4), 595–601.

Gross, N., Mason, W. S., and McEachern, A. W. *Explorations in role analysis: studies of the school superintendency role.* New York: John Wiley and Sons, 1958.

Guttman, L. The basis for scalogram analysis. In S. A. Stouffer, L. Guttman, E. A. Suchman, P. F. Lazarsfeld, S. A. Star, and J. A. Gardner (Eds.), *Measurement and prediction.* Princeton, N.J.: Princeton University Press, 1950a. Pp. 60–90.

Guttman, L. The problem of attitude and opinion measurement. In S. A. Stouffer, L. Guttman, E. A. Suchman, P. F. Lazarsfeld, S. A. Star, and J. A. Gardner (Eds.), *Measurement and prediction.* Princeton, N.J.: Princeton University Press, 1950b. Pp. 46–59.

Haefner, D. P. Arousing fear in dental health education. *Journal of Public Health Dentistry,* 1965, **25**, 140–146.

Hall, C. S., and Lindzey, G. *Theories of personality.* New York: John Wiley and Sons, 1957.

Hall, Sharon. The importance of choice and attitudinal discrepancy in the study of extreme attitudes. Unpublished master's thesis. The Ohio State University, 1964.

Hammond, K. R. Measuring attitudes by error-choice: an indirect method. *Journal of Abnormal and Social Psychology,* 1948, **43,** 38–48.

Harary, F., Norman, R. Z., and Cartwright, D. *Structural models: an introduction to the theory of directed graphs.* New York: John Wiley and Sons, 1965.

Hartmann, H. *Essays on ego psychology.* New York: International Universities Press, 1964.

Harvey, O. J. Some situational and cognitive determinants of dissonance resolution. *Journal of Personality and Social Psychology,* 1965, **1**(4), 349–355.

Harvey, O. J., Hunt, D. E., and Schroeder, H. M. *Conceptual systems and personality organization.* New York: John Wiley and Sons, 1961.

Heider, F. Attitudes and cognitive organization. *Journal of Psychology,* 1946, **21**, 107–112.

Heider, F. *The psychology of interpersonal relations.* New York: John Wiley and Sons, 1958.

Heider, F. Social perception and phenomenal causality. *Psychological Review,* 1944, **51**, 358–374.

Helson, H. Adaption-level as a basis for a quantitative theory of frames of reference. *Psychological Review,* 1948, **55**, 297–313.

Helson, H. Adaption-level theory. In S. Koch (Ed.), *Psychology: a study of a science,* Vol. 1. New York: McGraw-Hill, 1959. Pp. 565–621.

Hemple, C. *Fundamentals of concept formation in empirical science.* Chicago: The University of Chicago Press, 1952.

Hess, E. H. Attitude and pupil size. *Scientific American,* 1965, **212**(4), 46–54.

Hess, E. H., and Polt, J. M. Pupil size as related to interest value of visual stimuli. *Science,* 1960, **132**, 349–350.

Hicks, J. M., and Campbell, D. T. Zero-point scaling as affected by social object, scaling method, and context. *Journal of Personality and Social Psychology,* 1965, **2**, 793–808.

Hinckley, E. D. A follow-up on the influence of individual opinion on the construction of an attitude scale. *Journal of Abnormal and Social Psychology,* 1963, **67**, 290–292.

Hinckley, E. D. The influence of individual opinion on construction of an attitude scale. *Journal of Social Psychology,* 1932, **3**, 283–296.

Hittes, R. W., and Campbell, D. T. A test of the ability of fraternity leaders to estimate group opinion. *Journal of Social Psychology,* 1950, **32**, 95–100.

Hollander, E. P. Conformity, status and idiosyncracy credit. *Psychological Review,* 1958, **65**, 117–127.

Hollander, E. P. *Leaders, groups and influence.* New York: Oxford University Press, 1964.

Hollander, E. P. Some effects of perceived status on responses to innovative behavior. *Journal of Abnormal and Social Psychology,* 1961, **63**, 247–250.

Horowitz, E. L. The development of attitude toward the Negro. *Archives of Psychology,* 1936, **28**, No. 194.

Horowitz, E. L. "Race" attitudes. In O. Klineberg (Ed.), *Characteristics of the American Negro*. New York: Harper, 1944.

Horowitz, E. L., and Horowitz, R. E. Development of social attitudes in children. *Sociometry*, 1938, **1**, 301–338.

Horowitz, M. W., Lyons, J., and Perlmutter, H. V. Induction of forces in discussion groups. *Human Relations*, 1951, **4**, 57–76.

Hovland, C. I. Reconciling conflicting results derived from experimental and survey studies of attitude change. *American Psychologist*, 1959, **14**, 8–17.

Hovland, C. I., Harvey, O. J., and Sherif, M. Assimilation and contrast effects in reactions to communication and attitude change. *Journal of Abnormal and Social Psychology*, 1957, **55**, 244–252.

Hovland, C. I., Janis, I. L., and Kelley, H. H. *Communication and persuasion*. New Haven, Conn.: Yale University Press, 1953.

Hovland, C. I., Lumsdaine, A. A., and Sheffield, F. D. Experiments on mass communication. Princeton, N.J.: Princeton University Press, 1949.

Hovland, C. I., and Mandell, W. An experimental comparison of conclusion-drawing by the communicator and by the audience. *Journal of Abnormal Social Psychology*, 1952, **47**, 581–588.

Hovland, C. I., Mandell, W., Campbell, E. H., Brock, T., Luchins, A. S., Cohen, A. R., McGuire W. J., Janis, I. L., Feierabend, R. L., and Anderson, N. H. *The order of presentation in persuasion*. New Haven, Conn.: Yale University Press, 1957.

Hovland, C. I., and Pritzker, H. A. Extent of opinion change as a function of amount of change advocated. *Journal of Abnormal and Social Psychology*, 1957, **54**, 257–261.

Hovland, C. I., and Sherif, M. Judgmental phenomena and scales of attitude measurement: item displacement in Thurstone scales. *Journal of Abnormal and Social Psychology*, 1952, **47**, 822–832.

Hovland, C. I., and Weiss, W. The influence of source credibility on communication effectiveness. *Public Opinion Quarterly*, 1951, **15**, 635–650.

Hull, C. L. The goal-gradient hypothesis and maze learning. *Psychology Review*, 1932, **39**, 25–43.

Hyman, H. H., Cobb, W. J., Feldman, J. J., Hart, C. W., and Stember, C. H. *Interviewing in social research*. Chicago, Ill.: University of Chicago Press, 1954.

Hyman, H. H., and Sheatsley, P. B. Some reasons why information campaigns fail. *Public Opinion Quarterly*, 1947, **11**, 412–423.

Insko, C. A., Murashima, F., and Saiyadain, M. Communicator discrepancy, stimulus ambiguity, and influence. *Journal of Personality*, 1966, **34**(2), 262–274.

Janis, I. L. Effects of fear arousal on attitude change: recent developments in theory and experimental research. In L. Berkowitz (Ed.), *Advances in experi-*

mental social psychology, Vol. 3. New York: Academic Press, 1967. Pp. 166–224.

Janis, I. L Motivational factors in the resolution of decisional conflict. In M. R. Jones (Ed.), *Nebraska Symposium on Motivation.* Lincoln: University of Nebraska Press, 1959.

Janis, I. L., and Dabbs, J. M. Why does eating while reading facilitate opinion change?—an experimental inquiry. *Journal of Experimental Social Psychology,* 1965, **1,** 133–144.

Janis, I. L., and Feshbach, S. Effects of fear-arousing communications. *Journal of Abnormal and Social Psychology,* 1953, **48,** 78–92.

Janis, I. L., and Gilmore, J. B. The influence of incentive conditions on the success of role-playing in modifying attitudes. *Journal of Personality and Social Psychology,* 1965, **I**(1), 17–27.

Janis, I. L., Hovland, C. I., Field, P. B., Linton, H., Graham, E., Cohen, A. R., Rife, D., Abelson, R. P., Lesser, G. S., and King, B. T. *Personality and persuasibility.* New Haven, Conn.: Yale University Press, 1959.

Janis, I. L., Kaye, D., and Kushner, P. Facilitating effects of "eating-while-reading" on responsiveness to persuasive communications. *Journal of Personality and Social Psychology,* 1965, **1,** 181–186.

Janis, I. L., and King, B. T. The influence of role-playing on opinion change. *Journal of Abnormal and Social Psychology,* 1954, **49,** 211–218.

Janis, I. L., and Millholland, H. C., Jr. The influence of threat appeals on selective learning of the content of a persuasive communication. *Journal of Psychology,* 1954, **37,** 75–80.

Janis, I. L., and Terwilliger, R. F. An experimental study of psychological resistances to fear-arousing communications. *Journal of Abnormal and Social Psychology,* 1962, **65,** 403–410.

Janowitz, M., and Bettleheim, B. *Dynamics of prejudice.* New York: Harper, 1950.

Jecker, J. D. The cognitive effects of conflict and dissonance. In L. Festinger, *Conflict, decision, and dissonance.* Stanford, Calif.: Stanford University Press, 1964. Pp. 21–30.

Jones, E. E., and Kohler, R. The effects of plausibility on the learning of controversial statements. *Journal of Abnormal and Social Psychology,* 1958, **57,** 315–320.

Jones, L. V. A. A rational origin in paired comparison and successive interval scaling. Paper read at the Symposium on Recent Developments in Psychometric Scaling, New York City, September 4, 1957.

Jones, R. A., Linder, D. E., Kiesler, C. A., Zanna, M., and Brehm, J. W. Internal states or external stimuli-observers' attitude judgments and the dissonance-theory—self-persuasion controversy. *Journal of Experimental Social Psychology,* 1968, **4,** 247–269.

Jones, R. G. Forced compliance dissonance predictions: obvious, non-obvious, or non-sense? Paper read at the American Psychological Association, New York, September, 1966.

Jordan, N. Behavioral forces that are a function of attitudes and of cognitive organization. *Human Relations,* 1953, **6,** 273–287.

Kahn, R. L., and Cannell, C. F. *The dynamics of interviewing: theory, technique and cases.* New York: John Wiley and Sons, 1957.

Kaplan, A. *The conduct of inquiry: Methodology for behavioral science.* San Francisco, Calif.: Chandler Publishing, 1964.

Katz, D. Do interviewers bias poll results? *Public Opinion Quarterly,* 1942, **6,** 248–268.

Katz, D. The functional approach to the study of attitudes. *Public Opinion Quarterly,* 1960, **24,** 163–204.

Katz, D., McClintock, C., and Sarnoff, D. The measurement of ego defense as related to attitude change. *Journal of Personality,* 1957, **25,** 465–474.

Katz, D., Sarnoff, D., and McClintock, C. Ego-defense and attitude change, *Human Relations,* 1956, **9,** 27–45.

Katz, D., and Stotland, E. A preliminary statement to a theory of attitude structure and change. In S. Koch (Ed.), *Psychology: a study of a science,* Vol. 3. New York: McGraw-Hill, 1959. Pp. 423–475.

Katz, H., Cadoret, R., Hughes, K., and Abbey, D. Physiological correlates of acceptable and unacceptable attitude statements. *Psychological Reports,* 1965, **17,** 78.

Kelley, H. H., Hovland, C. I., Schwartz, M., and Abelson, R. P. The influence of judges' attitudes in three methods of scaling. *Journal of Social Psychology,* 1955, **42,** 147–158.

Kelman, H. Attitude change as a function of response restriction. *Human Relations,* 1953, **6,** 185–214.

Kelman, H. The induction of action and attitude change. In S. Coopersmith (Ed.), *Personality Research.* Copenhagen, Denmark: Munksgaard, 1962.

Kelman, H. Processes of opinion change. *Public Opinion Quarterly,* 1961, **25,** 57–78.

Kelman, H. The role of the group in the induction of therapeutic change. *The International Journal of Group Psychotherapy,* 1963, **13,** 399–432.

Kelman, H. C. Compliance, identification, and internalization: three processes of attitude change. *Journal of Conflict Resolution,* 1958, **2,** 51–60.

Kelman, H. C., and Hovland, C. I. "Reinstatement" of the communicator in delayed measurement of opinion change. *Journal of Abnormal and Social Psychology,* 1953, **48,** 327–335.

Kiesler, C. A. Attraction to the group and conformity to group norms. *Journal of Personality,* 1963, **31,** 559–569.

Kiesler, C. A. Choice, reward and attitude change. Unpublished manuscript, 1965.

Kiesler, C. A. Commitment. In R. P. Abelson, E. Aronson, W. J. McGuire, T. H. Newcomb, M. J. Rosenberg, and P. H. Tannenbaum (Eds.), *Theories of cognitive consistency: a sourcebook*. Skokie, Ill.: Rand-McNally, 1968.

Kiesler, C. A., and Collins, B. E. The effects of attitudinal discrepancy, reward, and choice on attitude change. Unpublished manuscript, 1965.

Kiesler, C. A., and Corbin, L. H. Commitment, attraction, and conformity. *Journal of Personality and Social Psychology*, 1965, **2**, 890–895.

Kiesler, C. A., and DeSalvo, J. The group as an influencing agent in a forced compliance paradigm. *Journal of Experimental Social Psychology*, 1967, **3**, 160–171.

Kiesler, C. A., and Mathog, R. Resistance to influence as a function of number of prior consonant acts. Unpublished manuscript, 1968.

Kiesler, C. A., Pallak, M. S., and Kanouse, D. E. Interactive effects of commitment and dissonance. Unpublished manuscript, 1967.

Kiesler, C. A., and Sakumura, J. A test of a model for commitment. *Journal of Personality and Social Psychology*, 1966, **3**, 349–353.

Kiesler, C. A., and Singer, R. D. The effects of similarity and guilt on the projection of hostility. *Journal of Clinical Psychology*, 1963, **19**(2), 157–162.

Kiesler, C. A., Zanna, M., and DeSalvo, J. Deviation and conformity: Opinion change as a function of commitment, attraction, and presence of a deviate. *Journal of Personality and Social Psychology*, 1966, **3**, 458–467.

Kimble, G. A. Hilgard and Marquis' conditioning and learning (2nd ed.). New York: Appleton-Century-Crofts, 1961.

King, B.T., and Janis, I. L. Comparison of the effectiveness of improvised vs. non-improvised role-playing in producing opinion changes. *Human Relations*, 1956, **9**, 177–186.

Kintz, B., Delprato, D., Mettee, D., Persons, C., and Schappe, R. The experimenter effect. *Psychological Bulletin*. 1965, **63**, 223–232.

Kornhauser, A. W. Changes in the information and attitudes of students in an economics course. *Journal of Educational Research*, 1930, **22**, 288–298.

Krasner, L. Studies of the conditioning of verbal behavior. *Psychological Bulletin*, 1958, **55**, 148–170.

Krasner, L., Weiss, R. L., and Ullman, L. P. Responsivity to verbal conditioning as a function of two different measures of "awareness," *American Psychologist*, 1959, **14**, 388.

Krech, D., and Crutchfield, R. S. *Theory and problems in social psychology*. New York: McGraw-Hill, 1948.

Krieckhaus, E. E., and Eriksen, C. W. A study of awareness and its effect on learning and generalization. *Journal of Personality*, 1960, **28**, 503–517.

Kutner, B., Wilkins, C., and Yarrow, P. R. Verbal attitudes and overt behavior involving racial prejudice. *Journal of Abnormal and Social Psychology*, 1952, **47**, 649–652.

Lana, R. E. A further investigation of the pretest-treatment interaction effect. *Journal of Applied Psychology,* 1959a, **43,** 421–422.

Lana, R. E. The influence of the pretest on order effects in persuasive communication. *Journal of Abnormal and Social Psychology,* 1964, **69,** 337–341.

Lana, R. E. Inhibitory effects of a pretest on opinion change. *Educational and Psychological Measurement,* 1966, **26,** 139–150.

Lana, R. E. Pretest-treatment interaction effects in attitudinal studies. *Psychological Bulletin,* 1959b, **56,** 293–300.

Lana, R. E., and Rosnow, R. L. Subject awareness and order effects in persuasive communications. *Psychological Reports,* 1963, **12,** 523–529.

La Piere, R. T. Attitudes vs. action. *Social Forces,* 1934, **13,** 230–237.

Leary, T. F. *Interpersonal diagnosis of personality: a functional theory and methodology for personality evaluation.* New York: Ronald Press Co., 1957.

Lecky, P. *Self-consistency: a theory of personality.* New York: Island Press, 1945.

Leiderman, P. H., and Shapiro, D. (Eds.). *Psychobiological approaches to social behavior.* Stanford, Calif.: Stanford University Press, 1964.

Lenski, G. E., and Leggett, J. C. Caste, class and deference in the research interview. *American Journal of Sociology,* 1960, **65,** 463–467.

Leventhal, H. Fear communications in the acceptance of preventive health practices. *Bulletin of The New York Academy of Medicine,* 1965, **41,** 1144–1168.

Leventhal, H., Jones, S., and Trembly, G. Sex differences in attitude and behavior change under conditions of fear and specific instructions. *Journal of Experimental Social Psychology,* 1966, **2**(4), 387–399.

Leventhal, H., and Niles, P. Persistence of influence for varying durations of exposure to threat stimuli. *Psychological Reports,* 1965, **16**(1), 223–233.

Leventhal, H., and Singer, R. P. Affect arousal and positioning of recommendations in persuasive communications. *Journal of Personality and Social Psychology,* 1966, **4**(2), 137–146.

Leventhal, H., Singer, R., and Jones, S. Effects of fear and specificity of recommendation upon attitudes and behavior. *Journal of Personality and Social Psychology,* 1965, **2**(1), 20–29.

Leventhal, H., and Watts, Jean C. Sources of resistance to fear-arousing communications on smoking and lung-cancer. *Journal of Personality,* 1966, **34**(2), 155–175.

Leventhal, H., Watts, J. C., and Pagano, F. Effects of fear and instructions on how to cope with danger. *Journal of Personality and Social Psychology,* 1967, **6,** 313–321.

Levin, S. M. The effects of awareness on verbal conditioning. *Journal of Exerimental Psychology,* 1961, **61,** 67–75.

Levine, J. M., and Murphy, G. The learning and forgetting of controversial material. *Journal of Abnormal and Social Psychology,* 1943, **38,** 507–517.

Lewin, K. *A dynamic theory of personality.* New York: McGraw-Hill, 1935.

Lewin, K. *Principles of topological psychology.* New York: McGraw-Hill, 1936.

Lewin, K. *Resolving social conflicts.* New York: Harper, 1948.

Likert, R. A technique for the measurement of attitudes. *Archives of Psychology,* 1932, No. 140.

Linder, D. E., Cooper, J., and Jones, E. E. Decision freedom as a determinant of the role of incentive magnitude in attitude change. *Journal of Personality and Social Psychology,* 1967, **6**(3), 245–254.

Lohman, J. D., and Reitzes, D. C. Deliberately organized groups and racial behavior. *American Sociological Review,* 1954, **19,** 342–344.

McClintock, C. G. Personality factors in attitude change. *Dissertation Abstracts,* 1958, **18**(2), 1519.

McClintock, C. G. Personality syndromes and attitude change. *Journal of Personality,* 1958, **26,** 479–593.

Maccoby, N., Romney, A. K., Adams, J. S., and Maccoby, E. E. *Critical periods in seeking and accepting information.* Stanford, Calif.: Paris-Stanford Studies in Communication, Institute for Communication Research, 1962 (cited in Festinger, 1964).

McDougall, W. An introduction to social psychology. Boston: John W. Luce and Co., 1917.

McGuigan, F. J. The experimenter: a neglected stimulus object. *Psychological Bulletin,* 1963, **60,** 421–428.

McGuire, W. J. The current status of cognitive consistency theories. In S. Feldman (Ed.), *Cognitive consistency.* New York: Academic Press, 1966.

McGuire, W. J. The effectiveness of supportive and refutational defenses in immunizing and restoring beliefs against persuasion. *Sociometry,* 1961, **24,** 184–197.

McGuire, W. J. Inducing resistance to persuasion: some contemporary approaches. In L. Berkowitz (Ed.), *Advances in experimental social psychology.* New York: Academic Press, 1964. Pp. 191–229.

McGuire, W. J. A multiprocess model for paired-associate learning. *Journal of Experimental Psychology,* 1961, **62,** 335–347.

McGuire, W. J. Nature of attitudes and attitude change. In G. Lindzey and E. Aronson (Eds.), *Handbook of social psychology.* Reading, Mass: Addison-Wesley, 1968.

McGuire, W. J. Personality and susceptibility to social influence. In E. F. Borgatta and W. W. Lambert (Eds.), *Handbook of personality theory and research.* Chicago, Ill.: Rand-McNally, 1967.

McGuire, W. J. A syllogistic analysis of cognitive relationships. In M. J. Rosenberg, C. I. Hovland, W. J. McGuire, R. P. Abelson, and J. W. Brehm, *Attitude organization and change.* New Haven, Conn.: Yale University Press, 1960. Pp. 65–111.

McGuire, W. J., and Papageorgis, D. The relative efficacy of various types of prior belief-defense in producing immunity against persuasion. *Journal of Abnormal and Social Psychology,* 1961, **62,** 327–337.

Maltzman, I. Theoretical conceptions of semantic conditioning and generalization. In T. R. Dixon and D. L. Horton (Eds.), *Verbal behavior and general behavior theory.* Englewood Cliffs, N.J.: Prentice-Hall, 1968.

Manis, M. The interpretation of opinion statements as a function of recipient attitude. *Journal of Abnormal and Social Psychology,* 1960, **60,** 360–364.

Margenau, H. *The nature of physical reality.* New York: McGraw-Hill, 1950.

Marlowe, D., Frager, R., and Nuttall, R. L. Commitment to action-taking as a consequence of cognitive dissonance. *Journal of Personality and Social Psychology,* 1965, **2,** 864–868.

Mercado, S. J., Guerrero, P. D., and Gardner, R. W. Cognitive control in children of Mexico and the United States. *Journal of Social Psychology,* 1963, **59**(2), 199–208.

Milgram, S. Behavioral study of obedience. *Journal of Abnormal and Social Psychology,* 1963, **67,** 371–378.

Milgram, S. Group pressure and action against a person. *Journal of Abnormal and Social Psychology,* 1964, **69,** 137–143.

Milgram, S. Liberating effects of group pressure. *Journal of Personality and Social Psychology,* 1965, **1,** 127–134.

Miller, E., and Swanson, G. *Inner conflict and defense.* New York: Holt, 1960.

Miller, N. Acquisition of avoidance dispositions by social learning. *Journal of Abnormal and Social Psychology,* 1961, **63,** 12–19.

Miller, N. Contrast effects between communicators. Unpublished paper presented at the annual meeting of the Midwestern Psychological Association, 1966.

Miller, N. Involvement and dogmatism as inhibitors of attitude change. *Journal of Experimental Social Psychology,* 1965, **1**(2), 121–132.

Miller, N., and Devine, V. A personality interpretation of involvement effects: broad and narrow latitudes of rejection as a personality trait. Unpublished paper, mimeographed. University of Minnesota, 1968.

Miller, N., and Levy, B. H. Defaming and agreeing with the communicator as a function of emotional arousal, communication extremity, and evaluative set. *Sociometry,* 1967, **30**(2), 158–175.

Miller, N., and Zimbardo, P. G. Issue involvement and opinion change. Paper presented at the annual meeting of the Midwestern Psychological Association, 1964.

Miller, N. E. Learnable drives and rewards. In S. S. Stevens (Ed.), *Handbook of experimental psychology.* New York: John Wiley and Sons, 1951.

Miller, N. E. Liberalization of basic S-R concepts: extensions to conflict behavior, motivation, and social learning. In S. Koch (Ed.), *Psychology, a study of science,* Vol. 2. New York: McGraw-Hill, 1959.

Miller, N. E., and Dollard, J. *Social learning and imitation*. New Haven, Conn.: Yale University Press, 1941.

Mills, J. Interest in supporting and discrepant information. In S. Feldman (Ed.): *Cognitive consistency*. New York: Academic Press, 1966. Chapter 1.

Mills, J., Aronson, E., and Robinson, H. Selectivity in exposure to information. *Journal of Abnormal and Social Psychology*, 1959, **59**, 250–253.

Minard, R. D. Race relationships in the Pocahontas coal field. *Journal of Social Issues*, 1952, **8**, 29–44.

Morgan, J. J. B. Attitudes of students toward the Japanese. *Journal of Social Psychology*, 1945, **21**, 219–227.

Morrissette, J. O. An experimental study of the theory of structural balance. *Human Relations*, 1958, **11**, 239–254.

Mowrer, O. H. The psychologist looks at language. *American Psychologist*, 1954, **9**, 660–694.

Munn, N. L. *Psychology, the fundamentals of human adjustment*. Boston: Houghton Mifflin Co., 1961.

Murphy, G., Murphy, L. B., and Newcomb, T. M. *Experimental social psychology*. New York: Harper, 1937.

Nagel, E. *The structure of science*. New York: Harcourt, Brace, and World, 1961.

Nettler, G., and Golding, E. H. The measurement of attitudes toward the Japanese in America, *American Journal of Sociology*, 1946, **52**, 31–39.

Newcomb, T. M. *The acquaintance process*. New York: Holt, Rinehart, and Winston, 1961.

Newcomb, T. M. An approach to the study of communicative acts. *Psychological Review*, 1953, **60**, 393–404.

Newcomb, T. M. The cognition of persons as cognizers. In R. Taguiri and L. Petrullo (Eds.), *Person perception and interpersonal behavior*. Stanford, Calif.: Stanford University Press, 1958. Pp. 179–190.

Newcomb, T. M. Individual systems of orientation. In S. Koch (Ed.), *Psychology: a study of a science,* Vol. 3. New York: McGraw-Hill, 1959. Pp. 384–422.

Newcomb, T. M. The prediction of interpersonal attraction. *American Psychologist*, 1956, **11**, 575–586.

Niles, P. The relationship of susceptibility and anxiety to acceptance of fear-arousing communications. Unpublished doctoral dissertation. Yale University, New Haven, Conn., 1964.

Nunnally, J. C., and Bobren, H. M. Variables governing the willingness to receive communications on mental health. *Journal of Personality*, 1959, **27**, 38–46.

Orne, M. T. The nature of hypnosis: artifact and essence. *Journal of Abnormal and Social Psychology*, 1959, **58**, 277–299.

Orne, M. T. On the social psychology of the psychological experiment: with particular reference to demand characteristics and their implications. *American Psychologist,* 1962, **17,** 776–783.

Osgood, C. E. Cognitive dynamics in the conduct of human affairs. *Public Opinion Quarterly,* 1960, **24,** 341–365.

Osgood, C. E. *Method and theory in experimental psychology.* New York: Oxford University Press, 1953.

Osgood, C. E., and Suci, G. J. Factor analysis of meaning. *Journal of Experimental Psychology,* 1955, **50,** 325–338.

Osgood, C. E., Suci, G. J., and Tannenbaum, P. H. *The measurement of meaning.* Urbana: University of Illinois Press, 1957.

Osgood, C. E., and Tannenbaum, P. H. The principle of congruity in the prediction of attitude change. *Psychological Review,* 1955, **62,** 42–55.

Ostrum, T. S. Perspective as an intervening construct in the judgment of attitude statements. *Journal of Personality and Social Psychology,* 1966, **3,** 135–144.

Papageorgis, D., and McGuire, W. J. The generality of immunity to persuasion produced by pre-exposure to weakened counterarguments. *Journal of Abnormal and Social Psychology,* 1961, **62,** 475–481.

Peabody, D. Two components in bipolar scales: direction and extremeness. *Psychological Review,* 1962, **69,** 65–73.

Pettigrew, T. F. The measurement and correlates of category width as a cognitive variable. *Journal of Personality,* 1958, **26,** 532–544.

Pettigrew, T. F. Social psychology and desegregation research. *American Psychologist,* 1961, **16,** 105–112.

Powell, F. A. Latitudes of acceptance and rejection and the belief-disbelief dimension: a correlational comparison. *Journal of Personality and Social Psychology,* 1966, **4,** 453–456.

Powell, F. A. Source credibility and behavioral compliance as determinants of attitude change. *Journal of Personality and Social Psychology,* 1965, **2,** 669–676.

Price, K. O., Harburg, E., and McLeod, J. M. Positive and negative affect as a function of perceived discrepancy in ABX situations. *Human Relations,* 1965, **18,** 87–100.

Price, K. O., Harburg, E., and Newcomb, T. M. Psychological balance in situations of negative interpersonal attitudes. *Journal of Personality and Social Psychology,* 1966, **3**(3), 265–270.

Prothro, E. T. The effect of strong negative attitudes on the placement of items in a Thurstone scale. *Journal of Social Psychology,* 1955, **41,** 11–17.

Prothro, E. T. Personal involvement and item displacement of Thurstone scales. *Journal of Social Psychology,* 1957, **45,** 191–196.

Rankin, R. E., and Campbell, D. T. Galvanic skin response to Negro and white experimenters. *Journal of Abnormal and Social Psychology,* 1955, **51,** 30–33.

Rhine, R. J. A concept-formation approach to attitude acquisition. *Psychological Review,* 1958, **65,** 362–370.

Rhine, R. J. The effect of peer group influence upon concept-attitude development and change. *Journal of Social Psychology,* 1960, **51,** 173–179.

Rhine, R. J., and Silun, B. A. Acquisition and change of a concept attitude as a function of consistency of reinforcement. *Journal of Experimental Psychology,* 1958, **55,** 524–529.

Riecken, H. W. A program for research on experiments in social psychology. In N. F. Washburn (Ed.), *Decisions, values and groups,* Vol. 2. New York: Pergamon Press, 1962. Pp. 25–41.

Riesman, D. Orbits of tolerance, interviewers and elites. *Public Opinion Quarterly,* 1956, **20,** 49–73.

Riesman, D., and Ehrlich, J. Age and authority in the interview. *Public Opinion Quarterly,* 1961, **25,** 39–56.

Robinson, D., and Rohde, S. Two experiments with an anti-Semitism poll. *Journal of Abnormal and Social Psychology,* 1946, **41,** 136–144.

Rogers, S. The anchoring of absolute judgments. *Archives of Psychology,* 1941, **37** (Whole No. 261).

Rokeach, M. The double agreement phenomenon: three hypotheses. *Psychological Review,* 1963, **70,** 304–309.

Rokeach, M. *The open and closed mind.* New York: Basic Books, 1960.

Rokeach, M., and Rothman, G. The principle of belief congruence and the congruity principle as models of cognitive interaction. *Psychological Review,* 1965, **72,** 128–142.

Rorer, L. G. The great response-style myth. *Psychological Bulletin,* 1965, **63,** 129–156.

Rosen, S. Post-decision affinity for incompatible information. *Journal of Abnormal and Social Psychology,* 1961, **63,** 188–190.

Rosenberg, M. J. An analysis of affective-cognitive consistency. In M. J. Rosenberg, C. I. Hovland, W. J. McGuire, R. P. Abelson, and J. W. Brehm. *Attitude organization and change.* New Haven, Conn.: Yale University Press, 1960. Pp. 15–64.

Rosenberg, M. J. When dissonance fails: on eliminating evaluation apprehension from attitude measurement. *Journal of Personality and Social Psychology,* 1965, **1**(1), 28–42.

Rosenberg, M. J. Hedonism, inauthenticity and other goads toward expansion of a consistency theory. In R. P. Abelson, E. Aronson, W. J. McGuire, T. M. Newcomb, M. J. Rosenberg, and P. H. Tannenbaum (Eds.), *Theories of cognitive consistency: a sourcebook.* Skokie, Ill.: Rand-McNally, 1968.

Rosenberg, M. J., and Abelson, R. P. An analysis of cognitive balancing. In M. J. Rosenberg et al., *Attitude organization and change.* New Haven, Conn.: Yale University Press, 1960. Pp. 112–163.

Rosenberg, M. J., Hovland, C. I., McGuire, W. J., Abelson, R. P., and Brehm, J. W. *Attitude organization and change: an analysis of consistency among attitude components.* New Haven, Conn.: Yale University Press, 1960.

Rosenthal, R. *Experimenter effects in behavioral research.* New York: Appleton-Century-Crofts, 1966.

Rosenthal, R. Experimenter outcome-orientation and the results of the psychological experiment. *Psychological Bulletin,* 1964, **61,** 405–412.

Rosenthal, R. On the social psychology of the psychological experiment: the experimenter's hypothesis as unintended determinant of experimental results. *American Scientist,* 1963, **51,** 268–283.

Rosenthal, R. Projection, excitement, and unconscious experimenter bias. *American Psychologist,* 1958, **13,** 345–346. (Abstract)

Saadi, M., and Farnsworth, P. R. The degrees of acceptance of dogmatic statements and preferences for their supposed makers. *Journal of Abnormal and Social Psychology,* 1934, **29,** 143–150.

Sarnoff, D. The experimental evaluation of psychoanalytic hypotheses. *Transactions of the New York Academy of Science,* 1965, **28,** 272–290.

Sarnoff, D. Reaction formation and cynicism. *Journal of Personality,* 1960, **28,** 129–143.

Sarnoff, D., and Corwin, S. Castration anxiety and the fear of death. *Journal of Personality,* 1959, **27,** 374–385.

Sarnoff, D., and Katz, D. The motivational bases of attitude change. *Journal of Abnormal and Social Psychology,* 1954, **49,** 115–124.

Schachter, S. Deviation, rejection, and communication. *Journal of Abnormal and Social Psychology,* 1951, **46,** 190–207.

Schachter, S. *The psychology of affiliation.* Stanford, Calif.: Stanford University Press, 1959.

Schachter, S., and Singer, J. E. Cognitive, social, and physiological determinants of emotional states. *Psychological Review,* 1962, **69,** 379–399.

Scott, W. A. Attitude change by response reinforcement: replication and extension. *Sociometry,* 1959, **22,** 328–335.

Scott, W. A. Attitude change through reward of verbal behavior. *Journal of Abnormal and Social Psychology,* 1957, **55,** 72–75.

Scott, W. A. Attitude measurement. In G. Lindzey and E. Aronson (Eds.), *Handbook of social psychology* (rev. ed.). Reading, Mass.: Addison-Wesley, 1968.

Secord, P. F., and Backman, C. W. *Social psychology.* New York: McGraw-Hill, 1964.

Segall, M. The effect of attitude and experience on judgments on controversial statements. *Journal of Abnormal and Social Psychology,* 1959, **58,** 61–68.

Selltiz, C., Edrich, H., and Cook, S. W. Ratings of favorableness of statements about a social group as an indicator of attitude toward the group. *Journal of Personality and Social Psychology,* 1965, **2,** 408–415.

Sherif, C. W. Social categorization as a function of latitude of acceptance and series range. *Journal of Abnormal and Social Psychology,* 1963, **67,** 148–156.

Sherif, C. W., Sherif, M., and Nebergall, R. E. *Attitude and attitude change; the social judgment-involvement approach.* Philadelphia, Pa.: W. B. Saunders Company, 1965.

Sherif, M., *The psychology of social norms.* New York: Harper, 1936.

Sherif, M., and Cantril, H. *The psychology of ego-involvements.* New York: John Wiley and Sons, 1947.

Sherif, M., and Hovland, C. I. *Social judgement: assimilation and contrast effects in communication and attitude change.* New Haven, Conn.: Yale University Press, 1961.

Sherif, M., Taub, D., and Hovland, C. I. Assimilation and contrast effects of anchoring stimuli on judgments. *Journal of Experimental Psychology,* 1958, **55,** 150–155.

Singer, J. E. Motivation for consistency. In S. Feldman (Ed.), *Cognitive consistency.* New York: Academic Press, 1966.

Singer, R. D. Verbal conditioning and generalization of prodemocratic responses. *Journal of Abnormal and Social Psychology,* 1961, **63,** 43–46.

Skinner, B. F. *Science and human behavior.* New York: The Macmillan Company. 1953.

Skinner, B. F. *Verbal behavior.* New York: Appleton-Century-Crofts, 1957.

Smith, B. L., Laswell, H. D., and Casey, R. D. *Propaganda communication and public opinion.* Princeton, N.J.: Princeton University Press, 1946.

Smith, E. E. The power of dissonance techniques to change attitudes. *Public Opinion Quarterly,* 1961, **25**(4), 626–639.

Smith, M. B., Bruner, J. S., and White, R. W. *Opinions and personality.* New York: John Wiley and Sons, 1956.

Solomon, R. An extension of control group design. *Psychological Bulletin,* 1949, **46,** 137–150.

Speilberger, C. D. The role of awareness in verbal conditioning. In C. W. Ericksen (Ed.), *Behavior and awareness.* Durham, N.C.: Duke University Press, 1962. Pp. 73–101.

Speilberger, C. D., Levin, S. M., and Shepard, Mary. The effects of awareness and attitude toward the reinforcement on the operant conditioning of verbal behavior. *Journal of Personality,* 1962, **30,** 106–121.

Spence, K. W. *Behavior theory and conditioning.* New Haven, Conn.: Yale University Press, 1956.

Spence, K. W. The nature of the response in discrimination learning. *Psychological Review,* 1952, **59,** 89–93.

Staats, A. W. An outline of an integrated learning theory of attitude formation and function. In M. Fishbein (Ed.), *Readings in attitude theory and measurement.* New York: John Wiley and Sons, 1967.

Staats, A. W. Emotions and images in language: a learning analysis of their acquisition and function. In K. Salzinger (Ed.), *Research in verbal behavior.* New York: Academic Press. 1969.

Staats, A. W., and Staats, C. K. Attitudes established by classical conditioning. *Journal of Abnormal and Social Psychology,* 1958, 57, 37–40.

Staats, A. W., and Staats, C. K. Effect of number of trials on the language conditioning of meaning. *Journal of General Psychology,* 1959, 61, 211–223.

Staats, A. W., Staats, C. K., and Biggs, D. A. Meaning of verbal stimuli changed by conditioning. *American Journal of Psychology,* 1958, 71, 429–431.

Staats, A. W., Staats, C. K., and Crawford, H. L. First-order conditioning of meaning and the parallel conditioning of a GSR. *Journal of General Psychology,* 1962, 67, 159–167.

Staats, A. W., Staats, C. K., and Heard, W. G. Denotive meaning established by classical conditioning. *Journal of Experimental Psychology,* 1961, 61, 300–303.

Staats, A. W., Staats, C. K., Heard, W. G., and Nims, L. P. Replication report: Meaning established by classical conditioning. *Journal of Experimental Psychology,* 1959, 57, 64.

Staats, C. K., and Staats, A. W. Meaning established by classical conditioning. *Journal of Experimental Psychology,* 1957, 54, 74–80.

Staats, C. K., Staats, A. W., and Heard, W. G. Attitude development and ratio of reinforcement. *Sociometry,* 1960, 23, 338–350.

Stanley, J. C., and Klausmeier, H. J. Opinion constancy after formal role-playing. *Journal of Social Psychology,* 1957, 46, 11–18.

Stanton, H. R., and Litwak, E. Toward the development of a short form test of interpersonal competence. *American Sociological Review,* 1955, 20, 668–674.

Steiner, I. D., and Johnson, H. H. Category width and responses to interpersonal disagreements. *Journal of Personality and Social Psychology,* 1965, 2(2), 290–292.

Steiner, I. D., and Johnson, H. H. Relationships among dissonance-reducing responses. *Journal of Abnormal and Social Psychology,* 1964, 68, 38–44.

Steiner, I. D., and Rogers, E. D. Alternative responses to dissonance. *Journal of Abnormal and Social Psychology,* 1963, 66, 128–136.

Stogdill, R. *Individual behavior and group achievement.* New York: Oxford University Press, 1959.

Stotland, E., Katz, D., and Patchen, M. The reduction of prejudice through the arousal of self-insight. *Journal of Personality,* 1959, 27, 507–531.

Suchman, E. A. The intensity component in attitude and opinion research. In S. A. Stouffer et al. (Eds.), *Measurement and prediction* (Vol. 4 of *Studies in social psychology in World War II*). Princeton, N.J.: Princeton University Press, 1950.

Sumner, W. G. Folkways; a study of the sociological importance of usages, manners, customs, mores, and morals, Boston, Mass.: Ginn and Company, 1906.

Tajfel, C. Anxiety and the conditioning of verbal behavior. *Journal of Abnormal and Social Psychology*, 1955, **51**, 496–501.

Tannenbaum, P. H. Attitude toward source and concept as factors in attitude change through communications. Unpublished doctoral dissertation, University of Illinois, 1953.

Tannenbaum, P. H. The congruity principle revisited: studies in the reduction, induction, and generalization of persuasion. In L. Berkowitz (Ed.), *Advances in experimental social psychology*. New York: Academic Press, 1967, Vol. 3, pp. 270–320.

Tatz, S. J. Symbolic activity in "learning without awareness." *American Journal of Psychology*, 1960, **73**, 239–247.

Taylor, J. B. What do attitude scales measure: the problem of social desirability. *Journal of Abnormal and Social Psychology*, 1961, **62**, 386–390.

Taylor, J. B., and Parker, H. A. Graphic ratings and attitude measurement: a comparison of research tactics. *Journal of Applied Psychology*, 1964, **48**, 37–42.

Thibaut, J., and Kelly, H. *The social psychology of groups*. New York: John Wiley and Sons, 1959.

Thistlewaite, D. Attitude and structure as factors in the distortion of reasoning. *Journal of Abnormal and Social Psychology*, 1950, **45**, 442–458.

Thistlewaite, D. L., de Haan, H., and Kamenetsky, J. The effects of "directive" and "nondirective" communication procedures on attitudes. *Journal of Abnormal and Social Psychology*, 1955, **51**, 107–113.

Thistlewaite, D. L., and Kamenetsky, J. Attitude change through refutation and elaboration of audience counter-arguments. *Journal of Abnormal and Social Psychology*, 1955, **51**, 3–12.

Thomas, W. I., and Znaniecki, F. *The Polish peasant in Europe and America*, 2 vols. (2nd ed.). New York: Alfred A. Knopf, 1927.

Thorndike, E. L., and Rock, R. T., Jr. Learning without awareness of what is being learned or intent to learn it. *Journal of Experimental Psychology*, 1934, **17**, 1–19.

Thurstone, L. L. Attitudes can be measured. *American Journal of Sociology*, 1928, **33**, 529–554.

Thurstone, L. L. Comment. *American Journal of Sociology*, 1946, **52**, 39–40.

Thurstone, L. L. Theory of attitude measurement. *Psychological Review*, 1929, **36**, 222–241.

Thurstone, L. L., and Chave, E. J. *The measurement of attitude*. Chicago, Ill.: University of Chicago Press, 1929.

Torgerson, W. S. *Theory and methods of scaling*. New York: John Wiley and Sons, 1958.

Triandis, H. C. Exploratory factor analyses of the behavioral component of social attitudes. *Journal of Abnormal and Social Psychology,* 1964, **68,** 420–430.

Triandis, H. C., and Fishbein, M. Cognitive interaction in person perception. *Journal of Abnormal and Social Psychology,* 1963, **67,** 446–453.

Troldahl, V. C., and Powell, F. A. A short-form dogmatism scale for use in field studies. *Social Forces,* 1965, **44**(2), 121–215.

Underwood, B. J. Interference and forgetting. *Psychological Review,* 1957, **64,** 49–60.

Underwood, B. J. *Psychological research.* New York: Appleton-Century-Crofts, 1957.

Underwood, B. J., and Shultz, R. W. *Meaningfulness and verbal learning.* Philadelphia, Pa.: Lippincott, 1960.

Upshaw, H. The effect of variable perspectives on judgments of opinion statements for Thurstone scales. *Journal of Personality and Social Psychology,* 1965, **2,** 60–69.

Upshaw, H. S. Own attitude as an anchor in equal-appearing intervals. *Journal of Abnormal and Social Psychology,* 1962, **64,** 85–96.

Verplanck, W. S. The control of the content of conversation: reinforcement of statements of opinions. *Journal of Abnormal and Social Psychology,* 1955, **51,** 668–676.

Volkmann, J. Scales of judgment. In J. H. Rohrer and M. Sherif (Eds.), *Social psychology at the crossroads.* New York: Harper, 1951. Pp. 273–294.

Wagman, M. Attitude change and the authoritarian personality. *Journal of Psychology,* 1955, **40,** 27–45.

Walster, Elaine. The temporal sequence of post-decision processes. In L. Festinger, *Conflict, decision, and dissonance.* Stanford, Calif.: Stanford University Press, 1964. Pp. 112–128.

Walster, Elaine, Aronson, E., and Abrahams, D. On increasing the persuasiveness of a low prestige communicator. *Journal of Experimental Social Psychology,* 1966, **2,** 325–342.

Waly, Patricia, and Cook, S. W. Effect of attitude on judgments of plausibility. *Journal of Personality and Social Psychology,* 1965, **2,** 745–749.

Ward, C. D. Attitude and involvement in the absolute judgment of attitude statements. *Journal of Personality and Social Psychology,* 1966, **4,** 465–476.

Ward, C. D. Ego-involvement and the absolute judgment of attitude statements. Unpublished master's thesis, University of North Carolina, 1962.

Ward, C. D. Ego-involvement and the absolute judgment of attitude statements. *Journal of Personality and Social Psychology,* 1965, **2,** 202–208.

Watson, G. B. The measurement of fairmindedness. *Teachers College, Columbia University Contributions to Education,* 1925, No. 176.

Webb, E. J., Campbell, D. T., Schwartz, R. D., and Sechrest, L. *Unobtrusive measures: Nonreactive research in the social sciences.* Chicago, Ill.: Rand-McNally, 1966.

Weick, K. E. Reduction of cognitive dissonance through task enhancement and effort expenditure. *Journal of Abnormal and Social Psychology,* 1964, **68**(5), 533–539.

Weick, K. E. When prophecy pales: the fate of dissonance theory. *Psychological Reports,* 1965, **16**(3), 1261–1275.

Weiss, R. F. A delay of argument gradient in the instrumental conditioning of attitudes. *Psychonomic Science,* 1967, **8**, 457–458.

Weiss, R. F. Persuasion and acquisition of attitudes: models from conditioning and selective learning. *Psychological Reports,* 1962, **11**, 709–732.

Weiss, R. F., Buchanan, W., and Pasamanick, B. Delay of reinforcement and delay of punishment in persuasive communication. *Psychological Reports,* 1965, **16**, 576.

Weiss, R. F., and Pasamanick, B. Number of exposures to persuasive communication in the instrumental conditioning of attitudes. *The Journal of Social Psychology,* 1964, **63**, 373–382.

Weiss, R., Rawson, H., and Pasamanick, B. Argument strength, delay of argument and anxiety in the "conditioning" and "selective learning" of attitudes. *Journal of Abnormal and Social Psychology,* 1963, **67**, 157–165.

Weiss, W. The effects on opinions of a change in scale judgments. *Journal of Abnormal and Social Psychology,* 1959, **58**, 329–334.

Weschler, I. R. An investigation of attitudes toward labor and management by means of the error-choice method. *Journal of Social Psychology,* 1950, **32**, 51–62.

Westie, F. R., and De Fleur, M. L. Autonomic responses and their relationship to race attitudes. *Journal of Abnormal and Social Psychology,* 1959, **58**, 340–347.

Wever, E. G., and Zener, K. E. Method of absolute judgment is psychophysics. *Psychological Review,* 1928, **35**, 466–493.

Whiting, J. Resource meditation and learning by identification. In I. Iscoe and H. W. Stevenson (Eds.), *Personality development in children.* Austin, Tex.: University of Texas Press, 1960.

Whittaker, J. O. Opinion changes as a function of communication-attitude discrepancy. *Psychological Reports,* 1963, **13**(3), 763–772.

Woodmansee, J. An evaluation of pupil response as a measure of attitude toward Negroes. Unpublished doctoral dissertation, University of Colorado, 1965.

Wulf, F. *Über die Veränderung von Vorstellungen (Gedächtnis und Gestalt).* *Psychol. Forsch.,* 1922, **1**, 333–373. (Cited in E. R. Hilgard, *Introduction to psychology.* New York: Harcourt, Brace, 1962, 3rd ed.)

Zajonc, R. B. The concepts of balance, congruity, and dissonance. *Public Opinion Quarterly.* 1960, **24**, 280–296.

Zajonc, R. B., and Burnstein, E. The learning of balanced and unbalanced social structures. *Journal of Personality*, 1965a, **33**, 153–163.

Zajonc, R. B., and Burnstein, E. Structural balance, reciprocity, and positivity as sources of cognitive balance. *Journal of Personality*, 1965, **33**, 570–583.

Zavalloni, M., and Cook, S. W. Influence of judges' attitudes on ratings of favorableness of statements about a social group. *Journal of Personality and Social Psychology*, 1965, **1**, 43–54.

Zimbardo, P. G. The effect of effort and improvisation on self-persuasion produced by role-playing. *Journal of Experimental Social Psychology*, 1965, **1**(2), 103–120.

Zimbardo, P. G. Involvement and communication discrepancy as determinants of opinion conformity. *Journal of Abnormal and Social Psychology*, 1960, **60**, 86–94.

Zimbardo, P. G. The role of involvement in attitude formation and change. Unpublished research proposal submitted to National Science Foundation, 1961. (Dittoed)

Zimbardo, P. G., Cohen, A. R., Weisenberg, M., Dworkin, L., and Firestone, I. Control of pain motivation by cognitive dissonance. *Science*, 1966, **151**(3707), 217–219.

Zimbardo, P. G., Weisenberg, M., Firestone, I., and Levy, B. Communicator effectiveness in producing public conformity and private attitude change. *Journal of Personality*, 1965, **33**, 233–255.

Zubin, J., Eron, L. O., and Schumer, F. *An experimental approach to projective techniques*. New York: John Wiley and Sons, 1965.

Name Index

Abbey, D., 20
Abelson, R. P., 117, 156–157, 161, 166–167, 169, 171–175, 177, 183, 188, 231n
Abrahams, D., 107
Adams, J., 37, 148
Adams, J. S., 223
Adorno, T. W., 6, 317, 322, 327
Allen, V., 205
Allport, F. H., 10–11, 103
Allport, G. W., 2–4, 5–6, 156
Allyn, J., *see* Hardyck, J. A.
Anderson, N. H., 117
Aronson, E., 53, 55, 57, 62, 64, 71–76, 107, 115, 191, 193, 210–211, 217, 223, 226, 233, 235–236
Asch, S., 33–34, 62
Athey, K. R., 65
Atkins, A. L., 239

Back, K. W., 187, 227
Backman, C. W., 196, 206
Bain, R., 2
Bales, R. F., 17
Bandura, A., 332
Bem, D. J., 92, 128–133, 153, 212, 217–222
Benney, M., 65
Bergmann, G., 338
Berlyne, D. E., 189
Bettelheim, B., 310
Bieri, J., 239
Biggs, D. A., 99, 143
Binet, A., 13–15
Bishop, F., 324–325
Blake, R. R., 54
Blumer, H., 6

Bobren, H. M., 111
Bogardus, E. S., 14
Bogdonoff, M. D., 227
Braithwaite, R. B., 39
Bramel, D., 224–226, 235
Brehm, J. W., 117, 191, 199, 201–205, 209–211, 219–223, 227–228, 236
Brehm, M. L., 227
Briar, S., 239
Brock, T. C., 63, 72, 107, 117, 205, 211, 227
Brown, R. W., 117, 167, 191
Brown, W., 84
Bruner, J. S., 257, 302–304, 306–308, 312, 314–317, 325–326, 330–331, 333
Buchanan, W., 124
Burdick, H. A., 163
Burnes, A. J., 163
Burnstein, E., 165
Burtt, H., 37
Buss, A. H., 211
Butler, D., 332

Cadoret, R., 20
Caldwell, O., 7
Campbell, D. T., 2, 19–21, 32, 45–46, 49, 59–61, 66, 71, 73, 83–86, 88, 114, 144, 151, 308, 344
Campbell, E. H., 117
Campbell, N. R., 39
Cannell, C. F., 65–66
Canon, L. K., 224
Cantril, H., 65, 244
Carlsmith, J. M., 37, 41, 53, 55, 57–58, 62, 64, 71–76, 115, 193, 206–210, 212, 214–217, 219–220, 226, 233, 324–325

377

Subject Index